Marxism and the Metropolis

MARXISM
and the
METROPOLIS

New Perspectives in Urban Political Economy

Second Edition

Edited by

WILLIAM K. TABB
QUEENS COLLEGE, CUNY

LARRY SAWERS
AMERICAN UNIVERSITY

New York   Oxford
OXFORD UNIVERSITY PRESS
1984

Library of Congress Cataloging in Publication Data
Main entry under title:

Marxism and the metropolis.

  Bibliography: p.
  Includes index.
  1. Urban economics—Addresses, essays, lectures.
2. Marxian economics—Addresses, essays, lectures.
3. Cities and towns—United States—Addresses, essays,
lectures. I. Tabb, William K. II. Sawers, Larry,
1942– .
HT321.M24 1984   338.973′009173′2   82–25965
ISBN 0–19–503307–8
ISBN 0–19–503308–6 (pbk.)

Printing (last digit): 9 8 7 6 5 4 3

Printed in the United States of America

Preface

In 1975 the editors of this volume organized a conference on "New Perspectives on the Urban Political Economy." The best papers delivered at this conference were brought together in a book, *Marxism and the Metropolis: New Perspectives on the Urban Political Economy* (Oxford University Press, 1978). This volume was so successful that we have repeated the process. A new conference with the same title as the first was held at The American University in Washington, D.C., in May 1981. Most of the papers in this new edition of *Marxism and the Metropolis* were delivered at this second conference. Only four of the papers, and some of these with extensive revisions, appeared in the first edition. The second edition is, therefore, almost entirely new. Since the first conference in 1975 there has been a dramatic increase in the activity of scholars writing in the field of urban political economy. The sophistication of the analysis and the breadth of empirical research has developed explosively. Thus our present effort represents the substantially better quality and greater quantity of research that is presently being produced.

We initially had some misgivings about re-using the title *Marxism and the Metropolis* for this second volume. There were authors of selections in both volumes who would not identify themselves as Marxists. More importantly, we did not want any pressure to justify why everything put in the book was specifically Marxist. We wanted to put our attention to explaining the urban reality around us rather than defending a particular school of thought. We, like many progressive scholars in this country, have become much less concerned about whether we are really Marxist than whether we are really right. To emphasize the specifically Marxist character of this work risks the creation of chasms which then must be bridged.

Realizing all of these dangers, we have nonetheless retained the original title. The purpose of this present volume is to carry on the mission of the first edition. This latest effort is bigger and significantly better than our first, but it is designed to play the same role, to fill the same niche, as the first edition. In editing these papers, we have not gone out of our way to highlight what is or is not Marxist. Indeed, we have edited out the more ponderous Marxist jargon. The perspective offered by this book was far more controversial ten or even five years ago. Feeling less defensive about our intellectual foundation allows us to focus on analyzing cities rather than self-consciously justifying or even calling attention to the particular methodology that we are using. Nevertheless, the reader familiar with the thinking of Karl Marx will undoubtedly notice the heavy intellectual debt that every selection of this book owes to him, even those selections by authors who do not consider themselves Marxist.

The present book differs from the earlier one in another important respect. The research for the papers presented in *Marxism and the Metropolis* was carried out in the mid-1970s, when the fires of the 1960s ghetto riots were, figuratively speaking, still smouldering. The concerns of political economists and conventional social scientists as well focused on the inner city and the urban crisis arising from the concentration of the poor and minorities there. More recently, political economists found that their perspective offered insight into other aspects of urban economic development. Instead of the rhetoric of earlier years which, for example, viewed the suburbs as a place where people could "escape from capitalist reality," it was seen that the suburbs too are a part of—and now the larger part of—capitalist reality. Urban decay and poverty on the one hand is matched with buoyant economic growth and affluence in other parts of the city or in other regions. Political economists broadened their scope in recent years to explain both aspects of the contradictory reality of capitalism, and this is reflected in many of the papers in this book.

One of the criticisms of *Marxism and the Metropolis* was that it was too often inaccessible to undergraduates, the primary market for the book. For the present book, greater care has been taken with regard to unnecessarily arcane vocabulary, academic jargon, Marxist lingo, and statistical terms in order to insure that the book is easily read by a typical undergraduate in a four-year institution with little background in economics or statistics. At the same time, the papers presented are sufficiently sophisticated to be of interest to graduate students and professionals. The book is of interest to and accessible to economists, sociologists, anthropologists, urban planners, and political scientists as well as the general public.

It would be impossible to properly thank everyone who has contributed to this book since it grows out of an intellectual movement composed of hundreds of scholars and activists. The ideas that helped shape this volume are a collective product. We would, however, be remiss if we did not mention the marvelous editing skills of Nancy Amy who turned garbled prose into elegant communications. Many thanks also to Melissa Eisenberg who typed substantial portions of this volume, transforming nearly illegible drafts into usable manuscript.

New York   W.T.
Washington   L.S.
June 1983

Contents

Marxism and the Metropolis

New Perspectives
on the
Urban Political Economy

LARRY SAWERS

Acres of abandoned housing along the bustling expressway, row after row of brand new office towers in glistening glass and aluminum, the incessant buzz of the lawnmower drifting over quiet, tree-lined streets—these are the images of urban North America. The scream in the dark of the mugging victim as neighbors huddle behind locked doors, convention centers sprouting like mushrooms in one downtown after another, and countless teenagers hanging out at the suburban shopping mall—the nation's urban areas are filled with stark contrasts. How can one make sense of these contrasts, how can they be grasped simultaneously and put into a single framework? How can one bring into the same focus a Houston where new office buildings are now built several at a time rather than singly and a New York City where the government deliberately withdraws services from neighborhoods so that the urban rot will accelerate, the sooner to be done with them. How can one comprehend the current strong demand for luxury housing and fur coats and a record high inner-city unemployment rate? The prevailing conventional wisdom of the urban social sciences anesthetizes one to these jarring contrasts. This volume on the other hand seeks to offer a perspective that allows one to make sense out of the seemingly incongruent facts of urban life in the 1980s.

A large and rapidly growing body of scholarship from which this book draws has appeared in recent years. Dissatisfied with the conventional explanations of urban problems, these scholars (or political economists as they often call themselves) have molded a consistent perspective with which to examine the deterioration of urban life that we are now experiencing. Most of these scholars are from the United States and

France, but there are many others from England, Italy, Australia, Spain, and elsewhere. All of these scholars have been heavily influenced by the thinking of Karl Marx; some would call themselves Marxists and others would not. Much of the data on which these scholars build their theories has been gathered by conventional social scientists, with whom the political economists share many opinions and values. There are, however, persistent, sometimes subtle differences between the political economist and the conventional social scientist. This essay attempts to distill the principal themes of urban political economy and contrast them with conventional urban social science. In the interest of brevity, I have been forced to make generalizations which obscure the variety of thinking in both camps.

THE CITY AND THE MODE OF PRODUCTION

Perhaps the most central proposition of the new urban political economy is that the city is merely a reflection of the larger economic and social fabric, termed the mode of production. This may seem to be a fairly innocuous statement, but its ramifications are far-reaching. One significant implication is that cities in different societies or at different times are very different, therefore there can be no single analysis of cities or of urbanization. There must instead be an analysis of urbanization that is specific to each particular society at a particular time. (This has led some even to reject the use of the word *urban* since it implies uniformity across social formations.) This applies specifically to the study of cities in less developed countries, in socialist societies, or in earlier historical epochs. Political economists are careful not to project the experience of developed capitalist countries onto cities in very different circumstances.

Capitalism is not a single static system, but undergoes constant evolution. Political economists divide the history of Western capitalism into three stages: mercantile, industrial, and corporate. The nature of cities has changed dramatically as capitalism has evolved from one stage to the next. Many of the urban phenomenon that we see today—the office building boom in central business districts, urban renewal and gentrification, the decline of the industrial Northeast and the rise of the sunbelt—are all linked to the transition from industrial to corporate capitalism. The older industrial cities face decline if they cannot remake themselves in the image of corporate capital; the sunbelt cities that have already done so are prospering.

To say that the city reflects the social and economic structure in which it is embedded raises myriad questions. There are substantial differences between Northern European and North American cities, though both are located in developed capitalist societies. Even more to the point, there are substantial differences in every aspect of urbanization within the United States. Which aspects of the city reflect the larger social and economic structure and which reflect local historical or political forces? The earliest writings by political economists on this topic focused on the similarities between cities, and only later has attention been paid to the differences. The notion that the city reflects the mode of production in which it is found is a general orientation rather than a definitive statement, a starting point of the analysis rather than its conclusion.

The conventional urban analysis, on the other hand, tends to view cities as apart from the social environment in which they are placed. This leads to an ahistorical, ethnocentric view of urbanization. Cities which were founded at the dawn of civilization or in medieval France are seen to be organized on the same principles as Phoenix in the 1980s. The same kind of policies that work in Cincinnati or Tokyo are applied to Lima or Dakar. Furthermore, the ability to envision sweeping change in either the nation's cities or the socioeconomic structure as a whole is inhibited. Urban problems are seen as the inevitable consequence of industrialization. This technological determinism is related to what some have called spatial determinism, the inability to envision alternative forms of organizing economic and social life across space. Ignoring the cultural specificity of urban space means that historically specific urban problems are seen as products of nature, not of social relationships, which leads to a fundamental pessimism about the future. The political economic viewpoint, which sees the present social and economic structure and the cities that it has generated as merely one stage in the historical unfolding of human history, provides the basis for a profound optimism about society.

This tendency of conventional urbanologists to see only one tree rather than the whole forest leads to the notion that the current shape of the metropolis is a result of externally determined consumer preference. But preferences are not independent of the economic system; they are a part of the larger mode of production. The political economist seeks to understand the sources of preferences for suburban living and other preferences such as the taste to discriminate racially.

THE ROLE OF CLASS

A second major tenet of the new urban political economics is that in analyzing any urban problem and therefore in analyzing any mode of production, class relations are paramount. Classes are groups of people in similar economic circumstances. The political economist finds that typically, though not invariably, the analytically most important economic groupings are those which categorize people according to how their livelihood is earned. In a capitalist society, the two most important groups are those who receive their income from property and those who receive their income from wages. Within each group, of course, there are enormous divisions and there are many people who do not fit easily into either category. But the division of society into owners (industrialists, financeers, merchants and landlords) and workers is a powerful analytical tool.

The analytic division of society into owners and workers is not arbitrary. The diametrically opposed ways in which the groups receive their incomes leads to radically different interests, attitudes, and behaviors. The income of owners is property income: dividends, rent, interest, capital gains which can be loosely grouped under the heading "profits." The inexorable logic of capitalism forces owners to do whatever is in their power to gain profit so that it can be reinvested so as to gain still more profit so that it can be reinvested and so on in a never-ending cycle. Those who fail to expand their profits either by choice, incompetence, or bad luck are wiped out in the competitive struggle. Profit maximization and capital accumulation is, therefore, the overriding goal of owners of capital. Taken as a whole, workers spend their incomes (though some may save in order to even out consumption over their lifetime). Their direct interest is in consumption, in the uses to which the things they buy (or to which they otherwise have access) can be put. Workers as a whole, of course, have a very strong interest in society's saving and investment so that the level of consumption can continue to grow, but they have no interest in the profits or income of any individual capitalist as long as consumption can be maintained.

Accordingly, owners as a class must seek to organize society and more specifically urban space in order to enhance profit maximization. Workers' interests, however, are in organizing society and urban space in a way that permits a humane and rational ordering of consumption. Thus the needs of capital and workers conflict not merely head-on in the division of society's pie into wages and profits, they also clash in the way in which the organization of urban space is determined. An example of this is described by Gordon (essay 2 here) in which he analyzes the nineteenth century centralization of industrial production in cities and the twentieth century migration of industry to the suburbs and the sunbelt. In each case factory owners sought to place their facilities in such a way so as to minimize their exposure to worker militancy. The small industrial town of the early nineteenth century, the heart of the industrial city at the end of the nineteenth century and the beginning of the twentieth, and most

of the industrial Northeast at present is a scene of intense industrial conflict. Industrialists simply vote with their feet in order to find more docile
workers elsewhere. This, of course, has had and is now having a disastrous economic impact on the working class and on cities.

The lack of a class analysis leads to an error which might be called
the fetishism of space. Conventional urbanologists often speak in such
terms as the city versus the suburb, the competition of Dallas and Fort
Worth, or the zone of deterioration expanding into the encircling ring of
independent workingmen's homes. These are all fundamental distortions
of reality. Two parts of the earth's inanimate surface cannot have opposing interests. History is made only when groups of people have interests
opposed to those of other groups of people. Spatial fetishism plays a
prominent role in confusing the important social relations which shape
urban space.

THE GOVERNMENT AND CAPITALISM

The antagonism between owners and workers more often has an indirect
(rather than direct) effect on the city which is mediated by the government. The conventional wisdom views the government as a neutral arbiter
among competing interest groups, each with political power proportional
to its size and cohesiveness. The political economist, however, sees the
government not sitting astride the class struggle but playing an active role
in it.

The government typically expresses the interest of owners. There are
several reasons for this. Most of the high positions in government are
filled by persons who are themselves wealthy. Those who do not come
from the property-owning class can be effectively controlled by those
who do through bribes, campaign contributions, or promises of jobs after
retirement. Even if an independent-minded individual should rise to a
position of authority, that person's latitude in decision making is severely
restricted because most of the important economic decisions are made
directly by the owners of wealth, particularly decisions regarding the
level and location of economic activity. The government, if it is to protect
the prosperity of the economy and the livelihood of its constituents, has
no choice but to rationalize or even subsidize the process of capital accumulation. One of the ways it can do this is to co-opt or repress potentially
disruptive dissent.

This is not to say that a socialist mayor of Burlington, Vermont, or
Santa Barbara, California, cannot make modest reforms. The working
class is not powerless in the political arena. The ballot box does offer a

degree of leverage over the government. Although "public opinion" normally means the opinions of newspaper editors and politicians who are quoted by the news media, strongly felt positions of the working class can occasionally effect the political process. Even the reforms which are instituted to co-opt dissent, such as the War on Poverty of the 1960s, are expressions of the power of the popular will and can make a real difference in the lives of millions of people. The question is whether popular movements, having achieved specific reforms, become satisfied or worn out or whether they use their victories as a springboard for new battles.

Armed with the perspective that the government primarily serves the interests of capital, the political economist can easily make sense out of much of what governments have done in or to cities. In this volume, for example, Kleniewski and Sawers argue that urban renewal and most urban transportation policy has been initiated and planned by small groups of capitalists whose economic base was rooted in the central business district such as bankers, department store owners, utility executives, and downtown real estate interests. These owners had a very real stake in bolstering the value of downtown real estate, but in doing so served the interests of capital as a whole. The nineteenth century industrial city was no longer suited to the needs of corporate capital, and a restructuring process was required. The private sector has taken up the ball and run with it, as can be seen in the office building boom and the gentrification of the housing stock.

The jurisdictional fragmentation of the metropolis is another expression of the interests of the wealthy according to other essays in this book (Gordon, Markusen, and Hoch). At the turn of the century the major industrialists began building their new factories on the periphery of the major industrial cities. Prior to this, cities had had little difficulty in annexing the urban growth that had sprouted at their edges. The new suburban migrants, however, were a power to be reckoned with. Within two decades, throughout the industrial North, annexation laws were changed by state legislatures, effectively preventing cities from expanding their boundaries. The city became the central city surrounded by a ring of suburbs. Industry was protected from the fiscal burdens and progressive social legislation of central city government. The ability to insulate one's self from high central city tax rates became an added impetus to suburbanization; the ability of the wealthy to manipulate government thus leaves its trace on the built environment. The result of this form of suburban jurisdictional fragmentation is that conflicting classes do not confront each other directly over all political issues, because they are in different jurisdictions. The governmental structure has been manipulated in such a way as to prevent open class struggle.

Most of the other essays in this book in one way or another reflect the notion that the government primarily serves the interest of the wealthy. Tabb for example argues that the ability to shape the debate concerning the causes of the New York City fiscal crisis permitted the wealthy to intervene in a way favorable to their interests and foreclosed the option of a working-class oriented solution to the crisis. Maier in another paper about New York City shows how the city government has manipulated municipal employee labor unions in such a way that prevented the expression of rank and file interests, to the very obvious advantage of employers (both the city government and indirectly all employers in the city). Friedland, Piven, and Alford show how the government is shaped in order to serve the functions of rationalizing capital accumulation and managing dissent. They conclude that the fiscal crisis is merely a disguised form of class struggle, a mechanism by which the social wage or living standard of workers can be reduced. Drier in his paper on the tenants' movement documents the enormous power of landlords and real estate developers over the government.

It is important to keep in mind that political economists are not talking about just a bunch of greedy, unscrupulous people though some capitalists (as well as workers) do have these traits. Urban development is not conspiracy and theft, or at least not only conspiracy and theft. There is an economic system which encourages or forces people to act in certain ways. The issue is not theft but the extraction of profits. In order to mobilize politically it is necessary to point out the prime actors on the urban scene. The danger, however, is that these actors, rather than the system which stands behind them, become the villains.

The role of class and class conflict in shaping the urban environment has been discussed. Much of the conflict that one observes in cities takes the form of community conflict over rent control, traffic safety, health, land use, and so on. Political economists view most, though not all, of these conflicts as essentially disguised forms of class struggle. Whether or not the dictates of profit will determine the character of land use, the balance of power between landlord (part of the capitalist class) and tenant (almost entirely workers), and the level of the social wage (and who will pay the taxes that fund it), all boil down to struggle between owners and workers.

The lack of a class perspective plagues the conventional analysis of urban phenomenon. In some cases it simply leaves the analyst baffled. For example, when faced with the fact that the federal income tax code offers tax subsidies to wealthy homeowners and landlords that are many times greater than all of the government's subsidies to low income housing put together, one respected researcher says, "With respect to any conceivable policy objective, the pattern of tax benefits seems to be capricious and without rationale." The political economist, however, has little trouble understanding the rationale of these subsidies. Traditional approaches based on an assumption of class harmony also err by frequently overstating the benefits of government programs to the working class. It was several decades after the urban renewal program was implemented before it began to penetrate into the thinking of conventional analysts that the program robbed poor people of their housing, destroyed their communities, and raised the price of similar housing elsewhere in the city. Even that realization required the massive ghetto rioting of the 1960s, in which urban renewal was a major grievance, to bring this to public awareness. One can still easily find scholarly expression of the mistaken notion that urban renewal was a housing program that benefited poor people. Similarly, federal housing subsidies are typically viewed as benefiting the poor despite the fact that the overwhelming thrust of federal housing policy since the 1930s has been to benefit the well-to-do. The current massive subsidies of urban mass transit are typically seen as disproportionately benefiting low income persons despite the fact that the groups which benefit most from the program are downtown business interests, affluent suburban commuters, and corporations who use the central business district as their headquarters.

The lack of a class perspective further leads one to overstate the power of the government. First, the conventional analyst tends to see the government as the primary actor on the urban scene and to be blind to the role of capital. Urban renewal is typically viewed solely as a government program rather than a joint business-government venture with business possibly having the upper hand. The fact that downtown business interests wrote the urban renewal legislation and lobbied it through Congress in 1949 and that plans for specific urban renewal projects were frequently developed by private business groups before the involvement of public renewal agencies is not noted by the mainstream urbanologist—there is simply no place for such information in their frame of reference. Or the fact that the planning for much of the current urban transportation network in the nation's metropolises has been carried out by downtown business interests escapes notice by the conventional social scientist.

A second consequence of this lack of class analysis and consequent overstatement of the role of the government is in the area of policy prescriptions. The liberals' analysis of urban problems leads them to propose government-sponsored reforms. In contrast to the political economists' proposals, these reforms are to be implemented in a top-down fashion, without grass-roots mobilization or involvement. It is assumed that the government has the interests of all citizens at heart. But if the government primarily serves the interests of the wealthy as the political economists contend, then appeals which are merely humane or rational, but which do not have a mass mobilization backing them, will come to nought. Drier's paper on the tenants' movement illustrates this point convincingly. The political economists' perspective permits them not only to maintain a vision of sweeping change in the system as a long-term goal, but also a sense of realism about the reforms that can be implemented in the short term because they take account of the pivotal role of the wealthy.

THE ROLE OF URBAN PLANNERS

This essay has at several points touched on the role of the state in organizing the city. It is now appropriate to turn to the professional employed by the state whose explicit duty is to shape urban space: the urban planner. The first city planners in this century in the United States were not government officials but were in the employ of private capital. Their attention was drawn initially to the use of roads, parks, and zoning in order to mold the city. The first zoning laws enacted in the United States, for example, appeared in New York City during the 1910s. A group of downtown business interests had banded together to develop the legislation which would discourage industry and the workers it employed from encroaching on the prime real estate of the central business district. Those who were active in the zoning campaign served as a nucleus for a group of privately-sponsored planners under the auspices of the newly organized Regional Plan Association. They quickly developed a comprehensive plan for New York City. The plan actually implemented by the public official Robert Moses is almost an exact duplicate of the one presented to him by this group of capitalists. But New York is not an exceptional case. After 1930 corporate leaders began to use the state directly to achieve their ends. Layers of publicly employed professionals were gradually added to the core of privately sponsored planners. Private capitalists still play a direct and often pivotal role in the urban planning process, as the essays by Kleniewski and Sawers illustrate.

The function of the professional urban planner today is to plan the restructuring of urban space in such a way that the process of capital accumulation is rationalized; that is, so that the urban environment is an arena in which profits can be maximized. This is true whether or not the planner realizes his or her role. Planners supply technical expertise in the organization of this restructuring which increases the efficiency of the planning process. The ideological role of the planner, however, is to technocratize what is essentially a political process in which some people gain (capitalists and possibly others) and some people lose. Different ways of organizing or reorganizing the city lead to very different patterns of benefits and costs. The issue is thus fundamentally a political one.

THE WORKING CLASS DIVIDED

So far the working class has been spoken of as a single entity, but of course it is characterized by numerous divisions. The underlying reality of the vast majority of the people in this society is that they do not have the resources to exist without working for someone else. This is the material basis for their fundamental unity of interest. But the reality of capitalist life continuously generates and reproduces a fragmentation of this unity. The reasons for this are twofold. Capital as a whole has an interest in the continued fragmentation of the working class since a united working class would be invincible in any clash with capitalists. The continued domination of capital requires this fragmentation. Capitalists thus find it natural to segregate jobs by sex, discriminate against blacks in housing, or hire strikebreakers of a different race or ethnic group than that of the strikers in order to stir up racial or ethnic hatreds, since it is in their individual as well as class interests to do so. But workers do much of the capitalists' dirty work for them. Racism, sexism, anti-semitism, nativism, the oppression of homosexuals, are also ways in which workers turn on each other to the obvious advantage of capital. Whatever oppressive inclination workers may have, it is clear that they are powerfully reinforced by the economic insecurity of the workers' lot. Any upward mobility on the part of those not far below you on the economic ladder implies downward mobility for you. For many, downward mobility means not just tightening the belt a notch, but unemployment and deprivation. Where dramatic differences in living standards exist and those at the bottom live in abject poverty, the struggle to cling to or rise up the economic ladder can easily become vicious. More than anything else, this has to do with the competitive nature of the labor market and the endemic character of poverty in a capitalist society.

The many divisions between different categories of workers is reflected in the spacial organization of consumption and production within the metropolis. The spatial segregation of these different factions of the working class in turn solidifies and reproduces these divisions. Ashton's essay in this volume argues that the economically privileged workers were able to move to the suburbs and create governments and social institutions which helped protect their privilege. For example, suburban schools are typically better than central city ones, and this reinforces the ability of the next generation of suburbanites to gain the better jobs. Informal social structures perform the same function. This process operates not just between central city and suburb, but also within jurisdictions. The institution of the neighborhood school even within a jurisdiction plays the role of reproducing working class stratification. Indeed the neighborhood presents a large array of experiences, values, and social networks that go into the construction of what we call the human being. (By contrast, the lack of the neighborhood school in England has arguably helped to produce that country's lower degree of spatial fragmentation.) This mechanism operates not just for different income groups among the working class but also for different racial groups, for groups with different forms of tenancy (homeowners versus renters), for different religious groups, for those with unorthodox sexual orientation (there is a sizable and spatially segregated gay community in many cities, especially San Francisco), and so on. Economic tensions between these groups are often translated into struggles over "turf." Spatial segregation functions so as to perpetuate whatever tensions exist and to reproduce the economic differences between segments of the working class. This is true even for the sexual division among workers. Men and women typically live in the same residences, but during the working day are spatially segregated.

The spatial segmentation of various factions of the working class has some rather obvious benefits to the capitalist establishment. By reinforcing and reproducing divisions within the working class, its political power is reduced. In addition, the spatial segmentation of the working class allows the gains in the social wage to be isolated to a limited number of people. Privileged strata of the working class move to the suburbs where better quality public services can be had at a lower cost (tax burden). The spatial separation of different strata of workers into different jurisdictions discourages the generalization of this higher social wage.

Traditional views, by ignoring the systemic way in which these divisions within the working class are created, reinforced, or manipulated, fall into several errors. Liberal reforms typically underestimate the persistence of the various forms of oppression because they understate the benefits of oppression to various elements of society, in particular the property-owning class. Liberal reformers tend to overestimate the willingness of the government, which primarily serves the interests of capital, to do anything about the situation. As argued above, the political economists stress grass-roots mobilization as the key to successful efforts to change society. Accordingly, combatting the oppressive divisions within the working class is crucial since without unity the working class power is diminished. By beginning with a perspective which views class struggle rather than class harmony as the more fundamental reality of our present society, political economists necessarily place near the center of their political strategy the lessening of oppressive divisions in the working class.

THE CAPITALIST CLASS DIVIDED

All capitalists, because they receive their income in the same way, have an essential unity of interest and outlook. This is why it is appropriate to speak of them as a class. At the same time, the competitive nature of capitalism means that this class is inherently divided against itself. Different categories of the property-owning class play very different roles in the urban arena. In the eighteenth century, it was the merchant capitalist who dominated the economy, the polity, and thus the city. By the nineteenth century, it was the industrialist whose decisions shaped space, and specifically urban space. Because industrialists decide where production takes place, they have the ultimate say as to the spatial organization of the economy. However, it has not been since the first half of the nineteenth century that industrialists have directly organized urban space except in a handful of company towns. The early mill towns of New England (which included the mills as well as the housing) were built by the factory owners. By mid-century, other capitalists specializing in the production and leasing of housing took over its provisioning from the industrialist. The role of the landlord, real estate developer, and financier rose to prominence or became decisive according to some political economists. The accelerating spatial fragmentation of the capitalist class perhaps means that there is no longer a unified group that can directly organize the city.

One of the sources of divisions within the capitalist class is the chaotic character of capitalist development. The accumulation of capital is for the most part organized through markets. Despite powerful and endemic tendencies for monopolization and political centralization, the economy is still competitive. It is individual capitalists or enterprises acting in their individual interest which initiate most productive activity. This sets the stage for considerable disagreements within the owning class.

Much of the unsatisfying nature of the modern metropolis (both from the view of the working class and that of the capitalist class) results not from planning by a small cabal of capitalists, but from no planning at all. For example, society has invested enormous amounts of resources in the built (as opposed to the natural) environment. It is wasteful to discard these structures and to build new ones elsewhere. But the largely unplanned market for land continually forces this to happen, thereby generating enormous losses in efficiency for the economy as a whole. Older neighborhoods (Bedford-Stuyvesant), older cities (East St. Louis), older regions (the Northeast), and even older countries (England), are cast aside by the vagaries of the market. Once a few residents and businesses leave a particular area, it can become labeled a declining area. Once so labeled, financial credit for maintaining or upgrading the built environment dries up and still more are encouraged to leave. Once begun, the process snowballs out of control. Only some form of central coordination can prevent this scenario from being repeated over and over again. (It is this kind of analysis that leads many political economists to argue that any kind of planning, even if inevitably under the control of capitalists, is preferable to no planning at all.) This process, of course, leads to enormous stresses and strains among different factions of the capitalist class as some gain enormous fortunes and others are crushed.

The unplanned, chaotic nature of capitalist development leads to another consequence known familiarly as the business cycle. The restructuring of capital and the disciplining of labor which come about in a recession or larger transformation inevitably have spatial dimensions. The lack of planning in a capitalist society leaves no mechanism for regulating the overall contours of capital accumulation. As accumulation proceeds, excesses, which come from incompetence, venality, or just too many lemmings following the herd, inevitably build up. Further, too long a period of prosperity leaves the working class in a strong position to bargain for a higher individual and social wage. Every few years, a recession is required to enforce a rationalizing of capital and a disciplining of labor. Every few decades, a major transformation of the economy is required to deal with more fundamental contradictions which have emerged. The 1930s was such a period of transformation as was the 1970s and, so far, the 1980s.

The excesses that have been built up are, of course, found at particular points in space. The Penn-Centrals and Chryslers which must be devalued or destroyed have a physical location. Furthermore, the ability of the working class to gain concessions from employers is distributed unevenly over space. Detroit and Cleveland used to be hot beds of labor union organizing. The industrial Northeast is being abandoned because the technology embedded in its capital is obsolete and its working class has become accustomed to the protection of a labor union. These periods of restructuring in which many capitalists are destroyed and others rise to prominence greatly exacerbate the divisions within the capitalist class.

The existence of these divisions has led some political economists to argue that the government has considerable independence from any particular faction of capitalists. The government, in this view, plays the role of coordinating the diverse interests of all capitalists, rationalizing the accumulation process. It still acts in the interest of capital as a whole because of the structure of economic, political, and bureaucratic imperatives within which it operates. The structuralists who argue along these lines thus downplay the role of specific groups of capitalists such as the Highway Lobby; the participation of such groups in the political process is seen as a consequence, not a cause, of the objective coincidence of the interests of the government and the owning class. A limitation of this structuralist approach if narrowly construed is that it rivets one's attention on how the structural features of the capitalist system inexorably reproduce themselves without sufficient attention to the contradictions within the system. Structuralism has difficulty in comprehending the options or degrees of freedom that capitalists have to alter the structure of the system in different ways. Similarly structuralism, by overstating the self-perpetuating character of capitalism, gives little guidance to working-class movements in their attempt to change the system. Without a careful documentation of which group of capitalists is behind this or that policy, one's political responses can be misdirected. Furthermore, structuralists overstate the fragmentation of the capitalist class. There are a wide variety of institutions and organizations—trade associations, social clubs, *ad hoc* groups, political action committees, forums, interlocking directorates— which serve to integrate the capitalist class and permit it to take unified positions.

An over-simplified instrumentalist position, which sees the government as merely the instrument of one or another faction of capitalists, is also flawed. Narrowly construed instrumentalism only allows one to reason backward from specific policies to the interest groups which advocated them, without revealing why a particular policy was advocated by a particular group or why one faction of capitalists instead of another were able to prevail upon the government to do its bidding. Thus neither a structuralist nor an instrumentalist approach is appropriate; rather both viewpoints must be integrated so that a completely developed understanding of capitalist reality can be articulated.

UNEVEN DEVELOPMENT

One way to summarize this essay is to invoke the political economists' notion of uneven development. In any competitive struggle in which some succeed and others fail, those with the most formidable resources for waging the struggle will prevail. But in winning one battle, the victor has still more resources for the next. The differences between those who succeed and those who fail automatically tend to grow with each successive round in the competitive struggle. This is the basis for what some have called the law of uneven development. Since capitalism is a system characterized by competition, it is also a system in which uneven development abounds.

In the struggles between capitalists and workers, or within those two classes, unevenness prevails. This is reflected in all aspects of the capitalist city. Differences between neighborhoods, between city and suburb, between cities or regions seem to grow continuously. The stark contrasts that one finds in all aspects of urban life now come into focus. Capitalism is a system which must generate contrasts, opulence and poverty, dynamic growth and steady decay. An understanding of this process is the first step in ending it.

one

FROM
CITY TO METROPOLIS

Capitalist Development and the History of American Cities[1]

DAVID M. GORDON

Capitalism, as a mode of production, is the basic process of most of what we know as the history of country and city. Its abstracted economic drives, its fundamental priorities in social relations, its criteria of growth and of profits and loss, have over several centuries altered our country and created our kinds of city. . . . The division and opposition of city and country, industry and agriculture, in their modern forms are the critical culmination of the division and specialization of labour which, though it did not begin with capitalism, was developed under it to an extraordinary and transforming degree. . . . The symptoms of this division can be found at every point in what is now our common life.

—Raymond Williams (pp. 302–6)

This essay explores the historical links between capitalism and urban development in order to support the general proposition that capitalism, as a mode of production, has generated the modern metropolis. This essay presents a case study of the history of cities in the United States.

In turning toward that history, we quickly confront one informing idea in the orthodox social sciences. Most urban histories treat the growth of cities as a gradual, evolutionary, and ineluctable process. The outcomes seem destined. In any developing society, as Kingsley Davis writes with assurance, "urbanization is a finite process, a cycle through which nations go in their transition from agrarian to industrial society" (p. 9). Cities become continuously larger, more complicated, more specialized, and more interdependent. Hans Blumenfeld describes the determinants of this historical process:

> The division of labor and increased productivity made concentration in
> cities possible, and the required cooperation of labor made it necessary,
> because the new system called for bringing together workers of many skills
> and diverse establishments that had to interchange goods and services.
> The process fed on itself, growth inducing further growth (p. 42).

Because the United States has become the prototypical advanced industrial society, orthodox historians view American urban development as
the consummate reflection of this universal process of urbanization.

In the Marxian view, that history must be seen in a different light.
The Marxian analysis of the spatial division of labor suggests that no particular pattern of urban development is inevitably "destined," somehow
deterministically cast in a general spatial mold. Spatial forms are conditioned, rather, by the particular mode of production dominating the society under study; they are shaped by *endogenous* political-economic
forces, not by *exogenous* mechanisms. Marxians also argue that urban
history, like the history of other social institutions, does not advance in-
crementally, marching step by gradual step along some frictionless path.
Urban history advances *discontinuously,* instead of *continuously,* periodi-
cally experiencing qualitative transformations of basic form and structure.
During the capitalist epoch, in particular, the instability of the accumulation process itself is bound to lead to periodic institutional change. The
current economic crisis and its attendant urban crisis, from this perspective, are just another in a long series of these kinds of transformations.

This essay applies the Marxian perspective. According to that view,
we have witnessed three main stages of capital accumulation in the advanced capitalist countries: the stages of *commercial* accumulation, *industrial* (or competitive) accumulation, and advanced *corporate* (or monopoly) accumulation. I argue that urban development in the United States
has passed through *three corresponding stages*—each conditioned by the
dynamics of capital accumulation that characterize that stage. I argue that
the process of capital accumulation has been the most important factor
structuring the growth of cities; city growth has not flowed from hidden
exogenous forces but has been shaped instead by the logic of the underlying economic system. Finally, I argue that the transitions *between* stages
of urban development have been predominantly influenced by problems of
class control in production, problems erupting at the very center of the
accumulation process.

This connected set of historical arguments can be separated formally
into three main historical hypotheses about the relationships between capitalist development and urban form in the United States:

First, that three principal urban forms have characterized urban development in America, each corresponding to a determinate stage of capital accumulation. In order to emphasize the *logic* of these connections, I give each urban form, defined abstractly, the name of its conditioning stage of capital accumulation, referring respectively to *the Commercial City, the Industrial City,* and *the Corporate City.*

Second, that the changes from one dominant urban form to another were forged in the crucible of capitalist production, determined by the struggles between owners and workers over social relations of production in the capitalist workplace.

Third, combining these first two hypotheses, that the process of capitalist development more generally has created a uniquely capitalist urban form in the United States—that American capitalism has bred the American capitalist city.

I develop this argument in four sections. The first three trace the emergence of these three successive urban forms—the Commercial City, the Industrial City, and the Corporate City. The final section applies that historical analysis to explore the current crisis of American cities, arguing briefly that the relationship between capitalist development and urban form in the United States *lies at the roots of the current urban crisis.*

COMMERCIAL ACCUMULATION AND
THE COMMERCIAL CITY

During the final stages of the emergence of capitalism, merchant capitalists sought to increase their capital through *commercial accumulation.* They made profits through the exchange of commodities in the marketplace. Their profits depended on their capacity to "buy cheap and sell dear." Operating in the market, they did not typically intervene in the production process. They counted heavily upon political favors and franchises to strengthen their privileged intermediate positions in the marketplace. Because monopoly power in the market and political franchise through the State played such a critical role in determining the rate of commercial accumulation, tendencies toward uneven development among merchants, companies, cities, regions, or countries often emerged. Increasingly through this stage of "original accumulation," as capitalists' hungry pursuit of commercial profits grew more and more infectious, the dynamics of commercial accumulation became the major source of change in societies experiencing capitalist transformation.

I would propose in general that cities served four kinds of political economic functions in this stage of commercial accumulation:[2]

A *Political Capital* (and colonial control centers) became the site(s) of the mercantilist government, attracting court followers and mercantile lobbyists eager for commercial privileges.

The *Commercial Metropolis* housed the discounting, lending, accounting, and entrepreneurial functions supporting commercial exchange. (Tendencies toward the uneven development of commercial power among merchants were likely to produce an increasingly uneven geographic concentration of these support activities among cities.)

Ports served as Transport Nodes—as centers for the collection and distribution of commodities being supplied from geographically diffuse points in the hinterlands and carried to dispersed markets. (Merchants were able to consolidate their monopoly control over exchange most effectively if there were few and fixed channels for commodity transport; there were strong tendencies, therefore, for an increasingly uneven geographic concentration of transport functions among Transport Nodes.)

Since artisans producing luxury goods usually clustered in cities to gain access to their wealthy merchant and court-following customers, cities also served as *Craft Manufacturing Centers.*

These few simple observations are sufficient to analyze the emergence and crystallization of the Commercial City in the United States. The dynamics of commercial accumulation dominated American economic development from the colonial era through the middle of the nineteenth century. The American Commercial City evolved during those years.

Among Cities

Before Independence, American colonial cities served few economic functions. The first two general functions of Commercial Cities—those of the Political Capital and the Commercial Metropolis—were firmly lodged in London (see Albion; Nettels). Some seaports developed as Transport Nodes. Many artisans gathered in the colonial ports, producing luxuries for colonial merchants and administrators, but this Craft Manufacturing Center function was obviously limited by the slow growth of the indige-

nous merchant class itself.[3] The Transport Node function therefore dominated the distribution of people and economic activity both between city
and country and also among cities.

Because colonial cities were serving such limited functions, the urban
population did not grow very rapidly. Although total colonial population
increased more than tenfold between 1690 and 1790, the cities' relative
share of the colonial population actually declined.[4] Roughly 9 percent of
colonial Americans lived in cities and towns in 1690 (Bridenbaugh, 1971,
p. 6). One hundred years later, the relative urban share had fallen back to
only 5.1 percent. Although the main port cities grew in absolute numbers,
urbanization failed to keep pace "with the diffusion of hundreds of thousands of settlers into the back country" (Glaab and Brown, p. 26). There
was little to keep them down in the town.[5]

Given the singular importance of the Transport Node functions,
there were strong political-economic pressures which not only limited
relative urban population growth but also limited the *number* of major
cities. From the beginning, the British Crown strictly controlled town
charters. The Crown feared that British merchants would be unable to
control commercial transport if too many port cities developed. As early
as 1680, according to the governor of Virginia, the King was "resolved as
soon as storehouse and conveniences be provided, to prohibit ships trading here to land or unload but at certain fixed places" (Glaab and Brown,
p. 1). In the North, these early political-economic constraints limited the
growth of commercial ports during the colonial period to just four places—
Boston, New York, Philadelphia, and, somewhat later, Baltimore. Although these four ports grew from an average size of almost 10,000 to
nearly 22,000 between 1720 and 1775, few other cities were able to attain
populations of as much as 5000.[6] The four ports accounted for 66.9 percent of total urban population in 1790, while only 50,000 lived in all
other towns combined. The four ports captured 47.5 percent of urban
population growth in the thirteen colonies between 1720 and 1790. There
was little space in the economic tableau for other towns to develop.[7]

After Independence, the forces affecting urban development shifted.
Commercial accumulation still dominated the pace of economic development, but American merchants were able to gain control over a broader
range of commercial functions. As domestic and foreign trade expanded,
American merchants quickly replaced British merchants in the middle.
American cities added the Commercial Metropolis functions to their earlier roles.[8]

As a result, the growth of American ports exploded. The urban population increased from just over 200,000 in 1790 to more than 6 million in

1860. More important, the urban share of total population *reversed* its decline during the colonial period. Relative urban population rose from one-twentieth of the American population in 1790 to one fifth in 1860.

With trade growing rapidly, urban merchants competed frenetically to gain control over both the Commercial Metropolis and Transport Node functions. Potential commercial monopolists raced against their peers in other leading American ports. "A complex of city imperialisms arose," as Arthur Schlesinger, Sr., put it, "each scheming for dominion, each battling with its rivals for advantage" (p. 28).

During the first decades after Independence, the major ports were evenly matched in the battle for business. Each of the four main Northern cities participated in the urban trade boom, and each was able to grow more or less apace with the others. Between 1790 and 1810, the populations of Philadelphia, New York, Boston, and Baltimore each increased between 180 and 290 percent. Their absolute population growth alone accounted for 45 percent of total city population increase during those first twenty years.[9]

Soon enough, however, tendencies toward uneven development asserted themselves. New York merchants began to gain clear competitive advantage over their rivals. Thanks to the Erie Canal and to other important commercial innovations, New York commercial capitalists began to control more and more of domestic and foreign trade. Between 1800 and 1860, the New York Port's share of total U.S. foreign trade climbed from only 9 percent to 62 percent. Reflecting its growing role as the primary Commercial Metropolis, the city's population soared. By 1860, New York (including Brooklyn) contained over one million people, more than Philadelphia, Boston, and Baltimore combined.[10] Once again, commercial activity was almost exclusively determining the growth of American cities and the distribution of population among them.[11]

Within Cities

The dynamics of commercial accumulation had much less effect on the internal structure of American cities. Because merchant capitalists were not yet intervening directly in production, commercial accumulation was not yet directly affecting the social relations of production.

As a result, the port cities grew within the context of an earlier precapitalist set of social relations. The ports internally retained their precapitalist forms. In precapitalist cities, as Gideon Sjoberg writes, even business was "conducted in a leisurely manner, money not being the only desired end" (p. 8). Daily life, like the entrepôt around which it centered, was "shot through with chance" (Handlin, p. 11).

Within that precapitalist context, commercial accumulation had two simple direct effects which further specified the content of urban life. First, the economic functions of the port cities determined the groups of people who shared in this "random" urban life. The early port populations were dominated by three main occupational clusters: (1) merchants, associated political professionals like lawyers, and the domestic servants of the wealthy; (2) the artisans, journeymen, and apprentices of the craft trades; and (3) the laborers of the transportation sector, like seamen and draymen.[12] Second, the cities tended naturally to center geographically around the wharves, drawn centripetally to the locus of their main political-economic functions.

As the commercial cities grew, therefore, they began to assume a simple and characteristic urban form, laced with residual social relations not yet transformed by the dynamics of capitalist accumulation.

Most families owned their own property and acted as independent economic agents. Most establishments remained small, making it possible for nearly everyone to live and work in the same place. People of many different backgrounds and occupations were interspersed throughout the central city districts, with little obvious socioeconomic residential segregation. In the central port districts, the randomness and intensity of urban life produced jagged, unexpected, random physical patterns. Streets zigged and zagged every which way. Buildings were scattered at odd angles in unexpected combinations. (Even in Philadelphia, where William Penn's original street plan of 1681 had projected regular, spacious, extensive city growth, the intensive growth around the wharf had resulted in the creation of new unplanned streets around the docks.) It appears that a vibrant community life flourished throughout this central area. The cities featured "an informal neighborhood street life," in Sam Bass Warner's words, threaded by the "unity of everyday life, from tavern, to street, to workplace, to housing. . . ."[13]

Only one group failed to share in this central port-district life. Poor itinerants—beggars, casual seamen, propertyless laborers—all lived outside the cities, huddling in shanties and rooming houses. Too poor to establish themselves stably, moving frequently from town to town, they had little relationship to life in the urban center and little impact upon it.

By the beginning of the nineteenth century, in short, each of the major ports increasingly reflected the characteristic structural logic of the Commercial City. Each city was divided into two parts. One part coalesced around the wharf. Within that central district, many different occupational groups, filling the limited economic roles defined by the Commercial City, lived and worked in intimate, intermingling, heterogeneous contiguity. The second part formed a band around the central port district. In it lived the

transient, homogeneous poor. This urban form resulted from the simple
intersection between precapitalist social relations among independent economic agents and the limited occupational and locational consequences of
the dynamics of commercial accumulation.

Once this basic form was established, rapid urban growth took place
within it as long as the dynamics of commercial accumulation remained
dominant. Between 1800 and 1850, trade expanded rapidly but industrialization had not yet dramatically invaded the urban scene: factories were
being built in small towns, not in the large port cities. Some new occupational groups began to enter city life, but all of these groups continued to fit into the places and styles of the Commercial City. The wharves
continued to act as magnets, containing urban growth within the central
port districts. People pushed toward the docks as much as possible. "In
the area adjacent to the waterfront," George Rogers Taylor writes, "a
greatly increased work force lived under intolerably crowded conditions"
(1970, p. 132). Scattered evidence suggests that central-district residential
densities probably reached their peaks in the port cities in the 1840s and
1850s. "In some quarters," Pred concludes, they "approached or exceeded
those encountered in modern high-rise housing projects" (p. 196).

And still, the central districts retained their heterogeneity. New immigrant groups were rapidly assimilated into the flowing central-city life.[14]
Workplace and residence were still connected.[15] Socioeconomic segregation did not increase.[16] The ebb and flow of street life, however much
more crowded it had become, seemed to continue.[17]

The poor also remained itinerant and isolated on the outskirts. There
is no evidence that the poor had begun to move into the central districts—
where we know that they later began to live—through the 1840s and the
1850s.[18]

One major change in the form of the Commercial City did take place,
however, but it simply manifested the intensifying effects of the commercial dynamic. After Independence, as city populations began to boom,
land speculators cast their covetous eyes on urban property. The randomness of the earlier street and lot plans gave way to the "rationality" of
land speculation. Realtors' straightedges took the zigs out of the maps. In
Lewis Mumford's words, land speculators "treated the individual lot and
the block, the street and the avenue, as abstract units for buying and selling, without respect for historic uses, for topographic conditions, or for
social needs" (p. 421).

The map of Manhattan vividly witnesses this sudden turn. Below
Houston Street in Manhattan, streets flow in many directions at odd an-
gles. Streets above Houston Street were first plotted in the Commissioners'
Map of 1811. "Motivated mainly by narrow considerations of economic

gain" (Reps, p. 299), the commissioners laid out rectangular grids all the way up the rest of the island (to 155th Street). As the commissioners themselves explained, "the price of land" made it seem "proper to admit the principles of economy. . . . The effect of these plain and simple reflections was decisive" (Lyman, p. 113). Thus the "spatially determined" birth of the urban grid!

The Contradictions of the Commercial City

Cities grew very rapidly after Independence in the United States, but, despite their increasing size and complexity, they did *not* exhibit several of the ostensibly inevitable consequences of city growth in "modernizing" societies. For instance, American cities did not experience increasing physical separations among economic functions like work and residence. Nor did they exhibit increasing socioeconomic or ethnic residential segregation. Their poor people did not live in their central districts. And community life in the ports did not become demonstrably more impersonal and anomic.

This kind of emphasis, however heuristic for a skeptical reconsideration of spatial determinism, may convey a misleading impression about the quality of life for early American urban residents. In emphasizing the persistence of heterogeneity and the vibrancy of community life, I may appear to be romanticizing the "good old days" in the early American cities. But sharp conflicts did exist in the Commercial City. Their basic contour developed directly from the central contradiction of the process of commercial accumulation itself.

Commercial accumulation tended to generate uneven development among buyers and sellers. This tended to bring about, among other consequences, increasingly unequal distributions of wealth and income. Because different socioeconomic groups were living and working closely together in the Commercial Cities, these spreading inequalities became more and more physically evident—manifested in the luxury consumption of local merchants.

It appears that this evidence of inequality generated popular protest against it. As inequalities reached their peaks both during the Revolutionary period and during the 1820s and 1830s, popular protests also seemed to intensify. Most of these protests focused on demands for more equality.[19] Because these protests frequently had political effect, they tended to limit opportunities for further commercial accumulation.[20]

The recurrence of these kinds of protests prompts a final point about the Commercial City. Commercial accumulation both generated uneven development and consequently stimulated popular demands for more economic and political equality. This dialectic of uneven development and popular protest reveals a fundamentally *spatial* aspect to the contradictions of the commercial path to capital accumulation. Capitalists sought a mechanism for increasing their profits on the surface of economic life—tracing profitable connections along the sphere of circulation. Their successes, manifested in increasing wealth through persistently visible exchange, could not be hidden. Because the Commercial City retained the precapitalist transparencies of immediate, intimate, and integrated social relationships, commercial capitalist profits could not be masked. The quest for such a disguise—the urgent need for which was so dramatically witnessed in the streets of the Commercial City—played a central role in prompting the turn to a new and ultimately more opaque mode of capital accumulation.

INDUSTRIAL ACCUMULATION AND THE INDUSTRIAL CITY

Commercial Cities were obviously superseded. City life had fundamentally changed by the end of the nineteenth century. Why?

Following our application of the Marxian perspective, we can draw our first clues from the pace and pattern of capital accumulation. In the United States, the years between 1850 and 1870 witnessed a transition from the stage of commercial accumulation to the stage of industrial accumulation. Capitalists turned more and more toward making profits through industrial production itself—through the direct manufacture of the commodities that they exchanged on the market. In the United States, as in England before it, this consolidation of the capitalist mode of production depended on the final development of the factory system.

Industrial accumulation within the factory form depended centrally on two main factors. First, problems of both cost-minimization and labor discipline required the continual *homogenization* of the labor process; craft jobs were compressed into semiskilled operative work and almost all factory workers were subjected to the same discipline of factory control. Second, the system required the continual availability of a *reserve army of the unemployed*—jobless workers, available for immediate employment, whose presence could help discipline those inside the factory gates.

Given these requirements, it hardly seems surprising that cities became the central locus for factory production. Cities provided easy access to markets, facilitating the scale of production necessary to support homogenized labor processes. Cities also provided easy access to pools of reserve workers, much less accessible to employers in the countryside.

But which cities would house those factories? And what would they look like? Our analysis of the links between industrial accumulation and urban form obviously requires further specification before we can adequately answer those questions.

The Transition to Industrial Accumulation

The first major American factories—the textile mills of the 1830s and 1840s—were clustered along the rivers of New England in small cities like Lawrence, Lowell, Waltham, and Lynn. The factories depended on water power and were small by modern standards. As manufacturing production expanded, the factory cities extended along the rivers rather than piling more and more densely around the original centers of industrial production. When coal replaced water as a source of energy between 1850 and 1870 and when railroads began to knit together the economic countryside, factories were freed from the riverbanks. Where would capitalists pursue their profits?

Huge cities eventually dominated as the loci for factories. Orthodox economic historians have argued that factories concentrated in large industrial cities for some combination of four main reasons: (1) they could be near large numbers of workers; (2) they could secure easy rail and water access to essential raw materials, particularly coal; (3) they could be near industrial suppliers of machines and other essential intermediate products, including "innovations"; and (4) they could be near consumer markets for their final goods. All of these factors are captured by the conventional term from locational economics, "agglomeration economies." In essence, according to this view, factory owners will continually discover advantages to locating near other factory owners.[21]

But these hypotheses about agglomeration economies are not sufficient, by themselves, to explain continuing geographic concentration. Originally proposed as hypotheses about economies of scale, they can turn just as easily into hypotheses about analogous *dis*economies of scale. Too many industrialists located in one city can bid up the price of labor, for instance, superseding accessibility advantages. Dense concentrations around rail and water depots can cause congestion and chaos, obliterating savings in longer-haul transport costs. The same effects of congestion can impede intermediate commodity exchange, slowing transport within cities among suppliers and final producers. And too great a concentration of final producers near the same consumer market, finally, can potentially generate competitive, unstable, and self-destructive battles for market position and market share.

Where is the threshold? When are industrial cities likely to approach the point of diminishing returns to economic agglomeration? The main-stream view cannot answer this question *a priori*.

The relevance of these questions, posed initially at a theoretical level, can be dramatized historically. Evidence suggests that the transition to industrial accumulation was witnessing a *diffusion* of the advantages of urban factory location, not a centralization. Employers' access to workers was spreading because workers were becoming so mobile that labor supply fluidly followed demand. The railroad network expanded so rapidly during the 1860s and 1870s that most medium-sized cities quickly gained access to the major coal fields and sources of other raw materials. Major technological innovations were sufficiently simple and widespread by the decade after the Civil War, according to most historical accounts, that industrialists everywhere were equally able to take advantage of them. And access to consumer markets apparently played a minor role after the rail network improved; most major industries, particularly heavy industries, became increasingly concentrated in one or two cities, more and more isolated from their consumer markets around the country.[22]

Conventional arguments about agglomeration economies, in short, are so indeterminate that one cannot directly derive from them a clear projection of increasingly uneven concentration of manufacturing employment in increasingly large industrial cities. From what we have learned thus far, it appears that capitalists could have profited equally from location in factory cities of almost any size.

Indeed, in the early years of transition, this appears to have been the case. In 1850, many cities of different sizes housed burgeoning factory production. As industrial capitalism took hold between 1850 and 1870, many of these cities enjoyed rapidly expanding industrial production regardless of their former size. Between 1860 and 1870, for instance, manufacturing employment in the three largest cities increased by only 53 percent while it increased in the cities ranked 21st through 50th in population by 79.5 percent. There was no significant correlation between rate of employment increase and initial population-rank size.[23] The New Yorks, Chicagos, and Clevelands were growing rapidly, to be sure, but so were cities like Worcester, Jersey City, Indianapolis, and Dayton. Many cities, it seems, had a grip on the golden ring.

As the economy continued to boom after 1870, however, manufacturing began to concentrate in fewer and fewer large cities. By 1900, New York, Philadelphia, and Chicago each housed well over one million people. Manufacturing employment in those three largest cities grew by 245 percent between 1870 and 1900 while the number of industrial wage-earners in the cities ranked 21st through 50th in population grew by only

158 percent. The ten largest industrial areas increased their share of national value-added in manufacturing from under a quarter to almost two
fifths between 1860 and 1900.[24]

How can we account for this rapid centralization of manufacturing
employment without resorting to the kinds of relatively indeterminate *ex
post* explanations which the agglomeration hypotheses involve?

I hypothesize that a major reason for the concentration of manufacturing in the largest cities flowed from the dynamics of *labor control in
production*. At its most general level, the hypothesis proposes that large
cities became increasingly dominant as sites for capitalist factories because
they provided an environment which more effectively reinforced capitalist
control over the production process. Capitalists had to find *qualitatively
efficient* locations for their factories—locations, that is, which maximized
their control over the process of production and minimized workers' resistance to that domination (see Gordon, 1976). Medium-sized cities did
not fully satisfy this imperative. Larger cities satisfied it much better. And
so, more and more capitalists built their factories in those large cities.

This hypothesis can best be elaborated through two separable questions: First, what differences between medium-sized cities and large cities
account for their differential sustenance of capitalist production? And
second, what explains those underlying differences between the two kinds
of cities?

The first question is somewhat easier to answer. The problem of
labor discipline plagued capitalists continually after they began to institute the factory form of production. Artisans resisted the degradation of
work, and wage-laborers from preindustrial backgrounds struggled against
the insecure wages and working conditions which factory homogenization
continually imposed. Particularly as Civil War prosperity gave way to the
stagnation and depression of the 1870s, workers fought to resist layoffs
and wage cuts all across the industrial terrain.

In smaller and medium-sized industrial cities, employers had great
difficulty suppressing and overcoming these moments of worker resistance.[25] The power of the industrialist, in Gutman's words, "was not yet
legitimized and 'taken for granted'" (1963, p. 11). Many middle-class
residents, used to earlier, preindustrial relationships, resented the imposition of the relentless, uncompromising, impersonal disciplines of factory
life. When workers struck, newspapers, politicians, and the middle classes
often supported them. As Gutman elaborates, the non-industrial classes
"saw no necessary contradiction between private enterprise and gain on
the one hand, and decent, humane social relations between workers and
employers on the other" (1963, p. 48). As the Portsmouth, N.H., *Times*

explained, "We have very little of the codfish aristocracy, and industrious laborers are looked upon here with as much respect as any class of people" (quoted in Gutman, loc. cit.).

In the largest cities, it appears, relationships among the several classes were significantly different. Workers were, in the transitional years at least, no less likely to strike than workers in smaller cities. But the various strata of the middle class were much more hostile to the workers than their peers in smaller cities. Newspapers, politicians, and the middle classes usually opposed workers on strike. Facing such hostility, workers found it more difficult to fight their employers. Because "there was almost no sympathy for the city workers from the middle and upper classes," workers were weakened and "employers in large cities had more freedom of choice than their counterparts in small towns." One of the many results, according to fragmentary evidence, was that "strikes and lockouts in large cities seldom lasted as long as similar disputes outside of these urban centers."[26]

The implications of this hypothesis seem clear. Even if all other economic factors were equal—equalizing the factors of *quantitative efficiency,* or the amount of output employers could generate from given labor inputs—employers in large cities would be able to gain considerable advantage over their competitors in smaller industrial centers. Many workers were resisting the factory system. If employers in large cities were better able to overcome that resistance, they would suffer fewer losses during strikes, achieve greater discipline over their regular factory, and, in general, extract more surplus value from their workers. Even if employers were not particularly conscious of these relative advantages at first, those located in larger cities would be able to grow more rapidly and profit more steadily than their classmates in other locations. That dynamic alone would account for the growing concentration of manufacturing employment in those larger cities. And this explanation by itself, from the Marxian perspective, has precedence over other, more "technical" explanations based on agglomeration hypotheses. Economies of scale are little use to any employer, in the end, if he has not already solved the more basic problems of labor discipline. Factor cost-minimization makes little difference to the capitalist if he can't get his workers to labor diligently in the service of his own profits.

How can we account for these differences in class relationships and social environment between larger and smaller industrial cities?

Superficially, two explanations seem obvious. First, the greater physical segregation and impersonality of the larger cities seem to have isolated the working class and exposed it to community indifference or ostracism. Second, nonindustrial classes in smaller cities seem to have exhibited more militantly preindustrial values than their larger-city cousins.

These superficial differences are more difficult to explain. It appears that they need to be examined in different fashion for two separate groups of large industrial cities. In the Northeast, New York, Philadelphia, Boston, and Baltimore—the four dominant Commercial Cities—became the four leading industrial centers in that region. Two characteristics of their precedent dynamics as the leading Commercial Cities seem to have played an important role in isolating their increasingly numerous industrial workers. First, they had already attained considerable physical scale as port cities and, on balance, had begun to suffer from the increasing impersonality which large scale tends to implant. Second, many of the professionals, politicians, newspapers, and merchants of those ports had begun to acquire—after years of support for commercial accumulation—a growing sympathy for the calculus of profitability.

Across the Appalachian Mountains, the most rapidly growing industrial cities displayed exactly the opposite traits. Those industrial cities, like Chicago, Detroit, and San Francisco, that changed character most quickly were those which *least* exhibited preindustrial community relations. Those Midwestern cities, like Louisville, Cincinnati, Pittsburgh and St. Louis, that had already developed commercial and preindustrial production activities before 1850, were the cities most likely to expose capitalist production to the friction of residual solidarities between workers and the middle classes. Indeed, if one looks at the ten Midwestern cities which were largest in both 1850 and 1900, one finds that those with the *fewest* wage-earners in manufacturing in 1850 were precisely those whose industrial employment grew most rapidly between 1850 and 1900.

In either case, it turned out that the basis for industrial profits was best secured if and when a homogeneous industrial proletariat could be most effectively segregated from the rest of society. Ironically, in the American case, this appears to have been spatially possible in cities where Commercial City life had become either *most* or *least* manifest. Where it had been most manifest, cities had apparently become impersonal enough, and the relentlessness of commercial accumulation had sufficiently infected precapitalist community relations to facilitate this process of isolation. Where Commercial City relations had been least manifest, industrial capitalists were able metaphorically to establish their factories on *tabulae rasae*. In both cases, the transition to the Industrial City pointed in the same directions.

The Form of the Industrial City

As the largest cities became increasingly dominant, the form of the Industrial City crystallized. Its characteristics can be easily summarized.

First, huge factories were concentrated in downtown factory industrial districts, near rail and water outlets. (There were a few small industrial districts on the outskirts of some of the cities.)

Second, entirely new segregated working-class housing districts emerged. Located near the factories so that workers could walk to work, the housing was crammed densely together. In New York there were tenements. In Philadelphia there were row houses. In most other big cities there were wooden tenements. Whatever the specific features of the housing, it was typically clustered together in isolation from the middle and upper classes. Although some ethnic segregation by block began to emerge, almost all working-class ethnic groups were contained within the same isolated areas.[27]

Third, the middle and upper classes began to escape from the center city as fast and as far as their finances permitted. The wealthy and not-so-wealthy joined in "fleeing from the noise and confusion of the waterfront, the dirt, the stench, and the intolerably crowded conditions of the old central city" (Taylor, 1970, p. 134). Since the wealthy could afford to travel farther to and from work than the middle classes, residential socioeconomic segregation among those groups became more and more pronounced. The middle and upper classes were gradually arrayed in concentric rings moving along the transport spokes radiating from the center.

Finally, shopping districts arose in the heart of the city to provide centralized shopping outlets on which the middle and upper classes could converge for their marketing.

Working from this schematic view, we can easily see that the Industrial City represented a clear *reversal* of some of the most important tendencies reflected in the Commercial City form. The central city was now occupied by dependent wage-earners rather than independent property-owners. Producers no longer worked and lived in the same place; there was now a separation between job and residential location. There was no longer residential heterogeneity; instead, the cities had quickly acquired a sharp residential segregation by economic class. In the Commercial Cities, the poor had lived outside the center while everyone else lived inside; now, suddenly, the poor and working classes lived inside while everyone else raced away from the center. In the Commercial Cities, central-city life involved nearly everyone in easy communality; in the Industrial Cities, only the working classes participated in the increasingly intense, impersonal, and assaulting street life, and they had little choice.

Was this new urban form destined by technical and spatial necessities? Apparently not. Other, much smaller, less segregated cities might well have facilitated equally rapid industrial growth. It appears, in other words, that a wide variety of cities was initially meeting the tests of quantitative efficiency in industrial production. But capitalism requires workers' submission to their exploitation. Only in this kind of large Industrial City, it appears, could workers be sufficiently isolated for their resistance to be rubbed smooth. As one foreign observer commented upon surveying the central districts of Pittsburgh in 1884, "There are no classes here except the industrious classes; and no ranks in society save those which have been created by industry."[28]

The Contradictions of the Industrial City

Although the Industrial Cities grew rapidly, their growth did not proceed smoothly for long. As the end of the century approached, certain characteristic contradictions began to erupt. Accumulating friction began to threaten the speed of the industrial machine. These frictions assumed both quantitative and qualitative dimensions.

Quantitatively, some diseconomies of scale began to plague the increasingly crowded central cities. Before the second wave of immigration flooded the Industrial Cities after 1890, demand for labor was piling up more quickly than supply could meet it, and wages were beginning to rise. (The index of money wages rose from 66 in 1880 to 74 in 1890, despite falling prices.)[29] Transportation was getting increasingly clogged in some factory districts, and some manufacturers were beginning to complain about congestion. Increasing concentration was creating some pressure on land prices. And, to the degree that political machines were beginning to take advantage of the political isolation of the working classes, governmental corruption was beginning to affect business-property taxes.[30]

None of these sources of friction, for the time at least, seemed decisive. The flood of immigrants after 1890 reduced wage pressure. The rapid extension of electric trolleys during the 1890s helped relieve some downtown traffic congestion, easing the strain on intermediate goods supply. The urban construction boom of the 1890s increased building supply and eased land prices. And businesses began to handle the tax problem themselves, helping spur the "good government" movement after the turn of the century to gain increasing control from corrupt bosses.[31]

The qualitative contradictions were much more decisive. The latent explosiveness of the concentration of workers became more and more manifest. At first, the impersonality and isolation of the factory and working-class districts had helped subdue the industrial proletariat. Gradually, through the 1880s, the dense concentrations of workers began to have the opposite effects. As spreading mechanization and speedup drove industrial workers to increasing resistance during the 1880s, individual strikes and struggles began to spread, infecting neighboring workers. Isolated moments of resistance took increasingly "political" forms. Strikes bred demonstrations not only at the plants but throughout the downtown districts. As the Wisconsin Commissioner of Labor and Industrial Statistics observed about the growing movement for the eight-hour day in Milwaukee in 1886, "the agitation permeated our entire social atmosphere" (quoted in Brecher, p. 40).

The evidence for this relatively sudden intensification of labor unrest in the largest cities, spilling from one sector to another within the working class, seems reasonably persuasive. During the 1870s, most labor unrest took place in small towns, in the mines, and along the railroads.[32] During the early 1880s, according to Florence Peterson's review of the data, "strikes were comparatively infrequent in the United States" (p. 22). From 1885, the magnitude, intensity and form of strikes changed rapidly (see Peterson, pp. 27ff.). In Table 2.1, for average annual index of workers involved in strikes is tabulated for five-year periods between 1881–85 and 1901–5. (The data series is interrupted in 1905.) The data reveal a sharp increase in the numbers of workers engaged in strike activity during the 1880s and a steady quantitative increase after the first five years of the period covered. Data on character and location of the strikers are also suggestive. A rising percentage of strikes focused on disputes over "recognition" and "sympathy." The percentage of strikes "ordered by labor organizations" also rose. Most important, workers seemed to be gaining increasing strength; comparing the period between 1886 and 1890 with the years from 1897 to 1899—two junctures of relatively comparable prosperity—we find that the percentage of strike resolutions which were "unfavorable to workers" fell dramatically from 41.1 percent in the former years to 19.6 percent ten years later. It appears, finally, that many of these

Table 2.1. Workers Involved in Strikes, 1881–1905

	Index of Strikers, 5-Year Averages
1881–1885	56.8
1886–1890	118.6
1891–1895	125.8
1896–1900	124.0
1901–1905	187.4

Note: The index includes all workers involved in strikes for each year, 1927–29 = 100, averaged over 5-year periods.
Source: Peterson, p. 21, Table 1.

spreading and more militant strikes were taking place in the largest industrial cities. Exact data on urban location are not available, but two sources help suggest the general trends. First, strikes between 1881 and 1905 seem to have been concentrated intensely in Illinois, Pennsylvania, and New York, the sites of the three major industrial cities; 59.8 percent of workers involved in strikes over that period were located in those three states alone. Second, increasing numbers of the major industrial disputes surveyed in the comprehensive labor histories of Foner (1955) and Commons were concentrated in the largest industrial cities.[33]

As these contradictions began to erupt, in short, it appeared likely that the form of the Industrial City would have to change. Its original structure had been premised on its sustenance of capitalist control over production. The increasing centralization of the industrial proletariat that it promoted, however, was beginning to backfire. Labor control was threatening to dissolve. Something clearly had to give.

CORPORATE ACCUMULATION AND THE CORPORATE CITY

We now know that the Industrial City was itself short-lived. For about half a century, at least, our cities have been pushed in different directions. A new kind of city form has framed American urban development. Corporate skyscrapers have come to dominate the downtown districts of many cities. Factories have moved away from the central cities. Cities have become politically fragmented.

Once again, our application of the Marxian perspective leads us to begin our analysis of these changes with an examination of the pace and pattern of capital accumulation. Around the turn of the century—between 1898 and 1920—the United States experienced a transition from the stage of industrial accumulation to advanced corporate accumulation. The accumulation process, still grounded in the production and realization of surplus value, was being guided by the decisions of many fewer, much larger economic units. Those economic units—the giant corporations—now had sufficient size to permit a qualitatively new level of rationalization of production and distribution. Their size and scope led them increasingly to search for stability, predictability, and security. That search, I argue, played a central role in shaping the Corporate City.

The Decentralization of Manufacturing

Through the 1890s, as we saw, manufacturing had been concentrating in the largest central cities. Factories had been piling more and more densely

into downtown districts. Workers were crowding nearby. And some contradictions of that geographic concentration were beginning to erupt.

Suddenly, around 1898 or 1899, manufacturing started moving out
of the central city. In twelve of the thirteen largest industrial districts in
the country, a special Census study showed that manufacturing employment began to increase more than twice as fast in the "rings" of the industrial districts as in the central cities. Between 1899 and 1909, central-city
manufacturing employment increased by 40.8 percent while ring employment rose by 97.7 percent.[34]

These numbers refer to a real and visible phenomenon noted by contemporary authors—in Graham Taylor's words, to "the sudden investment
of large sums of capital in establishing suburban plants" (p. 6). Between
1899 and around 1915, corporations began to establish factory districts
just beyond the city limits. New suburban manfacturing towns were being
built in open space like movie sets. Gary, Indiana, constructed from 1905
to 1908, is the best-known example. Other new industrial satellite suburbs included Chicago Heights, Hammond, East Chicago, and Argo outside Chicago: Lackawanna outside of Buffalo; East St. Louis and Wellston
across the river from St. Louis; Norwood and Oakley beyond the Cincinnati limits; and Chester and Norristown near Philadelphia.[35]

Orthodox economic historians have conventionally explained the decentralization of manufacturing in the twentieth century as the product of
technological change. Somebody invented the truck, and the truck made
it more efficient to locate manufacturing outside the central city. Somebody else invented land-intensive automated processing machinery, they
add, which placed a premium on employer's finding cheap land outside
dense central-city manufacturing districts.

But these conventional explanations cannot explain this sudden explosion of satellite suburbs at the turn of the century. The truck certainly
had nothing to do with the development, since the truck was not an effective commercial substitute for freight transport until the late 1920s.[36]
There is no obvious evidence that there was a sudden rash of new inven-
tions prompting a shift to land-intensive technologies; indeed, there is
some evidence that the sudden decentralization took place *despite* shifts
to less land-intensive technology in some industries.[37]

Other "factor price" explanations also provide little help. I can find
no evidence either that land-cost increases had accelerated at the turn of
the century or that these increases were directly linked to the sudden decentralization. And one can hardly argue that the factories began to move
out to the suburbs because the working class had already begun to leave
the central cities for "dormitory suburbs." Workers were still tightly locked
in central-city tenement districts, they had not been moving out to the

suburbs, and many continued to live in the central city even after they had begun to work in the satellite factories.[38]

It appears that conventional economic historians have overlooked the major reason for the sudden dispersal of central-city factories. Throughout the late 1880s and 1890s, as we saw above, labor conflict had begun to intensify in the downtown central-city districts. Employers quickly perceived one obvious solution. Move!

In testimony presented before the U.S. Industrial Commission from 1900 to 1902, employer after employer explained the crystallizing calculus. Some examples:[39]

> *The President of Fraser and Chalmers Co. in Chicago:* "Chicago today is the hotbed of trades unionism. . . . If it were not for the high investment [manufacturers] have in their machines and plants, many of them would leave Chicago at once, because of the labor trouble that exists here. . . . In fact, in Chicago, within the last two months we have lost some of the very largest corporations that operated here."

> *Chairman of the New York State Board of Mediation and Arbitration:* "Q: Do you find that isolated plants, away from the great centers of population, are more apt to have non-union shops than in a city? A: Yes. Q: Do you know of cases in the State where they do isolate plants to be free . . . from unionism? A: They have been located with that end in view."

> *President of a contracting firm in Chicago:* ". . . all these controversies and strikes that we have had here for some years have . . . prevented outsiders from coming in here and investing their capital. . . . It has discouraged capital at home. . . . It has drawn the manufacturers away from the city, because they are afraid their men will get into trouble and get into strikes. . . . The result is, all around Chicago for forty or fifty miles, the smaller towns are getting these manufacturing plants. . . ."

Graham Taylor, in his study of the satellite-city movement written in 1915, confirms that employers were particularly concerned about the contagiousness of central-city labor unrest. The language of one of his examples is suggestive:

> In an eastern city which recently experienced the throes of a turbulent street-car strike, the superintendent of a large industrial establishment frankly said that every time the strikers paraded past his plant a veritable fever seemed to spread among the employees in all his workrooms. He

thought that if the plants were moved out to the suburbs, the workingmen would not be so frequently inoculated with infection (p. 23).

When factories did move to the industrial suburbs, Taylor notes (p. 101), workers were automatically more isolated than they had been downtown: "Their contact with workers in other factories, with whom they might compare work conditions, is much less frequent." In general, Taylor concludes the decentralization served its purpose and the unions were much less successful than they had been in the central-city districts (see, e.g., p. 101).

If labor trouble had been burgeoning since the 1880s, why did this movement wait so long and begin so suddenly? I would propose that the abrupt inauguration of industrial dispersal could not have begun until the great merger wave of 1898 to 1903. Movement to the suburbs required huge funds for new capital investment. The small entrepreneurial firms of the nineteenth century could scarcely afford plant expansion, much less wholesale reconstruction. Falling profits and prices in the late 1880s intensified the squeeze on their capital. The depression of 1893–97 further delayed what was beginning to seem inevitable. Finally, as corporations rapidly centralized capital after 1898, they acquired enough extra investment cash to be able to finance the new satellite-plant construction.[40]

I do not mean to imply that the sudden construction of the satellite cities represented some massively engineered, carefully calibrated class-wide conspiracy steered by the new corporate giants. Individual corporations understood the reasons for and the implications of their actions, to be sure. (Taylor concluded that "the industrial exodus . . . is, in its individual parts, a consciously directed movement" [p. 26].) But individual corporations were largely acting on their own, without central coordination or suggestion, perceiving and protecting their own individual interests. There were some examples of collective planning, Taylor notes, but "much more usual, if not so conspicuous, is the shifting of factories one by one to the edge of the city" (p. 71). The individual corporations did not need to be directed in their flight from the central-city labor turmoil. They had little choice.

The great twentieth-century reversal of factory location, in short, began because corporations could no longer control their labor forces in the central cities. As with the transition to the Industrial City, problems of labor control had decisive effects. U.S. Steel's creation of Gary metaphorically expressed the importance of this spatial effect. "The Steel Corporation's triumphs in the economics of production," Taylor concluded, "are only less impressive than its complete command over the army of workers it employs" (p. 227).

The Central Business District

The second major change in the twentieth century was the creation and growth of downtown business districts. What explains this development?

Conventional historians explain the growth of the central business districts with new versions of the same arguments about "agglomeration." Every complex society needs vast administrative organs coordinating its transactions, they argue, and many of these activities are best located near each other to permit "face-to-face" communication. These conventional explanations come close to the mark, but they do not fully reveal the importance of the transition to the Corporate City.

The first major expansion of downtown central business districts occurred in the 1920s. Downtown office space in the ten largest cities increased between 1920 and 1930 by 3000 percent. Tall skyscrapers suddenly sprouted; by 1929, there were 295 buildings 21 stories or taller in the five largest cities alone.[41] The towers began to dwarf their dominions.

The "face-to-face" explanation is not specific enough to explain this sudden spurt of skyscrapers. Why was there a dramatic increase in the need for close administrative contact during those years and not before? Technical explanations also provide little help. Both elevators and steel-beam construction had been applied since the first decade of the century. If technical innovations are sufficient explanations of tall buildings, why did construction await the twenties?

It appears that central business districts flowered in the 1920s because large corporations were not yet ready for them before then. Huge corporations had not consolidated their monopoly control over their industries until after World War I. Once they gained stable market control, they could begin to organize that control.[42] They were now large enough to separate administrative functions from the production process itself, leaving plant managers to oversee the factories while corporate managers supervised the far-flung empire. Having already spurred the decentralization of many of their production plants, they could now afford to locate their administrative headquarters where it would be most "efficient." They chose downtown locations to be near other headquarters, near banks and law offices, and near advertising agents. The presence of one cluster of administrative services quickly bred a forest of looming neighbors. The uneven centralization of headquarters locations quickly surpassed the concentration of industrial employment at its late nineteenth century peak. By 1929, according to McKenzie's figures, 56 percent of national corporations had located their headquarters in New York City or Chicago (p. 164).

From this perspective, there is nothing necessarily destined about central business districts and towering skyscrapers with their "face-to-face" communication. Those spatial forms develop as the sites for administrative control functions when *power gets very centralized*. During the stage of corporate accumulation, even in its first decades, economic power became very centralized indeed.

Suburban Fragmentation

The third major change in urban form during the twentieth century involved its political fragmentation. Conventional analysts emphasize the importance of residential decentralization as a source of this political suburbanization. People began to prefer suburban autonomy, in this view, over central-city domination.

Once again, we must be very careful about the timing of events. Up to the end of the nineteenth century, central cities habitually annexed outlying residential districts as people moved beyond the traditional city boundaries. Central cities continued to unify their political jurisdictions as they spread outward. This process of annexation continued steadily until the end of the century.

Then the continuing spread of the Industrial City suddenly slowed. Chicago completed its last major annexation in 1889. New York City did not physically grow after the great incorporation of Brooklyn in 1898. Philadelphia and Boston had discontinued annexation even earlier. Of the twenty largest cities in 1900, thirteen enjoyed their last geographic expansion by 1910.[43]

This rapid deceleration of central-city annexation cannot be explained by some exogenous shift in people's preferences about suburban autonomy. People had been fleeing the central city since the 1860s.[44] From the beginning, the refugees typically preferred autonomy and opposed annexation. Despite their opposition, extending suburban populations were simply reclaimed for the central-city government by legislative *fiat*. They were continually subjected, in Kenneth Jackson's words, to "the local or downtown brand of urban imperialism" (p. 449).[45]

What changed at the end of the century? Residential suburbanization did not accelerate. There was not yet a widespread use of the car. The electric streetcar developed rapidly through the 1890s, permitting somewhat more distant intra-urban travel, but it represented a simple improvement on a long succession of carriages and horse cars dating from the 1840s rather than a qualitative transformation of urban transit.

What changed most dramatically, it appears, was that manufacturers themselves began to move out of the central cities. Obviously they wanted to avoid paying central-city taxes. It was now in their interest to oppose further annexation. Given their influence over state legislatures, they easily satisfied their desires. Earlier residential opposition to annexation had not been strong enough to resist central-city aggrandizement. Now, with manufacturers switching sides, the scales dramatically tilted. After industrialists joined the movement against central-city extension, political fragmentation was the natural consequence.

The Form of the Corporate City

Once this transitional period had culminated in a stable pattern of urban reproduction, American cities had acquired a qualitatively new structure. It is reasonably easy to review the central political-economic features of the Corporate City.

If a city had reached maturity as an Industrial City during the stage of industrial accumulation, its character changed rapidly during the corporate period although its physical structure remained embedded in concrete. Its downtown shopping districts were transformed into downtown central business districts, dominated by skyscrapers. (Because corporate headquarters were more unevenly distributed than nineteenth-century industrial establishments, many Industrial Cities, like Baltimore, St. Louis, and Cincinnati, never captured many of these headquarters.) Surrounding the central business district were emptying manufacturing areas, depressed from the desertion of large plants, barely surviving on the light and competitive industries left behind. Next to those districts were the old working-class districts, often transformed into "ghettos," locked into the cycle of central-city manufacturing decline. Outside the central city there were suburban belts of industrial development, linked together by circumferential highways. Scattered around those industrial developments were fragmented working-class and middle-class suburban communities. The wealthy lived farther out. Political fragmentation prevailed beyond the central-city boundaries.

Many other, newer cities—particularly those in the South, Southwest, and West—reached maturity during the stage of corporate accumulation. These became the exemplary Corporate Cities. They shared one thundering advantage over the older Industrial Cities: they had never acquired the fixed physical capital of an earlier era. They could be constructed from scratch to fit the needs of a new period of accumulation in which factory plant and equipment were themselves increasingly predicated upon a decentralized model. (Orthodox historians explain the decentralization of manufacturing as a *result* of this new plant and equipment; I have argued that an eruption of class struggle initially prompted the decentralization and, by implication, that the new plant and equipment developed as a result of that dispersal in order to permit corporations' taking advantage of the new locational facts.) There was consequently no identifiable downtown factory district; manufacturing was scattered throughout the city plane. There were no centralized working-class housing districts (for that was indeed what capitalists had learned to avoid); working-class housing was scattered all over the city around the factories. Automobiles and trucks provided the connecting links, threading together the separate pieces. The Corporate City became, in Robert Fogelson's term, the Fragmented Metropolis. No centers anywhere. Diffuse economic activity everywhere.

These two models help underscore the significance of the *reversals* reflected in the Corporate City form. Manufacturing had been clustering toward the center of the Industrial City; now it was moving anywhere across the urban space. Working-class housing had been packed into dense central zones; now it was scattered around the metropolitan area and increasingly segmented. Central business districts had been dominated by shopping centers; now, in at least some cities, they were dominated by corporate headquarters. (The shopping centers, at least in the newer cities, were scattered everywhere.) The middle and upper classes had been fleeing but were continually reabsorbed; now, in the older cities, they fled more successfully into separate suburbs. Before, the city had crammed around its center; now, the Corporate City sprawled.

Once this new urban form crystallized, of course, many additional influences affected urban growth. Patterns of defense spending, federal housing policies, the power of the auto-energy-construction block, the shifting dynamics of urban-land speculation—these and many other factors contributed to the content of urban America after World War II (see, for example, Mollenkopf). All of these factors had secondary effects, however, in the sense that they tended to reproduce the structure of the Corporate City rather than to change or undermine it. The foundations of that urban form were so strong that simple political influences could not change its basic shape.

With that final observation, our study of the relationship between capitalism and the history of American cities can be brought to a close. I have argued that the Corporate City, like its antecedent urban forms, was premised on the requisites of capital accumulation. If we look up at the Corporate City from within its form, it seems fixed and unyielding. If we view it more critically over a much longer horizon, its form seems much more contingent. The Corporate City emerged as a historical solution to some eruptive crises in capital accumulation at the turn of the century. Its form began increasingly to correspond to the pace and pattern of a new stage of corporate accumulation. If we have learned that the Corporate

City emerged historically from the disarray of capitalism in crisis, it seems equally likely that we can best understand the current crises of the Corporate City with the same kind of probing analysis.

THE ROOTS OF THE CURRENT URBAN CRISIS

Some of the current urban crisis can be simply explained as a product of general economic crisis. When the economy plunges into a tailspin, for instance, city finances suffer badly and many in the cities go jobless.

It would be misleading to stop at that point. It turns out that the current urban crisis is not a *general* urban crisis at all. Some cities are suffering crisis, like New York, San Francisco, St. Louis, and Detroit, while others are not. Which ones are being hit the worst?

The preceding historical analysis points directly toward some obvious answers. The analysis of the emergence of the Corporate City suggested that American cities have been dominated during the twentieth century by either of two characteristic structures. Cities that reached maturity before the stage of corporate accumulation acquired what has become a relatively archaic physical structure. We can call them "Old Cities." Cities that reached maturity after the era of corporate accumulation had begun, gradually developed a more "modern" physical shape. We can call them "New Cities."

Though shaped by the same underlying logic, Old Cities and New Cities were bound to develop in different directions. New Cities inevitably captured more and more manufacturing. Even the suburbs of the older central cities could not compete with the more perfectly suited physical environments of the newer cities, and industry has continually moved out of the older metropolitan areas—out of the old Industrial Cities—into the newer regions of the Sunbelt.[46] Because corporate centralization continued, on the other hand, corporate headquarters continued to concentrate in a few central business districts. By 1974, although New Cities had stolen huge chunks of manufacturing employment away from Old Cities, New York and Chicago still hosted nearly one-third of the 500 largest corporations' headquarters. In New Cities, finally, annexation has never stopped. Industrialists had vested interests neither in the "original" central cities nor in the "expanding" suburban areas alone. Their economic interests were more or less equally distributed across the metropolitan plane. And so, given industrialist neutrality, opposition to central-city annexation never developed in the New Cities. The twenty most rapidly growing cities between 1960 and 1970 more than doubled their total land area between 1950 and 1970 (Jackson, p. 441).

Tracing some of those different directions, we can certainly map much of the current urban crisis. Relying on the careful statistical work of Alfred Watkins, we can distinguish between Old Cities and New Cities. Of the fifty largest metropolitan areas in the United States (ranked by 1970 population), twenty-five are Old Cities and twenty-five are New Cities. Since eleven of those cities reached maturity during the transitional decade between 1910 and 1920, their definitive categorization is problematic. For the purposes of this brief discussion, therefore, we can work more easily with thirty-nine cities whose "age" seems less ambiguous. Of these, seventeen are Old Cities and twenty-two are New Cities.

A first measure by which to locate the incidence of urban crisis involves the basic health of metropolitan economies. If employment and the labor force are shrinking, cities may be in trouble when general economic crisis strikes. Between 1960 and 1970, the labor forces of sixteen of these thirty-nine cities declined; fourteen were Old Cities. Counting another way, over 90 percent of the New Cities grew while 80 percent of the Old Cities declined. When crisis struck in the mid-seventies, it seems obvious that Old Cities were destined to suffer the worst.

If metropolitan economies are stagnating, social problems intensify. Richard Nathan has developed an index of social hardship for metropolitan areas by combining indices of several different problems like unemployment, poverty, and welfare. The hardship index compares the magnitude of these problems in central cities and their suburbs. The higher the index of central-city disadvantage, the more severe the social problems faced by central city governments. Ranked by this measure, thirteen of the seventeen *most* disadvantaged central cities are Old Cities and thirteen of the sixteen *least* disadvantaged central cities are New Cities.

Social hardship usually means mounting city expenditures. We can compare general municipal expenditures per capita for (at the time of writing) 1972. Within our group of cities, ten of the eleven central cities with the highest municipal expenditures per capita were Old Cities. The average in the Old Cities was 42 percent higher than in the New Cities.

With declining economies and exploding expenditure obligations, finally, we would expect that Old Cities would be more likely to get into serious fiscal trouble. With revenues lagging and expenditures climbing, Old Cities may be forced to short-term borrowing to balance their budgets. Sooner or later, the threat of municipal default or bankruptcy may loom. Municipal debt, in this sense, becomes the lightning rod for more general urban crisis. A comparison of short-term municipal indebtedness per capita dramatically understores the differences between Old Cities and New Cities. In 1973–74, fourteen of the sixteen most indebted cities were

Old Cities. The average municipal short-term indebtedness per capita in the Old Cities was 6300 percent greater than in the New Cities.

This discussion makes clear that the current urban crisis is neither universal nor surprising. It is a crisis of Old Cities in the corporate stage of capital accumulation. Capitalism has decreed that those cities have become archaic as sites for capitalist production. The process of capital accumulation is leaving them behind. Capitalists have found that they can better control their labor forces and make higher profits elsewhere. In the terms of this essay, it seems clear that the current crisis of the Old Cities stems, at its roots, from their increasing failure to sustain capital accumulation *on the capitalists' terms*. Given the more general argument that American capitalism has bred the American capitalist city, it seems clear that we shall continue to suffer urban crisis, trapped by the shifting economic fates of our respective cities, until we cast aside the logic of American capitalism itself.

We might as well begin now. Over the longer term there should be nothing sacrosanct about the physical and institutional structure of *either* Old Cities *or* New Cities. The forms of both were historically determined, in large part, by the needs of capital. Neither affords the basis for decent community life because both forms were historically conditioned by capitalists' efforts to isolate workers and then to divide them spatially. Rather than taking those urban structures for granted, we should begin instead to cast aside capitalist criteria altogether. The time has come to develop our own spatial forms.

NOTES

1. This paper draws upon a larger project. Because it has been considerably abridged for this book, it provides neither the historical detail nor the documentation it requires.
2. Price makes some comparable points, less abstractly, about American ports in the eighteenth century.
3. As both Tryon and Morris show, most manufacturing took place in rural villages and households.
4. Unless otherwise credited, all references in this paper to absolute and relative urban population and to individual city populations are based on U.S. Bureau of the Census (1939); Bogue; U.S. Bureau of the Census (1976).
5. This argument obviously conflicts with the general view that cities automatically grow continuously alongside "modernization."
6. According to Bridenbaugh, other cities reaching populations of 5000 or more included New Haven, Norwich, Norfolk, New London, and Salem (1955, pp. 216–17).
7. The fate of Southern cities supports this argument. Southern rivers provided direct access between the plantations and the ocean, so coastal

Transport Nodes were not required. As a result, Southern cities scarcely developed at all; in 1790, only 2.3 percent of the South Atlantic population lived in cities while 7.5 and 8.7 percent of the New England and Middle Atlantic populations, respectively, lived in cities.

8. A variety of factors combined to keep the Political Capital functions out of the port cities, lodged in an entirely new city, Washington, D.C., and small inland cities like Albany, N.Y., and Harrisburg, Pa.

9. Because of later developments, one must also note that New York did not even grow most rapidly among the four.

10. On New York's history, see Albion. For the figures on New York's share of trade, see Vernon (pp. 31, 32); Pred (p. 147).

11. Southern urban underdevelopment continues to support the argument. With New York merchants hogging the Commercial Metropolis functions supporting the cotton trade, there was still little role for Southern cities. By 1860, the relative urban share in the South had climbed to only 9.8 percent, while the New England and Middle Atlantic figures had risen to 28.8 percent and 25.5 percent respectively.

12. Price concludes (p. 133) that about one-quarter worker in the artisanal trades, another quarter in the transport occupations, and the remaining half in commercial support.

13. Warner (pp. 61, 21). This summary draws mainly on Bridenbaugh (1955); Warner (Part I); E. Foner (Chap. 2); Kulikoff; Price; Pred (Chap. 4).

14. See Warner (p. 56); Knights (pp. 49ff.); Schnore and Knights (p. 254).

15. See Warner (pp. 55ff.); Pred (pp. 207ff.).

16. See Warner (pp. 57ff.); Pred (pp. 200ff.), Knights.

17. Warner provides some glimpse of this continuity for Philadelphia.

18. Warner (p. 56) Pred (pp. 200ff.); Knights (p. 89).

19. See Maier for the Revolutionary period and Pessen for later.

20. The change in land-grant policy during the Jacksonian period, for instance, severely crimped land speculation in the West.

21. Pred provides the most careful review of most of these hypotheses.

22. See Pred (pp. 69–70) for some examples of this concentration.

23. These calculations are based on data from U.S. Bureau of the Census (1850, 1860, and 1870).

24. These data are based on U.S. Bureau of Census (1870 and 1900); Pred (p. 20).

25. The following paragraphs rely heavily on Gutman (1963, 1976).

26. Gutman (1963, p. 41). His conclusions are qualitative and cannot, however strong the evidence, be turned, it appears, into numbers.

27. For some particularly interesting evidence for Philadelphia, see Hershberg et al.

28. Quoted in Glaab (p. 236). This kind of Industrial City was not new. In England, Manchester had already pioneered its form in the first half of the nineteenth century, and Friedrich Engels had already perceived the essential social functions which that singular form was serving. See, for instance, Engels (p. 84).

29. Millis and Montgomery (p. 83).

30. For some discussion of these factors, see Pred (p. 43); Taylor (pp. 271, 311).

31. See Millis and Montgomery; Taylor (1970); Hays.

32. See Commons; Foner (1947).

33. These impressions cannot be precisely tabulated because the Foner and Commons presentations do not lend themselves to quantification. But the qualitative histories support the point.

34. See U.S. Bureau of the Census (1905 and 1910).

35. The maps in U.S. Bureau of the Census (1910) are instructive.
36. See McKenzie (p. 93); Tunnard and Reed (p. 238).
37. In the steel industry, for instance, open-hearth furnaces were used more frequently in the Gary plants than in the central-city plants, but those furnaces required smaller plant units, rather than larger ones, when installed within the factories. See Clark (p. 68).
38. Graham Taylor reports (p. 97), for instance, that only 31.3 percent of the workers in the Cincinnati satellite factories actually lived outside the central cities and that almost all the remainder lived in the traditional central-city working-class housing districts.
39. These examples are taken from U.S. Industrial Commission (vol. VIII, pp. 10; vol. VII, p. 878; and vol. VIII, p. 415) respectively.
40. I have not yet systematically investigated this hypothesis, but contemporary accounts do seem to suggest that only large corporations participated in the exodus.
41. See McKenzie (pp. 164, 222).
42. See Edwards; Chandler.
43. See Jackson (p. 443).
44. See Schnore.
45. More detail is provided in Jackson; McKenzie.
46. As Watkins concludes, "the suburban economy has proved too feeble a base from which the old metropolitan areas can regain their lost competitive advantage" (Chap. 2). His statistical analyses support those conclusions.

REFERENCES

Albion, Robert G., *The Rise of the New York Port, 1815–1860* (New York: Charles Scribner's Sons, 1939).

Blumenfeld, Hans, "The Modern Metropolis," in *Cities,* A Scientific American Book (New York: Alfred A. Knopf, 1965).

Bogue, Donald, *The Population of the United States* (Glencoe, Ill.: Free Press, 1959).

Braverman, Harry, *Labor and Monopoly Capital* (New York: Monthly Review Press, 1974).

Brecher, Jeremy, *Strike!* (San Francisco: Straight Arrow Books, 1972).

Bridenbaugh, Carl, *Cities in the Wilderness* (New York: Oxford University Press, 1971).

———, *Cities in Revolt* (New York: Oxford University Press, 1955).

Chandler, Alfred D., Jr., *Strategy and Structure* (Cambridge, Mass.: MIT Press, 1962).

Clark, Victor S., *History of Manufactures in the United States,* vol. III (Washington, D.C.: Carnegie Institution, 1929).

Commons, John R., *History of Labor in the United States,* vol. II (New York: Macmillan Company, 1918).

Davis, Kingsley, "The Urbanization of the Human Population," in *Cities,* A Scientific American Book (New York: Alfred A. Knopf, 1965).

Edwards, Richard C., "Corporate Stability and the Risks of Corporate Failure," *Journal of Economic History,* June 1975.

Engels, Friedrich, *The Condition of the Working Class in England* (Moscow: Progress Publishers, 1973).

Fogelson, Robert M., *The Fragmented Metropolis* (Cambridge, Mass.: Harvard University Press, 1967).

Foner, Eric, *Tom Paine and the American Revolution* (New York: Oxford University Press, 1976).

Foner, Philip S., *History of the Labor Movement in the United States,* vol. 1 (New York: International Publishers, 1947).

————, *History of the Labor Movement in the United States,* vol. 2 (New York: International Publishers, 1955).

Glaab, Charles N., ed., *The American City: A Documentary History* (Homewood, Ill.: Dorsey Press, 1963).

————, and A. Theodore Brown, *A History of Urban America* (New York: Macmillan Company, 1967).

Gordon, David M., "Capitalist Efficiency and Socialist Efficiency," *Monthly Review,* July–August 1976.

Gutman, Herbert G., "The Worker's Search for Power: Labor in the Gilded Age," in H. Wayne Morgan, ed., *The Gilded Age: A Reappraisal* (Syracuse: Syracuse University Press, 1963).

————, *Work, Culture, and Society in Industrializing America* (New York: Alfred A. Knopf, 1976).

Handlin, Oscar, "The Modern City as a Field of Historical Study," in A. B. Callow, Jr., ed., *American Urban History* (New York: Oxford University Press, 1969).

Hays, Samuel P., "The Politics of Reform in Municipal Government in the Progressive Era," *Pacific Northwest Quarterly,* October 1964.

Hershberg, Theodore, et al., "The 'Journey-to-Work': An Empirical Investigation of Work, Residence, and Transportation, Philadelphia, 1850 and 1880" (Unpublished paper, 1974).

Jackson, Kenneth T., "Metropolitan Government versus Political Autonomy," in K. T. Jackson and S. K. Schultz, eds., *Cities in American History* (New York: Alfred A. Knopf, 1972).

Knights, Peter R., *The Plain People of Boston, 1830–1860* (New York: Oxford University Press, 1971).

Kulikoff, Allan, "The Progress of Inequality in Revolutionary Boston," *William and Mary Quarterly,* July 1971.

Lyman, Susan E., *The Story of New York* (New York: Crown Publishers, 1964).

McKenzie, R. D., *The Metropolitan Community* (New York: McGraw-Hill Book Co., 1933).

Maier, Pauline, "Popular Uprisings and Civil Authority in Eighteenth-Century America," *William and Mary Quarterly,* January 1970.

Marglin, Stephen A., "What Do Bosses Do?" *Review of Radical Political Economics,* Summer 1974.

Millis, Harry A., and Royal E. Montgomery, *Labor's Progress and Some Basic Labor Problems* (New York: McGraw-Hill Book Co., 1938).

Mollenkopf, John H., "The Postwar Politics of Urban Development," in William K. Tabb and Larry Sawers, eds., *Marxism and the Metropolis* (New York: Oxford University Press: 1978), p. 117–52.

Morris, Richard B., *Government and Labor in Early America* (New York: Columbia University Press, 1946).

Mumford, Lewis, *The City in History* (New York: Harcourt, Brace and World, 1961).

Nathan, Richard P., and Charles Adams, "Understanding Central City Hardship," *Political Science Quarterly,* Spring 1976.

Nettels, Curtis P., "British Mercantilism and the Economic Development of the Thirteen Colonies," *Journal of Economic History,* Spring 1952.

Pessen, Edward, "The Egalitarian Myth and the American Social Reality: Wealth, Mobility and Equality in the 'Era of the Common Man.'" *American Historical Review,* October 1971.

Peterson, Florence, *Strikes in the United States, 1880–1936* (Washington, D.C.: U.S. Government Printing Office, 1938).

Pred, Allan R., *The Spatial Dynamics of U.S. Urban-Industrial Growth, 1800–1914* (Cambridge, Mass.: Harvard University Press, 1966).

Price, Jacob M., "Economic Function and the Growth of American Port Towns in the Eighteenth Century," *Perspectives in American History* 8, 1974.

Reps, John W., *The Making of Urban America: A History of City Planning in the United States* (Princeton: Princeton University Press, 1965).

Schlesinger, Arthur M., Sr., "The City in American History," in P. Kramer and F. L. Holborn, eds., *The City in American Life* (New York: G. P. Putnam's Sons, 1970).

Schnore, Leo F., "Urban Structure and Suburban Selectivity," *Demography* 1, 1964.

———, and Peter R. Knights, "Residence and Social Structure: Boston in the Ante-Bellum Period," in S. Thernstrom and R. Sennett, eds., *Nineteenth-Century Cities* (New Haven: Yale University Press, 1969).

Sjoberg, Gideon, "The Origin and Evolution of Cities," in *Cities,* A Scientific American Book (New York: Alfred A. Knopf, 1965).

Taylor, George Rogers, *The Transportation Revolution, 1815–1860* (New York: Rinehart and Co., 1951).

———, "Building an Intra-Urban Transportation System," in A. M. Wakstein, ed., *The Urbanization of America* (Boston: Houghton Mifflin, 1970).

Taylor, Graham Romeyn, *Satellite Cities: A Study of Industrial Suburbs* (New York: D. Appleton, and Co., 1915).

Tryon, Rolla M., *Household Manufactures in the United States, 1640–1860* (Chicago: University of Chicago Press, 1917).

Tunnard, Christopher, and Henry Hope Reed, *American Skyline: The Growth and Form of Our Cities and Towns* (Boston: Houghton Mifflin, 1955).

U.S. Bureau of the Census, *Seventh Census* (Washington, D.C.: U.S. Government Printing Office, 1850).

———, *Eighth Census* (Washington, D.C.: U.S. Government Printing Office, 1860).

———, *Compendium of the Ninth Census* (Washington, D.C.: U.S. Government Printing Office, 1870).

———, *Twelfth Census,* "Manufactures," (Washington, D.C.: U.S. Government Printing Office, 1900).

———, "Industrial Districts: 1905," *Bulletin* No. 101 (Washington, D.C.: U.S. Government Printing Office, 1909).

———, *Thirteenth Census,* vol. 10 (Washington, D.C.: U.S. Government Printing Office, 1910).

———, *Urban Population in the U.S. from the First Census to the Fifteenth Census* (Washington, D.C.: U.S. Government Printing Office, 1939).

———, *Historical Statistics of the United States,* rev. ed. (Washington, D.C.: U.S. Government Printing Office, 1976).

U.S. Industrial Commission, *Reports* (Washington, D.C.: U.S. Government Printing Office, 1900–1902).

Vernon, Raymond, *Metropolis 1985* (Garden City, N.Y.: Anchor Books, 1963).

Warner, Sam Bass, *The Private City* (Philadelphia: University of Pennsylvania Press, 1968).

Watkins, Alfred, "Urban Development in the U.S. System of Cities" (Ph.D. dissertation, New School for Social Research, 1977).

Williams, Raymond, *The Country and the City* (New York: Oxford University Press, 1973).

3

Urbanization and the Dynamics of Suburban Development Under Capitalism

PATRICK J. ASHTON

One of the most striking and significant social phenomena of the twentieth century has been the growth and proliferation of suburbs around large cities in the United States. From a limited and relatively rare social form at the beginning of this century, suburbs have developed into major growth poles for industrial and commercial investment and suburbanism has become a way of life for over ninety million Americans—by far a plurality of the population. The purpose of this paper is to show how this historical development is rooted in the dynamics of the capitalist mode of production and to demonstrate how the specific evolution of suburbs both reflects and contributes to more general contradictions within the economic system.

THE NATURE OF SUBURBS

Suburbs may be defined as politically independent municipalities located outside the corporate boundaries of large central cities but within an economically interdependent metropolitan area. While several different types of suburbs may be distinguished (e.g., bedroom, industrial, commercial), nearly all of them share two important characteristics: political independence and a relatively small scale. As forms of the state,[1] suburbs enjoy a number of independent powers, most significant of which are the ability to make and enforce laws and to levy taxes. The small scale of the suburb is made possible by its dependence primarily upon the large central city and secondarily upon other units within the metropolitan area. An individual suburb need not contain all necessary or desirable services and facilities since they can be obtained elsewhere. This smaller scale makes the suburb much more amenable to domination by a single interest group (or coalition of interest groups) than a large heterogeneous city. And the political independence of the suburb provides a vehicle for protecting and extending a particular group's self-interest.

Suburbs are thus potential conduits for power. But power is not distributed evenly in capitalist society. Its distribution is determined by the nature of capitalist class relations, which are in turn influenced by the level of development of the forces and the social relations of production. The political fragmentation of the modern metropolis is thus a reflection of the hierarchical stratification and uneven development of the capitalist mode of production. In what follows I will attempt to trace the political economic developments which have led to the current proliferation of suburbs.

THE SPATIAL DYNAMICS OF INDUSTRIAL CITIES

American society underwent a substantial transformation in the 1830s to 1860s. A predominantly agrarian, commercial society was recast as an urban industrial one. This development was driven, as Gordon shows (essay 2), by the transition to the industrial mode of capital accumulation. "The main elements in the new urban complex," observes historian Lewis Mumford, "were the factory, the railroad and the slum. . . . The factory became the nucleus of the new organism. Every other detail of life was subordinate to it" (p. 458). The factory did not occupy this position of dominance, however, on technical merits alone. Historical experience had taught capitalists that the factory was the most *profitable,* if not the most efficient and humane method of organizing production.[2] Thus, the basis for evolution of the factory was a politicoeconomic one. Nevertheless once chosen, the factory had ramifications that were social as well as physical, geographical as well as technological.

The most important consequence of the use of factories as production sites in nineteenth century U.S. cities was *centralization:* centralization of the actual physical plant, of productive facilities, of workers, of political control. First of all, the architecture of the factory was dictated by the major source of available energy: steam. Since every piece of machinery had to be connected to a central steam engine by means of belts or shafts, it was most efficient to put the machinery as close as possible to the source of power. Thus factories were built as compact, multistory units.

Second, the primary modes of commercial transportation limited locational flexibility. Since waterways and railroads—the only viable means of shipping large amounts of raw materials and finished goods—were relatively fixed in space, they demanded that production and distribution facilities be grouped around them. At the same time, these transportation arteries facilitated rapid growth of industrial production at urban nodes by providing relatively cheap coal for steam generation and by linking cities and regions to create national markets.

Third, enormous economies of scale were achieved by the centralization of the production process. In addition, the organization of the factory required a relatively large number of workers producing under one roof, as well as a large reserve army of the unemployed, in order to discipline those workers. Given the limitations of the existing transportation system, these workers and potential workers needed to live close to their workplaces. And since they could not outbid more powerful and wealthy groups in the market for space in the city, the development of overcrowded slum housing was all but assured.[3]

The rapid and continued growth of factories and industry swelled the urban population and further crowded the slums. Thousands of people left the countryside and streamed into the cities. Doubtless some were attracted by the excitement of city life or the promise of better wages. But many had no choice. Declining soil fertility east of the Mississippi and the lack of free land in the west pushed farmers off the land, as did expanding urban land use. And the uneven development characteristic of the capitalist market process resulted in the destruction of many small regional centers of trade and finance. Rural entrepreneurs as well as farmers increasingly became part of the urban proletariat.

The social relations of the factory came to dominate political life also. A great deal of the original investment in industrial infrastructure—roads, water mains, power systems, etc.—had been made by the entrepreneurs themselves. But faced with the rapidly increasing scale and complexity of production, capitalists sought ways to socialize these mounting costs. As capital has always done, it turned to the state for help. The fiscal powers of the state could be used to generate revenue for infrastructural investments, which would be politically defined as "public goods." To ensure this happening, capitalists attempted to consolidate their control of state and local government.[4]

The intensification of concentration at the center of the industrial city led to incremental outward expansion. And as the industrial economy spread into the countryside in the mid-nineteenth century, political control was not far behind. Urban capitalists encouraged the local government to pursue a policy of annexing the expanding fringes of the city. Not only did this extend urban administrative control, it increased the tax base of the city. Sometimes this policy was carried out at the local level, but more often it was implemented by state legislatures dominated by urban capitalists. The Pennsylvania state assembly, for example, voted in 1854 to increase the size of the city of Philadelphia from 2 to more than 129 square miles, effectively annexing twenty-eight separate boroughs, towns, and townships in the area.

In addition, annexation was also used to destroy or weaken urban rivals. Brooklyn, New York, for example, was itself an industrial city and annexed many surrounding towns and villages on Long Island. By 1898 it had grown to be the fifth largest city in the United States and represented a powerful rival to neighboring New York City. And so in 1898 the New York state legislature stripped Brooklyn of its political autonomy and awarded it to the city of New York. This completed New York City's annexation of over 250 square miles of its hinterland.[5]

Thus, the policy of annexation greatly expanded the size and scale of the industrial cities—in social as well as physical terms. But while political and economic control remained centralized in the old central districts— now called "downtown"—new needs, conditions, and interest groups were being created in these sprawling cities. This process of differentiation, in social as well as spatial terms, was as much a part of the growth dynamic of industrial urbanization as the process of centralization. Thus it was that the unfolding in space of industrial development and expansion set in motion forces antagonistic to itself—forces that would bring a virtual halt to annexation and spur the transition to a new form of urbanization by the beginning of the twentieth century.[6]

EARLY SUBURBS: REFUGES OF THE ELITE

By the middle of the nineteenth century, small upper-class communities were springing up in the countryside around the large industrial cities. The motivation for the creation of these communities was social, economic, and political. Rapid industrial development within the anarchic framework of the capitalist market had radically altered the quality of life in the cities. Factories belched smoke and cinders over the entire city, noxious chemicals filled the air, the rivers and canals were open sewers, and garbage and other forms of waste littered the streets. Workers, crowded into dismal, suffocating slums suffered the most. But even the living quarters of the rich in the central city could not escape contamination. Therefore, those who could escape, did.

The city government also faced constantly mounting financial demands during this period. On the one hand, there was the increasing demand for investment in the industrial infrastructure, as capitalists fought to socialize their costs. On the other hand, the tremendous influx of population from the countryside into the cities generated a huge new demand for services. Sewers, water, police, firefighters, libraries were required in amounts previously unimagined.[7]

Moreover, the proletarianization of artisans, craftsmen, and farmers frequently meant their pauperization, requiring public welfare programs. This need was enlarged and exacerbated by continually escalating immigration. While not all immigrants remained in the cities, many of those who did were poor. For example, in 1852 more than half of those requiring public assistance in eastern cities were Irish and German. In 1860, 86 percent of the paupers in New York City were of foreign birth (Glaab and Brown, p. 77).

While the tax burden did not fall predominantly on the rich, its sheer size and rate of growth presented the well-to-do with an economic threat. Furthermore, two major depressions and a general deflation in the economy in the last third of the nineteenth century made tax dollars harder to come by. But tax revenues were only one of the budgetary problems the cities encountered. Faced with spiralling demands for services and investments which constantly outran revenues, most cities borrowed heavily. In the decade after the Civil War, the fifteen largest cities in the United States experienced a population increase of 70 percent; their municipal debts, however, increased 271 percent (Glaab and Brown, p. 169). The mounting interest payments on this expanding debt represented an inelastic burden on the municipal budget.

The changing nature of the city politics provided another motivation for the exodus of the wealthy from the city. Though urban capitalists were never a large percentage of the population, in the early part of the nineteenth century their direct control over city government was relatively unchallenged. The urban population boom in mid-century, occasioned by internal migration and foreign immigration, made their control more problematic, however. With even a modicum of democracy, capitalists stood the chance of being outvoted on crucial issues by the rapidly increasing urban proletariat.

The well-established urban bourgeoisie could not blatantly impose its political will on the unruly masses, however, without posing a serious threat to its own legitimacy. As a result of this impasse, the political boss system arose. On the one hand, the institutionalization of the urban political machine protected capital's interest by diluting class consciousness and class conflict. Through pandemic bribery, graft, embezzlement, and kickbacks, thousands of ethnic small businesspeople and political operatives were given a stake (however modest) in the existing system. Politics, moreover, were placed on an ethnic, rather than a class basis. "Indeed," says Mollenkopf (p. 324), "if the urban political machines had not driven out both Yankee aristocratic rule and the fledgling American socialism, it is doubtful that the U.S. industrial revolution could have occurred with such speed and effectiveness."

On the other hand, the old bourgeoisie resented the loss of direct political control in the cities. Even more, they came to resent the massive and widespread corruption which not only offended their business sense and class morality, but came to represent an increasingly unacceptable overhead on the cost of city government.

So, motivated by a deteriorating quality of life, mounting taxes, and a loss of political control, the capitalist elite moved their residences out of the city and formed suburbs. Here in the countryside the small scale and political independence of the suburban municipality allowed them to reassert control over their environment.[8] But it would be wrong to assume that, because capitalists had removed their residences from the cities, they had abdicated power in city government. On the contrary. Because of the level of development of production technology and the class relations of the factory system, it was still necessary to locate industrial plants in the central cities. Thus, capitalists retained a prime stake in the politics of the city, and they did their best to see that their economic interests were protected.

The upper class was not the only group for whom residence in the city was unattractive. The deteriorating quality of life and mounting tax burden were a source of concern to all urban residents. The difference was that the wealthy were generally the only ones who could afford the time and commuting costs engendered by a residence in the suburbs. Initially, horse and carriage—a luxury out of the financial reach of most urban residents—or ferries were the only means of travel to these communities. With the development of railroads in the 1840s, railstop suburbs began springing up in the countryside. But again, it was only the relatively well-to-do who could afford the time and money to commute. Horse-drawn streetcars, which came into widespread use in the 1850s, permitted some elements of the middle class to move away from the city's core. The limitations of this mode of travel, though, meant that they could not move very far (three miles or less from the city center) and these would-be suburbanites were generally introduced into the city as a result of annexation.[9]

The large-scale development of electric trolley lines in the late 1880s involved real estate and land interests in the active promotion of suburbs and offered the middle classes their first real chance to escape the city. As

Walker (1978) shows, this phenomenon was largely spurred by "over-accumulated" capital searching for investment outlets. The way it often worked was that entrepreneurs built tracks out into the countryside, buying up the surrounding property as they went. Then, with fares set artificially low to encourage ridership, they offered the land for sale. Any losses they sustained from the operation of the trolley line were more than offset by their monopoly profits from the sale of the real estate. The majority of workers, barely able to scrape by financially in the urban slums, could not possibly outbid small businessmen and professionals for this new property.

However, these "streetcar suburbs" were frequently shortlived as independent communities. After they had sold off all the available land, the real estate entrepreneurs often let the trolley lines deteriorate. Moreover, the feverish speculation in this form of investment inevitably led to overbuilding and financial collapse. The new middle-class suburbanites, who were totally dependent upon the trolley lines, mobilized their poitical clout to get the central city to annex their area and to provide public subsidies for the trolleys.

The development of upper-class residential retreats and upper-middle-class streetcar suburbs during the nineteenth century did not represent a significant shift in the population. Most urban residents continued to live only a short distance from their workplaces. And since the existing class relations and level of productive and distributive technology decreed that these sites be centralized in the city, most urban residents lived in central cities. The widespread development of suburbs as social forms would flow from sweeping changes in the forces and social relations of production which began to manifest themselves near the turn of the century.

THE DECENTRALIZATION OF INDUSTRY

The most important causal factor for the widespread development of suburbs in the early twentieth century was the movement of industry out of the large cities. This decentralization process has been discussed by Gordon in his essay, so great detail is not necessary here. But it should be emphasized that this movement derived its origin and shape from the nature of the developing forces and social relations of capitalist production. The conditions which motivated capitalists to move their industrial facilities out of the central city were both technical and social. On the one hand, the despoliation of the city's physical environment for which the industrialists themselves were largely responsible—and which, ironically, had impelled them to remove their own residences—began to create added costs which the capitalists could not always successfully socialize. Furthermore, the growing tax burden of many cities threatened to cut into profits.

On the other hand, the escalating hostility of urban class relations provided capitalists with an even stronger motivation for getting out, as Gordon has indicated. The swelling size of the urban proletariat had had a profound effect on city politics, as previously noted. But more important, the growing organization and militancy of urban workers challenged capitalist prerogatives and threatened capitalist profits. Capitalists perceived that by moving their industrial facilities to suburban communities they could reassert both economic and political control.[10] Some industrialists tried to set up company towns, but the disastrous strike at Pullman in 1894 generally dissuaded them from this approach. Capitalists became content to use the small scale of the suburb and their own position of economic dominance within it (as "big fish in little ponds") as a less direct and less politically offensive means of ensuring that their own interests were satisfied.[11]

Despite capitalists' strong motivations to leave the city, however, the decentralization of industry would not have been possible without facilitating economic and technical developments. First, a massive and historically unprecedented wave of mergers swept over the economy right at the turn of the century. From a low point of 32 in 1897, the annual number of mergers and acquisitions soared to a peak of 1200 in 1899, before falling back to 225 in 1905. During this period, over 5300 industrial firms were consolidated into just 318 corporations (Dowd, pp. 70–72). This consolidation provided the surviving giant corporations with the massive amounts of capital necessary to build huge new industrial plants at the fringes of large cities (see essay 2 here).

Second, innovations in management and control of the production process during this same period dictated a new, more (technically) efficient form of factory architecture. The scientific management movement, though not totally successful in its own terms, nevertheless showed capitalists a new way to control workers in the production process: by rearranging the process so that workers would be deprived of overall knowledge of it, and would be restricted to limited, minutely specific tasks. In other words, to separate conception from execution. This in turn led capitalist managers to an examination of the ways in which machinery itself could be used to dictate the design and pace of the work process. The now-familiar assembly line was the ultimate result of the marriage of technology and capitalists' need for control at this time.[12]

Assembly lines, however, worked best in spread-out, one- or two-level factories. The existing compact, multistory plants in the central cities were not generally suitable for this purpose. Furthermore, the cost of land in the central city was far too expensive for this kind of space-extensive use. Electric power, which had been introduced in the 1880s, was employed to solve both of these problems. Unlike steam, which required the placement of machinery near the power source, electricity allowed tremendous flexibility in the placement of machinery, since electrical energy could be transported over great distances with little loss in efficiency. This also introduced great flexibility into the geographical location of the entire industrial plant.

In addition, the growing system of electric trolleys in major cities by the turn of the century permitted capitalists to decentralize their plants to the fringes of those cities, confident that workers would be able to commute from their homes in the central cities. The separation of conception from execution brought to fruition in assembly lines also meant that production activities per se could be dispersed to the fringes of the city, while corporate control functions that continued to require a centralized location could remain downtown.

The immediate effect of these developments was the beginning of the decentralization of industrial capital. And, given the strong motivations capitalists had for leaving the city, it is not surprising that they were quick to do so when the opportunity presented itself. Indeed, census data for the decade 1899–1909 shows that industrial employment in twelve of the thirteen largest industrial districts was already increasing more than 100 percent faster in the outlying zones than in the central cities (Taylor, p. 4).

In the 1920s, another strong impetus to the decentralization of industry was added. World War I had allowed large corporations to consolidate their monopoly control over major industries. These corporations expanded greatly in size and scale, penetrating new markets and diversifying product lines. This, coupled with the continuing application of technical control in the workplace, generated the need for a large, centralized white-collar workforce. Thus it was that every major city experienced an office-building boom downtown in the 1920s, fueled by monopoly-generated "overaccumulated" capital looking for secondary investment outlets. As the downtown area was transformed into a central business district, industrial land uses were increasingly forced out, either through speculation-induced inflation in land values, or through consciously imposed zoning regulations.[13]

One final factor that facilitated the decentralization of industry was the development of truck transport during and after World War I. This greatly increased locational flexibility, as factories no longer had to be built along railroads. Highways could be built more quickly, more cheaply, and to almost any location. Note, though, that trucks came along after the decentralization process was well under way. Thus they, along with automobiles—as we shall see in the next section—*facilitated, but did not create* suburbanization, as so many bourgeois social scientists would have it.[14]

An important political result of this decentralization process was a virtual end to the policy of annexation in the Northeast and Midwest. Upper-class residential communities had been resisting annexation by central cities with varying success almost since the Civil War. It was the large-scale migration of industrial capital to the suburbs at the beginning of this century, however, which decisively killed annexation. Not only was escape from the city and its social context the primary motive behind decentralization, but the industrial capitalists possessed the economic and political clout in both the new local governments and in state legislatures to assure that the political independence of the suburbs would be maintained.[15]

STATE SUBSIDY AND THE SUBURBAN BOOM

As industry moved out of the city, many workers followed to be near their jobs. When relatively inexpensive automobiles became widely available, even more workers were able to move out beyond the reaches of urban mass transit. At the same time, capitalists became more flexible in locating their decentralized production facilities, confident that a newly mobile labor force could follow them almost anywhere. As more and more people moved to the suburbs, commercial capital decentralized to take advantage of new or shifting markets. And more industrial capital moved out to make use of growing suburban labor markets.

In the suburbs, both capital and labor demanded more and better roads. As they were constructed at public expense, decentralization became more and more feasible. And as the auto, rubber, oil, and construction industries grew in size and power, they acquired the economic and political clout to force the building of still more roads—which not only encouraged suburban migration, but tended to make the automobile an economic and social necessity for each new resident.[16]

The development of suburbs, then, was an interactive process: each element both nourished and fed off of the others. Together they generated an economic boom which profoundly altered the social, political, and geographical character of urban America. On the economic front, suburban development made a significant contribution to the ongoing stability

of American capitalism. Baran and Sweezy (pp. 218–238) argue that capital investment in the automobile and all its spinoffs (including suburbs),
though largely unanticipated and unplanned, rescued the U.S. economy
from a period of growing stagnation and underwrote the economic boom
of the 1920s.

Indeed, in 1900 when there were only about 14,000 autos in the
entire country, roughly ten percent of the U.S. population lived in suburbs.
In 1915, with 2.5 million autos registered, new non-farm residential construction totalled $950 million and there were 414,000 non-farm dwell-
ing-unit starts—most of them in the suburbs. The growth rate of suburbs
exceeded that of cities for the first time in 1920. In 1925 new non-farm
residential construction jumped to $4.5 billion and non-farm dwelling-unit
starts totalled 752,000. From 1926 to 1929 new mortgage loans annually
exceeded $5 billion. At the time of the collapse in 1929 there were more
than 26 million autos on the road and the population of suburbs was
growing twice as fast as that of central cities.[17]

The Great Depression of the 1930s reined in suburban development
in dramatic fashion. The suburbs registered only a slight gain in population during the stagnant decade (the central cities, on the other hand,
actually lost population). Economic activity in the suburbs, as elsewhere,
was sporadic at best. In its attempt to revive the sagging U.S. economy,
the federal government enacted various legislative measures during the
1930s which had a significant impact on suburbanization. The overall
effect of the federal legislation was to create both explicit and implicit subsidies for low-density, detached, owner-occupied, single-family housing,
to the virtual exclusion of other types of dwelling units. And since space
was generally lacking in the central cities, the federal government was
effectively subsidizing the development of suburbs.

In 1934, for example, the Federal Savings and Loan Insurance Corporation (FSLIC) was formed. It guaranteed deposits in savings and loan
associations which were granted preferential interest rates to enable them
to attract savings with which to finance owner-occupied housing. That
same year, the Federal Housing Administration (FHA) was also created.
This agency provided guaranteed, self-liquidating mortgages for newly
constructed homes. Furthermore, it required low down payments and set
up amortization rates which were realistic for middle-class incomes.[18]

These measures did not have an immediate effect, however. The generally pervasive economic stagnation of the 1930s held back suburban
development, despite the existence of incentives. The advent of World
War II got the economy moving again, but the growth of suburbs was held
in check as the country focused its productive resources on war matériel.

During the war period, however, the federal government once again engaged in activities which would later represent a massive subsidy of suburbanization. Between 1939 and 1946 the federal government built an average of over $2.5 billion worth of industrial buildings every year. This was more than twice the average of private industry for the same years (Kain, pp. 7–10). Lacking adequate space in the cities, most of these plants were constructed in the suburbs. When the war ended, these production facilities were turned over to private industry, often at nominal cost.

State subsidy of suburbanization continued and increased after the war. In addition to expanded support for low-density single-family homes (through the creation of Veteran's Administration guaranteed mortgages), the federal government embarked on a massive program of highway construction. The effect of the new interstate freeway system in cities was the destruction of many older neighborhoods and the creation of a convenient means of access to central city jobs for suburban residents. And the creation of the Federal Highway Trust Fund ensured that freeways would be self-propagating. As more freeways were built, more automobile travel was encouraged. The consequently increased revenue from the gasoline tax swelled the coffers of the Highway Fund. Strict controls (at least until the 1970s) dictated that its burgeoning budget be used only for more highways—effectively diminishing alternative modes of transportation.

Predictably, these massive state subsidies fueled the rapid decentralization of both industry and population. By the 1960s the decentralization of jobs had escalated to the point where the central cities were actually suffering net losses in employment. Between 1954 and 1963, in the 24 metropolitan areas with populations greater than 1 million, the central cities lost more than 500,000 jobs while the suburbs were gaining over 1.5 million (Masotti and Hadden, 1974, p. 9).

The decentralization of urban households was every bit as dramatic. By 1950 the population of suburbs was growing ten times as fast as that of central cities; nearly one in four Americans was a suburbanite. Sixty-four percent of the nation's total population increase in the 1960s took place in the suburbs. By 1970 seventy-six million Americans lived in suburbs. They represented fifty-seven percent of the total metropolitan population and a plurality (37.6 percent) of the population of the nation as a whole.

The onset of economic stagnation in the 1970s slowed but did not reverse this suburban trend. Between 1965 and 1974, more than three million new jobs were created in suburbia; in 1973 nationwide suburban employment surpassed that of central cities for the first time. Similarly, the population of suburbs grew by 12.0 percent between 1970 and 1977, while that of central cities declined 4.6 percent. By 1977, 83.1 million Americans lived in suburbs, representing 39.1 percent of the nation's total population (Muller, p. 4).

Suburbanization, it is fair to say, was closely linked with the roughly three decades of unprecedented postwar prosperity. Under the aegis of the Pax Americana, U.S. multinational corporations gained access to cheap resources and new markets overseas (see Dowd, pp. 226–265). Stable, relatively high profits prompted the expansion of production at home, diversification, and a rapprochement with labor that traded rising wages for industrial peace. Rising wages, in turn, increased consumer demand for housing and durable goods. Provision of these goods by the construction, auto, appliance, real estate, and financial industries further contributed to rising wages and a snowballing process of growth.

Why should this growth have meant suburbanization? Could not it just as well have taken place in expanding central cities? The answer, it seems, is no. As we saw earlier, the spatial form of the industrial city no longer met the needs of capital—industry, remember, led the way into the suburbs at the turn of the century. Furthermore, postwar suburbanization represented a marriage of convenience between the immediate economic and political needs of significant segments of both the capitalist and the working classes. On the one hand, capitalists used the suburbs as a means of political and economic control; they manipulated or propagandized the working class into acquiescence with this strategy. On the other hand, significant elements of the working class acquired a genuine, (semi-) independent interest in suburbs and suburban development as a means of meeting individual and collective needs.[19] It is to this phenomenon that we now turn.

SOCIAL REPRODUCTION IN SUBURBS

The massive decentralization of the urban population occasioned by post-World War II suburban development was not simply a general movement of city-dwellers to the countryside. Rather, it tended to be a site-specific process. That is, particular groups of people tended to take up residence in specific suburbs. Conventional social scientists almost totally ignore this important fact. Consciously or unconsciously, their research obscures the dynamic of suburban development in two ways.

First of all, their discussion and data is usually presented in terms of central cities and "suburban rings" (see, for example, Schnore; Birch). On the one hand, this form of presentation ignores the variation in both the form and social composition of suburbs. On the other hand, it mystifies class relations by setting up a geographic contradiction as the basis for inequality rather than an economic one. For, although classes clearly have spatial locations, they are defined primarily by their relationship to the means of economic production.

Second, suburbs are often described by bourgeois social scientists as the logical outcome of some "natural" market process. Muth, for instance, argues that suburbs have been generated by essentially the same market forces as the central city. Furthermore, he argues that the distribution of income and resources among suburbs is largely what it would be if there were no political fragmentation. In my view, however, it is *precisely* this political fragmentation which explains the inequality in resources among suburbs.[20]

The movement of central-city residents to the suburbs represented, on the one hand, a genuine search for community. On the other hand, it reflected an attempt by some groups to socially reproduce privileges derived from the differentiation and hierarchical stratification of the labor force created by monopoly capitalism in this century.

Mollenkopf has cogently argued that the dynamic of social interaction and community formation is a crucial force in the development of the urban political and spatial economy. But although this dynamic is separate from, and opposed to, the dynamic of capital accumulation, it is ultimately subordinate to it. This means that the search for community is mediated by the existing institutions of economic production and accumulation. In the nineteenth century industrial city, these institutions provided the context for the formation of viable ethnic working-class communities in the city, as well as elite suburbs on the fringe. Twentieth century economic development mostly destroyed these ethnic communities and, as we have seen, precipitated the movement of first industry, then population to the suburbs.

These latter developments were in some sense generated, as well as accompanied by, the creation of a national consumer culture. The consolidation of monopoly capitalism in the second decade of this century provided giant corporations with the productive ability and the financial resources to satisfy as well as to create national markets. Advertising became a vehicle by which to encourage people to meet all their varied needs through consumption of commodities. Not coincidentally, the success of this strategy bolstered effective demand.

The needs for which commodity consumption was touted as the only solution included, of course, basic physiological ones like food, clothing, and shelter. But they also included needs for personal security, a sense of belongingness, and self-esteem. It is these three needs in particular that advertising has so skillfully exploited and manipulated. Pandemic alienation, rooted in production but expressed in all capitalist institutions, has made consumers more vulnerable to this sophisticated manipulation. More and more in this society, individuals are defined by what they consume.[21]

The effects on community of the generalization of alienated commodity consumption have been paradoxical. On the one hand, there has been a rejection of the traditional notion of community (which economic forces were dismantling anyway). Advertising encourages people to utilize consumption to express their individuality. The model of community put forth, such as it is, is patterned on the free market. In this view, sometimes called "community without propinquity,"[22] physical proximity and geographical ties are seen as unnecessarily confining; association, it is argued, should be freely chosen on the basis of an instrumental, utilitarian calculus.

On the other hand, people have continued to pursue some sort of geographical proximity and social community. Despite, and perhaps in part because of, the general homogenization of mass consumer culture, differential consumption styles have been identified and promoted by both advertisers and consumers. Those consumers wishing to be identified with high-status lifestyles and patterns of consumption have sought propinquity with each other and the exclusion of "outsiders." The suburb, with its small scale—which allows for a certain degree of consensus—and its historical identification with the elite, was an attractive vehicle for this purpose.

This is not to say that everyone who has moved to a suburb has done so for status consumption reasons. In fact, the immediate attraction of suburbs for most potential residents has to do with the generally better schools, lower crime rates, and cheaper prices for detached dwellings on larger lots than can usually be found in the central city. This latter feature is particularly important in an alienated, individualistic society like our own where informal social controls rarely work and the most efficient way to avoid problems of interaction is to distance oneself physically as well as socially from one's neighbors.

What is true at the level of the individual household is true at the level of the community as well. In the absence of mechanisms of social cooperation and orientations to pro-social behavior, suburban amenities can only be maintained through the exclusion of "undesirable" outsiders. And in an alienated, consumerist society, these outsiders tend to be identified on the basis of consumption patterns and lifestyles.

I do not mean to imply here that suburban residents are any more consumption-oriented than central-city dwellers or indeed than any other group of people in this society. Consumerism is in fact pandemic in advanced capitalist society. It is just that the small scale of the suburb makes it amenable to a kind of grass-roots control which, coupled with political independence, makes possible the protection of existing suburban advantages. It is this potential for the protection of the desirable features of suburban living which often makes consumption patterns and lifestyles more broadly salient features in suburbs.

The small scale and potential manipulability of the suburb have made it attractive for another reason, however. Certain groups within the urban population have been able to use the suburb to protect and reproduce privileged economic and social statuses derived from the workplace. As monopoly capitalism has developed in this century, it has created a complex system of hierarchical stratification in production. Workers at different locations in the hierarchy enjoy quite different levels of wages and benefits, differential job security, varying working conditions, and distinctly different amounts of control over their work. Given a highly individualistic and competitive labor market, it was perhaps inevitable that those workers with better jobs would try to protect their privileged access to them.

One way of accomplishing this was to maximize the social distinctions between themselves and other, less-privileged workers through the promotion of particular consumption patterns in a bounded geographical unit—the suburb. Even more important for the reproduction of privilege than these shared patterns of private consumption, however, was the suburb's promise of control over collective consumption. Here residents could consciously direct expenditures on items like education, health, and recreation in a manner geared to gain, protect, or expand privileged characteristics and competitive advantages derived from the workplace.

In order to make this system work, suburban residents have often sought to establish and maintain a certain degree of homogeneity within the community in order to both ensure consensual agreement about major priorities and to guard against "deviant" displays of consumption behavior. A number of mechanisms, both formal and informal, have been developed to accomplish this. Conscious manipulation of the suburb's independent legislative powers is perhaps the most important. A community can carefully control overall development, for example, through selective municipal expenditures on roads, sewers, drains, schools, and so forth. The cost of land and construction can be raised by large-lot zoning. Building costs can be further inflated by specifying minimum quality standards for construction materials which are significantly higher than industry minimums. The volume, type, and size of dwelling units can also be closely regulated.

Not only can various groups be excluded from a municipality, but investment capital can be lured by the prospect of special developments and services (for example, industrial parks with all utilities) and property tax breaks. Even with special reductions, though, corporate taxes provide a major source of revenue to many suburban municipalities. If enough capital can be recruited, individual property taxes can remain low while still assuring the residents that the level and quality of services will reproduce their privilege.[23]

Residential covenants provide another mechanism for maintaining the "character" of suburban communities. These agreements are often contracts which homeowners must sign as part of their deed. Formerly these protective covenants explicitly limited the type of people to whom residents could sell their houses. Although overt discrimination of this type has been outlawed since 1948, these kinds of arrangements are still perpetuated on an informal basis. Other types of agreements dictate the ways in which residents can use and develop their property. All of these types of protective covenants have been consistently upheld by the courts.

The foregoing conceptualization of suburbs does not mean to imply, however, that *all* suburban communities are the result of conscious decisions by particular groups to organize and incorporate for the purpose of reproducing some privileges or perceived advantages in the workplace. Rather, I would argue that the promise of the ability to achieve a measure of control over the social and economic environment has been an important attraction of suburban living and has exerted a major influence over the specific pattern of population decentralization.

Furthermore, I would not suggest that all or even some suburbs are completely homogeneous by class or status group. Communities can actually tolerate a rather large amount of internal diversity while maintaining a dominant ethos. It is the *possibility* of realizing and imposing their own values and mores that has impelled various groups to seek out suburbs as vehicles for the protection and reproduction of competitive advantages and social amenities.

It must also be noted that the desire of certain groups to use suburbs for the protection of privilege is not always directly realized. Rather, endeavors to this effect are mediated by real estate, land development, and banking interests. These interests share one common overriding motivation: profitability. It happens, however, that historically it has been highly profitable to construct communities that are relatively homogeneous by status group. Thus, we have the tract homes of the 1920s and 1950s, the sprawling single-family subdivisions of the 1960s, and the elaborate townhouse and condominium developments of the 1970s.

DIVISIONS WITHIN THE WORKING CLASS

Social and economic divisions among workers in this country have grown up simultaneously with the development of the capitalist mode of production. They are part and parcel of the very logic of the system. Capital investment according to the sole criterion of profitability produces a pattern of uneven development throughout the society. Workers reflect this as some of their number are paid better, work under more desirable conditions, receive more education or training, and have better fringe benefits according to the general location, specific needs, and overall profitability of their employer.[24]

In addition, social and cultural divisions among workers not directly produced by the economic system (for example, race and sex) have nevertheless been exploited and enlarged by capitalists in order to dilute the power of the working class. At various points in time workers have overcome these divisions and achieved class solidarity. But it is also true that short-run self-interest has forced workers in more privileged positions to expend a great deal of time and effort attempting to maintain or expand their advantages at the expense of other workers.

The implication for our present discussion of the growing importance of status distinctions among workers is this: as these distinctions become more and more significant in the labor market, workers possessing privileged characteristics will increasingly desire to consolidate, protect, and reproduce them. The move to the suburbs—not just any suburb, but one whose residents possess the appropriate status characteristics—is a way of accomplishing this. In their chosen suburb, status groups can engage in the lifestyles and consumption patterns which reinforce their status. Members of the various status groups tend to feel more comfortable—a sense of community, if you will—with those who possess similar homogeneous status characteristics. Thus, the class- and ethnicity-based neighborhood of the industrial city has given way to the status-conscious suburban community of the corporate metropolitan city as the dominant form of community organization.

Suburbs are also important because access to desirable jobs is controlled by segmented labor markets that have spatial characteristics.[25] The growing emphasis on credentials in the labor market has increased the importance of the educational system as a determinant of employment. And it is here that the suburb has played a crucial role, for the promise of control inherent in the small scale and political independence of the suburban municipality offers an unparalleled opportunity to workers with access to better jobs. An educational system can be developed, along with various supportive services, which effectively reproduces competitive advantages for themselves and, perhaps most important, for their children.

THE CONTRADICTIONS OF CONTEMPORARY SUBURBAN DEVELOPMENT

The phenomenon of suburban development in this century has been, as we have seen, a political and economic boon to capital in general, as well as to particular elements of capital. On the one hand, real estate, construction, and financial interests got rich building suburbs. The automobile, construction, and consumer durables industries got even richer maintaining them.[26] On the other hand, capital in general was able to use the suburbs as a form of social control, and to limit and isolate gains in the social wage to specific sectors of the working class. Moreover, suburbanization recruited working-class support for an effort to remake the obsolete industrial city.

As this implies, a substantial number of workers gained from, and therefore supported, suburban development. Many were able to realize the American dream of owning a single-family detached home, and to gain access to and control over institutions of collective consumption which could protect and reproduce the social and economic privileges they derived from their workplaces.

The process of suburban development, however, like other social processes in capitalist society, is a contradictory one. This means that certain irresolvable tensions are part of the process of development itself. Though these tensions can be effectively suppressed and perhaps forgotten in one era, they inevitably emerge to generate serious problems at a later date. Moreover, the very solutions which succeeded in suppressing contradictions at one time frequently emerge later as the most intractable barriers to further progress and the most salient points of structural tension and social conflict.

Suburbanization today faces such a crisis. Although suburban development continues relatively unabated, increasingly intractable problems are beginning to crop up. These contradictions pose unique difficulties and different types of challenges to capitalists and workers. In the last section of this paper I will examine important problems posed for capital and for workers by the contradictions of contemporary suburban development.

For capital, the basic contradiction of contemporary suburban development is that the pattern of suburbanization which was once so supportive of both capital accumulation and social control now poses a barrier to further success. First of all, suburban economic development currently seems to be choking on its own past success. The massive decentralization of the urban population after World War II spurred the further decentralization of industry. Retailing, too, escalated its exodus from the city by constructing ever-larger and more complex shopping malls in the suburbs. And in recent years, office functions have increasingly left the downtown central business district for minicities of commerce and finance located on major suburban transport nodes.

The result of this pattern of development has been the creation of a multi-nodal metropolis—a process some analysts have called "the urbanization of the suburbs" or the creation of "the outer city."[27] While this development has tended to be extremely profitable for the capitalists involved, it has "created suburban variants of the big-city problems which capital had hoped to escape" (Mollenkopf, p. 330). Among the most serious of these problems is that of congestion in the suburban transportation system.

The freeway and superhighway system that came into being in the postwar era was designed to facilitate traffic flow to and from the heart of the central city; it was not particularly conducive to inter-suburban journeys. As long as development, and therefore traffic was light, this was not a serious problem. The large-scale decentralization of population and economic activity to the suburbs, however, has made inter-suburban travel both more necessary and more problematic. From capital's point of view, transportation congestion poses a problem not only for the production and circulation of commodities, but for the reproduction of the labor force as well, as workers demand higher wages to compensate for increased commuting costs.

This latter problem is exacerbated for capital by the particular way that political fragmentation has divorced the place of residence from the place of work in the modern metropolis. Capitalists have very astutely used the political fragmentation inherent in the proliferation of suburbs to maximum advantage. They have used the competition for capital among suburbs to extort tax breaks, special services and investments, and other highly profitable arrangements from the privileged suburbs in which they have located their investments. But, as we have seen, the residents of these communities often attempt to keep other groups of workers from moving in in order to protect their own competitive advantages. As the location of production has increasingly become divorced from the residences of the workers, they have faced ever-increasing commuting costs, and have demanded higher wages in compensation.

In addition, the costs of commuting to work, coupled with the growing congestion of the metropolis make it difficult for many workers to get to their jobs. Thus, capitalists are confronted with problems of absenteeism and labor turnover which hurt production schedules as well as profits. Capitalists have tried to exert pressure on the suburbs to build more housing suitable for production workers; so far they have largely been unsuccessful. Their failure is not surprising, for although capitalists were a major force in the creation of the political fragmentation of the metropolis, they do not control the process completely. Thus suburbs now confront capital as a contradiction.

Capital also faces a contradiction posed by the fact that the urbanization of the suburbs has meant the decay of the central city, or as Schwartz puts it, "the suburbs are becoming industrialized without the bother of an industrial population" (p. 329). He might better have said without the bother of an industrial *surplus population,* since it is this group which is increasingly concentrated in the central city. The implications of this for capital are twofold. On the one hand, this increasingly black and poor surplus population presents a threat to urban social control and must be managed, either through the cooptation of welfare and the threat of coercion, or through the massive provision of heavily-subsidized jobs.[28] Either way, a tremendous amount of money is needed— money which is not to be found in the declining central cities.

On the other hand, monopoly capitalists have huge fixed investments in the decaying central cities. The size and scale of these investments dictates that they cannot be abandoned as easily as the elite and certain elements of the working class have abandoned their homes there. Capitalists must find ways to reverse the trend of decay in order to revive and guarantee the profitability of their investments. To do this, they need huge investments by the state in services and infrastructure. But the hard-pressed central cities have nowhere near adequate resources to do the job. In fact, their tax bases are declining as capital and middle-status households continue to flee to the suburbs.

In both of these cases, capital is confronted with a contradiction of its own making, for it was the decentralization of production facilities which began the movement of resources out of the city. And the political needs and power of capital ensured that the city would not annex these new areas. The central city's tax base has been further eroded by various non-taxable infrastructural investments (such as highways, public research facilities) demanded by capital. To overcome this contradiction and ensure the continued profitability of their central city investments, capitalists must rationalize the metropolis. They must appropriate the resources of the suburbs and plow them back into the central city.[29] But to do this means that they must break the power of the suburbs. Capital must destroy the political fragmentation which it helped create and which it has exploited so profitably. It must, in addition, disenfranchise blacks, who are finally coming to politically control central city governments. Whether or not this can be accomplished remains an open question. But the task will certainly be difficult.

For workers, the form and pattern of contemporary suburban development poses three basic contradictions. The first has to do with problems of individual consumption. The deconcentration and separation of places of employment, retailing services, and sites for recreation and leisure are sources of the continuing appeal of suburbs; yet at the same time these processes pose increasingly intractable problems for suburban residents. Workers cannot always leapfrog across the metropolis in hot pursuit of capital. Rapidly rising indebtedness limits their financial flexibility. And the increasing costs of construction and residential finance along with ballooning fuel costs further limit their options. Moreover, the rising costs of owning and operating private automobiles—a necessity given the near-universal inadequacy of suburban mass transit facilities—represents a further burden on the budgets of workers, both those who live in suburbs and those who commute from the central city.

Collective consumption has also become problematic in today's suburbs. While the political fragmentation of the metropolis has served the short-run interests of some elements of the working class quite successfully, the anarchy, unevenness, and stratification of capitalist development—which are both cause and effect of the spatial distribution of privilege—have recently come to haunt even relatively privileged workers. For as the residents of older suburbs are rapidly finding out, the marriage between capital and any given suburb is really only a temporary affair. Short-term gains have often become long-term losses as capital has discarded some suburbs for other, more profitable ones. Since the small scale of suburbs makes them extremely sensitive to even minor shifts in investment, the continuing migration of capital has spelled economic disaster for some suburbs. This loss of tax base imperils expenditures for the purpose of reproducing privilege.

But whether or not they directly lose part of their tax base, nearly all suburbs are affected by the general fiscal crisis of local government. The prospect of increasing taxes threatens to cut into individual consumption expenditures; declining or stable revenues in the face of ever-rising costs, however, imperil spending on collective consumption. A decline in the latter not only tends to undermine the reproduction of privilege in a suburb, but it potentially leads to a decline in municipal prestige, which in turn calls the status of residents into question.

The social prestige of suburbs is also affected by the spinoffs from private capital investment. Shopping malls, for example, are increasingly becoming mixed blessings for the community in which they are located.

On the one hand, they bolster the municipal tax base. But on the other hand, the massive traffic congestion which is more and more a regular phenomenon on the streets around these malls creates noise, pollution, and limits access for local residents. As a result, the prestige of the immediately surrounding community is lowered. Residents of suburbs without shopping malls, however, face increased commuting costs as retailing becomes more and more concentrated in these developments, as well as the loss of tax base in their own communities.

Finally, the spatial distribution of privilege represented by suburbanization is contradictory to the long-term interests of the working class as a whole. There have always been certain groups of workers who did not benefit from suburban development. Some of these workers have been unable to mobilize their resources to protect whatever competitive advantages they might possess. The majority of them have simply lacked advantages altogether. The exclusion of these workers from social, economic, and political resources by those who find themselves in more advantageous positions represents a continuing barrier to working-class solidarity. It is an obstacle which must be overcome in order to build a democratic, egalitarian society.

The contradictions of suburban development are becoming increasingly manifest. These contradictions cannot fail to compel changes in the present social arrangements. The important issue, however, is the nature and direction of these changes. Capitalists will use their considerable resources to attempt to bring about changes which will support their prerogatives and strengthen the capitalist system. The interest of the working class, however, does not lie with propping up capitalism; in the long run, workers must struggle to transform it. A thorough understanding of the origin and historical dynamics of the contradictions of capitalism as manifest in the phenomenon of suburban development can, hopefully, aid in this struggle.

NOTES

1. Following O'Connor, *state* is used here as a generic term referring to government at all levels. The generic is justified by the fact that all levels of government share a common relationship to the mode of production. The functions of the capitalist state are (1) to ensure profitable private capital accumulation and (2) to maintain social harmony. The capitalist state contributes indirectly to the profitability of private enterprise through projects and services which increase labor productivity (e.g., highways, education) and through projects and services which lower the reproduction cost of labor (e.g., urban renewal, unemployment insurance). The state legitimates the capitalist system through projects and services which maintain social order (e.g., welfare, police). The state at all levels is subject to political

pressure and manipulation—but more especially so at the local level where its smaller scale makes it more accessible to a greater variety of interest groups. At the same time, the increasing importance of collective consumption in contemporary society renders this pressure and manipulation all the more necessary. For an excellent discussion of the state at the local level and the ways it has been manipulated, see essay 4 by Markusen.

2. Marglin points out that the factory system as a method of organizing production was not historically or technologically inevitable. Rather, it was developed by capital because it offered the greatest amount of control over labor and, therefore, was the most profitable way to organize production. Once this system of labor control was in place, enormous technological advances became possible (see, for example, Edwards).

3. An important impetus to the development of urban slums was the creation of a free market in housing, whereby capitalists lowered the reproduction costs of labor, created new avenues of speculation, and mystified class relations. For a good discussion of this development, see Walker (1978, pp. 189–91).

4. Glaab and Brown (pp. 21–44) document numerous examples of state subsidy of capital improvements which maintained or increased the profitability of the manufacturing sector in the mid-nineteenth century.

5. For more details and statistics on this process of annexation, see Kotler (pp. 1–26) and Wood (p. 77).

6. For an extended theoretical discussion of the transition to a decentralized urban form, see Walker (1981, pp. 385–95).

7. For an excellent discussion and good documentation of the increasing demand for city services, see Glaab and Brown (pp. 66–186).

8. The spatial distancing of the residences of capitalist entrepreneurs from their business facilities was made feasible by an important change in the control structure of industrial production. As Edwards (pp. 23–36) notes, the increasing size and scale of the industrial production process during the last half of the nineteenth century made it impossible for a single entrepreneur or group of entrepreneurs to personally supervise all of their workers. Increasingly, they hired foremen and supervisors to do it for them. As capitalists became less involved in the detailed supervision of the production process, they could spend more time commuting.

9. Horse-drawn streetcars thus *did not* create suburbs, as some (such as Muller) would have it. In a broader sense, no form of transportation "created" any form of urbanization. This kind of technological determinism is, however, common in the bourgeois analysis of suburbanization (see Schwab for a recent example). Marxists, of course, view social relations and the forms of social organization that flow from the mode of production as far more important—shaping, among other things, the development and employment of technology. With regard to horsecars, for instance, Walker (1978, p. 179) shows that this mode of travel was technically feasible long before it was introduced on a regular basis. The key to its ultimate widespread employment in the 1850s, he says, is the creation of a demand for it, generated by the need to put space between socially differentiated groups, coupled with "overaccumulated" capital's need to find investment outlets in this period.

10. Writing in 1915, Graham Taylor furnished this contemporary account of capitalist's thinking:

> Some company officials act on the belief that by removing workingmen from a large city it is possible to get them away from the influences which foment discontent and labor disturbances. The

satellite city is looked to as a sort of isolation hospital for the cure
of chronic "trouble." In an eastern city which recently experienced the throes of a turbulent streetcar strike, the superintendent
of a large industrial establishment said that every time workers
paraded past his plant a veritable fever seemed to spread among
the employees in all his work-rooms. He thought that if the plants
were moved out to the suburbs, the workingmen should not be so
frequently inoculated with infection. (p. 23)

11. One of the earliest and most obvious examples of this approach was the
    development of Gary, Indiana, by U.S. Steel in 1905. The corporation
    formed a subsidiary land development company which laid out and de-
    veloped the community. The town was then incorporated and formal po-
    litical control was put in the hands of its residents. As both the largest
    employer and the largest taxpayer in town, however, U.S. Steel retained
    effective control. Greer discusses this development and shows the continuing
    dominance of U.S. Steel in the municipal politics of Gary.
12. On the introduction of scientific management and technical control into
    the production process, see the pathbreaking work of Braverman (pp. 85–
    248) and Edwards (pp. 90–129).
13. Using New York as an example, Fitch shows that the growth of urban
    planning in the United States was closely linked to an effort to maximize
    land values in the central business district. This required the removal of
    "undesirable" (that is, less profitable) industrial uses and working-class
    residences from the area.
14. See Muller for an example of this technological-determinist thinking.
15. See Markusen here (essay 4) for a more detailed discussion of this point.
16. Kwitney details the famous 1949 court case which revealed that General
    Motors, Firestone, and Standard Oil of California, among others, had
    joined together to secretly buy up and destroy hundreds of miles of urban
    trolley lines in order to increase reliance upon buses for mass transit. Ulti-
    mately, the inherent inadequacies of buses made access to automobiles a
    necessity.
17. For documentation of the growth of suburbs, see Wood (pp. 540–87),
    Glaab and Brown (pp. 246–71) and Masotti and Hadden (1974, p. 7).
18. For more on the development of the U.S. financial structure and its relation
    to suburbanization, see Harvey.
19. Hoch (essay 5) provides a good illustration of capitalists' use of suburbs
    for the purpose of social control in his examination of the process of sub-
    urban incorporation in the Los Angeles metropolitan area. Mollenkopf dis-
    cusses the need for capitalists to recruit working-class support for their
    growth strategies.
20. For a more extensive discussion of the historical treatment of suburbs in
    social science literature, see Ashton.
21. For an excellent discussion of the creation of a mass consumer culture in
    the United States and its social implications, see Ewen. On the alienating
    aspects of capitalist consumption, see Fromm.
22. Webber was an early popularizer of the term. For a radical critique, see
    Plant.
23. Not all suburbs, of course, compete for industry. The residents of certain
    middle- and upper-status residential communities militantly oppose the in-
    troduction of industry into their municipalities. This opposition has two
    motivations: (1) a desire to keep local service costs down, and (2) a desire
    to maintain and increase the already high values of their single-family

dwellings on large lots. Both of these drives have the effect of keeping the tax rate low in these communities.

24. Divisions within the working class have been created on the basis of ethnicity, economic sector of employment, and types of labor control and working conditions. For a discussion of the first type of division, see Aronowitz; Rothstein. On divisions by economic sector, see the pathbreaking work of O'Connor. For an analysis of divisions by types of labor control and working conditions, see Braverman and Edwards.

25. For an introduction to the concept of a segmented, or dual labor market, see Piore; Reich, Gordon and Edwards.

26. Larry Sawers (p. 56) calculates that about one quarter of annual gross national product in this country is currently dependent upon roads, cars, and trucks. When all related goods and services (such as building construction, duplication of consumer durables and municipal services, local administrative bureaucracies) are factored in, it is reasonable to assume that at least half of the annual GNP of the United States is directly or indirectly tied to suburbs and suburbanization. The truth of this assertion is made painfully obvious by the sensitive and central position occupied by the automobile and construction industries in the current economic crisis.

27. The first phrase is from a book of the same name by Masotti and Hadden (1973). The second phrase comes from Muller.

28. See the discussion by Hill (essay 13).

29. Some of these resources must be plowed back into suburbs as well. The small scale of the suburb makes its tax base vulnerable to both cyclical and secular economic fluctuations. In the current economic crisis, many suburbs are having trouble maintaining necessary infrastructure and services.

REFERENCES

Aronowitz, Stanley, *False Promises: The Shaping of American Working Class Consciousness* (New York: McGraw-Hill, 1973).

Ashton, Patrick J., "Toward a Political Economy of Metropolitan Areas." Unpublished Master's thesis, Michigan State University, 1975.

Baran, Paul A., and Paul M. Sweezy, *Monopoly Capital: An Essay on the American Economic and Social Order* (New York: Monthly Review Press, 1966).

Birch, David, *The Economic Future of City and Suburb* (New York: Committee for Economic Development, 1970).

Braverman, Harry, *Labor and Monopoly Capital: The Degradation of Work in the Twentieth Century* (New York: Monthly Review Press, 1974).

Dowd, Douglas F., *The Twisted Dream: Capitalist Development in the United States Since 1776,* 2nd ed. (Cambridge, Mass.: Winthrop, 1977).

Edwards, Richard C., *Contested Terrain: The Transformation of the Workplace in the Twentieth Century* (New York: Basic Books, 1979).

Ewen, Stuart, *Captains of Consciousness: Advertising and the Social Roots of the Consumer Culture* (New York: McGraw-Hill, 1976).

Fitch, Robert, "Planning New York," in Roger E. Alcaly and David Mermelstein, eds., *The Fiscal Crisis of American Cities* (New York: Vintage Books, 1976).

Fromm, Erich, *The Sane Society* (New York: Fawcett, 1965).

Glaab, Charles N., and A. Theodore Brown, *A History of Urban America,* 2nd ed. (New York: Macmillan, 1976).

Greer, Edward, *Big Steel: Black Politics and Corporate Power in Gary, Indiana* (New York: Monthly Review Press, 1979).

Harvey, David, "The Political Economy of Urbanization in Advanced Capitalist Societies—The Case of the United States," in G. Gappert and H. Rose, eds., *The Social Economy of Cities* (Beverly Hills: Sage Publications, 1975).

Kain, John F., "The Distribution and Movement of Jobs and Industry," in James Q. Wilson, ed., *The Metropolitan Enigma: Inquiries Into the Nature and Dimensions of America's "Urban Crisis"* (Cambridge, Mass.: Harvard University Press, 1968).

Kotler, Milton, *Neighborhood Government: The Local Foundations of Political Life* (New York: Bobbs-Merrill, 1969).

Kwitny, Jonathan, "The Great Transportation Conspiracy," *Harper's,* February 1981.

Marglin, Stephen A., "What Do Bosses Do? The Origins and Functions of Hierarchy in Capitalist Production," *Review of Radical Political Economics,* Summer 1974.

Masotti, Louis H., and Jeffrey K. Hadden, eds., *The Urbanization of the Suburbs* (Beverly Hills: Sage Publications, 1973).

———, *Suburbia in Transition* (New York: New Viewpoints, 1974).

Mollenkopf, John, "Community and Accumulation," in Michael Dear and Allen J. Scott, eds., *Urbanization and Urban Planning in Capitalist Society* (New York: Methuen, 1981).

Muller, Peter O., *Contemporary Suburban America* (Englewood Cliffs, N.J.: Prentice-Hall, 1981).

Mumford, Lewis, *The City in History* (New York: Harcourt, Brace and World, 1961).

Muth, Richard R., "The Distribution of Population Within Urban Areas," in Robert Ferber, ed., *Determinants of Investment Behavior* (New York: National Bureau of Economic Research, 1967).

O'Connor, James, *The Fiscal Crisis of the State* (New York: St. Martin's Press, 1973).

Piore, Michael J., "The Dual Labor Market: Theory and Implications," in David M. Gordon, ed., *Problems in Political Economy: An Urban Perspective,* 2nd ed. (Lexington, Mass.: D. C. Heath, 1977).

Plant, Raymond, "Community: Concept, Conception, and Ideology" *Politics and Society,* 1978.

Reich, Michael, David M. Gordon, and Richard C. Edwards, "A Theory of Labor Market Segmentation," *American Economic Review,* May 1973.

Rothstein, Richard, "The Urban Ethnic Working Class," *Green Mountain Quarterly,* November 1975.

Sawers, Larry, "Urban Form and the Mode of Production" *Review of Radical Political Economics,* Spring 1975.

Schnore, Leo F., *The Urban Scene* (New York: The Free Press, 1965).

Schwab, William A., *Urban Sociology: A Human Ecological Perspective* (Reading, Mass.: Addison-Wesley, 1982).

Schwartz, Barry, "Images of Suburbia: Some Revisionist Commentary and Conclusions," in Barry Schwartz, ed., *The Changing Face of the Suburbs* (Chicago: University of Chicago Press, 1976).

Taylor, Graham R., *Satellite Cities* (New York: D. Appleton & Co., 1915).

Walker, Richard A., "The Transformation of Urban Structure in the Nineteenth Century and the Beginnings of Suburbanization," in Kevin R. Cox, ed., *Urbanization and Conflict in Market Societies* (Chicago: Maaroufa Press, 1978).

———, "A Theory of Suburbanization: Capitalism and the Construction of

Urban Space in the United States," in Michael Dear and Allen J. Scott, eds., *Urbanization and Urban Planning in Capitalist Society* (New York: Methuen, 1981).

Webber, M. M., "Order in Diversity: Community Without Propinquity," in L. Wingo, ed., *Cities and Space* (Baltimore: Johns Hopkins University Press, 1963).

Wood, Robert C., *Suburbia: Its People and Their Politics* (Boston: Houghton-Mifflin, 1958).

Class and Urban Social Expenditure: A Marxist Theory of Metropolitan Government

ANN R. MARKUSEN

An incisive analysis of the fiscal crisis of older U.S. central cities in the 1970s requires an understanding of the Marxist theory of the state. This paper seeks to explain, from a Marxist perspective, the dynamics of the state at the local level. In place of conventional social-science models of pluralism (political science) and competition (economics), the Marxist model used here builds on the concepts of class conflict and the historical development of political form under U.S. capitalism. The contribution of this paper is its elaboration of the Marxist theory of the state, heretofore applied almost exclusively to national government, to include an analysis of a unique American phenomenon: the fragmented urban governmental structure.

The impetus to undertake this investigation was the desire to comprehend why cities like New York and Detroit presently confront serious fiscal crises. Since the same brink-of-bankruptcy condition does not characterize European city governments, it is most probable that the specific form of the government at the local level in the United States is a very powerful force in exacerbating urban fiscal crisis. An inquiry into the origins of this form reveals that it has evolved from the resolution of past class conflicts, each of which in turn was shaped by existing political form. This history provides a means of strengthening the Marxist theory of the state, by illuminating the relationship between state structure and class conflict.

This is an extended treatment of ideas presented at the Conference on Urban Political Economy, at the New School for Social Research, New York City, February 16, 1975, and included in *Kapitalistate: Working Papers on the Capitalist State,* No. 4/5, Summer, 1976.

HOW MAINSTREAM SOCIAL SCIENCE EXPLAINS U.S. METROPOLITAN POLITICAL FRAGMENTATION

The class homogeneity and political autonomy of suburban development challenge mainstream social science because they undermine an approach which celebrates pluralism in the political process. Suburbs confront even the casual observer with the class character of U.S. society.

Political scientists and economists alike attempt to explain and applaud the existence of fragmented, autonomous local governments in metropolitan areas. Political scientists herald the structure as a successful solution to the corruption and bureaucratic unresponsiveness of big-city government, and as a nostalgic movement back toward rural living and New England town-hall politics (Wood; Warren). This idyllic model describes only suburban governments and ignores central-city political conflicts. Furthermore, it cannot explain why successive groups of recent migrants to cities fail to gain access to suburban democracy. The lack of a historical perspective that carefully documents the emergence of separate political units cripples the strength of such an analysis.

Empirical evidence indicates that this view focuses on a trivial (and most likely fictitious) aspect of suburban political structure. Residents of suburbia, paradoxically, treat with apathy and indifference the political apparatus which appears to be so accessible. Political scientists, despite their pluralist theory, document the uniformity and dullness of suburban politics and ascribe it to the homogeneity of populations (Keats; Wood).

Conventional economists' approval of the multiplicity of independent metropolitan local governments echoes the political scientists' emphasis on choice and pluralism. During the 1940s and early 1950s, public finance theorists could find no mechanism equivalent to the market with which to model resource allocation in the public sector (Samuelson). The marketplace tool kit was salvaged in part, however, when Tiebout pointed out that such pessimism was not warranted on the local level (Tiebout). The existence of multiple local governments, he claimed, introduces competition into the consumption and production of local public services. Customers (residents) express their preference for a particular package of public services by voting with their feet, i.e., moving to the utility-maximizing suburban location. In Tiebout's view, local governments act as firms, forced to produce efficiently the optimum level and mix of output by threat of resident out-migration.

The empirical evidence shows such arguments to be supple acrobatics indeed. If Tiebout's view were correct, suburban political units would exhibit a wide variety of public-service packages, available to residents of every income and ethnic group. In fact, the most striking characteristics of suburban units are their homogeneity, exclusion of other income and ethnic groups, and nearly identical public-service mixes, with quality of service rising quite consistently with class composition of residents (Newton). A hierarchy of suburbs, ranked by class characteristics, can be identified in all U.S. metropolitan areas. In this political atmosphere, the local government does not act like a firm, as Tiebout proposes, responding to areawide market forces of supply and demand. Rather, it behaves as a conscious constructor of its own local market through influence on the cost and demand features of its constituency (Markusen). Marxist analysis, with its focus on historical and materialist methods, can illuminate the logic beyond such observed outcomes. A Marxist model bests mainstream explanations by replacing the concept of individual with the concept of class.

THE MARXIST THEORY OF THE STATE

Simply put, the Marxist theory of the state sees the political structure of any society as a derivative of its economic system. In its early, simple form, the government represents the views and needs of the dominant economic class and legitimizes its economic power over other people (Lenin). Under capitalism, the state legalizes property rights, protects them with constabulary or military force, and thereby guarantees the expropriation of labor's product. Marxists today criticize the oversimplification of this model (Wright). With the elaboration of the concept of class, more recent Marxist models view the state as the crucible for conflicts among members of the dominant economic class as well as conflicts between classes and subclasses (Milliband; Bates).

In the United States, Marxists use the theory of the state to explain the growing size of the national government, its entry into the production sphere itself, and its continuing crises. Both imperialism and domestic recessions, fueled by intensifying monopolization of the private sector, evoke demands on the state from both capitalist and working-class groups: for subsidies, particular macroeconomic policies, state regulation, direct state production, and so on (O'Connor; Esping-Anderson, et al.). The state responds to these conflicts in ways that produce additional state structures, which become the immediate arena for future conflicts.

This paper attempts to use the elements of this analysis, particularly the concepts of class conflict, and contradiction, to develop an explicitly Marxist theory of the operation of the state at the local level in the United States. It begins by illustrating how class conflict in mercantilist and industrial-capitalist stages of U.S. development shaped the present *form* of the state at the local level.

THE CORPORATE TOWN:
INHERITANCE FROM MERCANTILISM

The United States federal system is unique among capitalist nations. Few other capitalist countries grant states or localities such extensive political autonomy. In Europe, local and regional officers are generally directly subordinate and responsible to the centralized national state. The peculiar American hybrid grew from European, mainly British, colonial policies and the political exigencies surrounding nation-building.

Local public corporate bodies date back to early feudal towns. On the European continent, the rising capitalist nation-states swept away urban self-governance, but in Britain and the United States, the emerging states' strength was, oddly enough, based on local partial autonomy. In England, forces of the developing nation-state manipulated the antagonism between the nascent trading town and the feudal manor. After the Norman invasion of 1066, the crown granted charters to towns in order to secure their independence from local landed gentry and their fealty to the new regime. These charters set up either an oligarchical municipal corporation or a hierarchical structure administered by a justice of the peace appointed by the crown (Harris).

English mercantile capitalists transplanted this corporate form of the city government to colonial America. They deliberately planned and chartered towns as agencies for English control over profits from mercantilist trade. Town charters forbade settlers from engaging in enterprise in competition with the British (e.g., privateering) and banned intracolonial mobility of immigrant labor to ensure a work force for local merchantilist shipping activity. Entire towns, highly socially stratified and tightly controlled, operated as market centers and military and administrative command posts for the colonial empire. From these bases, the English trading elite appropriated land and resources from the native Americans, extracted agricultural and forest products from the outlying areas (especially furs, wheat, and cotton), sold British manufactured goods, African slaves, and West Indian rum, and secured a profitable monopoly over trade (Glaab and Brown, pp. 1–6).

By the American Revolution, sixteen such corporate entities existed on the seaboard with charters originally granted under the authority of the English crown. The American Revolution linked these diverse communities and their hinterlands against a common enemy. Each had begun independently as a peripheral outpost of the dominant culture and had, over the space of 150 years, developed its own aspiring local elite and often a distinct political character. The founders of the new American state, in order to secure the allegiance of numerous emerging native capitalists who viewed each other and any state with suspicion, made substantial concessions to decentralized political structure, resulting in the federal system. The new federal system not only incorporated the existing charters, but vested state legislatures with the power to issue new city charters. Subsequently, state constitutions set up explicit provisions subordinating cities and towns to the state machinery but preserving the form and notion of the corporate town. The administration of local government passed from colonial governors to the emerging native merchant and capitalist classes.

FRAGMENTED METROPOLITAN GOVERNMENT: THE LEGACY OF U.S. INDUSTRIAL CAPITALISM

During the nineteenth century, industrial capitalism produced new class interests, which battled over the control of local government. The product of the various struggles is the contemporary maze of municipal local governments that are the institutional context for the present fiscal crisis of central cities. Cumulatively, the manifestations of this process begin with the push for city public services and municipal home rule, followed by the curtailment of outward extension of city political boundaries, the arrangements for easy incorporation of new political units on the periphery, and the separation of tax and expenditure domains between state and local levels. The forces underlying these developments are examined in turn below.

Growing City Budgets

After 1850, vigorously expanding industrial production triggered rapid development of U.S. cities. It imposed a tremendous need for physical infrastructure to enhance capital accumulation and to accommodate the swelling populations, most of which was immigrant labor. The responsibility for providing some of the power, water, and road needs for factory production was assumed by the local government. It was clearly in the interests of factory owners and merchants to disperse the cost of such infrastructure across the entire population rather than bear it as an internal cost of production.

At the same time, since capitalist production separated the worker from control over the means of production, unemployment emerged as a persistent phenomenon, along with mushrooming poverty, crime, and disease. When these reached levels that threatened the viability of cities, civic leaders (members of the merchant and capitalist classes) demanded that the city undertake programs for public health, sewage treatment, and police and fire protection. Urban education systems, produced and paid for at the local level, taught future workers skills needed in capitalist production and promulgated the ideology of individualism.

Conflict over Land Speculation and City Contracts

Because rapid urban development enriched those with political control, state legislatures became breeding grounds for special-interest legislation, granting lucrative public-sector contracts to private political entrepreneurs. In 1870, for example, three-fourths of the pages of acts passed by the New York State legislature related to cities and villages. A representative of the 1867–1868 New York State Constitutional Convention pointed out that "seven-eighths of all revenues are disbursed by those who hold state appointments and are in no way responsible to the people of the city. . . ." (McBain, p. 40). The Evarts Commission, set up in 1877 to investigate graft in New York City, concluded that

> Cities were compelled by legislation to buy lands for parks and places because the owners wished to sell them; compelled to grade, pave and sewer streets without inhabitants and for no other purpose than to award corrupt contracts for the work (McBain, p. 9).

Capitalist class representatives who did not share in the spoils but had to pay for them through property taxation complained bitterly about such graft and provided the political base for the municipal "home rule" movement (1865–1900). Up until 1900 their efforts resulted in little more than state provisions (statutory and constitutional) limiting in small ways the absolute control by state legislatures and providing for the election of some local officials. The ideological impact of their call for home rule, couched in terms of Jeffersonian democracy and self-determination, had greater consequences. In the 1880s, a Harvard academic, John Fiske, traveled the country popularizing local rights and "delighting audiences by tracing back the town meeting of New England to the village assemblies of the early Aryans, making federalism that began with those local units the key to heaven and earth" (Wickman, p. 70). The appeal of the issue tended to obscure whose interests the movement served. But the principle of home rule took root, especially in rural areas.

Interest in home rule among urban capitalist interests faded around
the turn of the century and was replaced by politics aimed at defeating
Tammany Hall and similar regimes. However, home rule had become a
universal state constitutional feature, creating a political structure which
was to impede metropolitan political integration in the future. The home-
rule arrangement originated in class conflict over control of the state
versus local levels of government but created a precedent which would
shape twentieth-century urban class conflict by permitting proliferation of
semiautonomous local units of government.

Residential Segregation

Long before the first peripheral independent suburb appeared, urban residences began to segregate spatially. Horse-drawn cars and then electric
trolleys permitted decentralization of residence in place of an older urban
pattern where classes lived in close proximity. Land speculators and trol-
ley-line owners promoted new class neighborhoods in order to receive
large capital gains on the land along the trolley lines. Warner documents
neighborhood segregation in Boston from the mid–nineteenth century on.
(English industrial towns developed similarly [Engels].) There, contractors built housing on the periphery for members of the merchant, capitalist, and professional classes because they could afford the construction
of larger houses and because the transportation system favored the location of the more leisured and occupationally stable groups on the periphery while requiring a central location of the poor and occupationally
mobile working class.

Elsewhere in this volume, Gordon and Ashton investigate the dynamics of continued out-migration of both workplace and workers over
the last century. What is relevant for the present purpose of tracing political proliferation is the tendency for this pattern of residential segregation
by class to repeat itself continually, marking neighborhoods in fine degrees of differentiation and providing the spatial basis for independent
political incorporation. This differentiation proceeded at a hectic pace,
since population burgeoned and no old housing stock existed to absorb it
or soften segregation with the inertia of tradition.

Class-segregated neighborhoods thus became the spatial context for
class-segregated suburbs. *Class* here refers not only to the basic division
between capitalist and worker, fundamental to Marxist analysis of the
operation of capitalist production, but to the subclasses within each class.
Ashton, above, describes the divisions within the U.S. working class and
their importance for the developing spatial array of suburbs. If this separation of residences had not taken place, it is unlikely that political inde-

pendence and insulation would have been advantageous. Instead, other methods of organizing the public sector would have emerged.

Conflict over Access to City Government

The potential accessibility of local government machinery to working-class populations also explains its unique structure in the United States. Remoteness and scale of the national government allow capitalist interests to construct and manipulate it easily. For national politics, Marx's famous quip about democracy—that it is the political system where once every four years the working class is allowed to vote for one or two members of the ruling class—is appropriate. But at the local level, relatively smaller size and geographical proximity render government power more accessible and potentially responsive to the working population. In fact, many cities in the late–nineteenth and twentieth centuries were ruled by political organizations solidly rooted in the immigrants who were flowing into Eastern cities. There is some evidence that earlier (mid–nineteenth century) political forces in favor of annexation and consolidated urban political structure were capitalists eager to enlist aid against Tammany Hall–type governments (Feshbach; Kotler, pp. 14–20). However, efforts to dilute the political power of pro-working-class groups by expanding the jurisdiction of the city did not succeed. The incorporation of the five boroughs that now make up New York City did not lessen Tammany's control, as its architects had hoped.

Progressive mayors, such as New York's Fiorello LaGuardia, exemplified the best of worker-based city regimes within the larger capitalist structure. During the 1930s, LaGuardia pushed for large numbers of public-service jobs, wiped out the $31,000,000 deficit of the city with business and public-utility taxes, and expanded city relief to include clothing, subsidized milk distribution, and health care. LaGuardia's proposals were accompanied by statements such as "If the right to live interferes with profits, profits must necessarily give way to that right," and "The economic principles of yesterday are as obsolete as the oxcart" (Franklin, p. 99). Despite such intentions, "left" city-government control merely demonstrated the difficulty that political units face when they attempt major reforms within the larger capitalist economy. Even when in firm control, worker-oriented regimes could not radically reorganize the city budget, because workers' jobs depended on the health of the private sector. Business emigration threatened any local government attempting to cut back on social-infrastructure expenditures, to transfer the burden for them back on business beneficiaries, or to raise business taxes for expanded social services.

Class Conflict over City Tax Burden

Struggle among classes and subclasses over distribution of the tax burden of growing city budgets provided the ultimate impetus to fragmented local government. At the national level, the growth of social expenses and social accumulation can be financed by deficit spending, so the burden does not cut directly into the operating capital of the private sector nor into consumption funds of the capitalist class. While diversion of funds from the private sector to the public sector does take place, it is voluntarily transferred by capitalist institutions and owners via the bond market. This procedure is welcomed by capitalist interests, because they are guaranteed a return on this loan of their capital.

At the local level, governments are legally forbidden to finance growing operating budgets with deficit spending. Deficit financing by state and local governments resulted in frequent bankruptcy in the early nineteenth century, so state constitutions limited debt to capital expenditure only. In addition, state and local government deficits would hinder the national attempt to pursue a stabilizing fiscal policy. Since World War II, hardpressed city regimes and their corporate backers have lobbied successfully for substantial federal and state revenue-sharing, accounting for up to 40 percent of big-city budgets today, and have collaborated in the surreptitious financing of operating costs by burying them in capital accounts. During the era critical for the establishment of independent suburban entities, however, local expenditures for social accumulation and social expenses had come principally from sources within the constituency.

Within the local political jurisdiction, the bases for such taxes were the capital funds of business entities and the consumption funds of the capitalist and working classes. The latter include amounts spent on class reproduction. Because taxes affect disposable income, the conflict over who should pay local taxes is an extension of the struggle between profits and wages. If the capitalist interests can arrange for the transfer of various costs of production to the city budget and escape the tax bill for them, they successfully enhance profits at the expense of wage-earners. This appears to be a fight over consumption funds, rather than over the returns to production, but is essentially the same conflict. Instead of occurring in the workplace, this conflict takes place in the local political arena. Given the features of city government detailed above, capitalist interests did not directly control the public means of production. City governments were, and in some cases still are, arenas where classes and subclasses, less unevenly matched in power, fought to secure the benefits of social production and expenses while escaping the costs. The construction of independent local-government production units insulated capitalist-class production and consumption funds from the risk of losing this battle and at the same time created a powerful weapon, exit, to tame working-class-oriented regimes.

Denouement: Suburban Autonomy and Proliferation

These class conflicts accompanying capitalist development in the United States and contemporary political exigencies, from inherited colonial and federalist structure to home-rule ideology, have resulted in a political configuration unique among capitalist countries: strong separate suburban government units that serve class-based neighborhoods but avoid production-associated costs that central cities incur. The first well-documented appearance of an independent political suburban government is that of Brookline, Massachusetts, in 1873. Warner, in his account of outward suburban expansion around Boston in the latter half of the nineteenth century, notes that the change from the tradition of central-city annexation of residential areas on its periphery to independent suburban incorporation occurs abruptly when state-level provisions for independent utilities ends suburban dependence on the city for basic public services such as water and sewers. Brookline was the first suburb to insist upon its independence:

> By the 1880's, with but one exception, no suburban town ever again seriously considered annexation. . . . It was already apparent in the 1880's that to join Boston was to assume all the burdens and conflicts of a modern industrial metropolis. To remain apart was to escape, at least for a time, some of these problems (Warner, p. 164).

The political fragmentation that followed the emergence of class-bound residential neighborhoods takes place only after new jurisdictions can get public services from a source independent of the central city.

In the same era, states adopted constitutions and laws that established uniform treatment of local government structure, instead of individually chartering each city. These laws facilitated the proliferation of independent suburbs by making it easy to incorporate as an independent "home-rule" political entity and difficult for the larger central city to absorb peripheral growth through annexation or consolidation (Markusen, Chap. 7). While there is little historical evidence available on the sources of organized support for such provisions, it probably came from groups wishing to protect local autonomy, like the residents of Brookline. Even without such explicit support, the American tradition of democracy and localism, shored up by the legal principle of home rule, would be sufficient explanation for the evolution of these institutional arrangements. By 1930, every state legislature in the country had adopted some form of legislation accomplishing this. In general, it put the decision to join or not to join the central city in the hands of the residents of the annexable area, leaving the parent who had spawned the child helpless to participate in determining their joint future. Thus, the home-rule movement, which aimed to strengthen the central city against state manipulation, culminated ironically in the weakening of the city by engendering suburban parasites.

The enabling legislation that fostered independent suburban political structure was not a historical accident nor was it prompted by a nostalgia for the town meeting. The latter was merely the ideology accompanying the development. Passage of such legislation lay with the historical strength of suburban-rural coalitions in state legislatures, and their motives were material rather than ideological.

The politically independent suburb first appeared about 1870 on the East Coast and established itself as a prototype for metropolitan structure across the country. Decade after decade, political struggles culminated in the repetition of this pattern in major cities. Detroit had no politically independent suburbs until World War I, but then developed forty-odd such entities in the next forty years. Suburb-ringing is still occurring, particularly in the West, although a few cities like Oklahoma City, Dallas, Houston, and Phoenix are attempting to avoid ringing by massive early annexations. Consolidation, the joining of previously independent local governments, has succeeded only where racist motives are suspectable (e.g., Jacksonville, Richmond).

THE CONTRADICTORY FUNCTIONS OF METROPOLITAN POLITICAL FRAGMENTATION

This fragmented political apparatus, the inherited product of past conflicts, continues to shape class conflict. Its role in directing the placement and intensity of the present fiscal crisis of the cities cannot be understated. A simple Marxist theory of the operation of the state at the local level can be stated as follows.

The fundamental force in shaping political life is the conflict of class interests associated with the contemporary mode of production. This conflict often takes place within the shell of institutions remaining from previous conflicts and which are important in the specific form of the present conflict. In the United States today, class structure under monopoly capitalism encompasses important subclasses which obscure the unity within a class, create intraclass conflicts, and diminish class consciousness while breeding subclass identification. Suburban geographical and political isolation nurtures subclass consciousness, and diffuses the public-sector struggle between capital and labor over a multiplicity of groups.

In the current urban fiscal crisis, the salient function of suburban governments is to insulate class consumption and capital from the costs of social accumulation and social expenses in the central city, thereby forcing the poor to finance their own oppressive police force and welfare system. The suburban government actually constructs its own public-service market by employing policy tools such as zoning in which class aims for levels and types of social consumption and class reproduction can be achieved by excluding high-cost residents and attracting those with ample resources. At the same time, the independence of the suburban government allows it to use these same exclusionary tools to enhance the private-sector functions of suburbia—the class assimilation of children by restricting their playmates and experience, the removal of class conflict from living situations, and the preservation of asset value of housing. But it also jeopardizes central-city finances and the rational use of metropolitan space.

An example will illustrate the argument. Public safety, meaning primarily the safety of private property, is a social expense necessary under capitalist production relations. It accounts for an average of one-third of all municipal expenditures (excluding schools). Originally a private expense, this function shifted to the state sector (although there are still large numbers of private guards). Construction of separate political units responsible for public safety involved a substantial shift of the burden of this cost. The benefiting classes could escape the costs of public safety that the city provided to their industrial and mercantile properties in the central city, thus leaving the working class and the reserve army of unemployed (precisely the groups from whom such property was to be protected) to pay for the safety of their oppressors' property. Furthermore, non-property-crime control and other poverty-related safety expenses would also be paid for by the same class.

Suburban insularity in turn diminished the costs of policing class conflict by segregating classes spatially and developing locally controlled police forces. In early U.S. cities, the rich and the poor lived quite close together, creating a potential for violence. When political autonomy followed residential segregation, the local police force became controllable via consensus and therefore dependable in any violent situation (Silver).

In addition to escaping the tax burden for social expenses like public safety, health, and welfare, suburban residents have also been able to help themselves to any number of city-financed services without contributing tax support (Neenan). Some of these services are associated with the daytime presence of commuters to the central city—street maintenance, traffic control, waste and pollution control, and water systems. Others are the extensive culture and recreational facilities that the central city provides to all metropolitan residents—parks, zoos, concerts, parade facilities, libraries, and museums—which are only occasionally compensated for by payment of fees.

As independent suburban governments increased in number, their differentiation from the central city grew apace. Autonomous local budgets not only allowed suburban class interests to escape the social expenditures of the central city while enjoying the benefits; it also allowed them to enjoy levels of social consumption and reproduction far above those of city residents by pooling parts of their consumption fund to produce high-quality public service for a limited group of recipients. It is not only an insular high income level that creates this opportunity; it is also the ability of local governments to exclude high-cost populations who would affect its production of local public services. This is most significant in education systems where excluding working-class and minority children from the constituency lowers the cost of providing a "good" education; no special education or compensatory programs are required. Class reproduction through the public education system is important to most suburban residents, from the professional subclass on down. These groups fight jealously to keep their tax dollars out of the unproductive sectors like welfare and in class-reproduction and -consumption sectors like education.

Similarly, excluding "crime-prone" populations and escaping aging physical structures lowers the cost of providing public safety—police and fire services. Even changes in technology, such as the substitution of the police cruiser for the cop on the beat, put a premium on suburban locations; it's cheaper to operate cruisers in suburbia than in the central city. Exclusion of high-cost populations and low-income residents is achieved by using policy tools such as exclusionary zoning and building codes to manipulate both the supply and demand features of local markets for social output. In this sense, the local government attempts to *create* its own market for public-sector output.

Far from acting as an impersonal firm trying to attract a population with an efficiently produced public-service package, the local government acts in class interests to fashion the very market it serves. It is strongly partisan, for instance, about who its customers are, as opposed to the disinterested firm of neoclassical theory, which is interested only in its customer's ability to pay the price. Even if families are willing to pay, the local government tries to exclude them if they are poor (because then they will be apt to get a larger portion of the public output than they pay for under most local tax systems) and if they are apt to raise the costs of production. Regressive taxation, large-lot zoning, strict building codes, discriminatory public-service distribution schemes, and urban renewal all contribute to the ability of local governments to shut out other classes and protect the public-sector class-consumption and -reproduction aims of its constituents.

All suburban governments thus try to attract residents better, not worse, off than current residents. Since better-off residents can always be wooed elsewhere, the result is a tendency for rather strict internal homogeneity to develop within each suburb. This development relegates the poorest and least mobile people to the central city, which is then left with the residents least able to pay and most dependent upon public-sector services. Since they must pay for their own city services, the arrangement ensures that the local public sector, despite its redistributive posture, will not significantly alter the division between wages and profits, nor end the unemployment that keeps wages down.

The growing participation of land speculators and construction interests accompanied the construction of these separate and disparate markets. The gains from insular social consumption in the suburbs can accrue to developers and landlords through their ability to capitalize the value of public-sector differentials into housing price and rent (Oates). Beginning in the 1920s it became profitable to extend the privileges of suburban public- and private-sector insularity to the better-paid members of the working class, but at premium rents (Harvey, pp. 169–70). The expansion of home ownership also meant that housing, including the tax and service value capitalized, became the only asset and chief means of economic security for working people who could afford it. Therefore, it became increasingly difficult for any group to stay in the central city because of the high level of public-sector taxes and low level of benefits, not only because of their effect on current consumption, but their devaluation of this asset as well. With few exceptions, only those who cannot escape, do not. Working-class suburbanization has contributed to the public-sector fragmentation of local government, often militantly defending it, and thus to the construction of a complicated network of class-stratified public-service units surrounding the metropolitan area. A detailed study of Detroit and forty-seven of its suburbs shows remarkable internal homogeneity within suburbs (measured by deviation from mean per capita income) and strong statistical relationships between high social-cost measures (educational background, poverty populations), low wealth status, and public-service levels across the metropolitan area (Markusen, Chap. 7).

The movement of industrial and mercantile establishments to suburban jurisdictions is largely a response to private-sector gains, as Gordon argues elsewhere in this volume, but taxes and public services do play an important role. Many corporations leave in the central city those portions of their operations which require extensive public-investment outlays while removing to suburban locations those which do not. To avoid paying for the social-consumption expenditures of their own work force in these suburban locations, they cooperate with local class-consumption interests to exclude their lower-paid workers from living in the same jurisdiction in which the plant pays property taxes. The existence of fragmented political units allows corporations to play off one jurisdiction against the other to secure preferential tax and expenditure arrangements in what public-finance theorists call tax-base competition (Harrison).

Progressive city administrations continue to face frustration in their attempts to end public-sector fealty to corporations. Detroit's progressive black mayor, Coleman Young, recently offered Chrysler Corporation a long-run property-tax break if it would simply continue to run its city assembly lines. A Michigan study confirms that intraurban tax differentials do make a significant difference in location decisions of businesses (Survey Research Center). In the recent New York City crisis, corporate hegemony reveals its ultimate power. Because the corporate and banking sectors hold the bonds that the city cannot pay, they can legally manipulate the city budget to cut back social expenses, require harsh measures against public-sector labor, preserve social infrastructural outlays that enhance corporate activities, and rule out substantial business-tax increases as a way of solving the fiscal crisis.

Although suburban dispersion would have proceeded outward in stratified neighborhoods regardless of the state-sector conflict, it is clear that public-sector forces exacerbate the outward movement and add to the degeneration of metropolitan cohesiveness. The process is thus self-reinforcing; the existence of class neighborhoods makes possible the creation of independent political units, and these in turn encourage the creation of class-segregated suburbs. The consequences for central-city fiscal crisis are obvious. The deformed local version of the state, therefore, adds a spatial dimension to the capitalist crisis, since anarchy of production in the public sector weakens the fabric of the entire community. The drive outward results in the waste of public-sector facilities already built and fails to incorporate public-sector economies that would be emphasized in a rational, planned system.

THE FUTURE OF THE STATE AT THE LOCAL LEVEL

What will happen in the future? The phenomenon investigated here is not a static political condition. The present plethora of political units is the result of one hundred years of class interests constructing and maintaining separate public-service sectors. In the future, it is possible that new class interests generated by monopoly capitalism will produce still different pressures on local political structure.

Corporate reliance on elaborate administrative, financial, and control functions continues to tie them to the agglomeration of facilities downtown. Certain operations, particularly actual production facilities and warehousing, will continue to locate in suburbia, but large numbers of corporate jobs will remain in the central city. Thus the corporate sector seeks new ways to control the local public sector in addition to its threat to emigrate. Corporate interests have used the New York City fiscal crisis to secure for themselves a legitimate, direct, and dominant position in the budgetary process. To the extent that this domination succeeds and is replicated across the country, the corporate sector has less need for the maintenance of independent suburban political jurisdictions.

At the same time, the existence of fragmented political units encumbers the coordination and administration of national and multinational corporations. Local governments can be a big nuisance in planning expansion and location decisions. Dealings with suburban units to secure zoning changes and infrastructural commitments are often unpredictable and time-consuming. Some corporate leaders complain about the lack of metropolitan regional planning and appear to be increasingly in favor of regionalized political structure. Thus a struggle may ensue between suburban subclasses militant in their desire to preserve their local public-sector autonomy and large capitalist interests pushing for planned, rationalized, metropolis-wide government.

A third change is itself the result of class segregation in suburban areas: the ascendancy by black urban populations to political power in some of the larger cities. This development appears to have different results for urban structure among different regions. In the South, urban areas like Richmond, Dade County (Miami), and Jacksonville have quickly consolidated the preexisting political units to prevent minority hegemony in the central city. In the North, the dominant class interests apparently feel that black central-city governments can be dealt with satisfactorily because of their dependence on private-sector jobs and taxes. No structural change appears to be imminent.

A final change is an increasingly parochial and defensive attitude on the part of suburban and exurban residents, who are beginning to oppose growth in their communities because of high infrastructural costs associated with it, potential overuse of facilities they enjoy, and subtle fear of incursions by other groups who might ultimately undermine the "fabric" of the community and erode property values. Despite liberal efforts to throw out the property tax as the main financial base for municipal and educational expenditures, to force busing across distrist lines, and to disperse low-income housing into otherwise homogeneous neighborhoods, the subclass interests in suburbia seem to be solidly arrayed against erosion of their preferential status.

The outcome of all this is likely to be a further hybrid: special districts for planning urban land use and constructing urban infrastructure in the interests of the business community, and the maintenance of separate political units for some local public-consumption and class-reproduction functions, particularly public safety, education, and welfare. Maintenance of separate units for the latter will mollify suburban residents for their loss of control over land use and planning.

The last fifteen years have been ones of almost unremitting urban crisis. Clearly the urban public sector is one of the important receptacles for the display of capitalist crisis. The growing pressures on the urban public sector generated by infrastructural demands of the private sector and the growing costs of labor and community pacification are exacerbated in the United States by the structural arrangements that make local governments responsible for them, limit the financial resources available for these purposes, and badly maldistribute the burdens across the political units within an urban area.

The urban crisis is not congenial for corporate capitalism, as evidenced by the regular presence of local capitalist interests on committees concerned with urban problems, e.g., Henry Ford's membership on the Detroit Renaissance Committee. But capitalist interests have made efforts to turn the crisis to their ends, culminating in the recent attempts to control the actual city budget-making process itself through formally established organs. This is a two-edged knife, however. The attempt to cut urban social expenses like welfare may heighten the class conflict within the city. Similarly, the attempt to stop wage and benefit gains by public-sector workers may heighten the visibility of the struggle between capital and labor even as it affects workers in this sector. Some temporary resolution of these conflicts will occur, most likely via greater federal financing of social expenses, continuing a trend begun in the 1930s, and increased regulation of labor disputes in the public sector by ostensibly publicly minded arbitration boards. Nevertheless, there is not likely to be a satisfactory outcome to the basic urban crisis, structural or other. In fact, urban political units may become explicit mouthpieces for class interests and arenas for class conflict, a development which argues in favor of considering community organizing as part of a revolutionary strategy. While there is no possibility of "solving" the urban structural problem under capitalism, community organizations' struggles within the United States and the experience of existing socialist states undoubtedly suggest many steps forward—for example, the neighborhood courts and housing micro-brigades in Cuba.

SUMMARY

Democracy in the United States is subverted at the local level by a unique development—the cordoning off of various subclasses into political units populated by their own kind wherein constituents equally escape the costs that might be imposed by participation of those worse off. Central-city populations are left the privilege of voting to impose the costs of social-capital and class-containment expenses upon themselves. This is simply, in different form, democracy for the rich, although it involves minor gains for subsets of the working class. Real class differences under capitalism are obscured by a subdifferentiation of class enhanced by segregated residence and by the particular consumption and class-reproduction activities that accompany that residence.

Insular suburbia has been a salient feature of urban America for a hundred years, and an important contributor to central-city problems in the last thirty. This investigation has traced its relation to the capitalist mode of production and reflected on its likely fortunes in the future. If nothing else, perhaps it will stimulate further Marxist analysis of local political structure, under both socialist and capitalist modes of production, which might produce a full-bodied analysis and a strategy for urban action.

REFERENCES

Bates, Timothy, *Economic Man As Politician: Neoclassical and Marxist Theories of Government Behavior* (Morristown, N.J.: General Learning Press, 1976).

Engels, Friedrich, *The Condition of the Working Class in England in 1844,* (London: Swan Sonneschein & Co., 1892).

Esping-Andersen, Gosta; Roger Friedland; and Erik Olin Wright, "Modes of Class Struggle and the Capitalist State," *Kapitalistate,* Summer 1976.

Feshbach, Dan, "Notes on Annexation" (Mimeographed, 1974). Library of City and Regional Planning Department, University of California, Berkeley.

Franklin, Jay, *LaGuardia* (New York: Modern Age Books, 1937).

Gitlin, Todd, "Local Pluralism as Theory and Ideology," *Studies on the Left,* October 1965, pp. 21–45.

Glaab, Charles, and A. Theodore Brown, *A History of Urban America* (New York: Macmillan Company, 1967).

Harris, George, *Comparative Local Government* (London: Hutchinson University Library, 1948).

Harrison, Bennett, and Sandra Kanter, "The Great State Robbery," *Working Papers for a New Society,* Spring 1976.

Harvey, David, *Social Justice and the City* (Baltimore: Johns Hopkins Press, 1973).

Keats, John, *The Crack in the Picture Window* (Boston: Houghton Mifflin, 1957).

Kotler, Milton, *Neighborhood Government: The Local Foundations of Political Life* (Indianapolis: Bobbs-Merrill Co., 1969).

Lenin, Nikolai, "The State and Revolution," in Arthur Mendel, ed., *The Essential Works of Marxism* (New York: Bantam Books, 1961).

McBain, Howard Lee, *The Law and the Practice of Municipal Home Rule* (New York: Columbia University Press, 1916).

Markusen, Ann, "The Economics of Social Class and Metropolitan Local Government" (Ph.D. Thesis, Michigan State University, 1974).

Miliband, Ralph, *The State in Capitalist Society* (New York: Basic Books, 1969).

Neenan, William, "Suburban–Central City Exploitation Thesis: One City's Tale," *National Tax Journal*, June 1970.

Newton, Kenneth, "American Urban Politics: Social Class, Political Structure and Public Goods," *Urban Affairs Quarterly*, Dec. 1975.

Oates, Wallace, "The Effects of Property Taxes and Local Public Spending on Property Values: An Empirical Study of Tax Capitalization and the Tiebout Hypothesis," *Journal of Political Economy*, Nov.–Dec. 1969.

O'Connor, James R., *The Fiscal Crisis of the State* (New York: St. Martin's Press, 1973).

Samuelson, Paul A., "The Pure Theory of Public Expenditures," *Review of Economics and Statistics*, Nov. 1954.

Sawers, Larry, "Urban Form and the Mode of Production," *Review of Radical Political Economy*, Spring 1975.

Silver, Allan, "The Demand for Order in Civil Society: A Review of Some Themes in the History of Urban Crime, Police, and Riot," in David Bordua, ed., *The Police: Six Sociological Essays* (New York: John Wiley and Sons, 1967).

Survey Research Center, *Location Decision and Industrial Mobility in Michigan* (Ann Arbor: University of Michigan Press, 1961).

Tiebout, Charles, "A Pure Theory of Local Expenditures," *Journal of Political Economy*, Oct. 1956.

Warner, Sam Bass, *Streetcar Suburbs: The Process of Growth in Boston, 1880–1900* (New York: Atheneum, 1973).

Warren, Robert, "A Municipal Services Market Model of Metropolitan Organization," *Journal of the American Institute of Planners*, Aug. 1964.

Wickman, W. Hardy, *The Political Theory of Local Government* (Columbia: University of South Carolina Press, 1970).

Wood, Robert, *Suburbia: Its People and Their Politics* (Boston: Houghton Mifflin, 1958).

Wright, Eric Olin, "To Control or to Smash Bureaucracy: Weber and Lenin on Politics, the State and Bureaucracy," *Berkeley Journal of Sociology*, 1974–75.

City Limits: Municipal Boundary Formation and Class Segregation

CHARLES HOCH

Everyday more than 50,000 people go to Vernon where they sew bathing suits, make chemicals, process meat, manufacture aluminum pistons and operate trucking terminals and warehouses. And every night 50,000 people leave Vernon for homes elsewhere because only about 100 people live in Vernon. . . . A Vernon Chamber of Commerce official describes the 5.06 square mile city, with pride, as a "lovable sewer." (*Los Angeles Times,* Dec. 24, 1978)

Rolling Hills, a city of about 2,000 people and half as many horses, on three square miles of choice view acreage atop the Palos Verdes Peninsula is frequently described as an exclusive suburb of Los Angeles which is putting it mildly. . . . After all, there aren't many suburbs that have gates manned by guards 24 hours a day on all entrances into town, and a city ordinance that threatens a $500 fine and the possibility of six months in the county jail for any outsiders trying to sneak in uninvited. (*Los Angeles Times,* Feb. 11, 1979)

The contrasting images these two quotations evoke illustrate dramatically the existence of class segregation among suburban municipalities in Los Angeles County. But what these images do not tell is the story of how municipalities like these were born. In essay 4 here, Ann Markusen argues that inequality among municipalities is the product of the uneven economic development of capitalist urbanization in which class relations determine the political allocation of space. But she does not explain how the two were joined. That is the purpose of this paper.

My argument is that the formation of local governments, in particular municipalities, incorporate class relations. This is not to say that classes are the only political actors, but that class positions and the relationships of competition and struggle between them determine the kinds of institutions and issues that political actors could use in their efforts to create a new municipality. Specifically, I contend (1) that the legal structure of incorporation favors members of the capitalist class, (2) that the organizations effectively supporting or preventing incorporation are capitalist and middle-class organizations, and (3) that the political effects of these incorporations are distributed unequally according to the class composition of the new municipalities. On a more general level I will argue that one of the most significant effects of the incorporations is that they provide a form of territorial political cohesion for small employers and members of the middle class, while simultaneously fragmenting the capacity for such cohesion among members of either the working or capitalist classes at the local level.[1]

The paper has been divided into four parts. The first part briefly introduces the reader to the political and economic context surrounding suburban growth in Los Angeles county, while the second discloses the class bias of the rules for incorporation. The bulk of the argument emerges in part three which contains the accounts of how class organizations influenced the formation of new suburban municipalities. Part four summarizes the fiscal and political outcomes this proliferation of municipalities produced.

SUBURBAN GROWTH AND FRAGMENTATION IN LOS ANGELES COUNTY

The magnitude of post-war suburban growth throughout California, especially in Los Angeles County, created severe fiscal problems for municipal governments. The demand for urban services grew enormously in the post-war years as the spread of subdivisions began to outstrip the revenue-producing capacities of municipalities. However, despite the cost, the underlying commitment to growth shared by local municipal officials precluded placing limits on the provision of infrastructure. They were forced to raise property taxes to meet expenses. The increased rates, however, encouraged development in unincorporated areas just outside municipal boundaries where the property taxes were lower. Since Los Angeles county was fully equipped to provide urban services to unincorporated communities, the new subdivisions seemed to have the best of both worlds; urban services and low taxes.

Municipal officials, however, did not acquiesce. Like amoeba in search of food, they stretched out jurisdictional limbs to engulf new developments piece by piece. The imperative was growth. By the early 1950s hundreds of annexation disputes had erupted in the county. One dispute in particular produced an important legal innovation. In order to avoid annexation to the city of Long Beach, an attorney for the developer of the suburban community of Lakewood, together with county officials, devised a plan whereby the community could incorporate as a city but continue to contract with the county for the same services it had received before incorporating. The 1954 plan protected Lakewood from being annexed, kept the same services, and as a bonus provided the community with police power and taxing authority. The plan sparked an explosion of incorporation attempts. By 1960, sixty-one suburban incorporation attempts had been launched producing 26 new municipalities. More than 60 percent of these attempts were concentrated in a 250-square-mile area east of Los Angeles, which I call the San Gabriel region (see Fig. 5.1). Between 1940 and 1970 the population in this area increased 832 percent to 1,108,572, while the proportion of agricultural land decreased from about 52 percent to less than 3 percent. The San Gabriel region provides an excellent case for the study of suburban political fragmentation (Hoch, 1981).

CLASS STRUCTURE AND MUNICIPAL FORMATION

The criteria of ownership that define the basic relation of class structure within capitalist production also defined the legal structure of municipal incorporation in California. Only those who owned property could initiate the process of municipal formation. On the one hand, the possession of land determined who was eligible to define the city boundaries and the form of government structure proposed for adoption. On the other hand, the value of the land owned within the proposed city units determined the degree of control available to each owner. This prevented non-landowning residents from forming a municipality on their own.

The legal requirements for municipal formation in California include a petition phase, a hearing phase, and an implementation phase. In the petition phase at least 12 property owners are required to petition the county clerk for permission to incorporate a new municipality. The municipality must include at least 500 residents and possess boundaries that do not overlap other municipalities. A map outlining electoral districts for council officials within the new municipality may also be submitted. When permission is provided by the clerk, the initial petitioners are given 50 days to gather signatures of aproval among the owners of land within the

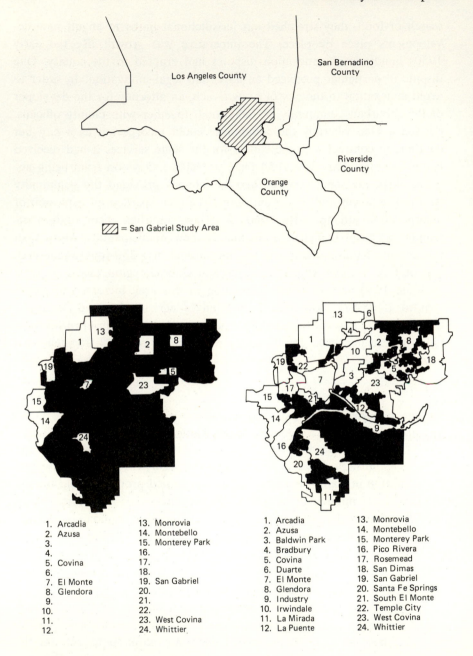

1. Arcadia	13. Monrovia
2. Azusa	14. Montebello
3.	15. Monterey Park
4.	16.
5. Covina	17.
6.	18.
7. El Monte	19. San Gabriel
8. Glendora	20.
9.	21.
10.	22.
11.	23. West Covina
12.	24. Whittier

1. Arcadia	13. Monrovia
2. Azusa	14. Montebello
3. Baldwin Park	15. Monterey Park
4. Bradbury	16. Pico Rivera
5. Covina	17. Rosemead
6. Duarte	18. San Dimas
7. El Monte	19. San Gabriel
8. Glendora	20. Santa Fe Springs
9. Industry	21. South El Monte
10. Irwindale	22. Temple City
11. La Mirada	23. West Covina
12. La Puente	24. Whittier

Figure 5.1

proposed city. A successful petition requires the approval of owners possessing at least 25 percent of the privately owned parcels and accounting
for at least 25 percent of the total assessed value of the land within the
proposed boundaries. By manipulating the location of the geographic
boundary for the proposed municipality, petitioning landowners can include only those large landowners of valuable property who have indicated their support for incorporation attempt, while excluding those owners who oppose.

The hearing phase places obstacles in the way of such a selective use
of boundary formation. If incorporation proponents want to ensure approval in this phase, they must have drawn the initial boundaries to include land owned by more supporters than opposition. A protest by
more than 50 percent of the property owners could scuttle the incorporation attempt. The proponents must also win the approval of the County
Board of Supervisors. This usually means convincing the Board to abstain
from a veto. However, the Board is limited in the criteria it could apply
to justify any deletions of territory from the proposed municipality. Board
members might respond to appeals from protestors to remove their land
from the municipality if it would not create a jurisdictional hole inside the
proposed municipality (political criterion); or the Board might apply
geographic requirements that the boundaries be contiguous and regular
(administrative criteria). At this point the structural advantages of ownership are no longer sufficient to obtain legal approval.

By the implementation phase, ownership is no longer either necessary or sufficient to be a political factor. The incorporation must be approved by the registered voters who live within the proposed boundaries.
The referendum approving or rejecting the incorporation is accompanied
by the election of local officials and the selection of the particular form
of local government (usually either mayor-council or city-manager form).
Although the petition and hearing phases include a structural bias favoring the owners of valuable land, the implementation phase does not.
However, when these advantages are exercised by owners acting together,
they are an effective force even at the implementation phase.

CLASS ORGANIZATION AND MUNICIPAL FORMATION

Organization and Class

Organizations that participated in the formation of municipalities in the
San Gabriel region are listed in Table 5.1. Class organizations were those
whose membership and leaders were drawn from the same social class,
and whose objectives reflected the interests of that class.

**Table 5.1. The Class Composition and Political Objectives
of Organizations Involved with Incorporation**

Organization	Class Composition	Political Objectives
Industrial*	Capitalist	Lower Production Costs
Commercial*	Small Employers, Proprietors	Better Control of Markets
Public Relations	Managers and Public Officials	Rationalize Formation of New Cities
Homeowner*	All	Protect Residential Homogeneity
County Government	Managers and Public Officials	Retain County Services
City Governments	Small Employers, Proprietors Managers and Public Officials	Geographic Growth of City

* Indicates those organizations that sponsored incorporation attempts.
Note: The class distinctions are taken from Wright, 1978.

Industrial Organizations

Throughout California the major proponents of industrial land consolidation and subdivision were also the largest landowners in the state: the
railroad corporations. In Los Angeles county the Atchison, Topeka and
Santa Fe Railroad in conjunction with several other large industrial landowners had formed organizations like the Central Manufacturing District
and the Santa Fe Land Improvement Company to plan for and organize
the industrial development of largely unincorporated suburban land. These
industrial development organizations were composed of corporate landowners interested in developing their land for industrial use. Some were
agribusiness landowners consolidating land for sale and lease as regional
industrial parks, while others were corporate executives interested in se-
curing industrial land for expansion. These organizations sponsored municipal incorporation they believed would protect industrial uses and lower
the costs of production.

Commercial Organizations

After World War II suburban commercial growth first occurred in existing shopping areas. (Suburban shopping centers came on the scene in the
mid 1950s.) Old businesses expanded and new ones opened up along
"Main Street." Small commercial employers and service professionals

sought to mobilize the apparently boundless opportunities for small-scale investment that suburban growth made possible. The class autonomy of small employers and middle-class proprietors had been constantly undercut and surpassed by the concentration of capital in corporations throughout the twentieth century. But the fragmented and chaotic growth of the suburbs offered new opportunities for small-scale investment. Small employers and proprietors formed local chambers of commerce. Too small to create corporations capable of exercising monopoly control in a sector of the national market, they created an organization that would help them secure a spatial monopoly of trade in a local community. The small employers and merchants collaborated to capture a local market by reducing competition among each other within the local market area and by enhancing competition with businesses in neighboring community market areas (Vidich, 1970, p. 53). Between 1940 and 1957 the number of active chambers of commerce in Los Angeles county nearly doubled from 55 to 105 with the vast majority of this increase occurring in the expanded suburban areas (Dinerman, 1958).

Public Relations Firms

These were firms that usually managed electoral campaigns for candidates at the state or national level. The employment of such firms in incorporation campaigns at the local level indicates both the seriousness of the stakes involved for the incorporation proponents and the fact that the proponents were willing to pay thousands of dollars to achieve municipal status. The objectives of the firms conformed to the class objectives of their clients. Members of the firms were managers trained in business schools and public bureaucracies. The firms provided feasibility studies outlining the fiscal benefits and costs of cityhood, conducted resident opinion surveys, organized incorporation election campaigns and, if the election was successful, often provided advice for the new city council on how to develop the bureaucratic and legal links with other government agencies. The managers adopted corporate management principles and techniques to structure the incorporation efforts.

Homeowners Associations

Unlike the industrial and chamber organizations, which tended to both reflect and unify particular class interests, homeowners associations tended to refract and fragment the class interests of community residents. Instead of place serving as a means of class cohesion, it was instead a means of high-lighting and protecting intra-class differences. By the mid 1950s close to 70 percent of all the households in the San Gabriel region were made up of homeowners. Possession cut across class lines. Single-family home-ownership integrated suburban residents into a neighborhood life-style defined mainly by a pattern of consumption and segmented into a hierarchy of neighborhoods reflecting building cost and lot size. Resident homeowners formed associations on the basis of their interest in protecting marginal differences in housing consumption. These were for the most part newly formed communities with a commitment to home ownership, basic services, and low taxes.

County Government

The Los Angeles county board of supervisors were generally attentive to the interests of capitalists and small employers alike and were loath to mediate political disputes between them. The incorporation battles were frequently these kinds of disputes. In such cases the board would usually support capital. State law enabled them to delete territory from within the proposed municipal boundaries. Since a city must have at least 500 residents to qualify for cityhood, reducing the boundaries to include less than this minimum effectively vetoed an incorporation. Managers and employees of the county supported virtually any kind of incorporation as long as it adopted the Lakewood Plan of contracting for county services. County administrators looked the other way when county employees participated illegally in the organization of incorporation campaigns. The managers and public officials supported the political fragmentation of the suburbs as long as they remained dependent on a centralized and rationalized system of urban services.

City Government

While the county government supported the formation of new cities, existing suburban cities took the opposite view. Their growth objectives tended to place them in competition with the newly forming cities. The class position of the officials representing the existing cities was the same as the chamber of commerce leaders organizing the new municipalities. The major difference of course was that the city officials could use the jurisdictional authority of the city to implement their growth objectives. The intra-class competition between these organizations became a battle of annexation versus incorporation. During the 1950s, the 11 original municipalities in the San Gabriel region made 689 annexations, acquiring over 27 square miles of new territory, more annexations than had been made for all cities in Los Angeles county during the previous 100 years.

THE POLITICS OF INCORPORATION

Forty-six incorporation attempts were undertaken in the San Gabriel region between 1950 and 1963. Four were sponsored by industrial organizations, 21 by chambers of commerce and 21 by homeowners' associations. When the results of these attempts are analyzed in relation to the different phases of municipal incorporation (see Table 5.2) several findings stand out: the industrial efforts never failed, chamber attempts failed occasionally, and all homeowner attempts failed with only one exception. Incorporation campaigns without the sponsorship of a class organization simply could not enter the game. But how did this work? How did the industrial and chamber organizations mobilize the rules of city-making in their favor?

Political Struggle at the Petition Phase

In the 1950s industrial landowners in suburban regions across the United States were concerned lest suburban sprawl short circuit the increasing spatial expansion of industrial plants on the urban periphery (Muncy, 1954). In Los Angeles county industrial landowners enjoyed the relatively effective protection of county zoning restrictions until 1954, when the successful incorporation of Lakewood as a contract municipality stimulated incorporation efforts. Industrial organizations did not initiate incorporations. Nearby chambers of commerce usually did.

In the case of the proposed city of Duarte, the chamber proponents foolishly included concentrations of extractive industry on one end and residential estates on the other (see Fig. 5.2). The industrial and residential estate owners not only managed to block the chamber attempt by withholding petition approval, but each quickly drew up their own plans for incorporation.

Table 5.2. Successful Incorporation Efforts (in percent)

	Organization		
	Homeowner	Chamber*	Industrial
Start	100	100	100
Petition	5	66	100
Hearing	5	66	100
Implementation	5	38	100
Total Number	21	21	4

* Ten of these attempts include unsuccessful first or second efforts for the same geographic area. Only one geographic commmunity in this group failed to incorporate.

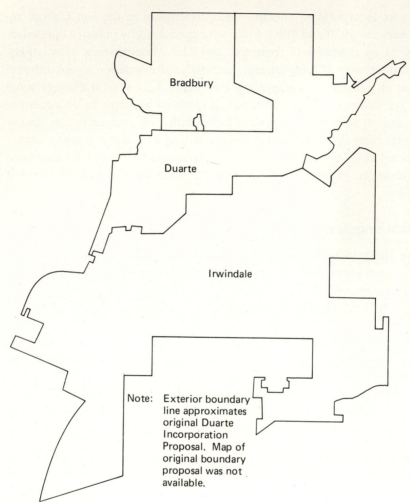

Original Boundaries of Cities of
Bradbury, Duarte and Irwindale

Bradbury

Duarte

Irwindale

Note: Exterior boundary
line approximates
original Duarte
Incorporation
Proposal. Map of
original boundary
proposal was not
available.

Figure 5.2

   Industrial and residential estate owners had little difficulty in meeting
or frustrating the petition requirements. A city with thousands of homeowners required that thousands of petition signatures be collected. Incorporating a city of industries or residential estates usually required less
than 200 and in some cases less than 50 signatures. Since there were just
a relatively small number of owners who possessed large and valuable
land holdings, soliciting or withholding approval was easy to organize.
For example, in each of the three largest industrial cities created in the

San Gabriel area, the signatures of only five landowners were needed to account for more than 35 percent of the land value for the entire area.

Homeowner associations, without the organizational focus and resources of industrial organizations and chambers of commerce, found the petition phase to be an insurmountable barrier. Homeowner groups filed boundary maps to legally protect their community for fifty days, anticipating annexation or incorporation attempts. Mounting a serious incorporation effort did not even seem possible. When chamber-sponsored efforts failed at this step it was either due to conflict with industrial owners or a successful legal interdiction by a neighboring municipality.

Political Struggle at the Hearing Phase

Industrial incorporations provoked vociferous protest at public hearings, but none aroused as much condemnation as the proposed City of Industry. The City of Industry proponents had drawn the city boundaries to exclude all but 624 residents (including 169 inmates of a sanitarium), and to include the most valuable commercial and industrial land in the San Gabriel region. In an interview with local reporters, the spokesperson for the incorporation committee laid out the objectives of the industrial landowners with surprising candor.

> Perhaps the largest concentration of industry in the State of California will exist in the city we propose . . . and while we are more than satisfied with the administration of county government which we now enjoy, we wish to remain the distinct area that lies within our proposed boundaries. Our sole aim is to attract additional industry and it is hoped that we can maintain complete freedom from the tax burdens which confront other cities. By the creation of this new industrial entity, we hope that in due time we can reduce extensively, if not eliminate entirely the personal property tax. (*LaPuente Journal,* May 1956; see also Warren, 1964, 368–69)

As news of the new incorporations attempt spread, both incorporated and unincorporated communities bordering the proposed municipality of Industry were quick to protest. Members of neighboring chambers of commerce were shocked. They imagined the center of a viable city as a marketplace with industry located on the periphery providing jobs and fiscal balance. An exclusive industrial municipality threatened the political autonomy of the small employers, proprietors, and professionals, as well as their hopes of creating and controlling balanced municipalities.

At the public hearing local officials and chamber representatives argued that the 169 mental patients could not be counted as residents and that the proposed City of Industry therefore lacked the minimum requirement of 500 residents to qualify for incorporation. Furthermore, they charged that the boundaries were drawn so as to capture revenue generating land uses such as new regional shopping centers, while avoiding the expenses of a large resident population. Although the protestors were numerous and their arguments true, the Board of Supervisors approved the incorporation proposal anyway; removing only the most blatant geographic tentacles as an act of symbolic appeasement.

The year after incorporation (1958), there were only 53 industrial establishments in the City of Industry with 3286 employees. By 1970 there would be over 330 establishments with more than 50,000 employees. For the most part these would include headquarters, branches, divisions, or subsidiaries of national or regional corporations attracted by the availability of large parcels of well-served industrial land, the proximity of relatively low-cost labor, and the political stability offered by a local city government dedicated to industrial needs (Stanford Research Institute, 1964).

Three fourths of the forty-two incorporation attempts undertaken between 1950 and 1970 occurred in the last four years of the 1950s. An incorporation attempt in one community set off similar attempts by neighboring communities. The owners of industrial land, recognizing their advantage in the incorporation process, usually mobilized their attempts first.

Although none of the proposals to incorporate enclaves of industry were seriously threatened at any phase of the incorporation process, two of the eight successful chamber-sponsored incorporations did manage to retain some valuable industrial land despite the protest of the owners. One of these was the City of La Mirada.

La Mirada was a new suburban community that had been planned by a single developer as a balanced community including a mix of residential, commercial, and industrial activities. However, the community was located adjacent to a large industrial area whose owners, the Santa Fe Railroad and several oil companies, petitioned to incorporate all the industrial land in the vicinity and the City of Santa Fe Springs, including that which had originally been included as part of the La Mirada community. Several resident businessmen and professionals from La Mirada were outraged and began their own incorporation campaign. Hopes of including industrial land in the proposed residential municipality were slight until a conflict erupted in the incorporation proceedings for Santa Fe Springs between industrial land owners and dairy farmers. The farmers successfully lobbied the County Board of Supervisors to exclude their property from the proposed City of Santa Fe Springs. The omission left a large portion of an industrial park owned by a subsidiary of the Santa Fe Railroad outside of the revised boundaries of the industrial city. Wasting no time, the La Mirada proponents submitted boundaries for a municipality that included this prime industrial land. This move pre-empted the legal advantages enjoyed by the large industrial landowners at the petition phase.

The City of Santa Fe Springs went on to incorporate without the industrial land, but the political struggle to recapture it had just begun. The lawyers for the industrial landowners and the new City of Santa Fe Springs mounted legal skirmishes against the sometimes faltering efforts of the La Mirada proponents to keep their incorporation attempt alive; and as the date for the public hearing drew near, the industrial owners launched an all-out public relations campaign in the local newspapers attacking the incorporation proponents. Such "external interference" quickly became a political issue with the La Mirada proponents orchestrating the incorporation campaign into a heated class conflict between the residents and the outside industrial owners. The conflict peaked during the public hearings. The first meeting ended in adjournment when the four supervisors present split two to two over the decision to approve the removal of the industrial land from the proposed City of La Mirada. The hearing was extended to the following week when the fifth member of the Board could be present to vote. In the interim the proponents were able to mobilize significant participation and support against removal of the industrial property. Feelings ran so high at one rally that the two supervisors who had voted in favor of removal were hung in effigy. When the Board reconvened they voted four to one approving the incorporation proposal for the City of La Mirada with the industrial land intact. While the La Mirada incorporation victory was an exception it does illustrate the class competition embodied in the boundary disputes and that the exercise of capitalist political power could be checked by political organization of small-business persons anxious to protect and control their local economic interests.

Political Struggle at the Implementation Phase

Electoral opposition to incorporation was strongest in the large, chamber-sponsored municipalities. Homeowner groups anxious to retain low property taxes were suspicious of the Lakewood Plan. Here the organizational resources of the chambers of commerce were crucial. The chambers hired public relations firms to prepare reports documenting the virtues of the Lakewood Plan, organized meetings at which county employees could reassure the worried, conducted mailings that illustrated how tax savings would be realized without service cuts. Opinion poll results for several communities prior to the incorporation elections revealed that those who supported incorporation did so out of fear of annexation, a desire for low

Proposed City of Rosemead
Boundaries: 1954 and 1956

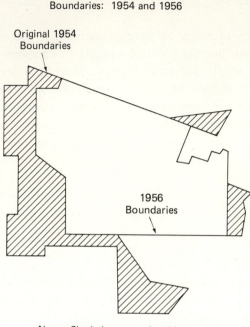

Note: Shaded areas omitted in second
attempt to avoid pockets of
electoral opposition.

Figure 5.3

taxes, and an interest in protecting the homogeneity of a community. Residents perceived incorporation as a means of neighborhood protection. Once opponents were convinced that they could not retain unincorporated status, resistance tended to dissipate. The exception to this were neighborhoods whose residents possessed a higher socioeconomic status than the majority of the residents in the proposed city. It was residents from these neighborhoods who were able to mobilize a geographically concentrated block of opposition votes, often large enough to outweigh the combination of much smaller margins of electoral support in the other neighborhoods.

Those proponents whose proposals were rejected by the electorate either learned from these electoral failures and amended the proposed boundaries to exclude geographic pockets of electoral opposition in later attempts or they continued to lose incorporation elections. The cities of Rosemenad and Temple City were examples of the former, while the community of South San Gabriel was a victim of the latter (see Fig. 5.3).

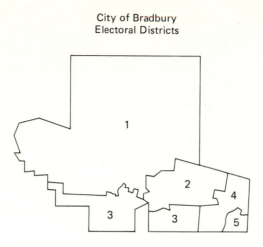

City of Bradbury
Electoral Districts

Figure 5.4

The proponents for incorporating the industrial suburb of Santa Fe Springs and the exclusive Bradbury estates utilized a different strategy. Instead of excluding pockets of voters who might vote against incorporating, they created electoral districts within the proposed municipalities. They gerrymandered the district boundary lines so as to place the majority of the electorate in a minority of the electoral districts. While this procedure had little direct effect on the incorporation vote, which was city-wide, it did influence the simultaneous election of city council officials where the vote was by ward. The hope was to direct the incorporation opponents' energy into electing their own representatives rather than concentrating on mobilizing the opposition to incorporation itself (see Fig. 5.4).

The fact that chambers of commerce were the majority proponents of incorporation was seldom an issue in the incorporation election campaigns. Chamber members were usually aware of the class distance between themselves and most residents. In one case the members selected a spokesperson who had been a local union leader with the express purpose of diffusing any charges of class bias. Chambers were successful in having their incorporation proposals accepted as a legitimate effort to protect the common good. In fact small employers, proprietors, and professionals were elected to fill 75 percent of the city council offices in all the incorporation elections in the San Gabriel region although by the most generous of estimates less than 25 percent of the residents were from these groups.

MUNICIPAL CLASS SEGREGATION
AND FISCAL INEQUALITIES

The thirteen new municipalities created in the San Gabriel region enhanced class, wealth, fiscal, and land-use differences among all twenty-
four suburban municipalities within the region. I compared the extent to
which differences in these variables were greater among new municipalities than among the municipalities incorporated before 1950 for the census
year following the municipal incorporation boom, 1960 (see Table 5.3).

For each variable the differences in coefficient values among the new
municipalities was at least twice as large as the differences among the
older municipalities. The new municipalities exhibited a greater degree of
specialization. Moreover, the exclusive upper-class residential enclaves and
industrial centers which had been successfully formed possessed larger
concentrations of wealth and were able to generate greater amounts of tax
revenue *per capita* with relatively less sacrifice than the older, more balanced suburban municipalities. In the San Gabriel region five of the thirteen new municipalities were specialized in this way: four industrial and
one residential. In effect the industrial and residential estate owners were
able to gain land use control over the most valuable territory in the region.
Through jurisdictional formation they were able to avoid the social costs
of a large population and acquire the fiscal benefits of valuable residential
industrial and commercial real estate (Hill, 1974; 1977).

While the fiscal benefits of incorporation were realized disproportionately by members of the capitalist class, the political benefits were
more widely dispersed. In particular, the small employers and merchants
who dominated the chambers of commerce were able to obtain political
authority within their local market areas. The economic base of local retail and service activities that were directly linked to a geographic com-

**Table 5.3. Previously and Newly Incorporated Municipalities
in the San Gabriel Region, 1960**

	Coefficients of Variation	
	Previously Incorporated N = 11	*Newly Incorporated N = 13*
Class	.33	.93
Wealth	.23	2.05
Revenue	.32	1.78
Land Use	.31	.74

Source: Hoch, 1981, Appendix C.

munity now received the privileged consideration and support of municipal government. In many cases, chambers of commerce received funds
from the city treasury since the personnel and policies of both agencies
shared the same commitment to local growth and development. The economic and political interests of small employers, self-employed entrepreneurs and professionals were identified as the public interest (Zisk,
1973).

Ironically, the predominantly working-class residents of these communities did not rise up in protest to the establishment of middle-class
political control or to the lopsided fiscal inequalities established within the
municipal enclaves of the capitalist class. This was consistent with the
relative inactivity of community working-class organizations in the 1950s
and 1960s as compared to the activity of middle-class organizations, even
though it may have been inconsistent with the long-term economic interests of the working class. The struggles among capitalist and middle-class
organizations shaped the boundaries of the new municipalities; boundaries
which became barriers to the local organization of working-class community politics. The municipality focused the political organization and
participation of its residents on problems and issues *within* the city. Since
political issues were raised in a jurisdictional context that defined them as
community issues, the tendency was for these issues to become *exclusively*
community issues (Newton, 1975; 1978).

Although members of the capitalist class were victorious in their incorporation efforts, the nature of the political struggles revealed a lack of
class control by national and regional capital over the structure of local
government in Los Angeles county. The chaotic fragmentation of local
government generated a multitude of new political demands as each municipal administration sought to expand its influence and enhance its economic base. Although politically stable in the short run, the arrangement
was economically expensive in the long run. One major result was that
capital as a whole was forced to pay more than it otherwise would for the
organization of production space. For example, although most suburban
municipalities were more than willing to provide fiscal and land use concessions to attract "clean" industry, they were just as willing to use the
same governmental powers to resist the location of undesirable or "dirty"
industries (Molotch, 1976, p. 328). Recent efforts by national capital to
persuade the federal government to pre-empt the land-use powers of local
government have met with little success (Plotkin, 1980).

Molotch (1978) and Cox and Nartowicz (1980) are only half right
when they argue that local coalitions of small employers, property developers, and middle-class investors form mainly to appropriate rent in return
for organizing space for corporate investors. These local coalitions also

have their own commercial and industrial interests to protect, and local government is a powerful ally. Although lacking the broad economic base necessary to challenge the national political power of monopoly capital successfully, these groups have been able to use local political authority to protect and strengthen their limited and distinctly territorial economic base against systematic, if not periodic, control of national capital.

NOTES

1. I have addressed the pluralist explanations of metropolitan governmental fragmentation in detail in my dissertation. Throughout the text here I have not noted the primary sources I used in my research. For the most part data was drawn from incorporation documents, local newspapers, public testimony, and the files of local municipal or country clerks. Detailed reference to these sources is given in the dissertation (Hoch, 1981).

REFERENCES

Cox, K. R., and F. Z. Nartowicz, "Jurisdictional Fragmentation in the American Metropolis: Alternative Perspectives," *International Journal of Urban and Regional Research* 4, 1980, 196–209.

Dinerman, B., "Chambers of Commerce in the Modern Metropolis," *Bureau of Government Research Observor* 2, 1958.

Hill, Richard Child, "Separate and Unequal: Governmental Inequality in the Metropolis," *American Political Science Review* 68, December 1974.

———, "State Capitalism and the Urban Fiscal Crisis in the United States," *International Journal of Urban and Regional Research,* 1 (1), 1977, 76–100.

Hoch, C. J., "City Limits: Municipal Boundary Formation and Class Segregation in Los Angeles Suburbs" (Ph.D. dissertation, University of California at Los Angeles, 1981).

Markusen, Ann, "The Economics of Social Class and Metropolitan Government" (Ph.D. dissertation, Michigan State University, 1974).

Molotch, Harvey, "The City as Growth Machine: Toward a Political Economy of Place," *American Journal of Sociology* 82, Sept. 1976, 309–332.

Molotch, Harvey, "Capital and Neighborhood in the United States," *Urban Affairs Quarterly* 14, 1979, 289–312.

Muncy, D. A., "Land for Industry: A Neglected Problem," *Harvard Business Review* 32, 1954, 51–63.

Newton, Kenneth, "American Urban Politics: Social Class, Political Structure and Public Goods," *Urban Affairs Quarterly* 11, 1975, 241–264.

———, "Conflict Avoidance and Conflict Suppression: The Case of Urban Politics in the United States," in Cox (ed.), *Urbanization and Conflict in Marketing Societies* (Chicago: Maaroufa Press, 1978).

Plotkin, Sidney, "Policy Fragmentation and Capitalist Reform: The Defeat of National Land Use Policy," *Politics and Society,* 9 (4), 1980, 409–446.

Stanford Research Institute, *City of Industry: Its Economic Characteristics and Significance, 1957–1970* (South Pasadena, Calif., 1964).

Vidich, A. J., and J. Bensman, *Small Town in a Mass Society* (New Jersey: Princeton University Press, 1970).

Warren, Robert, "Changing Patterns of Governmental Organization in the Los Angeles Metro Area" (Ph.D. dissertation, University of California at Los Angeles, 1964).

Wright, Erik O., *Class, Crisis and the State* (London: New Left Books, 1978).

Zisk, Betty, *Local Interest Politics: A One Way Street* (New York: Bobbs-Merrill, 1973).

two

POLITICAL STRUGGLE AND HOUSING

6

Austerity, Shelter, and Social Conflict in the United States

RICHARD T. LeGATES and KAREN MURPHY

Beginning in the 1970s, a period of fiscal crisis and austerity replaced the period of economic growth and increasing affluence which had characterized conditions in the United States during the three decades following World War II. Social conflict increases over which groups—rich or poor, white or black, young or old—will receive larger or smaller slices of a shrinking pie. Shelter represents the single largest expenditure item in most households' budgets and the availability, adequacy, and cost of shelter are matters which deeply touch all Americans. This paper examines what is happening in the U.S. housing sector, the nature of changes between today's conditions and those of both the recent period of affluence and prior periods of crisis (the Depression and World War II), and the nature of housing conflict today.

THE NEW ERA OF AUSTERITY IN U.S. HOUSING

In the 1980s you need more than a weatherperson to tell which way the wind is blowing. The complex cross-currents of change in housing are best approached in terms of key indicators. How much housing is being built? Of what kind? How much does it cost to buy or rent shelter? What is happening with interest rates? Before we can construct theory about housing conflict we need to have essential facts firmly in hand.

This article is adapted from an article which appeared under the same title in 5 *International Journal of Urban and Regional Research* No. 2 (1981). Detailed documentation and references to information sources may be found in the original article.

New construction of housing (both for ownership and for rent) is a matter of central concern. Housing analysts use housing starts as a measure of homebuilding activity. (Almost all starts are completed.) One might expect that during hard times there would be few housing starts, and indeed that was the case in earlier crisis periods such as the great depression and both World Wars. But in the current fiscal crisis the facts are more complicated. Surprisingly, overall the 1970s saw more housing starts than any prior decade in U.S. history. However, since 1970 the curve showing annual housing starts looks like the Coney Island roller coaster. In 1970 there were about a million and a half starts, by 1972 starts were up to about two and a half million, then down to barely three quarters of a million in 1975, up over two million in 1978, and at this writing in early 1982 screaming downhill toward a low that may match the lowest production figures of the 1970s. Fluctuations this violent in annual production figures are unprecedented even in our notoriously cyclic housing industry. While both seasonal and long-term cycles are nothing new, short-term fluctuations of this magnitude are indicators of very troubled times.

What is being built has changed even more significantly than how much is being built. As prices escalate and real income stagnates, one might expect a shift in new homebuilding to accommodate low and moderate income people through a higher proportion of rental units, mobile homes, and small, modest units for owner occupancy. This has not occurred. The most important shift in what is being built is an almost total cessation of construction of new rental units since the mid 1970s. Mobile home shipments have not increased significantly since 1970. And the median square footage of newly constructed homes continues to rise. By the early 1980s the median square footage of newly built homes in the United States hovered around 1600 square feet—about double what is considered the norm in a modern industrial country with high housing standards such as Sweden. Not only are the houses being built bigger, they are more luxurious than before. We shall return to the *what is being built* question in a later analysis of housing conflicts. First, what about housing costs?

House prices are an essential area of concern, with the problem of housing affordability receiving ever increasing attention. The most commonly used indicator is the median sales price of a new single-family detached home. Between 1970 and 1980 such median prices tripled from about twenty-three thousand dollars in 1970 to about seventy thousand in 1980. The median sales price of existing homes began at a lower level (because they were used), but rose almost in parallel with median sale prices of new homes.

Several caveats concerning this tripling are in order. First, the nominal change needs to be deflated to adjust for inflation. In constant dollars the rise is much less steep. Second the 1980 home was not the same thing as the 1970 home: on average by 1980 homes were both bigger and more luxurious. A constant house identical to the average 1970 house would cost less than the median sales price for all 1980 houses. Thirdly, the approximately two thirds of the U.S. population who are members of households who own a home received a substantial windfall in appreciation of their homes during this period. For them the harsh effects of rapid price escalation are softened by the fact that they can cash in their old home when buying a new one. These realities suggest that many recent articles which say that most U.S. households can no longer afford homeownership are overstated.

Notwithstanding, home price escalation has been severe. House prices have risen substantially more rapidly than the consumer price index or real wages. While it is not true that the majority of U.S. households have been priced out of homeownership, it is true that price escalation has driven a deep wedge between the lucky majority of long-term homeowners, who have had the value of their homes increase and their real shelter costs decline, and the unlucky minority of renters and would-be first-time homebuyers who have been shut out.

Most people who have owned their home since 1970 have seen a very substantial rise in the value of their property. The rise is greater in some active markets (Honolulu, Washington, D.C., San Francisco) and less in some depressed ones (Detroit, St. Louis). For the country as a whole the value of owner-occupied, single-family detached housing increased by about $1.5 trillion between 1970 and 1980—an astonishing unearned increment in housing.

There is another important aspect to the long-term homeowner's situation. Most of these owners purchased their homes with 30-year, fixed-rate mortgages. This means they will continue to make the same monthly payment to pay off the principal and interest on their mortgage each month for thirty years. As inflation reduces the value of the dollar, it becomes easier and easier for them to make payments. For them housing is becoming more, not less, affordable.

Contrast this situation with that facing a young couple looking to buy their first home in the mid 1980s. A recent cartoon shows a realtor explaining to such a couple that the tiny house he is showing can now be bought through creative financing: "Your father puts down the first $100,-000. . . ." First-time homebuyers face the double whammy of house prices that have tripled and interest rates that have more than doubled. Which brings us to our third key indicator.

Interest rates are extremely important to homebuyers because most people must borrow very substantially to purchase a house. Even a small fluctuation in interest rates has a dramatic effect on monthly and total housing cost.

Interest rates rose from around 7% to 8% in the early 1970s to the 16% to 18% range by the early 1980s. Financial intermediaries—Savings and Loan Institutions, mutual banks, commercial banks—have recognized that if inflation continues at present rates it will greatly erode the value of the payments made toward the end of a mortgage term. In order to get at least the same overall real rate of return they have greatly increased interest rates. Even if the total real value of principal and interest payments were to remain constant (unlikely as banks cover risk and look for higher profits in troubled times), the incidence of real costs is tilted toward the beginning part of the mortgage: a devastating change for first-time homebuyers with limited income.

While the sharp increase in interest rates is making homeownership increasingly difficult or impossible for many first-time homebuyers, it appears that many financial intermediaries did not raise interest rates quickly enough to keep themselves afloat. The real inflation-adjusted return on most mortgages let in the early to mid 1970s is very low; indeed often negative. Since these intermediaries must now borrow to meet current needs at high interest rates, many are in difficulty. The early 1980s are seeing large numbers of mergers and acquisitions of distressed intermediaries.

Rents are a fourth key indicator of the health of the housing sector. Currently, rising rents are a source of tension in many cities, and debate and political action around rent control, rent stabilization, tenant unions, and rent strikes is mounting. Is rental housing becoming less affordable? Surprisingly, this central question has proven difficult to answer and remains broadly misunderstood and hotly debated.

Rents have been rising since the end of World War II and rose much more rapidly as the pace of inflation increased during the 1970s. The preferred rent indicator is gross rent (the contract rent plus the amount the renter pays for utilities and heating fuel). Contract rent (the amount the renter agrees to pay the landlord) may or may not include some utility costs. Nationally median gross rent is an accepted benchmark of rent rates. National gross median rent figures are available for each census, and beginning in the 1970s are available annually from the *Annual Housing Survey*. In 1950 median gross rent in the United States was $43. In 1979 it was $217; a four-fold increase. Median gross rents rose rapidly in the late 1970s. In 1976, for example the figure was $167, fully $50 below the 1979 level.

But how do these rent figures compare with inflation? What has been the constant dollar increase? Is the 1979 pool of renters the same group as the 1950 group? And are they renting the same thing? Finally what has happened with their purchasing power? As analysts move into these issues the situation becomes cloudier and the debate heats up.

First, nominal rental increases must be adjusted to account for inflation. The residential rent component of the Consumer Price Index measures rents on the same dwellings, which are resurveyed from year to year, with adjustments for major changes in the quality of the dwelling. By comparing the rental component of the CPI to the overall CPI it should be possible to form a judgment as to how rapidly rents have increased relative to all consumer items. Such comparison shows that rents have risen less rapidly than all consumer items. They have risen much less rapidly than sensitive items such as gasoline or home heating oil and less than median sale prices of new or existing homes. Based on these figures some analysts conclude that renters have gotten a good deal, and that concern about rising rents rather than other fast-rising consumer essentials is misplaced.

Second, the category "renters" has changed over time. At the close of World War II about 45 percent of all U.S. households were renters; today only 33 percent are. Households with the greatest purchasing power have shifted from rental to ownership status. Even through the late 1970s there continued to be a net shift in favor of homeownership from the top of the rental ladder, though this ended in early 1982. Today the pool of remaining renters consists mainly of poor, near-poor, and lower-middle-income households, significantly minority and female-headed. It also contains a much smaller group of relatively well-off persons who are young and did not enter the potential homeownership market until after the great increase in prices and interest rates of the late 1970s. Analyses such as that in the President's Commission on Housing Report which ask the question what has happened to the pool of Americans who were renters in 1950 conclude that this group has done relatively well. Analyses which look at the situation of current renters are less sanguine.

Third, what is being rented has changed. Just as the house of the 1980s is larger and more luxurious than the 1950s house, so is the rental unit. At the end of World War II much of the nation's housing stock was old and often lacked plumbing and other essential elements. Moreover, after fifteen years of depression and war much of it was poorly maintained and substandard. During the succeeding thirty years much of the worst rental stock was demolished, most of the remaining old stock was rehabilitated, and new larger units with more amenities were built. Since 1975 there has been little new rental construction. The President's Commission Report concludes that quality improvements accounted for about as much of the increase in rent payments as did cost increases. That conclusion significantly fails to distinguish between the period up to 1975 and since that time.

Finally, renters' ability to pay has changed over time. The primary source of income for most renters is from wages (as distinct from non-wage income). So long as real wages increased as rapidly as real income, renters experienced no loss of purchasing power. Through 1975 this was the case, at least with respect to constant quality rental units. Since 1975 real wages have remained essentially constant while real rents have risen. Moreover a sharply increasing unemployment rate radically reduces the rent-paying ability of the unemployed. An indication of the seriousness of the latter problem is that the overall national unemployment rate by Spring 1982 was over 9 percent and most of this unemployment hit the third of the nation's households who are renters.

Many analysts, including the President's Commission on Housing, Anthony Downs of the Brookings Institution, and George Sternlieb of Rutgers University, conclude that in both absolute and relative terms renters have gotten a good deal in recent years: that they are paying reasonable amounts for their shelter, that costs have not increased exorbitantly, and that they are in little need of assistance. The overall thrust of the President's Commission Report is that renters needs should receive lower priority than the needs of homeowners. Downs and Sternlieb would like to see rents increase to stimulate new rental construction and investment in the maintenance of rental property. How have renters really faired in relation to owners of individual homes and owners of rental property? Have they really gotten a good deal?

The key question here is How do the real costs of owning compare with the real costs of renting? The cost of renting is relatively easy to measure, as the renter makes a measurable rent payment and receives shelter in return, without complicated tax and capital gains advantages to consider. Homeownership cost is complicated by the fact that immediate mortgage and other payments yield not only a place to live, but also tax advantages and potential capital gains from appreciation. Recently the U.S. Department of Housing and Urban Development has attempted to compute what they call the net effective cost of homeownership, or the cost including tax and appreciation. Their analysis concluded that the net effective cost of homeownership declined during most of the 1970s, reaching a postwar low in 1978. With large increases in interest rates since 1978, HUD concludes that the net effective cost of homeownership has begun to increase since 1978. The general pattern of net effective cost of rental property should roughly follow that of owned property. Comparing

net effective cost of ownership of either individual homes or rental buildings to tenants' rent payments indicates that generally tenants have fared
poorly relative to owners of both individual homes and rental property.

To the extent that the renters-have-gotten-a-good-deal theory has
any validity, it is essential to add "so far." In a period of rapid appreciation such as occurred throughout the 1970s in most U.S. rental housing
markets, owners of rental property are not primarily interested in the
profit they make from rental receipts; they are primarily interested in the
capital gains potential as a result of the resale value of their buildings. In
San Francisco during the second half of the 1970s, the value of apartment
buildings was increasing 20 percent or more a year, on average. Depending upon the amount of their own money invested in the building and their
tax brackets, owners of these buildings stood to gain four to five times as
much each year, or even more, from appreciation as from rents. Most
buildings purchased during this period had a negative cash flow—that is,
the money taken in from rents did not cover the cost of mortgage payments, taxes, management, maintenance, insurance, and other operating
expenses. The crucial factor for investors in such a climate was continued
rapid appreciation. Rent income was important not for the money actually
generated, but for its effect on the building's sale price. So long as appreciation continues there is a natural lid on rent increases. But when appreciation slows or stops, as has recently occurred in San Francisco and
many other markets, landlords who are strapped for cash and unable to
realize the capital gains they expected will be desperate to increase rents.
This has already happened in many markets; the conflict between tenants
and owners is at flash point.

In summary a look at the macro-level indicators of change in housing in the United States since 1970 shows the following important features: (a) high overall new production, but with violent peaks and
troughs and a particularly deep trough moving into the 1980s, (b) a
dramatic shift in what is being produced away from new construction of
rental units, (c) a tripling of the nominal median sale price of single-
family detached homes, which translates to substantial real cost increases
even when adjusted to constant dollars and for a constant quality house,
(d) continued increases in the average size of units being built and the
number of amenities they have, (e) a two-and-one-half-fold increase in
nominal interest rates, greatly increasing the front-end cost of borrowing
money for housing (though not keeping pace with the real cost of lending
to financial intermediaries), and (f) rents rising less rapidly than the consumer price index, but since 1975 more rapidly than real income and
until about 1978 or 1979 more rapidly than the net effective cost of ownership.

Helpful as these indicators are in helping us sift out what is significant and true about current conditions, there is another side to the housing
equation: the people who will live in them.

DEMOGRAPHIC INDICATORS OF CHANGE

Changes in the number of households needing shelter; the size and composition of these households; the way in which they are distributed geographically and between cities, suburbs, and rural areas; and lifestyle
changes related to housing consumption intersect with the changing housing stock to create conflict.

Three important shifts in the location of the U.S. population are
particularly noteworthy: (a) households are moving from the Northeast,
North Central, and Atlantic seaboard regions of the country (the frostbelt) to the South, Southwest, and Pacific states (the Sunbelt); (b) households are moving away from some (usually older) metropolitan areas to
rural areas, small towns, and other metropoli; and (e) central cities continue to lose population. Between 1970 and 1975 approximately 6 percent of the central city resident population relocated to the suburbs and
an additional 1 percent moved to non-metropolitan areas.

Housing policy analysts are particularly concerned with the number
of *households* (not *people*) seeking shelter. In the nineteenth century,
when many people lived in large, extended family groupings, fewer housing units were needed for a given number of people than today when
more people live as singles or in small households without children, grand-
parents, or other in-laws. Through the 1970s and 1980s the number of
households continue to rise. As household formations have increased the
average household size has continued to decrease. Increasing rates of
divorce; people choosing to marry late, to marry but not have children,
or not to marry; and other lifestyle changes help explain this phenomenon
of smaller households. In 1940 the average household size was 3.67 persons; in 1970, 3.14 persons; and by 1976 only 2.89 persons: This helps
explain the apparent paradox of a city like San Francisco, which experienced a 10 percent decrease in population between 1970 and 1976, but
simultaneously saw an increase in the number of households and demand
for housing units! Household formation and household size are closely
linked to changes in lifestyle. Consider that traditional nuclear family
households grew by only 6 percent between 1970 and 1976, while total
household growth was 15 percent and households headed by a single
woman increased by 33 percent. By far the fastest growing household
type is what could be labelled the alternative lifestyle household, com-

posed of two or more unrelated individuals. Over the same six-year period this household category increased by 67 percent.

An additional factor stimulating housing demand is the number of households making up the 25- to 35-year age category. Households in this age category represent an important demand for both ownership and rental units. Between 1970 and 1985 this age group will increase by 58 percent.

These demographic changes are of great importance for housing policy. They suggest that we will need more housing in fast growing (sunbelt) regions; less in the frostbelt. It doesn't help much to have enough units net if they are in the wrong place. Similarly, we will see pressures increasing on non-metropolitan areas. And demand for both small units and units which can accommodate alternative lifestyle groupings should increase.

These indicators of change in the housing sector—volatile production fluctuations; massive cost increases; a trillion and a half dollar unearned increment for homeowners; the pricing out of new households from the ownership market; rents rising unevenly, overall less rapidly than the Consumer Price Index, but recently at a rate above increases in real income, all point to potential conflict over who gets what in the increasingly disturbed housing economy.

THIRTY YEARS OF POSTWAR HOUSING AFFLUENCE

The way in which conditions today are changing can be better understood by comparison to the thirty-year period of unprecedented affluence and economic expansion in the United States and the way in which good times affected housing.

During the postwar period the U.S. emerged as a global superpower, nearly tripling its GNP. The housing sector received a proportional share of this increase in general affluence. From the end of the Second World War to the mid 1970s, *absolute* private fixed investment in residential uses increased massively, in proportion to the general rise in the GNP. *Proportionally,* fixed investments in residential uses remained quite stable. The proportion of GNP invested in housing has remained at between 3 percent and 6 percent annually. In short, there has been a steady, modest assignment of capital to shelter during this period. The country has not strained to meet shelter needs; nor has it assigned them as low a priority as some countries with more pressing problems or more disturbed economies.

The overall improvement in U.S. housing conditions which occurred

during this period was significant. The number of units added to the national housing inventory outpaced new household formations by healthy
margins; the number of units classified as substandard declined substantially, to the point where housing quality appears a residual issue in the
United States by most indicators; and the number of overcrowded dwelling units also shrunk, though more modestly. The average size of newly
constructed homes increased, and substantial upgrading of the existing
housing stock occurred.

An even more impressive aspect of the postwar affluent period is
that the above changes were achieved *without cutting into total household
income*. Average median gross rent as a percentage of income declined
slightly between 1950 and 1960 and again between 1960 and 1970.

The above improvement in housing conditions was far from even.
It was extremely maldistributed by region, income group, race, and gender
of the head of household. More investment occurred in the South and
West than in the East and North; more than two thirds within Standard
Metropolitan Statistical Areas; and disproportionately the dollars went to
improvements for middle- and upper-income households, the majority of
which were white. Female-headed households were among those least
benefitted by this period of affluence in housing, and as this group has
become larger their housing status takes on added importance.

For the majority of the population for whom conditions were improving, shelter was not a source of conflict. For significant, but limited,
groups such as long-term renters in the urbanizing fringe and residents
of inner-city areas selected for urban renewal, however, conflict was
severe.

Fundamental to understanding why conflict was limited and selective
is the role of suburban development during the postwar period. The
majority of suburban investment directly benefitted middle- and upper-
income groups. It was used principally for the construction of single-
family detached homes.

A principal reason why this use of capital for suburban development
did not generate overt social conflict was that as overall shelter conditions
were improving, inner-city renters did not resent the maldistribution of
the available increment as much as they would have if their own situation
were worsening. Also important was the fact that most of the land on
which development took place was either vacant or sparsely settled, limiting turf fights between existing residents and newcomers around issues of
territory and lifestyle.

The two types of suburban housing conflict which occurred during
this period of affluence did not involve the majority of Americans. For

the relatively small number affected, though, conflict was severe. First, suburbanization brought newcomers into competition with the much smaller group of previously fringe residents. Resident tenants of farms, pockets of poverty, and small communities engulfed by metropolitanization were frequently hurt. Second, in the limited cases in which government attempted to decentralize low and moderate income housing to suburbs, conflict was sometimes severe. Less than 1 percent of housing units built in suburbs during the period of affluence were subsidized units for low- and moderate-income persons.

Shelter conflict in urban neighborhoods during the period of affluence was more widespread and often bitter. Expenditures on urban renewal doubled every five years between 1949 and 1974. In many urban neighborhoods urban renewal plans called for a total change in the nature of the neighborhood. The social characteristics of the change were:

1. *Class*. Former residents of renewal areas were usually of extremely low socioeconomic status. Many were welfare dependent or unemployed. Most urban renewal involved transformation of either residential or mixed-use areas and their replacement with non-residential (commercial or industrial) uses. The class base of the interests behind these developments was totally different from that of the former residents—essentially upper- and some middle-income groups, which sometimes worked with organized labor, which often supported renewal projects due to the employment opportunities generated from these new growth policies.

2. *Race*. Displacees were primarily members of racial minorities; in-movers virtually all white. Hence the phrase "Negro removal" for urban renewal.

3. *Tenure*. Usually lower-income rental units were demolished to be replaced by non-residential uses. Thus tenure change was not a crucial element in the inner-city growth conflicts around urban renewal. Where residential uses were made of urban renewal land, the new units were primarily rental units, and almost always for much higher income persons than had been displaced.

4. *Government superstructure*. The state's role in urban renewal was explicit and massive. Local redevelopment agencies using federal renewal funds undertook land acquisition, relocation of former residents, demolition of structures, and preparation of land for resale. They bore the brunt of conflict on behalf of private interests who ultimately obtained the cleared and prepared land.

A more pervasive arena of conflict during the affluent years involved tenant-landlord relations. There was substantial conflict concerning the issues of housing condition (whether units met minimum standards of health and safety as measured by local codes), security of tenure (the right to be free of arbitrary evictions), and freedom to organize (the right to organize tenant unions, protest code violations to the authorities, and speak against a landlord's practices without fear of eviction or arbitrary rent raises in retaliation). Issues of housing *cost* played a much less important role during this period when real rents were stable or even slightly declining. Rent control was not a major issue in most parts of the country until the mid to late 1970s. During this period tenants were quite successful in obtaining reforms in tenant-landlord law, including adoption in state law of implied warranty of habitability doctrine which holds that a landlord is obligated to rent premises in habitable condition, and "retaliatory eviction" doctrine which prevents evictions in retaliation for tenant organizing or reporting code violations to the authorities. They were less successful in obtaining reforms related to security of tenure, though in public housing they were successful in establishing that evictions could only be for just cause. Since rent control was not pressed as an issue in most parts of the country, no progress occurred except in a few unusual jurisdictions.

Conditions have never been so favorable as during the postwar period of affluence. Another way of understanding what is unique about the current period is to look at similarities and contrasts with prior periods of crisis in housing during the twentieth century. The most severe crises in the housing sector (as elsewhere) occurred between the depression years of 1929–34 and the period of the Second World War, 1941–45.

LESSONS FROM THE GREAT DEPRESSION AND THE SECOND WORLD WAR

Five features of the two earlier crisis periods are particularly notable. First, massive shifts of capital away from new investment in housing occurred in both times of crisis. In 1925, the peak year of predepression housing construction, 937,000 units were built. In 1929, on the eve of the depression, the figure stood at 509,000 units. Production of new homes in 1933 had dropped to 93,000 units, less than a tenth of the number built in 1925. Gross private fixed residential investment dropped from $14.5 billion in 1929 to $2.9 billion in 1933. Similarly, during the Second World War, housing starts declined from 706.1 thousand units in 1941 to 141.8 thousand in 1944.

Second, although the housing sector was hard hit during times of crisis, recovery was rapid. The capacity of the post-slump economies to deliver new units is shown most dramatically by World War II statistics. In 1946 over a million housing starts occurred, about triple the number of units started the previous year and more than seven times the number started in 1944. During the war, gross private fixed residential investment declined to 13.5 billion in 1941 and 3.4 billion in 1944, but bounced back to 16.8 billion in 1946.

Third, the correlation between investment in housing and gross national product has been very weak during times of crisis. Because new construction is a capital intensive commodity, tied to availability of financing, it is particularly affected by declines in the availability of investment capital. During the war years GNP grew massively while investment in housing declined.

Fourth, austerity has produced surges of conflict over housing. During the great depression large portions of the residential stock were foreclosed, evictions mounted, and there was a marked increase in tenant militancy. Rising employment and patriotism dampened housing conflict during the Second World War, but nonetheless conflict over rent control was substantial in parts of the country which had the greatest influxes of war workers.

(To the country's benefit, both periods of austerity led to periods of intense political activity and ultimately significant structural change in the housing system.)

A final point relates to the interplay between tenure and economic crisis. The greatest tenure shift in U.S. history occurred during the Second World War. In the course of four-and-a-half years, from April 1940 to October 1944, the proportion of owner-occupied units in the United States rose 15 percent. It appears that a combination of rising employment, growth in real income, and limited availability of alternative outlets for consumer buying gave many households both the wherewithall and the incentive to purchase homes.

THE CHANGING NATURE OF HOUSING CONFLICT IN THE UNITED STATES

Previous sections have documented leading indicators of change in the housing sector and demographic bases of demand in the United States and contrasted conditions during the previous periods of affluence and earlier crisis periods with what is occurring today. We are now in a position to describe the nature of shelter conflict in the United States today and how it differs from earlier periods.

Long-term Homeowners versus New Entrants
and Potential Entrants

A major conflict has emerged during the new period of austerity between what may be termed long-term homeowners and all others. For convenience we may consider any household which owns a home purchased prior to 1975 a long-term homeowner. While price and interest rate escalation began somewhat earlier, the sharpest increases in both house prices and interest rates occurred subsequent to 1975. "New entrants" to homeownership are those who purchased after 1975. "Potential entrants" are households who have not yet purchased housing, but have sufficient accumulated wealth and high enough steady income that home purchase is, or under more normal circumstances would have been, an option for them. These three groups are very differently situated and have very different political interests.

Roughly two thirds of all U.S. households presently live in owner-occupied housing; one third rent. Most of the owners are long term. Thus the majority (about 60%) of all U.S. households are in this category. This group purchased homes at prices and interest rates much lower than today. For most of them, shelter costs are a manageable and shrinking percentage of real income, and their equity has risen rapidly due to price escalation of their owned homes.

Most households who are not long-term owners are renters with such limited assets and income so low that they cannot ever expect to make the downpayment required for homeownership or meet monthly costs of amortizing a mortgage. (This group has its own severe problems to which we will return in subsequent sections.)

The remaining two groups are much smaller. Between three quarters of a million and one million households a year became first time homebuyers after 1975, though at this writing in 1982 the number of such households has dropped significantly in the face of very high interest rates. Altogether post-1975 first-time buyers comprise a little less than 5 percent of all U.S. households. This group finds itself in a radically different situation from the long-term homebuyers. Most of these buyers purchased their homes at sharply higher purchase prices and at interest rates as high as double those of long-term buyers who had purchased only a few years earlier. Often they purchased with variable rate mortgages and/or creative financing, which typically involves short payback periods and balloon payments (a large amount of cash due at some period in the near future).

The late 1970s produced a rush into ownership by first time homebuyers who feared that if they did not get in at that time they would be forever priced out of the market. To get in, many borrowed downpayments from their parents, crossed their fingers in talking about their real situation to the local loan officer, gambled on continuing and increasing income from two wage earners who it was hoped would not lose their jobs or become sick, disabled, or pregnant. Even so many are stretching tight budgets to make mortgage payments. The hope of this group is that appreciation will make it possible to re-finance their homes at lower rates, that inflation will make it easier to meet monthly payments, or both. They have taken a large gamble.

Finally there is a significant pool of potential homebuyers—stable, employed households with substantial savings, healthy incomes, and job security, who in less troubled times would have purchased a home. At the present time this pool contains about 1 percent of the population, but it could expand at a half a percent or more each year during the 1980s. This group is gambling on (and politically sensitive to) a decrease in sale prices, a slowing of inflation, and new construction which will reduce the supply/demand imbalance. It stands in strong opposition to the long-time owners and new entrants.

There are many implications of the situation sketched out above. First, investment in holding existing housing units is replacing more socially useful investment. Rather than using capital and human inventiveness to build up industries, businesses, or to produce new housing either directly or through savings, which will permit others to undertake productive activity with borrowed capital, many households are calculating that their money is safest holding on to already-existing housing for speculative rather than use purposes.

Second, long-term homeowners are using equity gains to distort the kind of new housing production which is occurring. By the early 1980s most newly constructed housing was going to long-term owners who were trading up to larger and more luxurious units, not only to acquire better housing, but significantly because they consider it a prudent investment. This helps explain why, in a period of austerity, new production is of large, luxury units. This market distortion pits the interests of long-term owners directly against those of potential entrants.

Third, as the investment value rather than shelter value of housing dominates consumer decision-making, exchange value rather than use value dominates their calculations. This may lead to a misuse of existing units. In a provocative article, George Sternlieb and James Hughes argue that housing has become a "post-shelter" commodity; in other words, homebuyers consider the investment and resale potential of housing rather than its potential in meeting their own housing needs as their first priority in making a purchase. Thus, Sternlieb and Hughes argue, white households who would be content to live in a racially mixed neighborhood may choose to purchase in an all white neighborhood for fear that future buyers will not purchase in a racially integrated neighborhood.

The split between long-term, new entrant, and potential entrant poses very difficult problems. Given the lopsided predominance of long-term owners it is unlikely that reform legislation will be politically possible in the near future. If conditions deteriorate and the plight of potential entrants becomes more severe, conflict will increase. Already potential entrants are instead renting or buying older, inner-city homes, creating a second conflict situation between gentrifiers and those being displaced.

Gentrification

A recent Doonesbury cartoon brought a new word to the American public: "gentrification." In the cartoon Dan is asked on a radio talk show to explain the word gentrification to his audience. He explains that gentrification works like this: A developer buys a dilapidated house in a depressed neighborhood, fixes it up, and resells it to a young, middle-class couple. This encourages new "gentry" to buy into the neighborhood, and before long a fantastic real estate market booms where none existed before. When the interviewer asks "What happens to the low-income tenants who are displaced? Does anyone care?" Dan assures him, "Sure we do. . . . They move on to devalue other properties. Without them, the whole system falls apart."

About two and a half million Americans are involuntarily displaced in the United States each year. Gentrification is occurring selectively. In San Francisco and Washington, D.C., almost the entire city is gentrifying simultaneously, with enormous price escalation of all property, widespread physical revitalization, brisk turnover of properties, and dramatic socioeconomic transformation of many neighborhoods. In other cities the phenomenon is confined to a few prime neighborhoods: usually consisting of old, well-built, but somewhat run-down housing near centers of work and entertainment. Most of the housing stock involved is single-family row houses, or small multiples. In some economically distressed cities, little or no gentrification has occurred.

Gentrification is a direct result of the recent trends in housing and demography discussed above. As new construction costs soar the comparative value of a well-built older home rises. Young childless couples frequently enjoy city living. Row houses and large flats meet the needs of smaller households.

Studies of gentrification and displacement confirm some aspects of the popular image and contradict others. They answer many of the basic questions about the new phenomenon Dan introduced to the American public.

Who are the gentry? The studies confirm the popular image. Most incomers to gentrifying neighborhoods are young (25–34), white, middle-to upper-middle class, single or childless-couple households, earning good salaries (often with both members employed in the case of couples). Contrary to the popular image most did not move to the gentrifying neighborhoods from the suburbs. The back-to-the-city movement is a myth. Studies show that most incomers gave an address within the same city as their prior residence.

Who are displaced persons? This is a more heterogeneous group which departs from some stereotypes. It is often assumed that they are racial and ethnic minorities and either poor, or working class near-poor. But at least initially, gentrification tends to begin in lower-middle-class white neighborhoods, or neighborhoods which are predominantly white, but with some minorities. These neighborhoods house the elderly and young families with children, as well as other household types and people of other ages. Most residents have an employed head of household earning income which would place the household in the low to moderate range. Some are unemployed, welfare dependent, or retired. In some neighborhoods there are sharp distinctions among population subgroups. For example, low-income apartments, public housing projects, or residential hotels housing a different socioeconomic group may be mixed into a predominantly white, lower-middle-class neighborhood with substantial owner occupancy. In a number of cities studied, the former residents of gentrifying neighborhoods who were displaced are best characterized as low-status white-collar (not blue-collar) persons: secretaries, file clerks, key punch operators, and salespeople.

What happens to displaced persons? Dan in the Doonesbury cartoon said they move on to devalue other property. The studies show that most cluster close to their old neighborhood. Almost none resettle in the suburbs. Some report that their new housing is the same as or better than the old; many view their new housing to be worse after the move, particularly lower-income persons. Most end up paying more for housing. Some pay only a modest amount more; others as high as 50 percent more.

The new phenomenon of gentrification is standing some classical housing market theory on its head. Much has been written about how housing filters down during its life. In theory a newly constructed unit should be occupied by a high-income household who relinquishes a somewhat older and less desirable unit to a household just below them in income, who in turn release a somewhat less expensive and less desirable unit and so on. Thus, for each move by an affluent household into better housing there is a chain of moves which benefits people at every income level. Today we are seeing a form of reverse filtering in which low- to moderate-income households living in old but adequate housing are finding themselves outbid by newcomers.

Understandably many renters confronting gentrification and reverse filtering do not like it. Unlike property owners in gentrifying neighborhoods who find themselves torn between the potential to sell their property at a windfall profit and discomfort at transition of the old neighborhood renters stand only to lose in terms of forced relocation or higher rents. In many cities coalitions formed in gentrifying neighborhoods to try to hold onto affordable housing—particularly rental housing—for present residents and those like them. Counter-pressure groups composed of new residents or real estate interests formed up against them. In Boston's South End a committee called South End for South Enders has engaged in picketing and disruptive demonstrations. In Philadelphia, white ethnic gangs in the Fairmount neighborhood physically assaulted blacks who tried to purchase or even walk into the area, with the tacit approval of middle-class gentry who saw these toughs as a first line of defense against black intrusion into the area. In New Orleans a survey of residents new to fifteen gentrifying neighborhoods found that most expected the neighborhoods to be all white in a short period of time and opposed policies which would retain ethnic and income balance.

In addition to neighborhood change involving outsiders purchasing formerly owner-occupied housing and outbidding renters for the most desirable rental stock, the 1970s saw yet another related phenomenon: the conversion of rental housing to condominiums.

Condominium Conversion

Another point of conflict involves conversion of rental units to condominiums. This was a virtually unknown occurrence until the early 1970s, which saw the beginning of a sharply escalating boom in condominium conversions.

A condominium is a form of ownership in which individual units in a multi-unit building are individually owned. Each owner also owns a share in such common space as grounds, garage, roof, and utilities.

Until the early 1970s there were almost no condominiums in the United States. In 1970 fewer than one half of one percent of the population lived in condominiums. The few condominium units which existed served very special populations: retirees in Florida and other sunbelt states, owners of recreational condominiums, and the very rich who wanted an urban *pied-à-terre*. Almost all of the then-existing condominium units had been built as condominiums; not converted to condominium status from rental status.

Beginning in the early 1970s and accelerating throughout the decade a national epidemic of condominium conversions—sometimes referred to as "condomania"—occurred. Nationally, approximately 366,000 rental units were converted to condominium or cooperative status between 1970 and 1979. In the five-year period between 1970 and 1975, 86,000 units were converted, with 280,000 more in the following four years. In 1976, 20,000 units were converted; in 1977, 45,000; in 1978, 80,000; and in 1979, 135,000 units. Very recently a combination of high interest rates and local moratoria and other controls on the tempo of condominium conversion have slowed the trend. But continuing pressure for conversions is likely to resurface if interest rates drop.

Condominium conversions generate a variety of conflicts. When a building is converted, individual units are usually marketed at two to three times their sale price as part of a rental complex. A five-unit apartment which would sell for $250,000 can be divided into five condominium units which may be sold for $100,000 to $150,000 each. Residents are faced with the choice of purchasing or moving out. Purchasing a unit usually requires a substantial (20%) down payment and monthly mortgage payments which can be two to three times as high as the former monthly rent.

When conversions occur some tenants (almost always a minority) will choose voluntarily to purchase the unit in which they are living. They may want to do this for any of a number of reasons: (a) the unit will probably be less expensive than even the least expensive, available single-family detached house in the local market, (b) they will obtain security of tenure as an owner, (c) they will receive the appreciation if the unit increases in value (as in fact most converted units continued to do through the late 1970s), and (d) for tax advantages, particularly the deduction of mortgage interest payments will partially offset increased nominal costs. Recent evidence suggests that most tenants of converted buildings who chose to purchase during the 1970s are satisfied with their decision.

Most renters in converted buildings do not buy their units. Nationally HUD has estimated that about two thirds move out. This is particularly true of young renters who do not have enough funds for a downpayment or the income to meet the greatly increased monthly costs. Most young renters are in relatively low tax brackets and cannot take advantage of tax breaks to the same extent as higher income buyers. Some elderly households living on fixed incomes also cannot afford to purchase. Some who can afford to buy will not want to. Some feel that the unit is not a good deal or know that major problems with the building may surface in the future. Others prefer to be mobile for job, educational, or lifestyle reasons.

Recent studies suggest that there is an in-between group who do buy, but reluctantly. They purchase their unit not because they want to, but because they see no other choice.

This pattern produces two major conflicts.

First, many of the non-purchasing tenants are extremely hostile to the conversion, particularly if they are long-term residents or have limited income and restricted alternatives. To some extent their anger may be directed at incidental issues such as lack of adequate notice of the conversion, too little time to move, or high pressure tactics to get them out. More fundamentally they resent the loss of their housing and the feeling of powerlessness engendered by the conversion. Many bitterly oppose conversion because they correctly perceive that they will be displaced into a difficult housing market in which they may have to accept higher priced, less desirable, or more crowded living conditions.

Second, condominium conversion reduces the net rental stock and thus affects all renters to the extent that fewer rental units are available and supply/demand imbalance pushes up rents. The net loss of rental units when a conversion occurs will almost always be substantially less than the number of units converted because former renters (both from within and outside the building) have now become owners.

Nationally HUD has estimated that between 1970 and 1979 condominium conversions represented only 1.3 percent of all occupied rental housing units in the United States. Even in the 12 Standard Metropolitan Statistical Areas with the highest rates of conversion only about 2.7 percent of units were converted on average. But when one moves to the neighborhood scale the numbers jump. In prime conversion markets of Chicago, San Francisco, Washington, D.C., and elsewhere, as much as fifty percent of all rental units in some neighborhoods were converted in the space of a few years. Some suburban communities have seen large percents of all their rental units converted in the same way. When conversion activity of this magnitude occurs it usually stimulates political action by all tenants in a jurisdiction, led by tenants of converted buildings or buildings particularly threatened by conversion. In many cities tenants obtained moratoria on condominium conversions pending further study. Some ordinances now prohibit conversions unless there is an adequate rental vacancy rate; a set number of tenants in a building approve the conversion; or a set number of tenants agree to purchase their units. Some local ordinances now require a converter to offer elderly residents a lifetime rental opportunity in the building, to give residents special rights to purchase at reduced purchase prices, or to give relocation or other assistance.

Conflict over condominium conversions is closely related to the squeeze on first-time homebuyers and to gentrification. As people who would normally buy conventional single-family homes now buy condos instead or rent in gentrifying neighborhoods, they cut into the available rental housing stock. With almost no new rental construction, renters are finding themselves even harder pressed than the disfavored groups of homebuyers.

Availability and Affordability of Rental Housing

For the one-third of the U.S. population which rents housing, the great structural changes outlined above have profound and ominous implications. New household formation is adding to the demand for rental housing. At the same time almost no new rental housing is being built. Instead, some rental units (usually the best ones) are being removed from the rental market through conversion. Would-be homeowners who have been priced out of the market are outbidding the traditional pool of renters for what rental housing there is. Nationally there has been a contraction of vacancy rates and in many markets vacancies have slipped way below the five percent usually considered necessary to maintain normal fluidity in the rental market. This is altering the intensity of renter concern and shifting it to issues of availability and affordability. Maintenance of the rental stock and rent stabilization have replaced issues of physical quality and security of tenure as the central concern of the tenants' movement.

In the late 1970s many cities saw intense politics focussed on just holding on to what rental housing stock there is. Moratoria on condominium conversions and related ordinances limiting conversions are one aspect of this phenomenon. Anti-demolition ordinances and strategies to combat loss of units to vandalism and arson are others. These are essentially strategies aimed at maintaining the availability of rental housing. Even more intense has been the struggle to put a lid on rents.

Rent stabilization (less restrictive than rent control) ordinarily involves establishment of a base rent considered to allow owners of rental property a fair return on their investment and some form of controls on periodic rent increases to match inflation and pass along increases in maintenance, management, and taxes and any capital improvements to the property.

According to a recent article on the tenants' revolt, the momentum for rent stabilization in the late 1970s and early 1980s reached fever pitch nationwide. Over 110 New Jersey communities have enacted rent stabilization ordinances, as have cities in Alaska, California, Connecticut, the District of Columbia, Maine, Maryland, Massachusetts, and Virginia.

The structural reasons for the new emphasis on rent stabilization are clear from the changes discussed above. Consider the situation in 1950. In that year the U.S. Census reported that more than one third of all housing in the United States was dilapidated or lacking complete plumbing. At that time no state had passed legislation protecting tenants from evictions in retaliation for tenant organizing or reporting code violations to local authorities, and many states had archaic landlord-tenant laws permitting a variety of landlord practices which limited a tenant's security of tenure. Landlords in every state had an absolute right to repossess property rented on a month-to-month tenancy with 30-days' notice for whatever reason or for no reason at all. Some states permitted landlords to change the locks on a tenant's door, shut off utilities, or even move a tenant's possessions out onto the street without a court order. While the condition of units and security of tenure were major issues, rents were less problematic in 1950. Nationally the average renter in 1950 paid about 19 percent of income for rent, and during the period between 1950 and 1970 the proportion of real income (adjusted for increasing income and inflation) used for rent did not increase and even declined slightly. In this context tenants were primarily concerned with physical improvement in their units, at least to minimum standards of health and safety, and with eliminating the most oppressive landlord practices which intruded on security of tenure. Reduced rents have always been a part of the tenant agenda, but in a context of reasonably affordable housing, this was not a paramount issue. Furthermore, most tenant groups perceived that they simply lacked the votes to achieve rent stabilization throughout most of the thirty postwar years of affluence.

Today conditions have changed dramatically. The best available national statistics on housing quality are contained in the *Annual Housing Survey*—a sophisticated national survey of housing conducted by the Bureau of the Census and the U.S. Department of Housing and Urban Development each year. The 1979 *Annual Housing Survey* reported that less than 5 percent of the U.S. housing stock was dilapidated or lacked plumbing. Physical quality of units had shrunk in importance. Similarly, substantial progress was made during this period with respect to security of tenure. By the late 1970s most states had banned the most oppressive landlord practices. Lockouts, utility, shutoffs, and landlord self-help remedies are illegal in virtually all states today, often backed up with stiff civil and criminal penalties. By the late 1970s 38 states had adopted some form of law prohibiting eviction of tenants in retaliation for organizing tenant unions or informing authorities of code violations. While most tenants can still be evicted with thirty-days' notice for no cause, the two and a half million tenants of low-rent public housing can only be evicted for just cause and tenants in some jurisdictions are protected from eviction except under very limited conditions under rent stabilization laws. While issues of housing quality and security of tenure have not disappeared they have shrunk in importance. At the same time the issues of affordability and even the existence of a rental housing sector have emerged as the key concerns.

The above analysis suggests that both the availability of rental housing and affordability will remain the dominant problems in this sector throughout the 1980s and beyond. Pressure to preserve the rental stock by limiting conversion should intensify. Conflict over rent stabilization should increase as the effects of lack of production of new rental units are broadly felt. If price escalation slows so that landlords feel they must cover costs from rents rather than appreciation we can expect a major escalation of conflict in this area. To the extent that landlords choose to manage cash flow problems by undermaintenance, condition-related housing struggles may re-emerge with renewed intensity.

PROGRESSIVE HOUSING STRUGGLE
IN AUSTERITY CONDITIONS

Massive structural changes are occurring in the housing sector of the United States economy. Social and political conflict is already occurring, but it is moving in many different directions. What should be done? How can the energy released by the fissures now opening in many institutional structures be directed to make housing conditions better, rather than worse, or at a minimum assure that either the benefits of affluence are more equitably distributed or the burdens of continued austerity more justly borne?

Today many individuals and organizations are putting forward suggestions to help make housing more affordable. The suggestions range from building adobe structures, to rent control, to nationalizing Savings and Loan Institutions, to allowing banks to charge whatever interest rate on mortgages the market will bear. Many proposals which are diametrically opposed are held out as promoting housing affordability. For example most realtors and their lobbyists argue that permitting new home-buyers to assume existing loans (at lower than current interest rates) is essential to keeping housing affordable. On the other hand the financial intermediaries and their lobbyists argue that if this is done it will hurt their liquidity and long-term ability to survive and prosper. Who is right? This article cannot explain all the myriad solutions proposed. But it can lay out a framework to understanding them and an approach to evaluating their merits.

New Production For Use

Much of what is currently written about housing affordability focuses on increasing the supply of new housing. Advocates for builders' associations and others depict the problem as one of supply/demand imbalance. The idea here is that there are too few housing units for the people who need them. If new units are built prices will drop.

This kind of analysis does not explain what happened in the United States in the 1970s and solutions to the housing affordability problem grounded on such analysis are questionable. As indicated above the supply of housing in the United States increased rapidly during the 1970s, more rapidly than any previous decade. Housing starts outpaced new household formation by healthy margins. However house prices escalated rapidly, exactly the opposite of what theoretically should have happened according to the more-supply-lower-prices lobby.

Only about 2 percent of the U.S. housing stock is newly built in a given year. Even if production levels were doubled, effects on costs in the 96 percent of the existing stock would take many years to be felt. Thus new production does not provide even a medium-term solution to the housing affordability problem.

This is not to say that questions of *how much* of available resources should be used for new housing production are unimportant. This is a key normative question each society must ask for itself. Most countries socialist and capitalist, rich and poor, place new housing construction lower on their list of priorities than national defense and economic development and usually below other human services such as health and education. By world standards the United States invests modestly in new housing production and clearly has the wherewithall to spend more. The National Low Income Housing Coalition has calculated that the low-income housing budget cuts proposed by the Reagan administration for 1982 and 1983 are greater than the proposed 1983 increase in the defense budget. At this level the federal government has made a very significant guns-not-houses choice.

Moving from the macro-level allocation issue to the composition of whatever wedge of GNP is set aside for new housing production, it is clear that national priorities are askew. As indicated above in recent years we have primarily seen construction of large, expensive, and luxurious new housing units during a period of stagnant economic growth, level or declining real wages, high unemployment, and massively increased front-end financing costs for housing. New housing construction has served primarily as an investment outlet for people who have gained equity in their homes and want to trade up.

New production for use would focus available resources very differently. It would stress increased densities, smaller units with fewer amenities, and design modifications to provide adequate shelter at affordable costs. There are many devices to do this: density bonuses to encourage more compact growth, in-fill housing projects on vacant urban land, programs to inventory and recycle surplus government property, granny flats (modest units which can be placed in the back yard of existing houses), mini-condos, use of air rights to cut land costs, compact planned unit development, and a host of proposals to eliminate unnecessarily restrictive building code requirements which increase housing costs. Movement in these directions and away from use of whatever capital is allocated to new production from large, luxurious, housing is clearly in order.

While housing affordability is only weakly related to the supply of houses and the demand from people, it is intimately related to issues of the supply of investment outlets and demand for high returns on capital.

Redirecting Housing Investment

During the 1970s the *supply* of safe and profitable investment opportunities in the United States dropped. A plummeting stock market, unstable overseas climate, gyrating gold and silver markets, and tottering auto industry all limited the traditional outlets for investment capital. Meanwhile the amount of capital looking for outlets remained high—indeed grew. Housing was one of the few investments during the 1970s which appeared safe to investors, particularly small investors without access to sophisticated counseling. The enormous price escalation in housing is better explained in terms of capital bidding up the price of the limited pool of relatively safe investment outlets.

Currently many conservative, neo-conservative, and liberal analysts have concluded that there is too much capital invested in housing. During the 1980s we can expect a variety of devices to try to siphon off capital from housing and encourage investment to flow in other directions. If blunt policy instruments are used—such as limiting the amount of funds available for mortgages—the entire housing sector could be damaged further. If policy instruments discriminate between types of housing (for example, shifting investment away from further cost escalation generally

and further investment in new housing production), they could both benefit the economy and make the housing situation better.

Redistributing the Unearned Increment in Housing

While there is an emerging concensus that too much capital has been invested in housing recently there is little or no recognition of the enormous
unearned increment in housing and almost no policy initiatives which address this fact.

As indicated above the approximately sixty percent of the U.S. population who were members of households qualifying as long-term homeowners have received about a $1.5 trillion unearned increment as a result
of price escalation in the United States during the 1970s.

Why not recapture some of this unearned increment? It could then
be used either to address the housing needs of those who have been shut
out by the changes or for other purposes deemed socially useful such as
elimination of the federal budget deficit. If long-term homeowners were
allowed to keep an amount equivalent to what they would have earned if
they had their own money invested in a T-bill instead of housing and only
the balance recovered, there should still be about a trillion dollar recovery: enough to eliminate the 1983 Reagan budget deficit ten times over
or substantially eliminate the entire U.S. housing affordability problem.

There is no technical problem with recapturing windfall profits.
Donald Hagman of UCLA has catalogued windfall recovery devices not
only from the United States, but also other English-speaking countries.

Two basic approaches are to: (a) increase real property taxes (essentially an excise tax on the annual consumption of shelter) and (b) increase capital gains taxes on sale. Of these two devices capital gains taxes
have the advantage of recapturing windfall profit only at the point when
profit is realized. Presently homeowners—the numerical majority in the
U.S. and most states—have succeeded in reducing, not increasing, property
taxes through initiatives such as California's Proposition 13 and Massachusetts' Proposition 2½. Similarly the Reagan administration's new accelerated cost recovery program makes more, not less, favorable treatment
of capital gains on the sale of real property. Politically the votes are not
there to achieve reform at the present time.

Another way in which some portion of the unearned increment might
be recovered for the U.S. treasury would be through changes in the federal income tax laws to reduce favorable tax treatment for some classes
of owners who do not need what are in effect large housing subsidies.
U.S. taxpayers are subsidizing all owners of housing by permitting various deductions from federal income taxes which would otherwise be owed.

The largest of these tax breaks is the deduction of mortgage interest payments, which amounts to a highly regressive subsidy for homeownership, amounting to over $30 billion a year. This is often justified on the ground that homeownership is a public good and should be encouraged. But can we afford to continue to subsidize ownership of large and luxurious housing and second homes when a third of the nation, which does not own, faces such difficult times in housing? If homeowners were permitted to deduct interest only on an amount up to what is necessary to purchase one modest (for example, 900 square feet) home this would have a significant impact on redirecting investment away from luxury construction. The amount of increased federal income tax revenue would not approach the trillion dollars discussed above, but could greatly ease the housing needs of lower and lower-middle-income households if it were used for housing subsides. The very rich who want to live in very expensive housing and own more than one house should be permitted to do so, but not at the taxpayer's expense.

Managing the Existing Housing Stock

Since only about 2 percent of the U.S. housing stock is newly built each year, most strategies should focus on the other 98 percent. Since new units cannot be built at costs which match those of much of the existing stock this housing should be seen as an irreplaceable resource.

Many new interventions are emerging to assure that this irreplaceable resource remains both physically available and affordable. Some measures are aimed at simply keeping what housing stock there is intact. In the most distressed neighborhoods loss of housing through abandonment, vandalism, and arson is a severe problem. In revitalizing areas the escalation of land values and house prices often makes it economically advantageous to demolish older and more affordable housing and replace it with either luxury housing or commercial buildings. Moratoria on demolitions and permanent controls are springing into existence in many cities to retard or limit demolitions.

Another stock management issue involves conversion of existing housing—both physical alteration and changes of ownership or use status. The existing pool of affordable housing can be protected from elimination through conversion. Most common are condominium conversion ordinances which limit the number of conversions which may take place and the terms on which tenants are treated. Some cities have also limited conversion of residential hotels to tourist facilities or conversion of apartments to commercial use. Some cities have taken positive steps to promote conversions in the other direction—changes which will increase the pool of affordable housing. An interesting development involves programs to legalize small rental units within existing houses. So-called in-law units can usually be added by making modest structural changes and at little cost. They can be rented at affordable rents and still turn a reasonable profit for the owners. Such units make a more efficient use of the existing housing stock and an excellent resource, for elderly persons, students, single working people, and childless couples.

More important and more controversial than measures to preserve what housing is *available* are measures to assure that available housing remains *affordable*. Rent stabilization has emerged as one of the most bitterly contested issues at the local level. Another set of devices involve transferring ownership of multi-family housing or undertaking new construction under different ownership arrangements. Thus nonprofit housing development corporations may undertake housing for some sectors of the population (elderly, low and moderate income) without the profit motive. Another technique is to build or convert units to limited equity cooperative status. Under this form of ownership housing units are cooperatively owned, and the owner who moves out may take out of the project the original investment plus a fair return (for example, an amount to adjust for inflation or what the owner would have received in a T-bill). Participants in limited equity cooperatives do not realize speculative gain and the units will continue to be resold at affordable amounts in perpetuity.

CONCLUSION

As in all times of crisis and change there are opportunities as well as dangers in the U.S. housing system in the 1980s. While the massive unearned increment in shelter may remain through the decade with large profits pocketed by owners and continued distortion of the new production system, progressive political organization may achieve some redistribution of the unearned increment, and production for use. While gentrification may lead to forced displacement of low- and moderate-income renters, minorities, and working-class and low-status white-collar workers, it may provoke a new level of organization and progressive alternatives by minorities. While pressure on the existing irreplaceable stock may result in condominium conversions and demolitions, it may provoke comprehensive strategies to insure the availability and affordability of this stock, including widespread use of nonprofit housing corporations and limited equity cooperatives. Correct analysis of the changes which are taking place and action consistent with that analysis can affect the shape of shelter in the United States in the decade to come.

REFERENCES

Alonso, W., "The Population Factor and Urban Structure," Cambridge, Mass.: Harvard University Center for Population Studies (Working paper no. 102, 1977).

Auger, D., "The Politics of Revitalization in Gentrifying Neighborhoods," *Journal of the American Planning Association,* 45, no. 4, 1979.

Cybriewski, R., "Social Aspects of Neighborhood Change," *Annals of the Association of American Geographers,* 68, 1978, 17–33.

Diamond, D. B., Jr., "Taxes, Inflation, Speculation, and the Cost of Home-ownership," *Journal of the American Real Estate and Urban Economics Association* (Fall 1980).

Downs, A., *The Future of Rental Housing in America* (Washington, D.C.: The Brookings Institution, 1979).

Grebler, L., and F. Mittlebach, *The Inflation of Housing Prices: Its Extent, Causes, and Consequences* (Lexington, Mass.: Lexington Press, 1979).

Hartman, C., D. Keating, and R. LeGates, *Displacement: How to Fight It* (Berkeley: National Housing Law Project, 1982).

LeGates, R., and C. Hartman, *Displacement* (Washington, D.C.: U.S. Legal Services Corp., 1981).

Lowry, Ira S., "Inflation Indexes for Rental Housing" (working draft, Santa Monica, Calif.: The Rand Corp., 1981).

Sternlieb, G., *Urban Housing in a Post-Shelter Environment* (San Francisco: Federal Home Loan Bank Board, 1978).

U.S. Department of Housing and Urban Development, *The Conversion of Rental Housing and Condominiums and Cooperatives* (Washington, D.C.: Government Printing Office, 1980).

7

Large Builders, Federal Housing Programs, and Postwar Suburbanization

BARRY CHECKOWAY

I

It is customary in the literature on postwar American suburbanization to neglect the decision process and institutional context by which suburban places were established and developed. In one popular image, for example, postwar residential suburbs "exploded" on the American landscape or appeared as the sudden product of unspecified or invisible hands. Once there were rural farmlands and small villages at the edge of the city, then suddenly there were Levittown, Part Forest, and even Los Angeles, all the overnight work of get-rich-quick developers or families in flight (Editors of *Fortune,* 1958). In another image, postwar suburbs resulted from a virtual "tidal wave of metropolitan expansion." Suburbanization was no overnight explosion at all, but only the latest episode in a secular shift of metropolitan population from center to periphery and an ad hoc decision process fragmented and diffused among a large number of separate decision-makers (Blumenfeld, 1954; an earlier example is given in Warner, 1962). In yet another image, postwar suburbs resulted from the shifting preferences of consumers. Suburban development prevailed because the

Reprinted from the *International Journal of Urban and Regional Research* 4:1 (1980).

This paper was presented at the 1978 annual meeting of the American Political Science Association. Among those who commented on earlier versions are Bernard Frieden, Herbert Gans, Mark Gelfand, Chester Hartman, Seymour Mandelbaum, Roger Montgomery, Heywood Sanders, Allen Wakstein, Frederick Wirt, Michael Zuckerman, and colleagues at the Childhood and Government Project at the University of California at Berkeley.

public demanded it, directed government to provide incentives for suburban production and consumption, and fueled a revolution in the residential construction industry (Dobriner, 1958; Donaldson, 1969; Masotti
and Hadden, 1973). Suburbanization appears as a product of "forces"
originating elsewhere. It has an uncanny, dramaturgical quality. It appears
irreversible.

In all this, there has been little effort to conceptualize postwar suburbanization as a product of decisions and institutional interactions. Yet there
was no magic in the appearance of postwar suburbs. On the contrary, at
any moment metropolitan form is the product of understandable processes
put in motion and perpetuated by its key decision-makers. But there are
few accounts that approach suburbanization as a process rather than as
something to be taken for granted, and little is known about its principal
postwar participants, their interests and aims, their partners and hand-
maidens. There *are* studies of the decision behavior of home-buying consumers, but few which examine the prior, precipitating decisions in this
period (an exception is Clawson, 1971; see also Harvey, 1973).

This essay reports a search for the historical background of the decisions and institutions that together "built the suburbs." Who were the
key actors? What factors influenced their decisions? What interests and
values were involved? Who participated in—and who was excluded from—
the process? And what are the lessons of this history? The focus is on
large residential builders and how they were supported by the federal government. They do not comprise all those who participated in postwar
suburban development, but they are among the most important. They have
been selected for their importance in postwar suburban *residential* development.[1]

II

The growth of many postwar suburbs was precipitated by decisions of
large residential builders to select and develop suburban locations. There
was nothing new about suburban development in America. What was new
in this period was the developed capacity of large builders to take raw
suburban land, divide it into parcels and streets, install needed services,
apply mass production methods to residential construction, and sell the
finished product to unprecedented numbers of consumers. These decisions
are best explained in terms of the changing market conditions of housing
and developed technological capacity of housebuilding itself.

There was a shortage of adequate housing in postwar America. In
1947 it was estimated that between 2,750,000 and 4,400,000 families

were living with other families and 500,000 more were occupying transient or non-family quarters. Although estimates of the quantity of housing required to replace deteriorated structures and stay abreast of population and family increases ranged between 1,000,000 and 1,500,000 units per year, the building industry was unable to construct more than 500,000 units per year. Housing surveys in 1947 found more than 6,000,000 low-income urban families either searching for better housing or planning to do so (Rosenman, 1946; Newcomb and Kyle, 1947; Hauser and Jaffe, 1947; Bauer, 1948).

Several factors were cited to explain the housing shortage. Some analysts attributed it to wartime conditions and military priorities which had virtually stopped civilian residential construction and created shortages among postwar consumers (Abrams, 1948). Others attributed it to increases in family formation and birth rates which had resulted in a population that was eager for better housing (Glick, 1957; Taeuber and Taeuber, 1958). Others attributed it to postwar prosperity and a rising standard of living which had resulted in a growing demand for more products and consumers with purchasing power to back up demand (Saulnier et al., 1958; Haar, 1960; Miller, 1965). Yet others attributed it to the shortcomings of the residential construction industry. Housebuilding was dominated by small and local firms lacking the capacity to reduce shortages and reach demand. The typical small builder could not employ a permanent labor force, develop a research staff, bargain for materials in volume at lower cost, or buy a substantial area of land for large-scale development.[2] Housebuilding was, in a popular contemporary image, the "industry capitalism forgot" (*Fortune,* 36, August 1947, 61–7).

The national production of housing increased significantly in the period that followed. In the decade after 1950 more than 15,000,000 new housing units were started. The rate of new residential construction in 1950–59 was approximately twice that in 1940–49, six times that in 1930–39. The number of new housing units started was 515,000 in 1939, 1,466,000 in 1949, and 1,554,000 in 1959. In 1946, housing production almost quadrupled; in 1950 the housebuilding industry produced more

Table 7.1. New Housing Units Started in the U.S. by Decade, 1930–59

	New Housing Units Started
1950–59	15,068,000
1940–49	7,443,000
1930–39	2,734,000

Source: US Bureau of the Census, 1966, 18.

houses than in any one year in history. Although the shortage remained, production advances were nonetheless significant (Maisel, 1953, 11ff).

Important in postwar production advances were basic changes in the residential construction industry. What distinguished the period was an increase in the number, size, and importance of large residential builders. Postwar studies by Sherman Maisel in the San Francisco Bay Area documented the primacy of these builders. Maisel examined all Bay Area residential builders in 1949–50 and identified four basic types by size. A builder was classified as large if he annually completed 100 or more houses, had a volume of more than $1,000,000 and more than $600,000 in total assets, and employed 100 or more workers and a large overhead staff. Maisel found that although small builders were the most numerous type, they were of less overall importance than the small number of larger builders that built most of the houses and dominated the market. In 1949, large and medium builders comprised only 2 percent of the local total but accounted for 55 percent of the houses produced. Follow-up studies showed that between 1950 and 1960 large builders increased their share to 74 percent of all houses produced. By 1960 large builders built three out of every four houses in this area (Maisel, 1953; follow-up studies include Herzog, 1963, 19–32).

The Bay Area findings typified the national pattern. Several builders had developed gradually and grown before 1940, and others were born of the defense programs that followed. In 1939 it was estimated that there were 480 large and medium builders that together accounted for less than 20 percent of the houses produced nationally. In 1949 there were 3750 builders of this size and they accounted for 45 percent of the total number of units built. This was more than six times greater in 1949 than in 1939 (Maisel, 1953, chapter 2). Fully 70 percent of the houses built in 1949 were built by only 10 percent of the builders. Large builders

Table 7.2. Number of New Housing Units Started and Percentage Built by Large Builders, 1938–59

	New Housing Units Started	Percentage of Houses Built by Large Builders
1959	1,554,000	64
1949	1,466,000	24
1938	406,000	5

Sources: 1938 data from US Bureau of Labor Statistics (1940); 1949 data from US Department of Labor (1954); 1959 data from National Association of Homebuilders (1960, 17). Data on the housebuilding industry in this period is generally unavailable. On this point, see Maisel (1953, 3–9).

alone accounted for 5 percent of all houses built in 1938, 24 percent in
1949, and 64 percent in 1959. This period thus saw a significant increase
both in the number of large builders and in the number of houses built
by them.

The large builder was distinguished by his size, scale, and operating
structure. These were not small and local craftsmen but large, often national operators identified more with automobile industrialists than with
small operators of their own field. The typical large builder reduced costs
through direct buying of materials, purchased in carload lots, maintained
large inventories, developed new and more efficient subcontractual relationships, and specialized his labor force. He applied government financial aids and housing research to his work. Government research laboratories cooperated with large builders to make advances in materials and
equipment (Anon, 1954, 42–56; Dietz, 1959 et al., 1959), in land development and site planning (Spring 1959), and in faster and less costly
methods (Sasaki, 1959; Whyte, 1958). Mass production and prefabrication promised factory engineering, standardized dimensions, preassembled
units and prefitted systems.[3] It also promised more rapid construction and
higher production.

The large builder also was distinguished by his suburban orientation.
Mass production required large tracts of land typically found near the city
limits or in suburban areas beyond. In the suburbs was open and available
land at the right price and without restriction, and the promise of excellent transportation by automobile and expressways. Retail, manufacturing, wholesale, office, and service establishments all sought suburban locations in the postwar period. Given the orthodox market assumptions and
locational principles, postwar suburbanization was a logical alternative to
investment in the central city.[4]

The overall result was a significant increase in postwar American
suburban development. In 1950 the growth rate of suburbs was more than
ten times that of central cities. Between 1950 and 1955 the total metropolitan population increased by 11.6 million people, 9.2 million of whom
were suburban. Between 1950 and 1956, 64 percent of the net national
increase in housing was in metropolitan areas. Of this, 19.4 percent was
in central cities, 80.6 percent was in suburbs. New residential construction
was by far the most important single factor of change: the total volume
of new construction in suburbs was almost three times that in central
cities in this period (U.S. Bureau of the Census, 1958; 1966; U.S. Department of Labor, 1959). It was among the great population migrations
in American history.

Large-scale residential development spearheaded and symbolized the
movement. Orange County, California, increased in population by 65 per-

cent between 1940 and 1950. The increments outside Los Angeles alone were phenomenal. Torrance increased by 124 percent, Lynwood by 133 percent, Monterey Park by 140 percent, Arcadia by 154 percent, Montebello by 171 percent, Manhattan Beach by 175 percent, Compton by 198 percent, and Hawthorne Covina by 350 percent. Levittown, New York, had more than 51,000 people living in 15,000 identical houses by 1950. Park Forest, Illinois, housed 30,000 on 2400 acres 30 miles south of Chicago by 1956. In 1957 the editors of *Fortune* estimated that suburban land was being bulldozed at a rate of 3000 acres per day. It was a triumph for the suburbs and the large builders who built them.

III

Levitt and Sons exemplified the growing potential of large residential builders in postwar suburbanization. The firm had been founded in 1929 by Abraham Levitt, whose early background in real estate helped him to recognize the profitability of large-scale housebuilding operations, and by his two sons, Abraham and William. In the 1930s, Levitt had built custom homes for affluent families in suburban Long Island and Westchester County, New York, and the company continued to build by conventional methods until the Second World War. A wartime ban on most civilian construction forced Levitt to build low-cost housing in government defense areas. This experience gave Levitt an opportunity to experiment with prefabrication, to grasp the principles of mass production, and to imagine a housebuilding scheme of unprecedented scale. By the end of the war, Levitt had grown in size, developed in capital, and was ready to expand (Gans, 1967; Larrabee, 1948; Levitt, 1951; Liell, 1952; Levitt, 1968).

In 1947 Levitt acquired 1400 acres of Long Island farmland about 30 miles from New York City and proceeded to revolutionize the housebuilding industry. By 1948 Levitt was completing more than 35 houses per day and 150 houses per week and rapidly selling the low-cost product. More than 17,000 identical houses for over 70,000 people were finally built side-by-side in uniform rows and sold for the same price of $7990. By 1950 "Levittown" was praised as "an accomplishment of heroic proportions" and the Levitt house was known as "the best house for the money in the United States."[5]

How did Levitt do it? Levitt adapted assembly line techniques to the mass production of housing. An army of trucks speeding along new-laid roads stopped and delivered neatly packaged bundles of materials at exact 100 foot intervals. Giant machines followed the trucks, digging rectangular foundations in which heating pipes were embedded. Each site then became an assembly line on which houses were built. Men, material, and machines moved past each site in teams, each performing one of 26 operations over and over again from site to site according to standards derived from systematic studies of time and motion. Every possible part and system was pre-assembled, prefabricated or precut to specification and size in the factory, and then brought to the site ready to assemble with machinery developed just for the purpose. As operations were shifted from site to shop, scheduling and delivery grew in importance. Materials reached the site only minutes before a team would arrive to perform its particular operation. Mechanization and labor-saving machinery, forbidden or prohibitive in traditional operations, were everywhere evident in Levittown. Levitt was less a builder, more a manufacturer of houses.[6]

Each Levittown house was controlled by Levitt from start to finish. Over several years Levitt had recruited executives with specialized competence in all aspects of housebuilding. Levitt also had developed a construction crew which was thoroughly familiar with company techniques and capable of any construction task. Construction workers were non-unionized and assured of steady employment. Such stability and permanence were atypical of the housebuilding industry.

Levitt applied vertical organization and rationalization as rigorously as housebuilding would allow. He altered traditional distribution channels and reduced costs. Lumber, for example, came from Levitt's own company and was cut from his own timber on his own equipment to the exact specification and size at which it later was used in assembling the house, enabling further savings in handling and freight. Nails and concrete blocks were made in Levitt's own factory by contractors working only for him. Those few materials not produced by Levitt were bought in carload quantities directly from manufacturers by Levitt's own wholesaler, eliminating middle-men and markups. The typical builder was entangled in a costly distribution web. Levitt in comparison eliminated charges and even influenced product design to suit his own needs.[7]

Levitt also had an enviable capital position and a profitable partnership with government. In addition to personal resources, he boasted the largest line of credit ever offered a privately owned American housebuilding firm. This proved an important competitive advantage at every stage. He had easy access to government credit and financial aids. For large builders like Levitt, the federal government offered billions of dollars of credit and insured loans up to 95 percent of the value of the house. Such builders easily received FHA "production advances" before purchases were made. Levitt was able to get FHA commitments to finance 4000 houses before clearing the land. Veterans using the G.I. Bill of Rights could buy in Levittown with no down payment and instalments of only $56 a month.

The completed Levitt house was attractive to consumers. Levitt spent more money on consumer research than any builder of small houses in history. The Levitt house—and Levittown itself—was meticulously designed to match consumer preferences. Each house was small, detached, single family, Cape Cod in style, and centrally located on a small lot in a development in the suburbs. To ensure the sale, each house came complete with radiant heating, fireplace, electric range and refrigerator, washer, built-in television, and landscaped grounds. All were included at no added cost. For middle-income consumers, Levittown offered a virtual dream house, and Levitt was the dream's entrepreneur.[8]

Levitt also rationalized and simplified his marketing and merchandising. Full-page advertisements directed customers to a display building adjacent to Levittown. Inside were carefully decorated model rooms and all the appliances, design innovations, and gadgets for which Levitt was known; a scale model of the completed development; and several salespeople to answer questions, offer advice, and take deposits. The entire financing and titling transaction was reduced to two half-hour steps, one to purchase and another to clear title. Contract forms already stamped with fixed title enabled clerks to sign up to 350 buyers per day. In minutes customers could be assured of a completed transaction. Levitt could get three banks, a mortgage broker, and the construction superintendent on a single telephone to arrange several thousand FHA and VA mortgages for veterans. Levitt handled all legal and real estate details and charged $10 flat for closing costs. For an inexperienced buyer entering the market for the first time and looking for investment security, Levitt offered a creditable commodity and proven reliability. In 1947 Levitt undersold his nearest competitor by $1500 and still earned $1000 profit on each $7990 house.[9]

In 1950 Levitt sought to expand further and to create an entire community somewhere on the eastern seaboard. Levittown, New York, was the largest housing development ever built by a single builder, but now he wanted to build more than houses alone. The scheme was detailed by Alfred Levitt in the *Journal of the American Institute of Planners* in 1951. The proposed community could incorporate past Levitt experiences and "the principles of good planning laid down by leaders in the field." It would include neighborhood residential areas divided by parks, playgrounds, and schools; an industrial area separated by a green-wooded shelter belt; and an interior expressway connecting the neighborhoods and

on which commercial facilities would be located. Because all land would
be owned in advance, it would be possible "to plan right down to the last
tree and shrub" (Levitt, 1968).

Construction originally was intended for Long Island and several
hundred New Yorkers had made cash deposits before examining the proposed plans or the model house. But the Korean national emergency
forced postponement of construction, and Levitt instead proposed to
adapt the plan to one of several critical defense areas around the country.
He sought a large area of land requiring little modification and easily converted to large-scale use. He also sought an active housing market, assurances of consumer demand, and access to government financial aids aimed
at large builders. Several sites were considered: all were suburbs.

Levitt decided to locate outside Philadelphia in Lower Bucks County,
Pennsylvania. This area offered agricultural land on the suburban fringe
of a large city which shared strongly in the postwar housing shortages. It
also offered assurances of government financial aids. A prior decision by
United States Steel to construct a major defense-related steel plant had
made the area eligible for designation as a critical defense area. But the
particular location was not key. It is fair to assume that any of several
similar suburban sites also would have been acceptable. (These decisions
are described in detail in Checkoway, 1977a, chapter 3.)

Levitt was the largest but not the only builder of his kind. Large
builders were increasing in number and production outside every major
city. Among them was John Mowbray outside Baltimore, Waverly Taylor
outside Washington, D.C., Don Scholz outside Toledo, Maurice Fishman
outside Cleveland, Irvin Blietz outside Chicago, J. D. Nichols outside
Kansas City, Del Webb outside Phoenix, Carl Gellert and Ellie Stoneson
outside San Francisco, and Dave Bohannon, Fritz Burns, and James Price
outside several cities. They symbolized a revolution in housebuilding and
were instrumental in postwar suburbanization. Maisel said of them:

> These are the new giants in an industry once populated by pygmies. Here,
> at the very peak of their housebuilding pyramid, are the leaders of con-
> struction who are not content merely to build houses. They construct
> communities. (Maisel, 1953, p. 95)

IV

State support of large residential builders by federal government programs
was crucial in postwar suburban development. For, in addition to the
changing market conditions of housing and the developed technological
capacity of large builders, some measures were required to guarantee the

mortgage money, share the risk, and ensure the profitability of the suburban enterprise. Although there was nothing new about government aids to private industry in America, postwar conditions combined to enlarge the federal role in the housing field.

The federal housing policy that followed was mostly suburban in its orientation.[10] The Housing Act of 1949 authorized $1 billion in loans and $500 million in capital grants for slum clearance and urban redevelopment over a five-year period. In 1949 Congress also increased the amount that could be insured under the FHA home mortgage program to $6 billion. In 1950 Congress increased the FHA mortgage insurance authorization by $2.25 billion, amended FHA sales housing programs to provide incentives for production of three- and four-bedroom houses, liberalized FHA terms on loans for manufactured houses and large-scale residential construction, established a new FHA program for homes in suburban and outlying areas, and reduced the low-rent public housing authorization to 75,000 units for the year. In 1951 Congress increased the FHA mortgage insurance authorization by $1.5 billion, authorized loans to facilitate the production of prefabricated houses and major components for new houses, authorized $60 million for loans and grants for facilities and services in critical defense areas, and further reduced the public housing authorization to 50,000 units for the year. In 1953 Congress increased the FHA mortgage insurance authorization by $1.5 billion, liberalized FHA terms on loans for new owner-occupied homes and in suburban area, and further reduced the public housing authorization to 35,000 units for the year and subsequent years. Early in 1954 Congress again reduced the public housing authorization to 20,000 units and added the condition that unwanted public housing under construction could be stopped by the locality. The Housing Act of 1954 increased all FHA mortgage insurance authorizations by another $1.5 billion, liberalized the amounts and terms of FHA sales housing mortgages, and established another FHA mortgage insurance program for single-family dwellings in suburban and outlying areas (U.S. Congress Subcommittee on Housing and Urban Development, 1975; see also the various works of Charles Abrams). The 1954 act was hailed by large builders as "an aid to private enterprise." Public policy is not what is stated or intended but what is actually done. Federal housing policy was mostly suburban in its orientation.

A class of consumers was ready to purchase new houses, and the federal government sought to effectuate their demands through special incentives and financial aids to large suburban builders. A Veteran's Emergency Housing Program was enacted in 1946 to facilitate the financing of priority housing for returning veterans. The prefabrication industry got an important boost under this program, as government contracts were offered to all prefabrication firms and several hundred thousand dwellings were finally built. The Housing and Home Finance Agency was established in 1947 and soon began cooperating with government laboratories, universities, and the largest builders to develop products, methods, and ideas for housing. The emphasis was on new single-family suburban houses. New construction was by far the most important factor of change in the national housing inventory in this period (U.S. Bureau of the Census, 1958, 14).

Another focus was on large builders. The federal government encouraged small builders to grow large and large builders to further grow to a size that would be economically more meaningful. To the builder ignored by past federal programs, noted Charles Abrams, "FHA brought a rare prize." And the larger the builder, the larger the prize. Large builders more easily received credit advances and more easily negotiated with the FHA. Large operators and powerful economic institutions were among the principal beneficiaries of federal programs. Small operators were either excluded, penalized, or driven from the market. Any builder who could promise a large quantity of mortgages was eagerly sought after by a federal program (Abrams, 1946, 232; Stone, 1973; Eichler and Kaplan, 1967).

Another focus was on suburban residential construction. FHA, a profit-making enterprise based upon bankers' standards, encouraged new building in the suburbs and discouraged development in the central city. Its overall concern for "economic soundness" shaped a belief that poor and minority neighborhoods were bad credit risks and placed further emphasis on homeownership, new construction, and large builders. Mark Gelfand documents how builders and buyers generally could take advantage of FHA home mortgage insurance programs only if they located themselves beyond the inner city.[11] The result was that the vast majority of FHA houses were built in the suburbs and the suburbs could not have expanded as they did in the postwar years without FHA.[12]

Other federal programs also promoted suburbanization. The federal highway program made possible the roads that made large tracts of suburban land more accessible for development. The roads and highways that resulted laced metropolitan areas and transformed farmlands and old villages into real estate for suburban developers (Gelfand, 1975, 222–35; Howard, 1957, 38–39; 1959; Mumford, 1968; Leavitt, 1970; Rae, 1971; Muller, 1976). Federal tax policies also promoted suburban construction. Federal income tax deductions on owner-occupied houses made government contribute a fifth or more of costs of homeownership and virtually subsidized the new suburban houses (Meyerson et al., 1962, 236–37; other federal suburban programs are described in Arnold, 1971).

The suburban orientation was the direct result of the effort to stimulate production in the housing field and the national economy. The focus on homeownership and new construction stimulated the production and consumption of house-related goods in the marketplace and the flow of capital in the entire economy. It allowed for capital outlays in public works, physical facilities, social services, transportation systems and more. It offered incentives to realtors, large builders, bankers, lumber dealers, highway contractors, automobile manufacturers and others. Postwar suburbanization was a "built form" and an economic instrument for production, and federal legislators were predisposed to facilitate the process.

V

Large builders also organized to determine the direction of the programs which benefited them. There was nothing new about their efforts. The National Association of Real Estate Boards (NAREB) from its inception had a standing committee concerned with federal legislation and was instrumental in the housing acts of the 1930s. (The standard work on NAREB is Davis, 1958. On NAREB influence in the 1930s, see McDonnell, 1957.) The National Association of Home Builders (NAHB) originated in NAREB and then developed as an independent organization concerned primarily with large builders and new suburban houses (Mason, n.d.; Lilley, 1973). Postwar shortages and the promise of federal intervention necessitated more active involvement in legislation. In 1942, the Realtor's Washington Committee was formed to represent, promote, and protect the industry's position in Congress. This committee was led by NAREB and NAHB and was backed by the U.S. Savings and Loan League, the U.S. Chamber of Commerce, the American Bankers Association, the Mortgage Bankers Association of America, the Building Products Institute, the National Retail Lumber Dealers Association, the Associated General Contractors, the National Association of Retail Lumber Dealers Association, the National Clay Products Association, the Producers Council, and other trade associations representing apartment house owners, building materials manufacturers, lumber industrialists, subcontractors, prefabricators and others. (The formation of the Washington Realtor's Committee is described in Davies, 1966, chapter 2.)

The housebuilding lobby became one of the most powerful political groups in Congress. It operated from a well-defined although not singular position. It sought to facilitate the production and sales of new suburban houses. It favored FHA, VA, and other programs to remove risks and ensure profits of residential construction, and opposed public housing as a "socialistic" threat to private enterprise. It employed pressure tactics which were fundamentally grass roots in nature. NAREB alone reported 44,000 members in 1100 communities, NAHB 16,000 members in 130 local chapters. Local affiliates placed Congressmen on boards of directors, thus contributing to congressional understanding of, and responsiveness to, their position. On any given day the lobby could flood Congress with letters, telegrams, and telephone calls from influential constituents in every part of the country. Local leaders were also major advertisers in local media, thus contributing to media willingness to report their position and lend editorial support. A full-time, well-paid Washington staff prepared leaders for participation in hearings and meetings, produced form letters for constituents to mail, conducted active public information programs, sponsored homeownership fairs and displays, maintained a constant flow of press releases and news feature stories, and wrote model curricula for school teachers. Large sums of money were spent on advertising to persuade consumers to prefer homeownership and new construction and to direct government to provide programs to facilitate these preferences.[13]

The housebuilding lobby influenced the legislation and programs that developed. It effectively delayed the Taft-Ellender-Wagner housing act for four years mainly out of oposition to the proposed public housing. When the bill finally reached the congressional floor as the Housing Act of 1949, the lobby worked to limit the number of public housing units authorized, to further aids to private housebuilding through expanded FHA and VA programs, and to assure inclusion as a national housing goal "that private enterprise shall be encouraged to serve as large a part of the total need as it can." It was estimated that more than $5,000,000 was spent by homebuilders in the struggle over this act. So aggressive were their tactics that a full-scale congressional investigation was conducted.[14]

The housebuilding lobby also influenced policy through administrative action. Homebuilders gave sustained support to administrative agencies such as the FHA and VA, which in return tended to respond to the policy suggestions of their support groups. Homebuilders also worked to supply agencies with most of their personnel and guidelines.[15] At the national scale, Harry Truman appointed as head of the FHA Raymond Foley, who referred to himself as "a champion of free enterprise in housing" and said "the chief activity of government in housing should be to aid and stimulate private enterprise." Dwight Eisenhower replaced Foley with Albert Cole, a long-term opponent of public housing who labelled federal housing legislation as socialistic and voted against the Housing Act of 1949. Cole was later replaced by Norman Mason, who came to government after a career as a building supply and lumber retailer (Keith, 1973, chapter 6). It was no surprise that the FHA adopted guidelines consistent with the building and real estate industry and fully accepted the racial practices of the private society.

The homebuilders' lobby also influenced policy through local implementation. The FHA was relatively decentralized in its administration, permitting closer connections between field directors and local real estate operators, financial institutions, and homebuilders. When the Housing Act of 1949 was finally enacted and authorized public housing, the lobby immediately worked to amend the legislation and to defeat its implementation through local opposition and referenda. As a result, only 283,400 of 810,000 authorized units were actually produced in the scheduled period, and the number of authorized units was reduced in each successive legislative year after 1949 (Davies, 1966, 123–32). At the same time, programs benefiting homeownership, new construction, and large builders increased greatly.

The production of new single-family suburban houses was not the only focus of postwar federal housing practice, but others were minor in comparison. Urban renewal and public housing, for all of their clamor and controversy, were secondary to the houses whose mortgages were financed and guaranteed by federal housing programs. These programs operated as an economic instrument to stimulate production and large builders were influential in developing the programs which benefited them.

VI

Most suburban studies attribute postwar suburbanization to the shifting preferences of consumers. Indeed, so common is the focus on suburban consumers that they are pictured as independent actors in a process in which they chose to participate. In this image, postwar suburbanization followed from the selective migration of individuals with unprecedented preferences for social homogeneity and conformity, compulsory neighboring and membership in voluntary associations, a return to religion and a Republican Party switch, and other attributes of "the new suburbia" (Marshall, 1973). It was "a new way of life," "a new state of mind," and "one of the major social changes of the twentieth century." There was shaped a virtual "image of suburbia" in the American public mind, and so frequently have its attributes been addressed that when we think of suburbs we typically think of these attributes.

Later analysts argued instead that suburbanization resulted not from selective migration but from other more independent factors. In this image, postwar suburbanization was explained as an effort to achieve middle-class status and upward social mobility (Dobriner, 1963), or a "new bourgeois style" (Dobriner, 1963, chapter 1) or the homeownership ideal (Gans, 1967; Berger, 1960). Leo Schnore, for example, rejected the "social psychological approach" and argued that differential housing opportunities are the major determinants of growth differentials between subareas of the metropolitan community (Schnore, 1968, 162). Herbert Gans (1962, 625–48) argued that there was little to distinguish the way of life in suburbs from cities, that those who sought suburbs mainly sought the best available house for the money (Gans, 1967, chapter 2), and that the nature of suburban community derived more from the consequent poulation mix than from selective migration (Gans, 1967, chapter 7). Postwar suburbanization was, in the revisionist image at least, "new homes for old values" (Ktsanes and Reissmann, 1959).

The problem in this analytic exchange is the assumption on which it is based. It is assumed by both the selective migration analysts and their revisionists alike that consumers were free to choose among several residential alternatives, that their choices reflected real preferences, and that their preferences were the independent factor in suburbanization. The only real point of dispute is whether the preferences resulted from "a new state of mind," or from middle-class mobility, or from some other factor. *Not* in dispute is the assumption that consumers were the independent factor in the suburban pattern that evolved. This paper breaks with this assumption.

The customary view of the postwar consumer residential choice derives from a history that is well known and widely accepted (Checkoway, 1977b, chapter 4). It contends that the consumer decision and consequent federal programs were a response to urban decline and housing shortages. Central cities were surrounded by seas of deterioration in which housing quality and municipal facilities were allowed to decline. Studies of Philadelphia, for example, found central areas so blighted that they were wholly undesirable for business or residence; the majority of houses were grossly deficient and dilapidated; fully one-third of all dwelling units were labelled unfit for human habitation and nothing short of demolition was recommended. Declining conditions were commonly identified with racially changing neighborhoods, lower property values, and an unsafe financial investment.

Suburban homeownership was believed more attractive. Consumers were turned away from conditions in the central city and toward the "suburban ideal." The suburbs offered a new, free-standing, well-equipped, carefully designed and attractively landscaped house, with ample yard space to play and garden. They also offered an escape from the city, a more wholesome environment, and a more neighborly community. The

American predisposition to "suburbia" was confirmed by contemporary surveys of the subject.

The suburbs also offered the best available financial investment. The growing demand for suburban housing steadily increased its relative value. A slightly higher initial price seemed little to pay for a better product and investment security. Indeed, it probably confirmed the quality of the product and security of the investment in the minds of those purchasing their first house. And given the suburban orientation of FHA and other federal housing programs, suburban homeownership offered virtually the *only* sensible investment location.

Postwar consumers easily recognized the significance of any announced decision by a large builder to locate in a metropolitan suburb. For those turned away from central Philadelphia, for example, Levittown promised a planned alternative, a suburban oasis at a distance from the city, and a pioneering opportunity in a wholly new environment. It also promised a known commodity, a national reputation, and proven reliability. The advertised image—of a detached house with flower-filled window-boxes surrounded by grass, trees, shrubs, high clouds, and no other houses in sight—was hardly resistible. When the first model houses were opened for inspection in December 1951, more than 50,000 people filed through during the very first weekend. As salesmen on loudspeakers urged buyers to return on another day, police were needed to keep crowds in line. Several families squatted for days outside the salesroom waiting for the chance to put a deposit on a house which had not yet been built. On the first two days alone, more than $2,000,000 worth of houses were sold. It was, as the national media reported, "the most spectacular buyers' stampede in the history of American housebuilding."[16] This is the customary view of the postwar consumer choice.

This paper suggests something different about the postwar consumer residential choice. It does not question that growing families *were* justifiably turned away from conditions in the central city; or that suburban housing *was* more attractive and a better investment; or that residential suburbs *did* offer an escape from the city and a wholesome arena for family and child rearing; or that increased consumer demand *did* affect federal housing programs and residential construction decisions. Houses in suburbs like Levittown *were* a bargain and *did* offer a version of the suburban ideal to consumers who had never before been able to achieve it. All of these images are easily confirmed in the literature.

This paper does question those studies which fail to explain the impossibility of inferring the spatial dynamics and decision behavior of large operators and government partners from the residential aspirations and satisfactions of the eventual suburban consumers, or which fail to specify the narrow range of alternatives actually available, or which fail to emphasize the fact that consumers were important but not decisive actors in the decisions which produced the choices they made. Consumers made a logical choice among alternatives developed elsewhere. The evidence that consumers aspired to, brought in, or expressed satisfaction with suburbs is not proof enough that they would have chosen to do so if a different set of alternatives had been available to them. The assumptions that consumers were free to choose among several residential alternatives, that their choices reflected real preferences, and that their preferences were the independent factor in postwar suburbanization, all ignore the fact that final decisions do not always reflect real preferences and that prior decisions may predetermine a narrow range of alternatives from which consumers can choose. (A general perspective on the fallacy of consumer sovereignty is given in Galbraith, 1971.)

It is wrong to believe that postwar American suburbanization prevailed because the public chose it and will continue to prevail until the public changes its preferences. Suburbanization prevailed because of the decisions of large operators and powerful economic institutions supported by federal government programs, and ordinary consumers had little real choice in the basic pattern that resulted. Postwar suburbanization resulted from a decision process and institutional context and the consequences and policy problems flow from the nature of the process. To alter the consequences, it is first necessary to alter the process.

NOTES

1. This is not to suggest that large residential builders were the only large operators in postwar suburban development. Other important actors—mortgage lending institutions and local suburban governments, for example—have not been selected for examination here but have been or will be treated elsewhere. I treat the role of large transportation and industrial operators in Checkoway (1977a) and of local suburban government in Checkoway (1977b). Michael Stone (1973) examines the role of mortgage lenders. The literature on suburban economic development is massive.

2. Among the general studies are Abrams, 1950; Maisel, 1953; Foote et al., 1960; Beyer, 1965. On housebuilding operations and constraints see Grebler, 1950; Kelly et al., 1959; and Meyerson et al., 1962. On local building practices see Killingsworth, 1950, 538–80. On obstacles to production advances see U.S. Congress House Subcommittee of the Joint Committee of Housing, 1946, especially pp. 144–64.

3. Between 1948 and 1954, the number of manufactured homes produced in the United States increased from 30,000 to 77,000 (Beyer, 1965: 244). The development of prefabrication is explored in Bemis, 1936; Bruce and Sandbach, 1945; and Kelly, 1951. Prefabrication principles are described

in Chapman, 1954; "Where Is Prefabrication?" *Fortune* 33 (April 1946), 12–32; "More Houses for Less Money," *Better Homes and Gardens* 28 (October 1949), 189–92; "Prefabrication," *Architectural Forum* 92 (April 1950), 160–64; "Prefabs Fill Special Needs," *House and Home* 2 (November 1952), 89–114.

4. It could be argued that economies of scale would have made large-scale development desirable in any given location. In this period, however, government programs [were] developed to bear the public costs of new residential construction, encourage homebuilders to grow larger, and give development a suburban orientation. This is discussed in section V of this paper.

5. The construction of Levittown, New York, is described in Larrabee, 1948; Liell, 1952; and in "Up From the Potato Fields," *Time* 56 (3 July 1950), 67–72.

6. See Larrabee, 1948; Liell, 1952; "4000 Houses a Year," *Architectural Forum* 92 (April 1950), 20–22; "Levittown on the Assembly Line," *Business Week* 1172 (16 February 1952), 26–27; "Biggest New City in the U.S.," *House and Home* 2 (December 1952), 80–91.

7. "A large company, in short, by its very size and prestige and integrity, can accomplish, can achieve, can perform, where individuals are helpless and disunited," wrote William J. Levitt (1948, 253–56).

8. The Levitt house and consumer research are described in Lader: The Most Popular Builder's House"; and "Levitt Keeps Experimenting with . . . ," *House and Home* 5 (February 1954), 118–23.

9. Lader: "Levittown on the assembly line." It is revealing to contrast Levitt practices with the more common practices described in Dean, 1945.

10. The evolution of federal housing policy is described in Wheaton, 1953; McKelvey, 1966; Gelfand, 1975. See also Friedman, 1968; National Commission on Urban problems, 1968; Frieden, 1968: 170–225; Hartman, 1975; and Checkoway, 1977c.

11. My debt to the work and prose of Gelfand (1975, especially pp. 216–22) is obvious.

12. La Guardia, 1935, 13–14; Bartholomew, 1939; 1940; "Rebuilding the Cities," *Business Week* (6 July 1940), 38–39; FHA *Homes in Metropolitan Districts* (Washington: Government Printing Office, 1942); "FHA Policies Said To Hinder Urban Rebuilding," *American City* 63 (March 1948), 120; Bauer, 1956; "FHA in Suburbia," *Architectural Forum* 57 (September 1957), 160–61; National Commission on Urban Problems, 1968, 99. See also Chatterjee et al., 1976.

13. The position of the housebuilding lobby is well described in testimony in U.S. Congress House Committee on Banking and Currency, 1954; and U.S. Congress Senate Committee on Banking and Currency, 1954. Lobbying activities and tactics are described in U.S. Congress House Select Committee on Lobbying Activities, 1949.

14. The influence and delaying tactics of the housebuilding lobby are described in Schriftgiesser, 1951, chapter 14. The political history of the Housing Act of 1949 is described in Davies, 1966, chapter 8; Keith, 1973, chapters 2–5; Meyerson et al., 1962, 272–89; and *Congressional Quarterly Almanac* 4, 137–44.

15. Herbert V. Nelson, executive director of the Washington Realtors' Committee, told a U.S. Senate Committee in 1950: "We put several hundred of our people, whom we found and persuaded to go into government service, into positions where they could give their services" (quoted in Abrams, 1965: 61). But Nelson is probably best known for his statement after

passage of the Housing Act of 1949: "I do not believe in democracy. I think it stinks. I don't think women should be allowed to vote at all. Ever since they started, our public affairs have been in a worse mess than ever before" (U.S. Congress House Select Committee on Lobbying Activities, 1949).

16. On public affairs in Levittown in the 1950s, see Checkoway, 1977a, chapters 4 and 5. On Levittown 20 years later, see Popenoe, 1977, chapters 5 and 6.

REFERENCES

Abrams, C., *The Future of Housing* (New York: Harper & Row, 1946).
————, "Housing—The Ever-recurring Crisis," in S. F. Harris, ed., *Saving American Capitalism* (New York: Alfred A. Knopf, 1948).
————, "The Residential Construction Industry," in W. Adams, ed., *The Structure of American Industry* (New York: Macmillan, 1950).
————, *The City Is the Frontier* (New York: Harper & Row, 1965).
Arnold, J. L., *The New Deal in the Suburbs: A History of the Greenbelt Town Program 1935–54* (Columbus: Ohio State University Press, 1971).
Bartholemew, H., "The Case for Downtown Locations," *Planners Journal* 4, 1939, 32–3.
————, "Present and Ultimate Effects of Decentralization upon American Cities," in *Mortgage Bankers Association of America Yearbook 1940* (Chicago: Mortgage Bankers Association of America, 1940).
Bauer, C., ed., *A Housing Program for Now and Later* (Washington, D.C.: National Public Housing Conference, 1948).
————, "First Job: Control New City Sprawl," *Architectural Forum* 55, 1956, 105–12.
Bemis, A. F., *The Evolving House* (Cambridge, Mass.: MIT Press, 1936).
Berger, B. M., *Working-Class Suburb: A Study of Auto Workers in Suburbia* (Berkeley: University of California Press, 1960).
Beyer, G. H., *Housing and Society* (New York: Macmillan, 1965).
Blumfeld, H., "The Tidal Wave of Metropolitan Expansion," *Journal of the Institute of American Planners* 20, 1954, 3–14.
Bruce, A., and H. Sandbach, *A History of Prefabrication* (Raritan, N.J.: John B. Pierce Foundation, 1945).
Chapman, G., "Public Acceptance of Prefabrication," *Appraisal Journal* 22, 1954, 57–68.
Chatterjee, L., D. Harvey, and L. Klugman, *F.H.A. Policies and the Baltimore City Housing Market* (Washington, D.C.: National League of Cities, 1976).
Checkoway, B., "Suburbanization and Community: Growth and Planning in Postwar Lower Bucks County, Pennsylvania" (Ph.D. dissertation, University of Pennsylvania, 1977). a
————, *The Politics of Postwar Suburban Development* (University of California, Berkeley: Childhood and Government Project, 1977). b
————, "The Failure of Citizen Participation in Federal Housing Programs," *Planning and Public Policy* 3, 1977, 1–4. c
Clawson, M., *Suburban Land Conversion in the United States: An Economic and Governmental Process* (Baltimore: Johns Hopkins University Press, 1971).
Davies, R. O., *Housing Reform During the Truman Administration* (Columbia: University of Missouri Press, 1966).

Davis, P. J. *Real Estate in America* (Washington: Public Affairs Press, 1958).

Dean, J. P., *Home Ownership: Is It Sound?* (New York: Harper & Row, 1945).

———, "The Myths of Housing Reform," *American Sociological Review* 14, 1949, 281–88.

Dietz, A. G. H., "Housing Industry Research," in Kelly et al., 1959.

Dietz, A. G. H., J. A. Murray, C. Koch, and B. Kelly, "Construction Advances," in Kelly et al., 1959.

Dobriner, W. M., ed., *The Suburban Community* (New York: Putnam, 1958).

———, *Class in Suburbia* (Englewood Cliffs, N.J.: Prentice Hall, 1963).

Donaldson, S., *The Suburban Myth* (New York: Columbia University Press, 1969).

Editors of *Fortune, The Exploding Metropolis* (New York: Doubleday, 1958).

Eichler, E. P., and M. Kaplan, *The Community Builders* (Berkeley: University of California Press, 1967).

Foote, N. N., J. Abu-Lughod, M. M. Foley, and L. Winnick, *Housing Choices and Housing Constraints* (New York: McGraw-Hill, 1960).

Frieden, B. J., "Housing and National Urban Goals: Old Policies and New Realities," in J. Q. Wilson, ed., *The Metropolitan Enigma* (Cambridge, Mass.: Harvard University Press, 1968).

Friedman, L. M., *Government and Slum Housing* (Chicago: Rand McNally, 1968).

Galbraith, J. K., *The New Industrial State,* revised edition (New York: New American Library, 1971).

Gans, H. J., "Urbanism and Suburbanism as Ways of Life: A Re-evaluation of Definitions," in A. Rose, ed., *Human Behavior and Social Processes* (Boston: Houghton-Mifflin, 1962).

———, *The Levittowners* (New York: Vintage Books, 1967).

Gelfand, M. J., *A Nation of Cities: The Federal Government and Urban America, 1933–1965* (New York: Oxford University Press, 1975).

Glick, P. C., *American Families* (New York: Wiley, 1957).

Grebler, L., *Production of New Housing* (New York: Social Science Research Council, 1950).

Haar, C. M., *Federal Credit Aid and Private Housing: The Mass Financing Dilemma* (New York: McGraw-Hill, 1960).

Hartman, C. W., *Housing and Social Policy* (Englewood Cliffs, N.J.: Prentice Hall, 1975).

Harvey, D. M., *Social Justice and the City* (London: Edward Arnold, 1973).

Hauser, P. M., and A. J. Jaffe, "The Extent of the Housing Shortage," *Law and Contemporary Problems* 12, 1947, 3–15.

Herzog, J. P., "Structural Changes in the Housebuilding Industry," in Real Estate Research Program, *The Dynamics of Large-Scale Housebuilding* (Berkeley: University of California Press, 1963).

Housing . . . U.S.A. (New York: Simmons-Boardman Publishing Corporation, 1954).

Howard, J. T., "Impact of the Federal Highway Program," in *Planning 1957* (Chicago: American Society of Planning Officials, 1957).

———, "Arresting the Highwaymen," *Architectural Forum* 60, 1959, 93.

Keith, N. S., *Politics and the Housing Crisis since 1930* (New York: Universe Books, 1973).

Kelly, B., *The Prefabrication of Houses* (New York: Wiley, 1951).

Kelly, B., et al., *Design and Production of Housing* (New York: McGraw Hill, 1959).

Killingsworth, C., "Organized Labor in a Free Enterprise Economy," in

W. Adams, ed., *The Structure of American Industry* (New York: Macmillan, 1950).

Ktsanes, T., and L. Reissmann, "Suburbia: New Homes for Old Values," *Social Problems* 7, 1959, 187–94.

La Guardia, F. H., "The Federal Work Program and the Cities," in *City Problems of 1935* (Washington, D.C.: U.S. Conference of Mayors, 1935).

Larrabee, E., "The Six Thousand Houses that Levitt Built," *Harper's Magazine* 197, 1948, 79–88.

Leavitt, H., *Superhighway—Superhoax* (Garden City: Doubleday, 1970).

Levin, J., *Your Congress and American Housing—The Actions of Congress from 1892 to 1951* (H. Doc. 532, 82nd Congress, 1952).

Levitt, A. S., "A Community Builder Looks at Community Planning," *Journal of the American Institute of Planners* 17, 1951, 80–88.

Levitt, W. J., "More Houses and Better Values," *Journal of the American Institute of Planners* 9, 1948, 253–56.

———, "Revolutionizing an Industry," in *Editors of Nations Business, Lessons of Leadership: 21 Top Executives Speak Out on Creating, Developing and Managing Success* (Garden City: Doubleday, 1969).

Liell, J. T., "Levittown: A Study in Community Development and Planning" (Ph.D. dissertation, Yale University, 1952).

Lilley, W. III, "The Homebuilders' Lobby," in J. Pynoos, R. Schafer, and C. W. Hartman, eds., *Housing Urban America* (Chicago: Aldine, 1973).

Maisel, S. J., *Housebuilding in Transition* (Berkeley: University of California, 1953).

Marshall, H., "Suburban Life-styles: A Contribution to the Debate," in Masotti and Hadden, 1973.

Mason, J. B., "A Brief History of Housing, 1940–1949: Decade of War and Progress" (Nationals Association of Home Builders Library, unpublished manuscript, no date.

Masotti, L. H., and J. K. Hadden, eds., *The Urbanization of the Suburbs* (Beverly Hills: Sage, 1973).

McDonnell, T., *The Wagner Housing Act: A Case Study of the Legislative Process* (Chicago: Loyola University Press, 1957).

McKelvey, B., *The Emergence of Metropolitan America, 1915–1968* (New Brunswick: Rutgers University Press, 1966).

Meyerson, M., B. Terrett, and W. L. C. Wheaton, *Housing, People and Cities* (New York: McGraw Hill, 1962).

Miller, H. P., *Income of the American People* (New York: Wiley, 1965).

Muller, P. O., *The Outer City: Geographical Consequences of the Urbanization of Suburbs* (Washington, D.C.: Association of American Geographers, 1976).

Mumford, L., *The Urban Prospect* (New York: Harcourt, Brace, Jovanovich, 1968).

National Association of Homebuilders "The Homebuilder—What Does He Build?" *Journal of Homebuilding* 14 (March 1960).

National Commission on Urban Problems, *Building the American City* (Washington, D.C.: Government Printing Office).

Newcomb, R., and H. C. Kyle, "The Housing Crisis in a Free Economy," *Law and Contemporary Problems* 12, 1947, 186–205.

Popenoe, D., *The Suburban Environment: Sweden and the United States* (Chicago: University of Chicago Press, 1977).

Rae, J., *The Road and the Car in American Life* (Cambridge, Mass.: MIT Press, 1971).

Rosenman, D., *A Million Homes a Year* (New York: Harper & Row, 1946).

Sasaki, H., "Land Development and Design," in Kelly, 1959.

Saulnier, R. J., H. G. Halcrow, and N. H. Jacoby, *Federal Lending and Loan Insurance* (Princeton, N.J.: Princeton University Press, 1958).

Schnore, L., *The Urban Scene* (New York: Free Press, 1968).

Schriftgiesser, K., *The Lobbyists: The Art and Business of Influencing Lawmakers* (Boston: Little, Brown, 1951).

Scott, M., *American City Planning since 1890* (Berkeley: University of California Press, 1971).

Spring, B. P., "Advances in House Design," in Kelly, 1959.

Stone, M., "Federal Housing Policy: A Political-Economic Analysis," in Pynoos, Schafer, and Hartman, 1973.

Taeuber, C., and I. B. Taeuber, *The Changing Population of the United States* (New York: Wiley, 1958).

U.S. Bureau of Labor Statistics, *Builders of One-family Homes in 72 Cities,* R-1151 (Washington, D.C.: Government Printing Office, 1940).

U.S. Bureau of the Census, *1956 National Housing Inventory: Components of Change, 1950–1956, United States and Regions,* vol. 1, part 1 (Washington, D.C.: Government Printing Office, 1958).

———, *Housing Construction Statistics, 1889 to 1964* (Washington, D.C.: Government Printing Office, 1966).

U.S. Congress House Committee on Banking and Currency, *Hearings,* H.R. 7839, 83rd Congress, 1954.

U.S. Congress House Select Committee on Lobbying Activities, *Hearings—The Role of Lobbying in Representative Self-Government,* 81st Congress, 1949.

U.S. Congress Subcommittee of the Joint Committee on Housing, *High Cost of Housing* (Washington, D.C.: Government Printing Office, 1946).

U.S. Congress Senate Committee on Banking and Currency, *Hearings,* S. 2889, S. 2949, S. 2938, 83rd Congress, 1954.

U.S. Congress Subcommittee on Housing and Urban Development, *Evolution of Role of the Federal Government in Housing and Community Development* (Washington, D.C.: Government Printing Office, 1975).

U.S. Department of Labor, *Structure of the Residential Building Industry,* bulletin no. 1170 (Washington, D.C.: Government Printing Office, 1954).

———, *Nonfarm Housing Starts, 1889 to 1958,* bulletin no. 1260 (Washington, D.C.: Government Printing Office, 1959).

Warner, S. B. Jr., *Streetcar Suburbs: The Process of Growth in Boston, 1870–1900* (Cambridge, Mass.: Harvard University Press, 1962).

———, *The Urban Wilderness: A History of the American City* (New York: Harper & Row, 1972).

Wheaton, W. L. C., "The Evolution of Federal Housing Programs" (Ph.D. dissertation, University of Chicago, 1953).

Whyte, W. H., "Urban Sprawl," in Editors of *Fortune,* 1958.

8

The Tenants' Movement

PETER DREIER

Public officials and planners seeking to develop, legislate, and enforce housing policy must contend with a variety of competing interest groups with different stakes in the outcome. This is true at both the national and local levels of government. Bankers, developers, realtors, homebuilders, and apartment owners have been well-organized in order to exert political influence (Checkoway, 1980; Bouma, 1962; Clay, 1979; Gelfand, 1978; Hartman, 1967; Lawson, 1980a; Lilley, 1980; Mollenkopf, 1975; Mollenkopf and Pynoos, 1980; Wolman, 1971). Homeowners, when their interests as taxpayers or neighborhood residents are threatened, have frequently mobilized as a political interest group, particularly in local politics (Cox, 1982; Boyte, 1980; Fellman, 1973). But tenants, on the other hand, have only occasionally been serious contenders on the political scene. Although they have constituted a majority of residents in most central cities, and many suburbs, renters' protest and political activities have been more episodic than those of other actors with a stake in housing policy.

Americans have long cherished the "American dream" of homeownership. Being a propertyless tenant, at the mercy of landlords, has never been part of that dream. Unable to afford their own home, renters face many problems: the constant threat of eviction, unaffordable and rising rents, and poorly maintained buildings. Thus the struggle between tenant and landlord has been a persistent one in American history (Heskin, 1981). But only occasionally has this conflict taken organized or political form—from struggles to extend the franchise (Williamson, 1960), to land seizures and protests over evictions (Heskin, 1981; Kim, 1978) to campaigns for code enforcement and rent controls (Dreier, 1979). In other words, social, economic, and political conditions have given rise to peaks of tenant consciousness, mobilizing tenants to protect and expand their rights. The period since the mid-1970s is such a period. As the housing crisis has deepened, turning many would-be homeowners into reluctant renters, and many long-term renters into angry consumers, activist tenant groups have mushroomed across the country.

This article explains the origins of the modern tenant's movement, its current status, and its political strategies and tactics.

HISTORY

Modern tenant activism began in the late 1800s with the rise of the industrial city and the emergence of tenants as a majority of the population in central cities. From the 1870s through the 1960s, tenant activism has been primarily found among the poor and working class, crowded into tenements and slums in the large industrial cities. Most tenant groups dealt with immediate crises in their own buildings—evictions, lack of heat, rent increases, delapidation—with the landlords as targets of protest. At times, these groups developed the stability and coherence to join together and direct tenant protest toward local government to force it to enact and enforce building codes and other reforms. Only in New York City, however, were tenants able to win rent control, which was initiated in 1920. There, citywide tenant groups aligned themselves with trade unions and radical political groups, and elected city officials who dealt with working-class issues. (Lawson and McLoughlin, 1975a; 1975b; 1976; Lawson et al., 1975; Lawson, 1980.) In the Depression, tenant groups were organized in most major cities by Socialists and Communists as part of their efforts to organize and politicize industrial workers and the unemployed. One of their favorite tactics was to block evictions by bringing large crowds to confront landlords or the police at the doorstep, making it impossible to remove the tenants and their possessions (Piven and Cloward, 1977). Beginning at the turn of this century, tenant groups were also aided by middle-class reformers who worked on behalf of tenement dwellers (Lubove, 1962). These reformers were not directly part of grass-roots tenant groups, but their efforts—conducting studies on slum conditions and lobbying for the establishment of city departments to inspect buildings and enforce codes—helped to publicize tenants' grievances and legitimize their protests. These reformers were also in the forefront of programs for public housing and slum clearance.

During and immediately after World War II, tenant activism slowed

down. During the war, labor unions and other protest groups united behind the war effort and tempered their protests. Because of the wartime
housing emergency, Congress enacted nationwide rent controls which
lasted through 1947 (Lebowitz, 1981). When President Truman lifted
rent controls, tenants in New York City fought to have the local government enact a rent control of its own; for the next 20 years, it was the
only city in the U.S. with rent control. Even then tenants had to organize
to keep the city from abandoning the program. In the rest of the country,
however, there was a lull in tenant activism until the 1960s. Housing conditions for most Americans improved dramatically. Federal housing and
highway policies created a postwar boom in homeownership, particularly
in the burgeoning suburbs. The percentage of tenants in the overall population dropped from 56 percent in 1940, to 45 percent in 1950, to 38
percent in 1960. (It hit 35 percent in 1970 and is there still.) During
this period of rising affluence, American homes got bigger and bigger—
more rooms, more appliances, more patios and porches, more garden
and lawn space. This upsurge in homeownership created a strong belief
that all except the very poor would soon realize the dream. As a result,
working-class and middle-class tenants had little stake in their roles as
tenants. For the most part, they saw themselves as soon-to-be homeowners, so there was little incentive to organize around rent hikes or building problems. The tenants left behind in the cities during the postwar
boom were disproportionately the poor and the minorities, but the nation
showed little concern for the plight of these groups.

The 1960s witnessed the next wave of tenant activism as part of the
broader civil rights, poor people's, and student movements. Unlike previous periods of tenant protest, it was not a time of economic crisis or even
of a severe housing shortage. Instead, it developed in a context of rising
expectations (National Advisory Commission on Civil Disorders, 1968).
As the standard of living improved for most Americans, the poor became
more aware of the gap between themselves and the affluent society. Even
if things at the bottom were getting *slightly* better, they were getting
much better for everyone else—or so it seemed in the ghettoes—and so
the gap seemed to grow even wider.

From 1955 until 1964, the civil rights movement focused most of its
activities on the South, concerned primarily with segregation in public facilities (restaurants, schools, buses) and voting rights for blacks. It was
not until 1964 that the movement turned North and began to address
problems like housing discrimination and slum conditions. It was no accident, therefore, that the revitalized tenant movement began with the
Harlem rent strikes of 1964–65 (Lipsky, 1970; Piven and Cloward,
1967; Naison, 1972; Lawson and McLoughlin, 1976). These strikes can

be seen as part of the civil rights movement, although its leaders had been involved in previous tenant and political activities. According to some accounts, the strikes involved more than 500 buildings and 15,000 tenants. They received nationwide attention and helped inspire tenant activism in other cities, primarily among low-income blacks. Out of these efforts developed the first nationwide group, the National Tenants Organization (NTO). Formed in 1969, it had within two years affiliates in most large and medium-sized cities. The NTO was concerned primarily with problems in public housing, but also with private slum housing (Marcuse, 1971). The NTO's heyday lasted only until the early 1970s when, like the broader civil rights and poor people's movement of which it was a part, it declined. The tenants' movement of that period was also a spillover of the student movement. Tenant organizations and rent strikes emerged in college towns, such as Berkeley, Madison, Ann Arbor, and Cambridge (Burghart, 1972). In Cambridge and Berkeley, where students mixed with large low-income populations, the activities spread beyond the student neighborhoods. In the Boston area, for example, as well as in other nearby cities, student and ex-student activists built tenant organizations in private and FHA-subsidized housing and helped enact rent control in Boston, Cambridge, Lynn, and Somerville in the early 1970s. Protests against urban renewal were another major focus of tenant activism.

The 1960s wave of tenant activism indicates some of the strengths and weaknesses of the tenants' movement. It also shows some of the ways that well-organized tenants can influence government. The tenants' movement of that period was primarily a protest movement among the poor, especially blacks. As in earlier periods, they were aided by middle-class reformers, primarily students and radical lawyers. Suspicious of direct involvement in electoral politics (e.g., running candidates, registering voters), the movement primarily engaged in public protest demonstrations and rent strikes.

These actions must be seen within the broader context of the growing militancy of the civil rights and black protest movements of the late 1960s. Riots in most major cities led the federal government to enact a war-on-poverty program. These included funds for organizers and legal services lawyers, housing rehabilitation, and rent subsidies. These funds provided significant resources for tenant groups, and helped fuel tenant activism. But when the riots subsided, the war-on-poverty funds began to shrivel, although some programs remained intact and a few (such as legal services) grew even larger. The momentum of the tenants' movement ended, and most tenant groups disappeared.

That wave of tenant activism, however, produced some important legacies. For one thing, it developed a large nucleus of trained tenant organizers and advocate planners (such as Urban Planning Aid in Boston) who were ready and waiting when conditions would make another wave of activism possible. It also improved housing and living conditions for many low-income tenants. Issues such as housing segregation, welfare rights, voting rights, rent subsidies, and tenant involvement in public housing management were placed on the political agenda. Reforms were introduced even if problems were not completely solved. Finally, and perhaps most importantly, tenant-landlord law was dramatically reformed. These reforms represented the first significant change in tenant-landlord law since the colonial period. Legal services lawyers (part of the war-on-poverty program) worked with tenant groups on the local and national levels to advocate more equitable law. Local legal services offices, as well as the National Housing Law Project, initiated legal battles and also helped organized tenants to help themselves.

They won important legal precedents, including "warranty of habitability" (making the landlord responsible for providing habitable conditions), and protection against evictions in retaliation for organizing other tenants or complaining to local authorities about unsafe conditions. Other reforms dealt with security deposits, the right to withhold rent, utility shut-offs, lockouts, the seizure of tenants' possessions, and standard leases. Other reforms dealt with discrimination against minorities, welfare recipients, families with children, and the elderly (Blumberg and Grow, 1978; Rose, 1973). Because laws are enacted at the local and state levels, these reforms were not adopted uniformly: they exist only in areas where tenants were most active and politicized. Legal challenges to exclusionary zoning—where minority groups and rental housing were excluded from suburban areas—was another outgrowth of tenant and civil rights activism.

These were important victories. They made tenant activism easier when it revived in the mid-1970s. But the tenant activism of the late 1960s failed to build on its successes. For one thing, it failed to develop stable tenant organizations with active members. Tenant groups tended to be crisis-oriented, and did not sustain themselves for the long haul. Also, by avoiding direct involvement in elections, tenants depended on keeping up pressure on politicians who had other concerns and constituencies, rather than being able to rely on elected officials who emerged or were directly accountable to tenant groups. Finally, the tenants groups depended heavily on government programs for support and resources; when these resources were withdrawn or reduced, the tenant groups suffered. Most of these limitations reflect the fact that the tenants' movement of that period was concentrated among the poor. They moved a lot (often because they were evicted for non-payment of rent), they voted infrequently, they lived from crisis to crisis, and they lacked disposable income to pay steady dues to a tenants' organization. Resources from government and liberal foundations lasted only so long as tenants protested and disrupted business as usual.

CHANGING CONDITIONS

Any successful social movement requires a combination of potentially explosive social conditions and appropriate strategic and tactical leadership (Freeman, 1979). A number of conditions have made the emergence of "tenant consciousness" and tenant organizing possible since the early 1970s.

The most general condition has been the explosion of grass-roots protest during the past decade. The image of the 1970s as a quiet "me decade," a reaction against the noisy protests of the 1960s, is misleading. Not only did many civil rights, student, and anti-war activists remain politically active through the 1970s, but a much broader spectrum of Americans joined the struggle for more rights and freedoms. Through the decade, environmental, women's, consumer, senior citizens, and neighborhood movements emerged, mobilizing millions of Americans around a wide variety of concerns and creating a political climate of what Bell (1976) calls "rising entitlements." There was, once again, a climate of protest in the nation, not just among the poor, but among the working- and middle-class as well (Boyte, 1980; Perlman, 1978). This momentum carried through into the 1980s with protest movements against nuclear arms, the dangers of toxic chemicals in communities and workplaces, and the Reagan Administration's fiscal and social programs. Indeed, many of the people who distrusted the radical protesters of the 1960s were among those joining the protests of the 70s and 80s. This new climate of protest reflects a changing public perception of both the role of citizens in decision-making and the role of government in protecting and expanding basic rights. Increasingly, Piven and Cloward argue, "(w)orking people who once looked to the marketplace as the arena for action on their economic grievances and aspirations now look more often to the state" (Piven and Cloward, 1982, p. 125).

The broader climate of "rising entitlements" was fueled by the federal government. Owing its 1976 election in part to the low-income vote, the Carter Administration revitalized many programs that provided staff and support services to grass-roots community and tenant groups. These include VISTA (Volunteers in Service to America), CETA (job-training), and the Community Services Administration. (Perlman, 1979). Carter appointed a National Commission on Neighborhoods, and the Department of Housing and Urban Development added a division concerned with neighborhood issues and citizen involvement. While most of these programs were targeted to low- and moderate-income groups, their presence had a spill-over effect. Low-income tenant groups with CETA workers or VISTA volunteers would free resources that could be used for organizing middle-income tenants. Tenant newsletters or self-help manuals published by low-income tenant groups would find their way to middle-income groups as well. Also, the legal reforms around tenant-landlord law achieved during the late 1960s and early 1970s—particularly protection against retaliatory eviction—made tenant organizing easier and less risky. The cadre of experienced organizers, advocate planners, and poverty lawyers from the 1960s came out of the woodwork, eager to make the tenants' movement an effective political force.

Tenants joined in this demand for expanded rights. Within the broader climate of protest, specific changes in the conditions of tenant life triggered a new round of tenant activism.

The current housing shortage is the worst since the end of World War II and shows no signs of significant improvement, but it is especially bad for tenants. For those who cannot afford to own a home, the housing crisis means higher rents, lower maintenance, and more overcrowding. Tenants are now paying more for less housing. In 1980, 52.9 percent of the nation's 27.5 million renter households were paying more than one quarter of their income for rent; this is an increase from 40 percent in just ten years (U.S. Census, 1981). The poor, who can least afford to cut corners on other items, pay the largest part of their incomes just to keep a roof over their heads. Among tenant households with incomes below $10,000, 82.5 percent paid more than one quarter of their income for housing.

The situation for renters is much worse than for homeowners because renters are generally less affluent. Tenants' average income in 1980 ($10,600) was only 53.5 percent of homeowners' ($19,800). As Table 8-1 shows, rates of homeownership increase steadily with income; most tenants who can afford to buy a house do so, although this is getting harder to do. Despite the growing number of middle-income renters, the concentration of tenants among the less affluent is still pronounced. In 1980, 67.6 percent of all renters—compared with 37.1 percent of all homeowners—had household incomes below $15,000. And 89.1 percent of tenants, but only 63.1 percent of homeowners, had incomes below $25,-000. (U.S. Census, 1981) Thus, very few tenants are tenants by choice. They are forced by economic circumstances—and by racial discrimination in the housing market—to rent their homes.

Table 8.1. Income, Race, and Homeownership (1980)
(Percentage Homeowners)

Income	All Households	White Households	Black Households	Hispanic Households
Less than $3,000	43.7	51.1	26.6	21.0
$3,000–$6,999	47.0	52.9	31.1	20.0
$7,000–$9,999	53.0	58.1	37.4	24.5
$10,000–$14,999	56.5	59.7	44.3	37.6
$15,000–$19,999	65.5	67.7	52.4	53.5
$20,000–$24,000	74.7	76.7	59.2	62.0
$25,000–$34,999	83.1	84.2	71.0	75.0
$35,000–$49,999	89.5	90.2	80.0	82.6
$50,000–$74,999	92.1	92.4	83.9	92.1
$75,000 and above	92.4	92.7	99.9	73.9
Total	65.5	69.7	43.9	42.4

Source: U.S. Department of Commerce, Bureau of the Census, Annual Housing Survey: 1980, Washington, D.C.: Government Printing Office, 1981.

Government favoritism for homeownership, which especially benefits affluent homeowners, widens the gap between homeowners and tenants even further. Owners benefit from significant tax benefits which allow them to deduct their mortgage interest rate and property tax payments from their federal income tax. In 1982, these homeowner tax deductions cost the federal government more than $39 billion. This hidden subsidy to homeowners is bigger than all direct federal housing programs—public housing, rent subsidies, indeed the entire budget of the federal Department of Housing and Urban Development—together. Moreover, these tax benefits are exceedingly regressive, benefiting affluent homeowners most, moderate-income homeowners less, and tenants not at all. About 30 percent of these benefits go to homeowners with incomes above $50,000 (less than five percent of all taxpayers), while about 74 percent of these benefits go to the 19 percent of taxpayers with incomes above $30,000 (U.S. Congress, 1981).

Tenants, in other words, have good reason to feel like second-class citizens. But three conditions, in particular, contributed to the emergence of tenant activism.

The *first* condition was the increase in long-term tenancies. As the costs of homeownership skyrocketed during the 1970s, many tenants became locked into renting. Over the decade, the average price of a single-family home rose from $23,400 to over $70,000—much faster than the increase in people's incomes. Whereas two-thirds of all households could afford to buy a single-family home in the 1950s, less than one-quarter could do so in the late 1970s (Frieden and Solomon, 1977). By 1981, according to one estimate, less than 10 percent could do so (Donohue, 1982).[1] For an increasing number of families, particularly those of the postwar "baby boom" generation, the American Dream was beyond their reach. A growing number—including the growing number of single, single-parent, and elderly households—would find themselves spending a long time (perhaps the rest of their lives) as tenants. For example, the percentage of homebuyers who were purchasing their first home decreased from 36.3 to 13.5 percent between 1977 and 1981 alone (Christian and Parliment, 1982). Families who do purchase homes (their median income was $39,196 in 1981) were paying a much larger share of their income to do so. But even so, the number of foreclosures and late mortgage payments have risen steadily, reaching a postwar peak in 1982 (Brooks, 1982). They will find themselves renters once again. Having grown up expecting to be homeowners, many middle-income tenants became frustrated with the relative powerlessness and insecurity of renting. Gradually, and grudgingly, they began to think of themselves as long-term, rather than temporary, tenants.

The *second* condition was the decline in tenant transiency. When housing choices are abundant and vacancy rates high, tenants who do not like their apartments vote with their feet: they move (Fredland, 1973; Goodman, 1978; Rossi, 1955). This transiency has made it difficult to organize tenant groups and to develop stable memberships and leaders. It leads, for example, to lower levels of political involvement and a smaller stake in community issues (Cox, 1982; Fellman, 1973). Tenants have much lower levels of voting participation than homeowners (Alford and Scoble, 1968; U.S. Census, 1979). By the mid-1970s, however, tenants had fewer options. Construction of rental housing began to decline, reaching almost a standstill by 1980. With the "baby boom" generation escalating the number of separate households looking for apartments, the nationwide rental vacancy rate reached a postwar low of 4.8 percent in 1979 (U.S. Comptroller General, 1979). In most cities it was even lower. Low vacancy rates make it more difficult for tenants to find an alternative apartment and more likely for them to stay where they are, even when they are dissatisfied with the apartment. This gives tenants a greater stake in making their apartments more livable.

The *third* condition was the growing number of tenants living in large buildings or apartment complexes owned by absentee companies. During the 1970s, the economics of apartment ownership and management began to change. Until then, the vast majority of apartment owners were relatively amateur landlords who owned one, or just a few, small apartment buildings. For many, is was not a full-time job, but a sideline to earn extra money perhaps for a home of their own. Many lived in their own apartment buildings, knew the tenants on a first-name basis, and might even have pegged rent levels to their tenants' ability to pay. Such personal, paternalistic relationships between tenants and landlords, although often strained, tended to inhibit tenant activism. It is difficult, in that situation, to see the landlord as an "enemy"; he or she may not have much more money than the tenant. It is also difficult to organize tenants when only a few of them share the same building or landlord (Gans, 1962; Krohn and Tiller, 1969; Vaughn, 1968).

During the 1960s and early 1970s there was a boom of suburban garden apartment complexes and of high-rise apartment buildings in cities (Neutze, 1968; Shafer, 1974). One major reason for the growth in large apartment buildings was the urban renewal and federally subsidized apartment programs. Apartments rented by middle-income tenants were part of large buildings and complexes increasingly owned by absentee companies and run by professional property managers. These changes altered the nature of tenant-landlord relations. They became more and more depersonalized. Rent checks were sent to faceless professional management firms rather than handed or mailed to an individual landlord. Absentee-owners, who buy apartments primarily for their short-term tax advantages, have less incentive than live-in landlords to make repairs and maintain their buildings. A large number of tenants under the same roof, or within the same complex, who have the same landlord creates the potential for the emergence of a critical mass of tenants who share grievances, form committees, and organize tenants' groups. This depersonalization of landlord-tenant relations and the growing scale of apartment life enhanced the potential for the development of tenant consciousness and activism. Most tenant activism is, not surprisingly, found in the larger buildings and complexes. This situation is similar to the emergence of industrial unionism, which only occurred when the large absentee-owned factory—with a large number of workers employed by the same company—replaced the small mill with employees and owners working side-by-side.

These changes—the explosion of grass-roots protest and the climate of "entitlements," the skyrocketing cost of homeownership, the low vacancy rates and rising rents, and the depersonalization of tenant-landlord relations—set the stage for the development of a new wave of tenant activism.

TENANT POLITICS

Tenant activism developed steadily, although unevenly, during the 1970s. By the end of the decade, building-level tenant groups existed in every

city and many suburbs, and citywide tenant organizations could be found
in most localities with a significant renter population. Stable statewide
tenant organizations existed in New York, Massachusetts, New Jersey
and California, and helped to give the movement a sense of identity and
coordination. In 1975, tenant leaders founded *Shelterforce* magazine, to
report on and encourage tenant activism and its editors took the first steps
toward formation of the National Tenant Union which was organized in
1980. In addition, many of the Alinsky-style grass-roots community organizations that mushroomed in the 1970s within low-income and working-class neighborhoods, took on tenant organizing as part of their multi-
issue agendas. While these groups, such as ACORN, Massachusetts Fair
Share, Somerville (Mass.), United Neighborhoods, HART (in Hartford),
and many others were not just tenant organizations, their concern with the
problems of older urban neighborhoods necessitated some interest in tenant issues. Also, a growing number of activist senior-citizen organizations (e.g. Gray Panthers, National Council of Senior Citizens) around the
country made tenant problems one of their priorities, reflecting the worsening housing situation among older Americans on fixed incomes (Cliffe,
1982).

Landlords also developed greater cohesiveness and coordination to
stem the tide (or the threat) of rent control and condominium conversion
control laws around the country. Homebuilders, mortgage bankers, and
real estate agents have been influential in local, state, and national politics
for decades, but until recently, apartment owners and developers have
not. Not surprisingly, landlords have been particularly well-organized in
New York City (where rent control has existed for decades) and have
sought to weaken or abolish rent regulation. Where tenants have been
most active, landlords have banded together, often under the aegis of the
local Chamber of Commerce or Real Estate Board. (Lawson, 1980b)
Increasingly, landlords have begun to develop their own networks and organizations. Real estate groups are among the largest contributors to both
local and national political campaigns (Dreier, 1982; *New York Times,*
1982). In 1978, the National Rental Housing Council was formed to provide local landlord groups with advice on media campaigns, legal tactics,
and research and arguments against rent control and pro-tenant demands,
as well as to lobby in Washington. In 1980, the NRHC changed its name
to the National Multi-Housing Council, reflecting the growing number of
condominium developers and converters among the landlord's ranks. Although it has been the large apartment owners and developers who have
taken the lead in this process, they have consciously sought to include
both "Mom and Pop" landlords and even homeowners in their efforts to

broaden their appeal as defending property rights from government and
tenant interference.

The burgeoning self-consciousness and activism among both tenants
and landlords at the local, state, and national levels has made tenant-
landlord conflict a significant feature of America's political landscape.
While space limitations preclude a comprehensive survey, it is possible to
provide, through selected examples, some sense of the dynamics and range
of contemporary tenant activism and landlord-tenant politics.

The New Jersey Tenants Organization (NJTO)—with 60,000 dues-
paying members, the toughest landlord-tenant laws in the nation, rent
control in more than 100 cities to its credit, and an impressive string of
electoral victories—serves as a model for the tenant movement around the
country.

The New Jersey tenants' movement was started in 1969, in the middle-income suburbs of New York City by residents of large apartment
complexes and in the slums of Newark and Passaic by residents of public
and private slum housing (Baar, 1977). During the 1960s there had been
a surge of multi-family housing construction, predominantly large garden-
apartment complexes, particularly in the suburbs near New York City.
But there was a shortage of moderately-priced apartments. Rent increases
dramatically outpaced the inflation rate. In late 1969, tenants in the predominantly middle-income complexes organized to protest large (20%–
40%) rent increases. They picketed and demonstrated, generating widespread publicity. By the end of 1970, the NJTO reported it had organized
43 rent strikes involving 20,000 tenants. In response to five of the strikes,
landlords dropped planned increases; in 30 cases, proposed increases were
spread over several years; in eight cases, tenants successfully negotiated
for better conditions. Strikes were particularly effective because under
New Jersey law, striking tenants cannot be evicted if they agree to pay the
rent to the court. Also beginning in 1970, 11,000 tenants participated in
a rent strike in public housing projects in Newark that lasted four years.
In August 1969, the slum areas of Passaic witnessed five nights of violent
demonstrations over unbearable housing conditions and rising rents. Landlords agreed to a moratorium on planned rent increases and to the city's
efforts to control rents.

This combination of low-income and middle-income tenant protest
created a powerful alliance. The leader of NJTO from 1970 until his
death in 1973 was Martin Aranow, a 33-year-old business-machine company president who lived in a luxury high-rise in suburban Fort Lee.
Aranow provided a clean-cut, middle-class image and charismatic leadership. He would often appear at press conferences and public meetings

with poor black tenants, to symbolize the base of the tenants' movement. Another leader was Ron Atlas, a young legal-aid poverty lawyer who used his legal skills to win unprecedented court decisions regarding tenant-landlord law and rent-control. When Atlas died in 1979, his younger brother John, also a poverty-lawyer, filled the gap.

From the outset, NJTO developed a three-pronged strategy to de-velop tenant power in New Jersey. It combined (1) direct action tactics, such as rent strikes, demonstrations, pickets, and rallies, associated with grass-roots community organizing; (2) electoral politics, endorsing pro-tenant candidates for local and state elections, who would enact tenants' rights legislation; and (3) litigation to establish protection for tenants engaged in direct action and to strengthen landlord-tenant law. The orga-nization's leadership recognized that all three were necessary to mobilize tenants and win victories. A strategy that relied too heavily on direct confrontations to gain concessions from landlords and political officials would ultimately fail. The problem was that the rent strike, by itself, failed to expand tenants' rights and build stable organizations and grass-roots leaders; it did not, for example, lead to any lasting control over rent increases or enforcement of housing codes. Tenants remained subject to arbitrary evictions at the end of their lease or, if they had no lease (as many low-income tenants do not), on a mere 30-days' notice. Many tenant leaders were harassed and evicted for organizing or even for com-plaining to the city's building department or other government officials. Thus, NJTO recognized early the importance of developing tenants as a voting bloc and engaging in electoral politics.

The political response to NJTO's early efforts to register voters and engage in election campaigns surprised even NJTO leaders. In 1970 alone, more than 40 landlord-tenant bills, including 4 rent-control bills, were introduced in the state legislature. Local tenants' organizations threat-ened recall elections for unresponsive public officials. In some towns, tenants captured control of the local government. By 1971, the NJTO was ready to launch a major legislative campaign and begin to fight for rent control. In the 1970 elections, NJTO and its local affiliates endorsed candidates for local and state offices. In an attempt to win tenant support for its candidates, the state's Democratic Party endorsed rent stabilization. Following the November state legislative elections the NJTO staged a "March on Trenton." Thousands of tenants and many of the successful NJTO-endorsed candidates rallied in the state capital and gave the orga-nization added public recognition.

The NJTO strategy proved to be a tremendous success. It won pro-tenant laws on the issues of security deposits, evictions for cause, receiv-ership, public disclosure of apartment ownership, and state income tax credits for tenants. More than 100 communities passed rent control laws even though NJTO failed to get the legislature to pass statewide rent control. Tenant leaders were elected or appointed to serve on local rent control boards, watching out for tenant interests and encouraging tenant groups to monitor rent board hearings, formulas for rent increase, condominium conversions, and landlords' claims of cost increases.

NJTO viewed election campaigns as organizing tools. At election times, the media and voters paid attention. Campaign workers knocked on doors and talked to people, not only about candidates and personalities, but also about tenant issues. Campaign workers distributed NJTO literature and thus promoted the organization. An independent poll of New Jersey voters found that NJTO's endorsement gave politicians substantial credibility.

Meanwhile, NJTO and its local affiliates continue direct action, organizing to mobilize tenants and build momentum and publicity. Early in its career, for example, NJTO wanted to call a statewide rent strike as a show of strength, but its leaders knew it lacked the resources to do so effectively. Instead, it decided to issue a call for a short-term rent moratorium, a delay in paying the rent. From their experience, NJTO leaders knew that a majority of tenants do not pay their rent on the first day of the month anyway, but wait a few days or more. NJTO's moratorium was widely reported in the papers. When reporters went out to interview tenants on the third and fourth day of the month, sure enough, most tenants had not paid their rent yet. Reporters labelled the moritorium a success. The publicity gave NJTO's credibility another important boost. People started calling and joining. In December 1980, NJTO began a campaign around smoke detectors. A year earlier it had successfully pressured the state legislature to pass a law requiring landlords to install detectors in every apartment. Two days before the law was to go into effect, NJTO's leaders called the press and issued the results of a statewide survey that revealed that only 10 percent of landlords had complied with the law. Coming in the midst of the coldest winter in recent memory—and a string of news stories about serious fires due to gas explosions when tenants tried to keep warm—the missing smoke detectors made a dramatic story. Thanks to NJTO, tenant issues are a daily staple of newspaper and TV coverage.

If the situation in New Jersey were unique, the success of NJTO would be of only passing interest. But the growing upsurge of tenant activism suggests that New Jersey's successes have broader implications. In California, for example, tenant groups have developed along similar lines. Home prices there were higher than elsewhere, while rental vacancies reached record lows. The tenants' movement exploded in 1978 following passage of Proposition 13, the tax-cutting amendment (Dreier, 1979). On the same day that Proposition 13 won a landslide victory statewide, rent control initiatives were defeated in Santa Barbara and Santa Monica even though tenants represented a majority of both communities. An analysis of voting results revealed that precincts that favored Proposition 13 voted against rent control, often by a similar margin. Throughout the state, in fact, voters who opposed rent control thought that property taxes were the cause of high rents. They expected Proposition 13 to hold down rents; landlords even made such promises. But the anticipated windfall of rent rollbacks did not materialize. In fact, many of California's million tenants received notices of rent *increases* shortly after Proposition 13 passed. This set the stage for a significant tenant backlash.

Throughout California, tenants who had been hit by increases organized meetings to demand that landlords share their property tax savings. Newspapers were filled with stories of outraged renters, embarrassed landlords, and politicians jumping onto the bandwagon. For example, Los Angeles Mayor Thomas Bradley, who had earlier lent his name to the anti-rent control campaign in nearby Santa Monica, called for a citywide rent freeze ordinance. As public clamor mounted, some landlords agreed to voluntarily reduce rents in order to avoid mandatory rollbacks and freezes. But tenant pressure did not subside. And when heavy real estate industry lobbying defeated a statewide bill requiring landlords to pass on Proposition 13 savings to tenants, the battle shifted to the local level. Tenant groups began to mobilize in communities across the state, demanding rent control. Experienced tenant leaders began to travel across the state, helping local groups. A state-wide organization, the California Housing and Information Network (CHAIN) was formed to coordinate local and statewide efforts. By 1981, more than 25 California communities, including Los Angeles and San Francisco, had already passed rent control laws and more were considering doing so.

The tenants' movement has been particularly successful in Santa Monica, a coastal city of 90,000 in Ronald Reagan's backyard. In 1980 the tenants' movement passed strong rent and condominium conversion controls, and elected several members to the City Council. A year later, it secured a majority on the Council (its slate included a minister, two union activists, and several tenant activists) and Ruth Yanatta Goldway, the leader of Santa Monicans for Renters' Rights, was elected Mayor. Once in office, they enacted a radical program that went beyond tenant problems. This included increased police foot patrols and improved municipal services; increased fees on Shell Oil's underground pipeline; pro-union policies, such as requiring a union label on all city stationery and negotiating a favorable contract with municipal unions; and resolutions opposing U.S. intervention in El Salvador and nuclear proliferation. The City Council named citizen task forces on crime, women's issues, and other problems. It appointed progressive activists to such critical positions as city attorney, city manager, rent control administrator, and other policy-making positions. The Council also dramatically changed the city's development priorities; for example, it required one developer to build a park, a day care center, and affordable housing units in order to obtain a permit to build a highly profitable hotel complex near the waterfront (Shearer, 1982; *Business Week*, 1981).

Although the tenants' movement is most advanced in New Jersey and California, similar activities were taking place in cities and suburbs around the country. New York City is the home of the oldest and one of the most effective tenant groups in the nation, the Metropolitan Council on Housing, started in 1959. Independently, tenants in Co-op City, a housing project in the Bronx, participated in a 13-month rent strike beginning in 1976. Eighty-six percent of the 15,372 families participated, withholding over $25 million in rents. The NYC tenants' movement spilled over to suburban Westchester, Rockland, and Nassau Counties, where several communities passed rent control laws. Local tenant groups formed a statewide New York State Tenants Coalition in 1973 to coordinate activities and work together in Albany (Lawson, 1980a).

In Massachusetts, where tenant groups had been active throughout the 1970s in the older industrial cities, a state-wide Massachusetts Tenants Organization (MTO) was formed in 1981, triggering tenant activism in the middle-income suburbs and small towns, as well as the inner cities, primarily around rent increases and condominium conversions. Soon MTO was organizing tenants in state subsidized housing and mobile home parks. Like many grass-roots groups that have emerged in the past decade, much of MTO's initial funding came from the Campaign for Human Development, an agency of the Catholic Church devoted to promoting low-income empowerment.

Washington, D.C., Boston, and Baltimore, among other cities, passed rent control laws in the 1970s.[2] In 1979 and 1980 alone, momentum for rent control existed in cities in at least 26 states, according to a report by the National Multi-Housing Council.

Another emerging problem—the conversions of rental apartments to condominiums—began to trigger tenant opposition and activism beginning in the late 1970s. Some 366,000 units were converted in the U.S. between 1970 and 1979, with 71 percent of these conversions taking place since 1977. At first concentrated in a few urban areas, by 1980 the phenomenon had spread to most metropolitan areas. Conversions are highly profitable for landlords, developers, and the banks that finance the process, but also result in widespread displacement. Most tenants cannot afford the price of condominiums, but with vacancy rates so low, they have difficulty finding other suitable apartments. Tenants' groups have supported laws which delay evictions by requiring a year or more notice, prohibit evictions or conversions altogether, or require tenant approval before conversions proceed. By early 1981, some form of tenant protection against condominium conversion had been passed in 24 states and the District of Columbia (Dreier and Atlas, 1981).

While the tenants' movement has primarily been concerned with protecting tenants from rent increases and evictions and improving conditions, other issues have emerged as well. In Boston, for example, the Symphony Tenants Organizing Project (STOP) came together to investigate and fight fires that had been plaguing their neighborhood for several years. It began by trying to get the housing and building codes enforced. It soon discovered, however, that many fires were deliberately set by landlords in order to collect the insurance from buildings that they had abandoned or allowed to deteriorate. By generating considerable publicity and pressure around this "arson-for-profit" scheme, STOP got action by law enforcement officials and insurance companies, including the arrest of 33 landlords, lawyers, insurance adjusters, public officials, and a state police lieutenant. STOP has continued to organize tenants around rent increases, evictions, and gentrification.

In many older cities, abandoned housing has triggered tenant activism, including a tactic known as "squatting," in which tenants take over abandoned buildings and simply refuse to move (similar to workers' "sit-down" strikes). This tactic is used primarily by low-income tenants. Owners of these buildings often have not paid property taxes, so many abandoned buildings are owned by the city government. Tenants have demanded that the city government allow them to fix these buildings with "sweat equity" and live there permanently. ACORN coordinated a multi-city campaign, including Philadelphia, Detroit, and Boston, along these lines in 1981. In New York City, several programs are designed to turn abandoned properties over to tenant and non-profit community groups (Schur, 1980). In most localities, squatting still meets official resistance, eviction, and penalties.

Some tenant groups have organized as unions, seeking collective bargaining between tenants and landlords. Typically, this strategy is in response to rent increases and poor maintenance. Tenants engage in a rent strike, as well as demonstrations and picketing, to force the landlord to sit down and negotiate with the tenant group. Tenants hope that the landlord's legal fees, along with withheld rents and public embarrassment (one Boston group spread "wanted" posters, with the landlord's photograph and name on them, throughout the city) will force landlords to bargain. Because tenants risk eviction for such actions, it is not a widely-used tactic unless they already have achieved laws protecting them from eviction—or have faith in a sympathetic judge. In Chicago, Boston, and elsewhere, tenants have negotiated settlements with landlords, contracts which recognize the tenants' union and through which tenants gain a greater voice over rent increases, maintenance, and other conditions. Yet in no city or state are tenants' collective bargaining rights written into law, although in 1978–81 Madison, Wisconsin, had a "Rental Relations Ordinance" that required landlords to bargain in good faith with any legally constituted union of their tenants. Unlike labor unions, which are protected by the National Labor Relations Act, tenant unions have no automatic right to be recognized when more than half of the tenants (in a building or with the same landlord) vote for a union.

Tenant groups have also organized against involuntary displacement due to "gentrification," when private developers (often with the aid of public subsidies or tax breaks) build an office complex, luxury residential center, hotel, or convention center, or other major project. These developments often displace low- and moderate-income tenants—either directly (by tearing down their housing) or indirectly (by "upgrading" the neighborhood, attracting higher-income residents and boosting rent levels or including condo conversions). These anti-displacement efforts, however, involve great difficulties, since typically such developments are seen as "revitalizing" the city, broadening the tax base, and improving blighted neighborhoods (Hartman and Legates, 1981). Tenants have little leverage, other than costly, complex and drawn-out court battles (usually to deny government subsidies to such projects) or direct-action civil disobedience (which can delay projects, but rarely stop them). The principal of revitalizing neighborhoods without displacement requires a direct challenge to free market principles (i.e., controls on land speculation, even public ownership of land). It is only where tenant groups and their allies have more direct influence on government policy—as in Santa Monica, where they control local government—that the pace and direction of local development can be altered to stop displacement due to gentrification.

The discussion so far has focused primarily on tenants in private housing, but tenants in public housing have also engaged in rent strikes, direct action, litigation, and electoral activity to improve living conditions, often gaining concessions from local housing authorities. In the U.S., however, public housing tenants make up a very small portion (4.3 percent) of all renters. In addition, the targets for tenant activism among these tenants differ from those tenants in private housing, making joint action unlikely. Public and subsidized housing, for example, is exempt from local rent control laws (a result of federal regulations), thus removing these tenants as allies on many issues. Although these tenants typically live in large complexes and share the same landlord (the local housing authority or a private developer under government sponsorship), they rarely form enough of a critical mass of tenants in any one locality to form an effective political bloc. Two of the largest mobilizations among subsidized housing tenants—the Co-op City Rent Strike in New York and the Tenants First coalition in Massachusetts—ultimately collapsed and the short-term victories evaporated. Public housing tenants have won concessions over project maintenance and tenant input in decision-making, but local housing authorities are ultimately dependent on the federal government for resources and public housing has not been a priority of federal policy-makers.

PROBLEMS AND LIMITATIONS

There are some built-in limitations to a social movement organized primarily around tenant self-interest. Tenant-landlord laws are still biased against tenants, and their ability to endure costly legal battles in court is limited by their relative poverty. Tenant groups face the challenge to change the laws and to exert influence on elected officials and policy-makers. Where tenant protest has moved beyond direct action, to the political arena—seeking regulation of rents, evictions, and condo conversions, for example—landlords have mobilized their considerable resources. During referenda campaigns on rent control, for example, landlord groups have outspent tenant coalitions by more than 50 to 1. Landlords have the resources to require tenant groups to spend a great deal of time raising funds to win or maintain rent control. In 1980, for example, California's landlords tried to undermine local tenant victories by sponsoring a statewide initiative that would have effectively eliminated local rent control ordinances. With help from their counterparts around the nation, the landlords outspent the rent control advocates $4.9 million to $45,000 with expensive television, radio, billboard, and direct mail media campaigns. CHAIN, the statewide tenants' network, coordinated an effective grassroots campaign to overcome these heavy odds and defeated the landlords' initiative 65 to 35 percent. Beginning in 1978, the landlords' National Multi-Housing Council provided local landlord groups with help in coordinating anti-rent control drives. A number of consulting firms have also emerged to run such campaigns. Landlords in 1980 and 1981 defeated rent control initiatives in Minneapolis, San Bernardino, Seattle, San Diego, and Oakland.

Another route for tenant groups has been to pressure the local government to pass rent or condominium controls, but here tenants face the reality that real estate groups exert considerable influence over local elected officials. Real estate interests have a big stake in local politics and provide candidates with large campaign contributions (Dreier, 1982a). Elected officials are thus reluctant to move against such a powerful group. Tenants may represent a majority of the population in many large cities, but traditionally they have low levels of voter registration and political participation. Only where tenants as a self-aware voting bloc can deliver on their threat to help their friends and punish their enemies has the tenants' movement made significant political gains.

The showdown between tenants and landlords has primarily been a local matter. But landlords, tired of fighting brushfire battles against tenants across the country, have recently sought to pass federal legislation to stem the tide of tenant activism. Following the defeat of the anti-rent control initiative in California in June 1980, the National Multi-Housing Council proposed federal legislation that would deny or limit federal housing funds to any city with rent controls. The NMHC proposal was recommended in 1980 by President Reagan's urban affairs task force, and in 1982 by his special Commission on Housing (both dominated by realtors and bankers), and introduced in Congress. Although it has been defeated each year, it has forced local tenant groups to devote a great deal of their meager resources to stopping the landlord-sponsored bill.

Other policies of the Reagan Administration have dealt a blow to the tenants' movement. Drastic cutbacks in VISTA, CETA, Legal Services, and the Community Services Administration—all anti-poverty programs—have cut off staff and support services that helped to build the tenants' movement in the 1970s. Some groups simply could not survive the cutbacks and disappeared; others are limping along on much lower levels of activity. The stronger groups recognized the need to become more self-sufficient and put more emphasis on dues-paying members and grass-roots fundraising (raffles, bake sales). But there are obvious limits to the ability of tenants to financially support any organization. It is the emergence of tenant activism among the middle-class that provides some potential for financial self-sufficiency, but it is also this group that remains most committed to the dream of homeownership. Increased support from church and liberal foundations cannot compensate for the reductions in government funds. Both *Shelterforce* and the National Tenants Union run on shoe-string budgets; neither has any full-time staff. Real estate groups, in contrast, have enormous resources to lobby, provide studies and research, hire lawyers and consultants, and offer campaign contributions. The Realtors PAC, sponsored by the National Association of Realtors,

was the largest industry PAC (in terms of money contributed) in 1982
(*New York Times,* 1982).

FUTURE DIRECTIONS

Although still in its embryonic stages, and unevenly developed across the
country, the tenants' movement has already made some impressive gains.
It has politicized tenants, won concrete victories that improve housing
conditions, built stable organizations that develop leaders with political
skills and self-confidence, and elected pro-tenant candidates to public
office. Still, there is much room for growth. On the large stage of American politics, the tenants' movement is still a minor actor. It is still primarily a local phenomenon. The sum of its local activities does not add
up to a significant political force at the national level, where major housing policy decisions get made. Federal decisions—tax laws, subsidies, revitalization programs, interest rates, public housing budgets—determine
the nature of local housing problems and the resources available to solve
them.

Where can and should the tenants' movement go? To chart its future,
any movement needs to consider two basic elements. *Strategy* refers to
a political approach to broaden the movement's support and popular
appeal and to win political victories. *Program* refers to a coherent set of
policies that the movement seeks to win that would improve living conditions and, hopefully, whet people's appetites to go even further. Despite some differences, there is a growing consensus within the tenants'
movement regarding these questions.

The thrust of the tenants' movement will continue to be at the local
and state level—rent control laws, eviction regulations, improved enforcement of housing codes, and changes in tenant-landlord law. Its success,
however, depends in part on national policies. If, for example, homeownership costs continue to remain beyond the reach of the majority of
new American households, the tenants' movement will be able to draw
on this pool of frustrated would-be homeowners. Recent Census Bureau
data reveal that for the first time in the postwar period, homeownership
rates declined in 1982 (Guenther, 1982). If this trend continues, the
tenants' movement will undoubtedly benefit. In addition, if the national
government decides to devote greater resources to the poor and to grass-
roots groups—such as the VISTA program and Legal Services—tenant organizations will share in the benefits, as they did under the Carter Administration. Finally, if federal cutbacks in rent subsidy and public housing

programs continue, low-income tenants are likely to participate in greater strength in various protest, squatting, and other activities.

Although the tenants' movement is contingent on such policy directions, its success is also shaped by strategic choices made by tenant group leaders, as well as by the decisions of various nongovernmental funding groups that have supported tenant and other grass-roots self-help efforts in the recent past (Freeman, 1979). The success of the Santa Monica and New Jersey tenants' movements, for example, has triggered growing interest among local tenants' groups in electoral politics. *Shelterforce* has devoted many articles in recent issues to electoral strategies and tactics, encouraging tenant groups to get involved in voter registration, to sponsor candidates' nights, to endorse slates of pro-tenant candidates, and to learn the nuts-and-bolts of electoral work.

Successful tenants' groups have been the ones to recognize that the movement's potential is limited by numbers. Although many cities have renter majorities, in no state do tenants represent even half the population. Thus many tenant leaders are recognizing that the continued strengthening of the tenants' movement itself must coincide with a larger strategy of building coalitions with other progressive grass-roots groups. The success of the Baltimore rent control initiative in 1979 was the product of a joint effort by tenants and civil rights organizations, for example. The leaders of the New Jersey Tenant Organization, have initiated coalition efforts with state-level trade unions, senior citizens, environmental and women's organizations, to develop a progressive political action committee to coordinate electoral efforts. If this effort—called the New Jersey Public Interest PAC—is successful, it may encourage other tenant organizations to begin reaching out to other single-issue groups. Parallel coalition efforts are already under way in Massachusetts, Illinois, and elsewhere.

The tenants' movement has its own agenda. For the most part, it is a defensive agenda, seeking to improve tenants' status relative to landlords. The tenants' movement has been criticized for its narrow focus on such issues as rent control and condominium conversion, code enforcement, and arson. There is a growing awareness among tenant groups—as illustrated by articles published in tenant organization publications and by issues discussed at tenant movement conferences—that tenants' problems are not isolated to tenant-landlord conflicts. They recognize the need for more comprehensive housing reforms—policies that deal with supply, zoning, tax reform, and related issues. But the ability of tenant organizations to address these broader concerns is limited—both by the local nature of most tenant organizations and by the insecure position of most tenants.

One cannot expect most tenant groups to address these larger issues until the movement's own relative narrow agenda is more secure. Tenant leaders thus see such issues as rent control and code enforcement as a means to mobilize and educate tenants, win concrete reforms, and whet their appetites for more. It is not surprising, therefore, that the tenant organizations that have achieved the greatest success on tenant issues—in New Jersey, California, and Massachusetts—have been the first to begin to form coalitions and address the more comprehensive questions of housing policy.

CONCLUSION

The current housing crisis is a testament to the failure of liberal social policy. Since the late 1940s, the housing industry, the trade unions, poor people's advocates, and housing reformers joined in an uneasy alliance in support of a national housing policy based on subsidies and tax breaks for banks and homebuilders (Checkoway, 1980; Marcuse, 1978). For several decades this policy seemed to work, at least for the growing number of people who could afford to own their own homes. This policy in effect "co-opted" the potential for a significant tenants' movement. For those left behind in the rush to the suburbs—the urban poor, the minorities, the elderly—the private housing industry had little to offer. Public housing and rent subsidy programs provided only minimal security for the poor. This strategy of relying primarily on private industry to meet the nation's housing needs assumed that homes could be delivered at prices that working-class and middle-class people could afford. By the mid 1970s, however, economic growth stagnated, wages and salaries leveled off, and the postwar strategy began to falter.

In the long term, neither liberals nor conservatives—who both accept the basic tenets of postwar housing policy—have little to offer except different versions of austerity and belt-tightening. But the current crisis provides an opportunity to place housing policy on the nation's agenda once again. Large corporate employers, for example, do not want to pay higher wages simply to permit their employees to put a roof over their heads. Already in some areas of the country, employers are alarmed because rising housing costs are driving away, or making it difficult to attract, skilled (particularly professional level) employees. Some companies are even offering long-term reduced mortgages, or downpayments, to lure potential employees to move (*Business Week,* 1981a; Lindsey, 1981). But employers do not want to directly subsidize these housing costs. As housing prices skyrocket, some sectors of the business community will call for cost-containment, as they have already done for the spiralling costs of health care. Of course, business leaders will resist direct government ownership and production of housing, as they have resisted excluding the private sector from participation in any national health insurance legislation. But the call for government to "do something" about housing costs will push politicians into looking for new solutions. Much as the decades-long struggle for Medicare and Medicaid set the stage for recent debates over the structure of health care institutions and the "right" to decent, affordable health care, we can expect a protracted debate over housing. These circumstances set the stage for major reforms.

The ultimate goal of the tenants' movement, as part of a broader progressive movement for social change, is public policy that views housing as a public utility and a basic right (Hartman and Stone, 1978; Dreier, 1982b; Achtenberg and Marcuse, 1981). Housing is not an isolated enclave, but is part of the larger economy, which allocates scarce resources according to political priorities. For the coalition-building strategy to work, tenant and other groups must recognize their mutual interest not only in providing affordable housing, but in dealing with related issues of employment, public health, social welfare, and the billions wasted on militarism. All this may seem a long way from a local rent strike, but it is actually the direction extension of the logic of the tenants' movement.

The American tenants' movement has made some significant gains in the last decade, but this amounts to only a small dent in the nation's housing crisis. But crises create opportunities, not only for the tenants' movement, but for other grass-roots movements as well. Whether it can become more effective—not only in its short-term goals of increasing "tenant power," but also in the long-term goal of creating a progressive coalition movement to democratize American society—remains to be seen.

NOTES

1. This follows the government rule-of-thumb of spending one quarter of one's household income on housing.
2. Baltimore's rent control initiative, passed by the voters in 1979, was later overturned by the courts on the grounds that only the city council, and not the voters, can enact this type of legislation under Maryland's constitution.

REFERENCES

Achtenberg, Emily, and Peter Marcuse, "Housing and Neighborhoods: Network Position Paper," Washington, D.C.: Planners Network, 1981.
Alford, Robert, and H. M. Scoble, "Sources of Local Political Involvement," *American Political Science Review* 62: 1968, 1192–1206.

Baar, Kenneth K., "Rent Control in the 1970's: The Case of the New Jersey Tenants' Movement," *Hastings Law Journal* 28: 1977, 631–83.

Bell, Daniel, *The Cultural Contradictions of Capitalism* (New York: Basic Books, 1976).

Blumberg, Richard, and James R. Grow, *The Rights of Tenants* (New York: Avon Books, 1978).

Bouma, Donald, "Analysis of the Social Power Position of a Real Estate Board," *Social Problems* 10: 1962, 121–132.

Boyte, Harry, *The Backyard Revolution* (Philadelphia: Temple University Press, 1980).

Brooks, Andrea, "Foreclosing on a dream," *New York Times Magazine* (September 25, 1982): 68ff.

Burghart, Stephen, ed., *Tenants and the Urban Housing Crisis* (Dexter, Mich.: The New Press, 1972).

Business Week, "America's New Immobile Society," July 27, 1981. a

————, "Radical City Council Has Business Fuming," October 26, 1981. b

Castells, Manuel, "Theoretical Propositions for an Experimental Study of Urban Social Movements," in C. G. Pickvance, ed., *Urban Sociology: Critical Essays* (New York: St. Martin's Press, 1976).

Checkoway, Barry, "Large Builders, Federal Housing Programmes, and Post-war Suburbanization." In this volume, p. 152–73.

Christian, James W. and Thomas J. Parliment, *Home Ownership: The American Dream Adrift* (Chicago: U.S. League of Savings Associations, 1982).

Clay, Phillip, *Neighborhood Renewal* (Lexington, Mass.: D. C. Heath, 1979).

Cliffe, Chip, "Seniors and Tenants," *Shelterforce* 7 (November, 1982).

Comptroller General of the United States, "Rental Housing: A National Problem That Needs Immediate Attention," Washington, D.C.: Government Printing Office, 1979.

Cox, Kevin, "Housing Tenure and Neighborhood Activism," *Urban Affairs Quarterly* 18: 1982, 107–129.

Donohue, James J., "Interest Rate Pressure on the First-time Homebuyer: The Affordability Question," *Mortgage Banking* 42: 1982, 10–17.

Dreier, Peter, "The Politics of Rent Control," *Working Papers* 6: 1979, 55–63.

————, " 'Rent-A-Politician' Exposed," *Shelterforce* 7: (July 1982a).

————, "The Housing Crisis: Dreams and Nightmares," *The Nation* (August 21, 1982b): 141–44.

Dreier, Peter, and John Atlas, "Condomania," *The Progressive* (March 1981): 19–22.

Dunleavy, Patrick, "Protest and Quiescence in Urban Politics: A Critique of Some Pluralist and Structuralist Myths," *International Journal of Urban and Regional Research* 1977, 193–217.

Fellman, Gordon, *The Deceived Majority* (New Brunswick, N.J.: Transaction Books, 1973).

Fredland, David R., *Residential Mobility and Home Purchase* (Lexington, Mass.: Lexington Books, 1973).

Freeman, Jo, "Resource Mobilization and Strategy: A Model for Analyzing Social Movement Organization Actions," in Mayer Zald and John Mc-Carthy (eds.), *The Dynamics of Social Movements* (Cambridge, Mass.: Winthrop Publishers, 1979).

Frieden, Bernard, and Arthur P. Solomon, *The Nation's Housing 1975–85* (Cambridge: Joint Center for Urban Studies of MIT and Harvard Universities, 1977).

Gans, Herbert, *The Urban Villagers* (Glencoe, Ill.: The Free Press, 1962).

Gelfand, M. J., *A Nation of Cities* (New York: Oxford University Press, 1978).

Goodman, John L., *Urban Residential Mobility: Places, People, and Policy* (Washington, D.C.: The Urban Institute, 1978).

Guenther, Robert, "Rate of Homeownership Falls, Possibly Signaling Big Change," *Wall Street Journal* (August 11, 1982).

Hartman, Chester, "The Politics of Housing," *Dissent* 14: 1967, 701–14.

Hartman, Chester, and Michael Stone, "Housing: A Radical Alternative," in Marcus Raskin, ed., *The Federal Budget and Social Reconstruction* (New Brunswick: Transaction Books, 1978).

Harvey, David, "Labor, Capital, and Class Struggle Around the Built Environment in Advanced Capitalist Societies," in Kevin Cox, ed., *Urbanization and Conflict in Market Societies* (Chicago: Maaroufa Press, 1978).

Heskin, Allan David, "The History of Tenants in the United States: Struggle and Ideology," *International Journal of Urban and Regional Research* 5: 1981, 178–203.

Heady, Bruce, *Housing Policy in the Developed Economy* (New York: St. Martin's Press 1978).

Hendershott, Patric, and James Shilling, "The Economics of Tenure Choice, 1955–79," Cambridge, Mass.: National Bureau of Economic Research, Working Paper No. 243, 1980.

Indritz, Tova, "The Tenants' Rights Movement," *New Mexico Law Review* 1: 1971, 1–145.

Katznelson, Ira, "Considerations on Social Democracy in the U.S.," *Comparative Politics* 11: 1978, 77–99.

Kim, Sung Bok, *Landlord and Tenant in Colonial New York* (Chapel Hill: University of North Carolina Press, 1978).

Krohn, Roger, and Ralph Tiller, "Landlord-Tenant Relations in Declining Montreal Neighborhood," *Sociological Review Monographs* 14: 1969, 5–32.

Lawson, Ronald, "Tenant Mobilization in New York," *Social Policy* 1980, 30–40. a

———, "The Political Face of the Real Estate Industry in New York City," *New York Affairs* 6: 1980, 88–109. b

Lawson, Ronald, and John J. McLoughlin, "Elaborating the Structure of a Social Movement." Paper presented at American Studies Association meetings, 1975. a

———, "History of Tenant Organizing in New York City in the Twentieth Century." Paper presented at the Missouri Valley Historical Conference, 1975. b

———, "Tenant Organizing in a Metropolis: Harlem as a Case Study." Paper presented at Social for the Study of Social Problems meetings, 1976.

Lawson, Ronald, John J. McLoughlin, and Joseph Spencer, "New York City Tenant Organizations and the Formation of Urban Housing Policy." Paper presented at the Organization of American Historians meetings, 1975.

Leavitt, Helen, *Superhighway—Superhoax* (Garden City: Doubleday, 1970).

Lebowitz, Neil H., " 'Above Party, Class or Creed': Rent Control in the United States, 1940–47," *Journal of Urban History,* 7: 1981, 439–470.

LeGates, Richard, and Chester Hartman, "Displacement," *Clearinghouse Review* 15: 1981, 207–249.

Lilley, William, "The Homebuilders' Lobby," in Jon Pynoos, Robert Schafer and Chester Hartman, eds., *Housing in Urban America* (New York: Aldine, 1980).

Lindsey, Robert, "Housing Costs Are Turning Off Flow of Americans to California," *New York Times* (December 31, 1981).

Lipsky, Michael, *Protest in City Politics* (Chicago: Rand McNally, 1970).

Lubove, Roy, *The Progressives and the Slums* (Pittsburgh: University of Pittsburgh Press, 1962).

Mandelker, Daniel, *The Zoning Dilemma* (Indianapolis: The Bobbs-Merrill Co., 1971).

Marcuse, Peter, "Goals and Limitations: The Rise of Tenant Organizations," *The Nation* (July 19, 1971): 50–53.

———, "Housing Policy and the Myth of the Benevolent State," *Social Policy* 8: 1978, 21–26.

Mollenkopf, John, "The Post-War Politics of Urban Development," *Politics and Society* 5: 1975, 247–295.

Mollenkopf, John, and Jon Pynoos, "Boardwalk and Park Place," in Jon Pynoos, Robert Schafer, and Chester Hartman, eds., *Housing in Urban America* (New York: Aldine, 1980).

Naison, Mark, "The Rent Strikes in New York," *Radical America* 1: 1972, 7–49.

National Advisory Commission on Civil Disorders, *Report* (New York: Bantam Books, 1968).

Neutze, Max, *The Suburban Apartment Boom* (Baltimore: Johns Hopkins University Press, 1968).

New York Times "Independent Groups Lag on Candidate Donations" (November 3, 1982): A22.

Perlman, Janice E., "Grassroots Participation from Neighborhood to Nation," in Stuart Langton, ed., *Citizen Participation in America* (Lexington, Mass.: D. C. Heath, 1978).

———, "Grassroots Empowerment and Government Response," *Social Policy* 10: 1979, 16–21.

Piven, Frances Fox, and Richard Cloward, "Rent Strike: Disrupting the Slum System," *New Republic* (December 1967): 11–15.

———, *Poor People's Movements* (New York: Random House 1977).

———, *The New Class War,* (New York: Pantheon, 1982).

Rose, Jerome, *Landlords and Tenants* (New Brunswick: Transaction Books, 1973).

Rossi, Peter, *Why Families Move* (Glencoe, Ill.: The Free Press, 1955).

Sawers, Larry, and Howard M. Wachtel, "Who Benefits from Federal Housing Policies?" in David Gordon, ed., *Problems in Political Economy: An Urban Perspective* (Lexington, Mass.: D. C. Heath, 1977).

Schafer, Robert, *The Suburbanization of Multifamily Housing* (Lexington, Mass.: D. C. Heath, 1974).

Schur, Robert, "Growing Lemons in the Bronx," *Working Papers* (July/Aug. 1980): 42–51.

Shearer, Derek, "How Progressives Won in Santa Monica," *Social Policy* 12 (Winter 1982) Pp. 7–14.

Sternlieb, George, and James W. Hughes, *America's Housing: Prospects and Problems* (New Brunswick: Center for Urban Policy Research, 1980).

Stone, Michael, "Mortgage Bankers and the Politics of Housing," in David Gordon, ed., *Problems in Political Economy: An Urban Perspective* (Lexington, Mass.: D. C. Heath, 1977).

U.S. Congress, Congressional Budget Office, *The Tax Treatment of Homeownership* (Washington, D.C.: Government Printing Office, 1981).

U.S. Bureau of the Census, *Annual Housing Survey: 1980* (Washington, D.C.: Government Printing Office, 1981).

———, *Voting and Registration in the Election of November 1978* (Washington, D.C.: Government Printing Office, 1979).

Vaughan, Ted R., "The Landlord-Tenant Relation in a Low-Income Area,"
   Social Problems 16: 1968, 208–18.
Williamson, Chilton, *American Suffrage from Property to Democracy 1760–
   1860* (Princeton: Princeton University Press, 1960).
Wolman, Harold, *Politics of Federal Housing* (New York: Dodd, Mead, 1971).

three

PLANNING
THE METROPOLIS

9

From Industrial to Corporate City: The Role of Urban Renewal

NANCY KLENIEWSKI

"To provide a decent home and suitable environment for every American family."

This was the stated goal of the Housing Act of 1949 which established the urban renewal program. Many observers have mistakenly concluded that the program was initiated by the federal government in order to provide housing for the poor. They are wrong on two counts: first, the program was not initiated by the federal government, and second, it was not set up to provide housing for the poor. A study of urban renewal programs and their results—nationally or city by city—cannot help but come to those conclusions.

Urban renewal was a program for urban economic growth and revitalization. It was designed to stimulate economic growth by making cities more profitable places for capital to invest. Urban renewal was not a housing program and did not have housing production as its goal except where housing fit into overall plans for economic development and growth.

Urban renewal programs were also largely initiated and carried out by local business-oriented groups with the assistance of federal and local governments. Urban renewal programs were not simply originated by the federal government and imposed on cities but were initially sought by local groups promoting urban revitalization.

In this essay we will look at the urban renewal program in Philadelphia as an example of the origin and role of urban renewal programs in the United States.

THE POSTWAR SITUATION OF THE INDUSTRIAL CITIES

By the end of World War II, the downtown areas of many U.S. cities were in decay. Their physical condition reflected their declining economies. Many industrial cities had had little capital invested in them during the decades of the Depression and WW II. They had been built up during the period of industrial expansion in the late nineteenth and early twentieth centuries but had experienced a reduction in the level of investment and building after the 1920s.[1] The decline of these older industrial cities is linked to the growth of suburbs and newer cities. Both phenomena are results of changes in the dominant type of investment—from the industrial pattern of the nineteenth and early twentieth centuries to the corporate pattern characteristic of the middle-to-late twentieth century.

During and after World War II, economic investment has increasingly followed a different pattern from that prevalent in the industrial period. This postindustrial, or corporate, pattern of investment has several features. First, the scale of production has been increasing due to corporate growth and mergers. Corporations have grown in size and have created larger and larger production facilities. Second, investment has become increasingly concentrated in a smaller number of companies. Thus, the increasing size of corporations has been accompanied by increasing concentration and centralization of investment capital. Third, management has become separated from actual production. Research, administration, marketing, management, and other nonmanufacturing functions of companies have been taken out of factories and centralized in special administrative centers, often corporate headquarters. Fourth, with increasing automation, proportions of manufacturing personnel have been reduced although proportions of administrative personnel have increased.

These trends in the pattern of corporate investment have contributed to the restructuring of the work force and the workplace in U.S. industries. In the area of employment, there has been a decrease in the relative demand for production workers in manufacturing—both skilled and unskilled—and an increase in the relative demand for service, management, and technical workers. In the area of the workplace, production and management have been physically separated into different buildings, different communities, and even different parts of the country or the world. The larger factories have increasingly been located in suburban areas; office location has been more flexible, but has tended to be centralized in cities rather than dispersed in suburbs.

The change in patterns of investment from the industrial period to the corporate period has had profound implications for the growth and decline of cities, metropolitan areas, and even larger areas of the country.

Several urban trends that became apparent in the postwar decade have been linked to corporate investment patterns. The first of these is the growth of suburbs relative to central cities. The increasing size and concentration of corporations as well as changes in the technology of production have led companies to favor large suburban sites for the location of plants. As industrial production has moved to suburbs, more investment in related areas, such as housing and retailing, has gone into suburban areas than into urban areas. Consequently, suburbs have gained relative to cities in certain employment opportunities (especially manufacturing and retailing), in population, and in revenues.

Second, new cities and metropolitan areas have grown up based on their attractiveness for corporate investments. Predominantly but not exclusively located in the South and West, new cities such as Houston and Los Angeles have economies based on energy, high-technology manufacturing, leisure activities, and defense production.[2] In their physical structure as well as their economic structure, the new corporate-era cities are different from the old industrial-era cities. They tend to be low-density and non-centralized, with a spread-out development pattern more suited to the production technologies and organizational requirements of modern large corporations. These new cities and their metropolitan areas are also proportionally gaining capital investments relative to the older cities and metropolitan areas.

Suburban development and the growth of new cities has had an enormous impact on the central cities of the older metropolitan areas. These older cities are not only receiving a share of investment smaller than the share they received in the past, but they are also experiencing active disinvestment as large corporations close plants located in the older cities and expand or open new facilities in suburban areas or the South. For the old industrial cities this has often meant that they have been left with deteriorated industrial buildings, roads, and railroads, a population of industrial workers displaced from their jobs, a decline in population, and a shrinking tax base. On the other hand, a number of older industrial cities have also received some new corporate-era investment—not necessarily in manufacturing but in management, research, and services.

THE ACCOMPLISHMENTS OF THE URBAN RENEWAL

Urban renewal legislation, passed by Congress in 1949, provided federal aid to localities for the clearance of blighted buildings, the assembly and preparation of parcels of land for re-use, and the resale of the land at a reduced price. Federal funds were usually distributed through local redevelopment authorities which had control (within federal guidelines) over the location and nature of the urban renewal projects. Although the legislation was ostensibly passed with the purpose of providing "a decent home and a suitable living environment for every American family," the main focus of most cities' redevelopment programs was economic development of the city rather than housing production.[3]

In Philadelphia, the urban renewal program was initiated in 1948 (even before the federal legislation) and by 1965 was being heralded as one of the most successful urban renewal programs in the country. The heyday of urban renewal was the decade 1952 to 1962 during the administration of two Reform Democratic Mayors, Joseph Clark and Richardson Dilworth, both avid supporters of urban renewal.

The urban renewal program in the city of Philadelphia during the Clark and Dilworth years had four main results: urban renewal stimulated investment in the central city, it bolstered the values of central city property, it spurred the transformation of central Philadelphia from an industrial city to a corporate city, and it initiated a change in the composition of the population living in and near the central city.

Urban renewal helped stimulate new investment in central Philadelphia by amplifying the effects of a building boom that had already begun in the two years after World War II. It is not clear whether urban renewal activities boosted the total amount of investment capital in the city or merely helped concentrate some of it in the center, but it certainly did help promote development in the central business district. Urban renewal offered subsidized land which helped make the central city more competitive in cost with suburban land, thus creating new investment opportunities in the central city. The intention was that the urban renewal projects would encourage additional private investment in related projects; for example, luxury housing would provide opportunities for investment in restaurants, and tourist parks would stimulate hotel construction. Since the city had stopped growing, demolition, and rebuilding was substituted for genuine economic growth.

Second, urban renewal helped keep up the values of central city property. These had been in danger of collapse, partly because of the old age of many of the buildings, and partly because of the proximity of other deteriorated properties. Urban renewal's new construction helped bolster the values of existing properties and its revamping of land uses helped generate higher demand and prices in neighboring areas. This was of great concern to the realtors, bankers, and insurance companies which had large investments in property in the central business district.

Third, and most importantly, urban renewal helped to physically transform Philadelphia from a city characteristic of the industrial era to one characteristic of the corporate era. As an industrial city, central Philadelphia was constructed during the nineteenth century. Thus the patterns of land use, the physical structures, and the infrastructure of transportation and other facilities was outmoded for the twentieth century. Using urban renewal, the city's business and political leaders systematically began to remove the industrial-era characteristics and replace them with corporate-era characteristics.

Old productive spaces such as manufacturing lofts, warehouses, wholesale distributors' outlets, and small independent businesses were eliminated. These were replaced (not necessarily in the same place, because land use was being rationalized for maximum investment potential) with office towers, university expansion, luxury housing, and specialized shops. New parks were created and the historical areas rehabilitated for increased tourism. The transportation structure was also changed, with narrow streets, railroad tracks, and wharves demolished in favor of parking lots, underground railroad tunnels, and wider streets.

In addition to the changes in the functions of the space, urban renewal projects also helped change the symbolic nature of the city. The old pattern of low brick buildings, narrow streets, and little open land was replaced by a new pattern of concrete skyscrapers interspersed with plazas and malls and a widening of some streets. This new structural arrangement symbolically suggests the concentration of power. The space adjacent to the most prominent building in the central city, City Hall, was previously occupied by the terminal of the Pennsylvania Railroad. Its new incarnation was as Penn Center—the "Rockefeller Center of Philadelphia"—complete with skating rink. The railroad, which had previously been one of the strongest bases of the Philadelphia economy, developed the property for use by banks, insurance companies, and other offices and commercial establishments in recognition of the new, corporate base of the central city economy.

The fourth accomplishment of urban renewal in Philadelphia was that it began to change the nature of the population in and around the central city from predominantly industrial working-class, unemployed poor, and racial minorities, to predominantly white, middle- to upper-middle-class and professional population. This shift in population is actually a corollary to the change in the physical structure of the central city from an industrial to a corporate pattern. The wealthier white residents increasingly moving to certain sections of the central city were the workers for the new economic structure: lawyers, government workers, university professors and students, physicians and middle-level managers, as well as nurses, clerical workers, and social service workers. The old industrial-era workers' housing was labeled "blight" and demolished.

In examining the demolition of housing that was the first part of the urban renewal program, one can see that in the central business district, urban renewal eliminated the skid row area, part of Chinatown, parts of Society Hill (which housed both white and black working-class and impoverished families), and the Triangle, which was an area of white working-class housing and industrial buildings. By far the largest number of housing demolitions occurred in the area just north of the central business district, called Lower North Philadelphia. This area was overwhelmingly populated by poor blacks living in, on the average, the worst housing in the city. Through the demolition phase of the urban renewal program, advocates of urban renewal hoped to "deconcentrate" this slum area. Demolition would lower the density and size of the poor black population in North Philadelphia and the inhabitants would be encouraged to move elsewhere. A plan was developed and initiated (but never completed) to relocate the poor blacks of North Philadelphia in a new community that would be created on unused land in the far southwest section of the city, Eastwick, near the airport. Housing for the growing black middle class, however, was planned and constructed in North Philadelphia. This consisted of a subsidized mortgage townhouse development adjacent to one of the universities.

If we examine housing construction during this period, we find that the housing built on urban renewal land primarily accommodated a higher-income population than the housing that was demolished. Some public housing for low-income families was built, but twice as much land was developed for private housing as for public housing.[4] In the central city especially, the housing that was constructed on urban renewal land was overwhelmingly suited for upper-middle-income groups. The luxury high-rise buildings of Society Hill Towers, Hopkinson House, the Penn Towne project, and Kennedy House were all early products of urban renewal. The success of these early high-rises also helped spawn several developments of high-priced townhouses, especially in the areas adjacent to Society Hill Towers.

Although the Redevelopment Authority itself did not construct housing but simply prepared and sold land, it acted as part of a unit coordinated by the City Planning Commission which helped develop and approve the plans for buildings constructed on urban renewal land. Therefore, although city agencies did not directly build this new housing for the upper middle classes in the central city, they subsidized, helped plan, and in general enthusiastically supported its construction. At one point, when a proposal was made to develop Society Hill as a mixed low-moderate- and upper-income development, rather than purely upper-income, the Mayor objected, saying, "We've got to get the white [leadership] back. We have to give the whites confidence that they can live in town without being flooded."[5]

The effect of the demolition phase of urban renewal was to reduce the number of poor and working-class people in and around the central city. In subsequent construction, the effect was to increase the number of middle-to-upper-income white residents in the central city. Besides the upper-income housing constructed on the urban renewal land itself, urban renewal initiated a process of gentrification[6] that lasted long after the actual urban renewal program had ended. Many working-class neighborhoods adjacent to the central business district began to attract wealthier residents as a result of the popularity of the high-rise developments. As the professional work force in the central city continued to grow, housing for this group became scarce. Individuals, developers, and eventually speculators began to move into nearby working-class areas that had basically sound housing, such as Queen Village, Washington Square West, and Spring Garden. The subsequent increases in rents, housing prices, and taxes in those areas began to force out the people who had been living there. Many of these displaced residents were members of ethnic groups (such as the Irish and Eastern Europeans of Queen Village, and the Hispanics of Spring Garden) whose communities were broken up by the process of gentrification.

Ironically, the city planners failed in their attempt to stimulate the private market to produce housing for the poor blacks they had removed from Lower North Philadelphia. They did succeed, however, in stimulating the private market for luxury housing in the central city, causing rents and property values to skyrocket in the late 1960s and early 1970s. Urban renewal thus provided the impetus for the revamping of the central city's population base as well as its physical structure.

In other cities the urban renewal program was used in much the same way as it was in Philadelphia. Pittsburgh, Hartford, Boston, and San Francisco also attempted to facilitate the change from an industrial sector to a corporate sector economy by removing industrial-era buildings and constructing office space, particularly in skyscrapers. San Francisco and Boston also greatly increased the amount of space in their central business districts by demolishing nearby residential areas to expand the commercial and business centers. Another common theme is that cities such as New York, Boston, and San Francisco built luxury residential properties to house their new corporate work force as the cities' economies changed. Some cities, like Newark, suffering from the same "image" problem as Philadelphia, tried to attract investment and upgrade their negative image by replacing blocks of deteriorated and abandoned old housing with modern superblock apartments. Cities with universities such as New Haven, Cambridge, and New York used urban renewal to encourage the universities to expand in the city rather than in the suburbs. They also encouraged the development of private research institutions that would operate in connection with the universities.

In short, whatever potential resources a city had that it could use to bring it into the corporate era, it used. In some places this was a university, in others, tourist attractions, corporate headquarters, or government offices. The cities in which urban renewal did *not* facilitate a shift in the local economy were those which had lost their industrial-era functions of manufacturing and retailing but had no corporate-era functions with which to replace them. Thus in many of the smaller old industrial cities, the legacy of urban renewal was nothing more than empty lots and public housing projects. What appears to have happened is that the elites of those cities already moving into the corporate era used the urban renewal program as a way of hastening that movement; however, the urban renewal program could only facilitate, not *cause,* corporate-era investment in the older cities.

THE SUPPORTERS OF URBAN RENEWAL

A common misconception of the urban renewal program is that it was developed by the federal government and imposed on the cities. Actually, the opposite is true: groups from the large cities developed the general outline of the program and then lobbied Congress and the state legislatures for the legislation.[7] Pennsylvania, for example, had enacted enabling legislation for urban renewal three years before the national law was passed in 1949, due to the lobbying efforts of groups from Pittsburgh and Philadelphia. Many of the same groups supported and worked for the national legislation as well as state laws.

Those local groups that lobbied for and supported urban renewal nationally had the primary intention of stimulating local economic growth. Harvey Molotch (1976) and John Mollenkopf (1978) have described these "pro-growth coalitions" as coalitions of local elites with an economic interest in growth, either because of their ownership of land or because growth would be profitable to their businesses. Some examples of groups typically found in pro-growth coalitions include bankers, developers, construction companies, realtors, retailers, newspapers, and hotel owners. Molotch argues that the main function of cities in our economy has been to produce economic growth so that profits can be made by the elites that control urban investments. In the case of the old industrial cities which were not growing but shrinking in the 1940s and 1950s, Mollenkopf describes how the local business groups promoted urban renewal as a substitute for actual growth in population. Investment and construction that would result from urban renewal was expected to stimulate other aspects of urban economies, such as entertainment, retail sales, newspaper circulation, and even university enrollments.

In Philadelphia as well as in other cities, a pro-growth coalition initiated, lobbied for, and directed the urban renewal program. Led by an organized group of local business leaders, the Greater Philadelphia Movement, the coalition also included some city planners, city officials, and the Philadelphia Housing Association, itself a coalition of philanthropic groups interested in housing and urban planning. These groups had become alarmed at the physical and economic condition of the city in the late 1940s, citing old and abandoned buildings, inefficient land uses, and slum housing as detrimental to the future of the city. They were concerned primarily that the old and unattractive central city had little potential to attract investment and secondarily that the conditions of the impoverished slum dwellers would be an increasing fiscal burden on the city taxpayers, thus stifling growth.

One spokesperson, William F. Kelly, President of the First Pennsylvania Bank, remarked,

> The future of our companies—all of them—is tied to the growth of our city. . . . The growth of our bank, its well-being in the years to come, depends on what is done here in Philadelphia. (Adde, 1969, p. 36)

Divisions within the business leadership of the city initially prevented the pro-growth coalition from encompassing the entire business elite. These deep and bitter divisions were due partly to a feud which had begun during the Depression and partly to a fundamentally different philosophy of investment resulting from a different base of capital. The split was represented in the conflict and competition between the Greater Philadelphia Movement and the Chamber of Commerce.

The Chamber of Commerce represented the traditional business leadership of Philadelphia. Although all kinds of businesses were represented in it, the leadership tended to be composed of large manufacturers and large retailers. The Chamber's attitude toward government was very conservative: it backed the Republican machine and it opposed government intervention in local economic affairs. The Greater Philadelphia Movement, on the other hand, represented the "Young Turks,"[8] the movers and shakers of the business community. Representing 100 Philadelphia-based firms, the board of the GPM had a membership composed predominantly of executive officers of banks and partners in large law firms.

Politically, the GPM advocated reform, including a new cooperation between business leaders and city officials. Urban renewal was only one part of the GPM's program for Philadelphia's revitalization. Physical revitalization through urban renewal and city planning was one important element of this program. The other was political reform through the adoption of a new city charter and support of reform Democratic candidates to oust the corrupt Republican machine. Thus the GPM was intertwined with several other groups, including the Citizen's Council for City Planning and the Citizen's Charter Committee as well as providing much of the base of support for the mayoral campaigns of reform Democrats Clark and Dilworth.

If physical, economic, and political reform was the program of the Greater Philadelphia Movement, then a public-private partnership was the means to accomplish the reforms. Leaders of the GPM realized that totally private renovation of the central city would be prohibitively expensive and would probably not result in a unified project. Competition between investors for parcels of land, land owners "holding out" for higher prices, and the difficulty of developing small, isolated plots would all contribute to increasing the costs and decreasing the potential profits of private investors. Thus they advanced a plan for cooperation between the private and public sector. Private investors would put up most of the capital for the projects' actual construction. The city government would plan and coordinate the projects and use its power of eminent domain to condemn land for redevelopment. The public sector would not substitute for the private investors but would perform tasks that individual investors could not do: planning so that land uses would be compatible, changing zoning restrictions, floating bonds for improvements in streets or water supplies, and perhaps most importantly condemning property, thus eliminating the costly and time-consuming problem of "holdouts."

Leaders of the pro-growth coalition did not believe that urban revitalization could be accomplished by private business interests without the participation of the local government. The Chamber of Commerce, however, was initially opposed to public involvement in redevelopment. Its leaders, and particularly its Board Chair Albert M. Greenfield, argued that private, voluntary redevelopment would suffice to revitalize the central city, and that the city government should limit its activities to improving water supplies and transportation. This position was an extension of the traditional orientation of the Chamber of Commerce, which operated on a rather narrowly construed notion of business interests—that the protection of individual businesses' profits was its main duty. To this end, the Chamber of Commerce resisted government intervention and the tax increases that would have supported it. It did not share the views of the Greater Philadelphia Movement either on the urgency of large-scale revitalization or on the necessity of public-private cooperation to achieve it.

Why did these differences emerge? What underlying factors affected the different positions of these two business leadership groups regarding the urban renewal program? Although there are particular historical events which may have influenced their positions, the most important difference between the two groups is that each represented a different sector of capital. The Chamber of Commerce leadership was primarily composed of large manufacturers and large retailers—those groups which had been prominent in the central city during the industrial-era but were now tending to disperse to the suburbs. The Greater Philadelphia Movement's leadership, in contrast, were more closely tied to emerging corporate sector firms, especially financial institutions and law firms. This sector's goal was to remake the central city into a corporate-era city—a transformation that would benefit their own firms. Changing over from the old industrial-era buildings and land-use patterns to the new corporate-era patterns facilitated the "modernization" of investment patterns in the central city.

The struggle between the Greater Philadelphia Movement and the Chamber of Commerce was over more than the physical restructuring of the central city. It also involved a political struggle for the leadership of the city government. The Chamber of Commerce for several decades had been the acknowledged leadership body of the city's business community and had cooperated closely with the traditional Republican machine. The GPM, in rising to challenge the Chamber's leadership, first opposed it politically by backing the reform Democratic candidates and then proposed its own program—publically sponsored redevelopment—which the Chamber resisted. In both the electoral contest and the battle for the urban renewal program, the GPM was victorious. These two victories helped consolidate the position of the GPM as the new leadership of the business community in Philadelphia. The strength of the old industrial elite and the political machine it supported had dissipated and the new corporate elite with the progressive reform administration it supported was in the ascendancy.

THE CONTRADICTIONS OF URBAN RENEWAL

Urban renewal could have been viewed as a success. It resulted, directly or indirectly, in the rebuilding of a substantial section of the central city and parts of several nearby areas (especially around universities and hospitals). It helped to maintain and eventually to increase property values in the central city. It provided the basis for an expanded tourist industry. Yet it produced so many problems and became so unpopular that the program was eventually dismantled. These problems resulted mainly from two different flaws in the urban renewal program: first, it was carried out at the expense of the poor, the working class, and racial minorities; and second, it did not fundamentally change the patterns of capital investment in the city. Although the example is drawn from the Philadelphia experience, these two contradictions arose over and over in the administration of urban renewal programs throughout the U.S.

Urban renewal was carried out at the expense of lower-income and minority groups in several ways. The city's stock of low-cost housing was actually reduced by urban renewal. In its first five years, the urban renewal program demolished over 9000 homes in urban renewal areas of Philadelphia. Although the majority of these were in bad condition, they were providing housing for people. It was several years before any replacement housing was built, and even as late as 1963, about 3000 fewer units were either planned or constructed in those areas than had been demolished (Community Renewal Program 1963, pp. 67–68). As a result of this decrease in available low-cost housing, many families were forced to pay higher rents or live in smaller quarters than they previously had been able to obtain. This housing shortage problem occurred in many other cities undergoing urban renewal, since, like Philadelphia, there was an attempt being made to "deconcentrate" slums, meaning to reduce the number of dwelling units in them. Programs were deliberately designed to rebuild fewer housing units than were demolished. The assumption that private developers would build additional housing to absorb the "excess" poor and minority population in new locations proved false.

The second way in which urban renewal was detrimental to minority and low-income groups was through displacement of households from their homes and neighborhoods. Initially, this was done directly, through eviction of the families whose dwellings were slated to be demolished. With only a minimal relocation program, which came after the first evictions, the Redevelopment Authority forcibly removed thousands of both renters and homeowners from their homes. Even after the evictions had ceased, however, displacement continued through gentrification. In many neighborhoods not directly affected by urban renewal, the effects of the program were felt indirectly as developers, speculators, and even private upper-middle-class homeowners invested in older central-city neighborhoods, expecting values to rise as a side effect of nearby urban renewal projects. As a result, rents, property values, and eventually taxes rose to a level that was prohibitively expensive for the groups that had previously lived there. Many ethnic communities and stable working-class neighborhoods were disrupted by displacement associated with gentrification as the poor black areas had been disrupted by displacement due to demolitions.

In the early years of the program, groups being displaced did not protest in an organized way, partly because they believed that they would soon see the construction of new low-income housing. After a few years, it became apparent that construction was to be oriented more toward economic development plans than toward low-income housing construction. Gradually a strong social movement began, first among blacks, claiming that urban renewal was really "Negro removal." Initially, black community groups in Philadelphia blocked the plan to relocate blacks from North Philadelphia to Eastwick. Later, through protest and negotiation, community groups obtained modifications in renewal plans that would have allowed university expansion in North Philadelphia to take several hundred additional homes. These initial protests against urban renewal formed the basis of an urban social movement among community activists in the city which is still challenging and protesting the city's housing and community development programs.[9]

The second fundamental problem of urban renewal is that it did not really stop urban decline. Population continued to decline in Philadelphia, as in the other older large cities, and the tax base continued to shrink. Although the urban renewal program helped to rebuild the central city, it did not change the overall pattern of urban decline. Rather than revitalizing the city as a whole, the urban renewal program simply reshuffled the city's wealthy and poor areas into new locations. Although physical deterioration in the central city was abated, it appeared elsewhere. Investment was obtained for the central city, but the areas which were perceived as less profitable were ignored. The total amount of investment was insufficient to rehabilitate all the deteriorated areas. James O'Connor (1973, p. 137) remarks that in most cities, urban renewal programs simply "reinforced the 'decisions' of the market place . . . [contributing] not only to the dynamism of the downtown districts but also to the decay of the remainder of the city." This was true also of Philadelphia.

A related problem is that the urban renewal program did not change the distribution of resources within the city's population. The patterns of wealth and poverty, good housing and bad, rehabilitation and deterioration, remained. Under urban renewal, no attempt was made to provide services, education, or employment for the poor, working class, and minorities. The initiators of urban renewal felt that the demolition of blighted housing would start a chain of events that would revitalize slum neighborhoods. They did not design a program to deal with poverty, merely with old, dilapidated housing.

All these problems and contradictions made the program very unpopular, in Philadelphia and nationally. People refused to be evicted, squatted in houses that were slated for demolition, blocked bulldozers, built "peoples' parks" on vacant urban renewal lots, and of course marched on city halls throughout the country. Whatever political gains cities had made by the construction of their office buildings, convention centers, and luxury apartments were eroded by the protests, riots, and other forms of challenge brought by those groups (especially blacks) who had been the most adversely affected by the program. The urban renewal program was therefore phased out, ending completely in 1974. Since that time, however, new policies and programs have been developed that continue the same patterns initiated by the urban renewal program. Although they no longer use the method of large-scale slum clearance, newer programs such as the Community Development Block Grants and the Historical Preservation Act have continued to subsidize the redevelopment of central cities, usually at the expense of low-income housing construction.

ALTERNATIVE PROGRAMS FOR
URBAN REVITALIZATION

What conclusions can be drawn about urban renewal? The major conclusion is that urban renewal was a plan to bring the physical nature of the older industrial cities into line with certain changes in the structure of the U.S. economy.[10] As we saw in the case of Philadelphia, there was a transformation of the city's economy based on the national shift of emphasis from industry to service. As the economy changed, the nature of the most powerful groups in the city changed also, from a manufacturing-based elite to a finance-capital and service-based elite. In addition to the physical transformation of the city, this new elite proposed a new mode of managing investment, shifting from totally individual private projects to a public-private partnership in collectively planned projects. Thus, as John Mollenkopf (1981, p. 16) noted, urban "renewal played midwife to the emerging corporate economy that now characterizes the major cities."

The second major conclusion that can be drawn is that the urban renewal program was part of a wider transformation of the economic, physical, political, and social character of the city. Physically, industrial-era housing and commercial properties were replaced by skyscrapers, plazas, and parks. Economically, manufacturing, especially heavy industry, was replaced by services such as corporate management, research, finance, education, health and entertainment. Politically, the Republican electoral machine was replaced by the reform Democratic movement. Finally, the social nature of the central city was partially transformed by the displacement of poor, working class, and ethnic populations and the addition of white, upper-middle-class professional groups. Urban renewal did not arise in isolation and it involved more than just the demolition of blighted property.

The third major conclusion we can draw is that some groups gained and some lost from urban renewal. Clearly, those poor and minority groups displaced from their homes were losers. But who gained? The members of the pro-growth coalition seem to have made gains: the reform politicians, realtors, and builders gained either economically or politically by the revitalization of the central city. In addition, several hospitals, universities, and other nonprofit organizations were beneficiaries of urban renewal land. White upper-middle-class professionals gained additional areas of the city as choices for their residences. It appears, then, that urban renewal not only did not help the poor but redistributed some of their assets (land) to wealthier groups.

If urban renewal was the "capitalists' plan" for the revitalization of older cities, could we develop a "peoples' plan" for renewal? Rather than encouraging gentrification, displacement, and housing shortages, could we control them? Could we provide more and better housing for the poor, working class, and minorities rather than favoring the economically better-off? A program for revitalization that would avoid the problems of urban renewal would have to include at a minimum the following four features:

1. It must be redistributive from the rich to the poor. Low-income households should receive subsidies to make up the difference between their incomes and their housing needs. Some of our current housing programs such as Section 8 and public housing are redistributive in this way, but the amount of money spent on them is far less than the money spent on the programs which benefit middle- and upper-income households, such as income tax deductions for homeowners.

2. It must include more public production of housing. As long as housing is primarily produced by private investors and developers for profit, housing for the poor will be scarce and in bad condition. One possibility is to socialize some segments of the housing market, as England has done in the construction of publicly financed Council Housing. Public housing in the U.S. has justifiably received a bad reputation; however, public housing need not be either depressing, demeaning, or dangerous. To be viable, public housing simply requires a sufficient commitment of economic and social resources.

3. A program for urban revitalization must provide for social control over housing production and allocation. That is, communities would channel resources according to social needs rather than encouraging in-

vestors to channel them for profit. Thus, planning would have a social rather than an economic function and would involve the participation of all the users of housing. Some forms of social accountability would have to be developed to ensure that the communities' needs were met.

4. It must lessen the community's reliance on large sources of capital. Economic development plans should stress support for small businesses, cooperatives, and labor-intensive industries. These both create more jobs than larger industries and also hold less threat of capital flight after a period of time. In addition, attempts should be made to re-employ displaced workers, both through retraining and through support for the establishment of new jobs for workers with their skills.

It is readily apparent that no U.S. city (even Burlington, Vermont, or Santa Cruz, California, which both have socialist mayors) is about to institute this program. City governments fail to consider proposals such as these because they fall outside the limits of political debate. Thus policy makers and planners—even liberal ones—are faced with a dilemma. They are limited in their attempts at urban revitalization because they need the cooperation of capital to make their programs work. This cooperation is forthcoming only when the programs provide an opportunity for profit. However, the very profitability of a project tends to make it incompatible with the needs of the poor. Thus, revitalization programs have so far tended to be controlled by private corporate interests; if not directly, at least to the extent that consideration of corporate interests sets the limits of the policy options.

So how to get public money out of the revitalized downtowns and back into the still-declining neighborhoods is a political question. To apply a suggestion Mollenkopf has made in another context, what is needed is

> a political movement explicitly based on putting in place new city spending priorities and land use patterns. . . . Such a party . . . would seek to change the framework of decision-making and the values implicit within it. . . . Whether such an alliance can emerge remains to be seen, but when all is said and done, this remains the task of city dwellers who would like to live in a truly humane city. (Mollenkopf 1978, p. 149)

NOTES

1. See Gordon essay 2 here for a full discussion of types of capital accumulation and their impact on the nature of cities.
2. See Perry and Watkins (1977), Sternlieb and Hughes (1975) and Sale (1977) for discussions of Sunbelt cities' economies.

3. See Hartman (1966) and Anderson (1964) on the amount of housing production. Also see Weiss (1980) about the intent of the urban renewal legislation.
4. Community Renewal Program, 1966, Table V-2.
5. Mayor Dilworth quoted in Lowe (1968), p. 352.
6. Gentrification is the process whereby wealthier groups move into areas previously occupied by less wealthy and/or minority groups.
7. Marc Weiss (1980) discusses this phenomenon. Lobbyists included some trade unions as well as numerous local officials, civic leaders, and business groups.
8. There actually was a group named the Young Turks which strongly advocated urban renewal and which had some members in common with the Greater Philadelphia Movement.
9. See Mollenkopf (1978) for an expanded discussion of the protests engendered by urban renewal and the contradictory roles of local government that contributed to the protests.
10. See Bluestone and Harrison (1980) for an analysis of economic impacts of different types of industries.

REFERENCES

Adde, Leo, *Nine Cities: The Anatomy of Downtown Renewal* (Washington, D.C.: Urban Land Institute, 1969).

Anderson, Martin, *The Federal Bulldozer* (Cambridge, Mass.: MIT Press, 1964).

Bluestone, Barry, and Bennett Harrison, *Capital and Communities* (Washington, D.C.: The Progressive Alliance, 1980).

Community Renewal Program, *The Redevelopment Authority Program 1945–1962* (City of Philadelphia, Community Renewal Program. Technical Report #6, 1963).

Gordon, David, "Capitalist Development and the History of American Cities," in W. Tabb and L. Sawers, eds., *Marxism and the Metropolis* (New York: Oxford University Press, 1983).

Hartman, Chester, "The Housing of Relocated Families," in J. Q. Wilson, ed., *Urban Renewal: The Record and the Controversy* (Cambridge, Mass.: MIT Press, 1966).

Lowe, Jeanne R., *Cities in a Race with Time* (New York: Vintage Books, 1968).

Mollenkopf, John, "Neighborhood Political Development and the Politics of Urban Growth: Boston and San Francisco 1958–78," *International Journal of Urban and Regional Research*, March 1981.

Mollenkopf, John, "The Postwar Politics of Urban Development," in W. Tabb and L. Sawers, eds., *Marxism and the Metropolis* (New York: Oxford University Press, 1978).

Molotch, Harvey, "The City as a Growth Machine: Toward a Political Economy of Place," *American Journal of Sociology*, #2, 1976.

O'Connor, James, *The Fiscal Crisis of the State* (New York: St. Martin's Press, 1973).

Perry, David C., and Alfred J. Watkins, eds., *The Rise of the Sunbelt Cities* (Beverly Hills, Cal.: Sage, 1977).

Sale, Kirkpatrick, "Six Pillars of the Southern Rim," in R. Alcaly and D. Mermelstein, eds. *The Fiscal Crisis of American Cities* (New York: Vintage Books, 1977).

Sternlieb, George, and James Hughes, eds., *Post-Industrial America: Metropolitan Decline and Interregional Job Shifts* (New Brunswick, N.J.: Rutgers University Center for Urban Policy Research, 1975).

Weiss, Marc A., "The Origins and Legacy of Urban Renewal," in Pierre Clavel et al., eds., *Urban and Regional Planning in an Age of Austerity* (New York: Pergamon Press, 1980).

10

The Political Economy of Urban Transportation: An Interpretive Essay

LARRY SAWERS

This paper presents a brief history of urban transportation in the United States over the last century. It is not just a history of technological change, of one transportation mode supplanting another, but sees technology as merely one part of an evolving socioeconomic totality. More specifically, the purpose is not so much to explain modal choice—the focus of most analysis of urban transportation—but rather to establish the common characteristics of all forms of urban vehicular transportation in a capitalist society.

In presenting this history there are certain themes which will be stressed. A high demand for mobility is an inherent part of our political economy. It is created by and in turn stimulates the accumulation of capital. Capitalist accumulation in the last century has produced a rapid increase in fragmentation and decentralization of the urban economy and this has in turn generated an explosive growth in the demand for mobility. A second point is that the purpose for producing new urban transportation facilities is to generate private profit. This is so even if it is the government which is actually producing the new facility. This often yields transit operators who can be fairly characterized as arrogant and rapacious. The turn-of-the-century traction trusts are a notorious example of this, but are certainly not unique. Frequently, the profit which is sought from the development of urban transportation derives not from the operation of the transportation facility itself, but rather from its effects on the market for land. From the early elevated railroads and trolley companies who extended their lines into the rural countryside for the purposes of land speculation to the present day downtown business interests who prevail upon the government to build core-oriented subway systems, this has been a recurrent theme. A corollary is that many urban transportation systems must be subsidized by the government because they were never intended to generate a profit on their own.

Third, the government plays a crucial role in the history of urban transportation. In the earliest years, its function was primarily reactive, only regulating the worst abuses of the traction trusts. By the second decade of this century, however, the government was playing an active role in urban transportation: building roads, consolidating the trolley and subway lines and by the 1960s building whole new transit systems (such as San Francisco's BART or Washington's METRO). In this process, the government has been primarily responsive to the dictates of capital accumulation and the needs of capitalists, either the transit operators themselves or other business interests with a stake in the shape of urban transportation. The outcome is frequently transportation services that are decidedly inferior and inappropriate from the consumers' point of view. At various points over the last century, working class movements have been able to influence urban transportation policy, but only after considerable effort.

In presenting this account my interest is to integrate the research findings of a large array of political economists and transportation specialists rather than an analysis of new historical evidence. This is an interpretive essay rather than strictly original research. It is hoped that old evidence presented in a fresh way will make the data appear as new.

CAPITALISM, MOBILITY, AND THE EARLY BOOM IN MASS TRANSPORTATION

Capitalist accumulation creates an enormous demand for transportation. One can first observe this with the turnpike and canal booms of the early 19th century and later, the railroad boom. By the end of the century, a similar transportation revolution had engulfed the nation's cities. The growth in inter-urban transportation had been brought about by pressure from an increasingly articulated regional (and even international) division of labor in a context of rapid economic growth. Similarly, the growth in urban transportation was generated by a fracturing of the city into a series of differentiated districts which produced an urban form quite different from the relatively homogeneous, mercantile city of the early part of the century. This took place in a context of explosive growth.

The causes of this process (which has been given the somewhat inappropriate label of suburbanization), are exceedingly complex and can only be touched on at this point. (See Section One of this volume and Walker, 1978; 1981.) Only a very brief summary will be presented here.

At the root of the rapidly developing fragmentation of the metropolis is the separation of work and residence. In the early part of the 19th century, most urban residents lived and worked in the same building. As capitalism developed, it destroyed petty commerce, the putting-out system, and artisanal manufacture. Production and commerce was centralized into ever larger entities. Until this happened, the demand for urban transportation could never be very great. The separation of work and residence was followed by ever more extensive specialization among capitalist enterprises. Thus transportation and communication between these specialized firms was required. There are a wide variety of powerful economic forces that spatially attract similar or complementary enterprises. There are other land uses that repel each other. These positive and negative externalities (or agglomeration economies and diseconomies) provided the motive force that divided up production and commerce within the metropolis and thus created a series of highly differentiated districts.

Not only did the separation of work and residence allow the balkanization of industry and commerce within the city, it also permitted people to congregate in relatively homogeneous neighborhoods. There were a variety of reinforcing pressures to do so, most of which relate directly to the class divisions within the population. Some groups of workers' residences clustered around their places of work. Other residential districts were not oriented toward the location of industry but developed in order to bolster the class position of those that lived within. Part of one's standard of living was (and still is) the neighborhood in which one lives since it is the neighborhood which provided social interaction, schooling for one's children (at least in the U.S.) and other public services. If the neighborhood was relatively homogeneous, it also provided the amenity of not being forced to view close up the poverty of those less fortunate than oneself and offered social status distance from one's inferiors in the class structure. In short, both capitalist enterprises and the population retreated into relatively homogeneous districts at an accelerating pace during the later part of the nineteenth century. But these separate enterprises and classes were knit together in an indesoluble economic system and their continued interaction was imperative. Thus the need for transportation so that the now separate activities could correspond.

This fragmentation of the city was associated with a deterioration of the vitality of community life within the city. The early 19th century city had, in comparison to the modern metropolis, a strong sense of community. There were multiple overlapping dimensions of race, ethnicity, class, and culture rooted in a homogeneous economic base which served to maintain the viability of community life. This community process continued into the late nineteenth and even twentieth century ethnic slum neighborhoods, but disappeared from other parts of the city. The community lost its economic base and then ceased to be the focus of the social, cultural, and economic life of the population. This decline in a sense of community led to a greater demand for transportation as the needs of the people were no longer met next door.

All of this took place in a context in which powerful decentralizing pressures were building. During the middle part of the century, however, an urban implosion occurred as the intensity of land use built to ever greater heights at the city's center. By the end of the century, a distinct central business district had formed. But even as this implosion was beginning, the first trickle of outward migration from the city can be observed. The leaders in this march to the urban periphery were the very wealthy who, as early as mid-century, no longer desired their fashionable townhouses at the very center of the city. As industry began to dominate, the well-to-do fled what had been commercial cities; vast slum districts were built up around factories. Street crime became a serious problem and epidemics of infectious disease repeatedly swept the city. By the 1890s, the trickle became a flood as successive layers of the working class reached a level of affluence that would permit the leisure time sufficient to allow commuting, the income to pay the horse car or trolley fares, and the savings to invest in the house that was usually purchased upon moving to the outlying districts. Workers moved to the suburbs to be closer to the factories which, after the turn of the century, increasingly located on the periphery of the city. One reason why workers were able to abandon the central districts of cities in the 20th century (and especially in the post World War II period) is because of the increasing stability of their employment (Feldman, 1981, p. 37). Workers who frequently change jobs can minimize their total travel time by locating centrally if their employment locations are spread throughout the city. Once unions guaranteed masses of workers some stability of employment (allowed movement from the secondary to the primary labor market), it became economical to relocate in outlying districts near one's job. This has left secondary labor market workers who change jobs frequently disproportionately located in the central city ghettos.

The movement of industry out of the city's center has a number of sources. Gordon's paper earlier in this volume shows that manufacturers were fleeing among other things a militant labor force in the central city. The growing scale of operation discouraged central location where land was scarce. The wave of mergers around the turn of the century created giant bureaucratic empires which needed headquarters in which to coordinate their farflung operations. Thus office activities began crowding out manufacturing from the central business district, a process as we shall see later that was greatly abetted by various government agencies. As the well-to-do and the industrialist settled on the outskirts of the city, they resisted their annexation by the central city which they had just fled. Their ability to carve out separate suburban jurisdictions with lower tax rates and better services gave others still more incentive to leave the city.

This outward growth of the city was characterized by a leapfrogging pattern caused by speculators withholding land from the market in the hopes of greater profits at a later date. This made the city much larger (and consequently increased the demand for transportation much more) than it otherwise would have been. Speculative activity is, of course, an inseparable part of capitalism.

As Walker has pointed out, in some ways this explosive fragmentation of the city is a process that, once started, requires no explanation. Once there was an urban implosion in the nineteenth century there would be certain groups which would attempt to separate themselves from the undesirable aspects of that process. Once the first few set in motion the process of decentralization, others would follow at an accelerating pace.

The enormous increase in mobility of people and commodities associated with capitalist development has two consequences. First, as transportation grows between communities (both within cities and between cities), society becomes homogenized. In particular, rural backwaters are incorporated into the mainstream. This has within it the potential for welding the population into a unified whole. At the same time, increasing mobility fragments society and in particular has been associated with a fragmentation of the twentieth century metropolis.

These consequences of increasing mobility tend to dissolve allegiance to region, community, class, extended family, and even the nuclear family and would appear to lay the basis for a growth in class conscious political movements. Indeed, early Marxists predicted this would happen. But there is a contradictory tendency within the same process. The rootlessness, alienation, and fragmentation of highly mobile urban living contributes to a sense of powerlessness rather than class consciousness and political mobilization. Which of these two contradictory tendencies predominates depends on the social and economic setting in which the process is embedded. Capitalism, as the argument so far has made clear, has favored the centrifugal, disintegrative tendencies of transportation.

The huge demand for mobility generated by capitalist development grew rapidly toward the end of the nineteenth century as the tempo of capital accumulation accelerated. The boom in urban transportation was not primarily a result of technological change. The reverse was the case—

the rapid growth in transit demand inspired a search for new technologies. The first horse-drawn urban transit company opened in Paris in 1663 and failed soon after because of lack of demand (Feldman, 1977, p. 34). The horse car lines first appeared in this country in New York in the 1830s but were little used for lack of demand. Even as late as 1840, no more than 25 percent of the industrial workers in that city worked outside the home (Pred). New York was, of course, the largest and most capitalistically developed urban center in the U.S., but even here there could be no significant demand for urban transit until capitalist development had reached a certain stage, specifically until the wage system had developed to the point that masses of workers no longer worked in their homes.

After 1880, the use of the horse car grew at a rapid pace. Between 1878 and 1881, many miles of elevated railroad were built in Manhattan, much of it out into the open farm land on the city's outskirts. (Transit developers, according to one account, were primarily interested in the capital gains on land near the train stops [Tunnard and Reed, p. 120].) Chicago saw its first elevateds in 1892. The technology employed here was essentially the same used for decades in inter-city travel. The first subway built in this country opened in 1897 in Boston but it was really a trolley (which in turn was nothing but an electrified horse car) that operated underground. The first heavy rail subway in the U.S. was built in New York in 1904, nearly twenty years after London began operating its system.

As pressures on urban transportation systems built to a crisis point, a technological breakthrough permitted a rapid growth of the industry. In 1888 the electric motor was successfully mounted in an old horse car, and the trolley was born. The importance of this invention should not, however, be overemphasized. It is true that the amount of electrified trackage grew with astonishing speed in the 15 years after the trolley's invention. By 1890, nearly 1000 miles of track were electrified and by 1893, over 7000 (McKay, p. 52). By the turn of the century, hundreds of cities had together nearly 30,000 miles of electrified track. Much of this, however, was track used previously by horse cars. The greater speed of the trolleys allowed significantly better service and passenger volume. But the invention should be seen as providing a quantitative rather than qualitative change in the industry. It is clear that the growth in urban transportation was led by demand and not supply.

By the 1920s, urban trolley systems extended so far into the countryside that they linked up with lines coming from other cities. One could travel on these "inter-urbans" from Boston to Chicago and up and down the East and West Coasts. But the boom in trolleys was mostly over by 1910.[1] Ridership increased very gradually till 1920 and declined thereafter. Trackage hit its peak of 45,000 miles in 1918. New subway lines continued to be built during the first three decades of this century, but growth in subway ridership leveled off after 1929. By the end of the 1920s, the first era in U.S. urban mass transit drew to a close. The demand for mobility was not sated by the trolleys and subways; they only whetted capitalism's appetite. But it was the internal combustion engine that dominates the next era in urban transportation history.

THE DEMISE OF THE TROLLEYS

Within two decades after the first commercially successful application of the electric motor to a converted horse car many systems were in serious trouble. There were so many bankruptcies of trolley systems during World War I that a presidential commission was established in 1919 to investigate the problem. By 1920, the year of peak ridership for trolleys, there were well over 100 trolley systems in receivership and hundreds of miles of track had been abandoned or junked (Smerk, p. 18). The nation's trolleys as a whole were returning only one percent on invested equity. The reasons that were established by the presidential commission for the trolleys' difficulties are essentially the same reasons still offered by historians and transportation economists even today.

In the early years, the trolley systems were not conservatively financed. Buoyant optimism reigned in the first decade or two. It was widely believed that the 5-cent fare and long-term franchises would be indefinitely profitable. This kind of excessive optimism, as we shall see, has plagued urban transportation up to the present day. The problem was compounded by the early and rapid consolidation of trolley companies into a small number of giant traction trusts controlled by financiers and bankers in the major urban centers. Each layer of mergers would be accompanied by watered stock. The holding companies that survived the process were left with serious overcapitalization. The only way that this "fictitious capital" could be destroyed was by bankruptcy and reorganization. The inflation that accompanied World War I proved the underlying weakness of the entire structure. As prices rose sharply, and in particular the price of borrowing money—so very important to a capital intensive industry—the weaker systems collapsed.

Another factor cited by the presidential commission was the "overbuilding into unprofitable territory or to promote real-estate enterprises, involved sometimes with political improprieties" (Smerk, p. 19). At least some trolley companies and maybe most were organized by persons who had absolutely no long-term interest in producing transportation services. The trolley lines were built into the outskirts of the city near land that was owned by the trolley company or its affiliates. This would bring about a rapid rise in the price of that land and the transit operators would then make their profits on capital gains in land. Indeed, these trolley systems from the beginning were subsidized by the profits made from rising land prices. As soon as the real estate was developed, the unprofitable nature of the transit service forced bankruptcy. Outraged citizens would then petition, sometimes successfully, to have the municipality take over and operate the ailing trolley lines.

A third factor was competition from the automobile and the jitney. In 1915 there were a little over 2 million automobiles and by 1920 there were only about 8 million (compared with well over 100 million today). The fact that this small number of vehicles could seriously undermine the trolley industry is a comment on its weakness. The competition from the auto took three forms. First, passengers who would have taken the trolley now were driving their own autos. Second, the auto created congestion which slowed down the trolleys, which were not maneuverable in traffic. Third, in some cities autos operated as jitneys. They would use the same routes as the trolleys, proceeding them down the street picking up passengers waiting for the slower trolley. This had a very serious short-term effect in many cities. The trolley companies turned to the government to outlaw jitneys wherever they had become a problem. (The owner-operators who drove the jitneys had little political strength to resist the powerful traction trusts.) The long-term impact of the jitneys is surely small except in situations where an already precarious trolley company was pushed into receivership by jitney competition and could not be successfully reorganized. Competition from the automobile initiated a process of cumulative decline which became self-reinforcing once begun. As ridership declined, the already precarious trolley companies were forced to cut back on service (headways, maintenance, routes). As service was reduced, still more people were thereby encouraged to abandon mass transit and buy autos. This in turn created still more congestion which slowed the trolleys still further, and so on.

The auto contributed to the decline of the trolley for another reason. Since much of the impetus for the development of trolleys was land speculation, and since the advent of the auto implied that urban development and the resulting appreciation of property values could no longer be tied to areas adjacent to the trolley lines, the transit operators' enthusiasm for expanding their systems was considerably reduced.

Another factor that the presidential commission mentioned was the pressure of wage costs. Pre-war wage levels were generally insufficient from the viewpoint of a "living wage" in the words of the commission, and fell during the war as inflation ate up spending power. The surge of union activity during and right after the war led to a rapid increase in wages which put still more pressure on the traction trusts. The commission, however, offered no evidence that transit wages rose more rapidly than those in other industries. Rising labor costs, however, continued to be blamed for the transit industry's woes, right down to the present day. Many proposals to deal with the nation's urban transportation problems, such as a revival of the jitneys, are economically feasible only because they offer the possibility of using non-union labor (see Due, p. 99).

The rise of the motor bus was a symptom of the lack of viability of the trolleys. Some trolley lines were converted to gasoline-powered buses as early as the late 1910s, but the real challenge by buses did not occur till the following decade. The bus offered a number of advantages when compared with the trolley. It was safer, since passengers could get on or off at curbside rather than in the middle of the street. The trolleys were dilapidated; since the trolley companies were seriously overcapitalized, there was little money for adequate maintenance. The bus was new; the disadvantages of the trolleys were obvious whereas the disadvantages of the bus were yet to be discovered. (At least some of the trolley's disadvantages were associated not with the technology but with the arrogance of the traction trusts—the arrogance of the bus companies was still in the future.) Perhaps the most important advantage of the bus was that, since it did not operate on fixed rails in the center of the street, it did not slow down auto and truck traffic to nearly the same degree as the trolley. This was a major argument in the so-called Whelan report written by a public works official in New York City in 1922 (Guerin, p. 8.) Public officials were thus under pressure to force conversion of trolley franchises to buses. The trolley was not so inefficient on its own terms. But the bus could more easily share scarce space in the city's streets with the rapidly growing number of autos. The shift to buses was encouraged and in some cases forced by eager public officials, like Mayor LaGuardia in New York City who took an aggressive stance against the trolleys and forced motorization in 1936 (Guerin, pp. 14–19).

An actor in this process whose role was not particularly important was General Motors Corporation (Sawers, 1979). Bradford Snell has argued that GM's subsidiaries bought up trolley franchises and converted them to buses in order to spur demand for vehicles produced by GM: it was the largest manufacturer of both autos and buses by the 1930s. GM's role, Snell argues, began in 1932 but did not gain much momentum until 1936 when GM helped set up National City Lines which carried out the motorization of New York's trolleys. What should be clear so far is that the trolley systems of the nation's cities were in desperate circumstances long before this period. Trolley ridership hit its peak in 1920 and declined gradually during the 1920s as motorization of old trolley routes accelerated. Buses carried 400 million passengers in 1922 and 2.5 billion in 1930 (Foster, p. 49). The industry was in severe difficulties by 1929 when the Depression began. Ridership fell as unemployment soared and workers either stayed at home or walked to work. The highly leveraged debt structure of the traction trusts were too shaky to withstand declining revenues. Auto registrations continued to rise in the 1930s despite the Depression. Many of the trolley systems that GM's affiliates purchased in the 1930s had been in receivership for years. The federal government also dealt a blow in 1935 when it passed the Public Utilities Holding Company Act which required electric companies to divest themselves of the trolley companies they owned, thus ending the cross subsidies that had kept many trolleys alive. The gasoline shortage and the revived economy of the 1940s kept the trolleys rolling for another decade, but even in 1945 ridership had not risen to the 1930 levels. Ten years later, trolleys had all but disappeared from U.S. cities. Many of the trolley companies that went broke in the 1930s were using the original rolling stock that the company had started with. The inability to put aside reserves for depreciation is eloquent testimony to the unprofitable nature of many trolley systems.

THE RISE OF THE AUTO

The explosive industrialization of the nineteenth century created the industrial metropolis, but the competitive capitalism of the earlier period gave way to a new epoch dominated by enormous industrial and financial empires. These gigantic bureaucracies required a district within urban areas where administrative and support functions could be organized. As early as the 1910s it was recognized that industry would have to be squeezed out of the downtown area, making way for the office towers which are the command posts of monopoly capital. Zoning, expressways, and later new rapid transit systems were the tools of the corporate and financial capitalists to claim the downtown area for its own use. This process is the making of the metropolis into the image of corporate capital, abandoning the earlier industrial base. The government was thus used by the capitalist class to spearhead and organize the accumulation process. The government's efforts sustained the process of restructuring capital. The office building boom in the CBD and the "gentrification" of surrounding residential areas are the result.

Automobile usage experienced an explosive growth during the 1920s, with registrations tripling during the decade. The auto is nearly useless without roads on which to drive it. The construction and operation of toll facilities by private capital in order to generate profit was not unknown, but the government played the primary role in road, bridge, and tunnel construction. It is thus with the role of the government that this account of the rise of the auto begins.

There are two decisively important fractions of the capitalist class that sought government production of roads. The first is known familiarly as the highway lobby and is composed of automobile manufacturers, trucking companies, petroleum producers and refiners, and road construction companies. These private capitalists are joined in the highway lobby by their allies in state and local highway departments which have narrow bureaucratic interests in road production. The highway lobby has put enormous pressure on federal, state, and local government officials to extend the nation's highway network for two reasons. Such an expenditure validates and encourages purchase and use of motor vehicles by consumers and business thereby benefiting the automobile manufacturers, the oil companies and the insurance companies. Other sectors of the highway lobby benefit from the actual construction of the roads (contractors, heavy equipment producers, oil companies which produce the raw materials for roads). Together these interests represent an enormous concentration of economic power, comprised of the largest and most powerful corporations in the country as well as thousands of lesser enterprises.

The highway lobby has been instrumental in the building of the greatest highway network in the world, and its pivotal role has been widely decried by liberal critics of the nation's transportation system and its heavy reliance on motor vehicles.[2] Another fraction of capital, however, has played a crucial role in the building of urban roads and its role has largely remained hidden from public awareness. Beginning in the 1920s, downtown business interests initiated a series of private planning efforts directed at building networks of arterial and circumferential expressways in cities. Their goal was to increase central business district property values and to help redirect the nature of land use in the central city specifically away from manufacturing and toward office functions.

The best documented example of this is in New York (Fitch). Around 1920 the Regional Plan Association was formed. The association, funded by a private foundation, was made up of representatives of major banks, department stores, and utilities. The sole manufacturer represented was the Otis Elevator Company, with its obvious interest in high-rise office towers. The actual plan for New York was drawn up by a committee whose staff included representatives of J. P. Morgan and First National Bank. Another member of the committee was a former chair of the Federal Reserve Board, an uncle of Franklin Delano Roosevelt, who was later to head the Public Works Administration during the 1930s where he played an important role in sending federal dollars to help build the roads the plan called for. Three other members of the committee had been leaders of the zoning movement during the 1910s. The drive to write a zoning ordinance, the first in this country, was spearheaded by the Fifth Avenue Association, a group of department store executives, bankers, and realtors. The aim of this organization was to push the garment industry and its workers out of Midtown Manhattan because of the depressing effect the industry had on property values.

These private individuals, acting not at the behest of government but at the direction of the most powerful sectors of capital in the city, developed plans for the New York region. Their 1929 plan has been fulfilled almost to the letter. It called for a stupendous effort in constructing a system of expressways throughout the region. (Also in the plan a large number of city parks were called for—tearing down slums for open space has a way of pushing up property values and crowding out the less desirable land uses; that is, workers' homes and light industry.) Robert Moses has often been reviled as the ruthless dictator at the controls of the bulldozers which destroyed neighborhood after neighborhood. In particular, he has been denounced for his insistence on building the Cross Bronx Expressway in a manner that destroyed the community through which it passed (Caro). The route of the Cross Bronx, however, had been prescribed in 1929 by the RPA in almost precisely the orientation it was to later take under Moses' direction. Similarly, with billions of dollars worth of other roads and bridges and tunnels, it was the RPA that had established their precise placement. When Moses dared disagree with the RPA's plan—for example, when he wanted to build a bridge instead of a tunnel at the Battery—he lost.

What happened in New York was not unique. Fitch (p. 259) argues that

> there was hardly a major city in the United States where planning was not strictly a privately sponsored, privately organized affair confined mainly to business, financial and real-estate circles, with a thin layer of planning professionals that tended to thicken over time.

Planning from 1910–1930 was a coalescing of various anti-working-class movements in transit, housing, and zoning. Gradually, after World War I, cities organized planning departments, but it was well into the post–World War II era before these were professionalized and given the authority to shape urban development.

It should be noted that the RPA's plan expressed the traditional thought of urban planners as a whole in the 1920s (Foster, pp. 20–49). It was widely believed that the trolley and the subway had caused the rapid growth of congestion of central cities and in particular the central business districts. More mass transit would only worsen congestion. The only hope for the nation's metropolises was the building of expressways and parkways that would permit decentralization to occur. Very early in the century, Burnham's City Beautiful movement (centered in Chicago) had developed plans for the central business districts of more than a score of cities, but most planners by the 1920s focused their attention on suburban areas. The expressways they envisioned would rejuvenate the city by accelerating suburban development and even restore the slum neighborhood they traversed. The suburban orientation of some planners was so great that they counseled abandonment of central districts as a conscious social goal since they believed urban problems there to be insurmountable (Foster, p. 20). The Regional Plan Association, of course, advocated expressways for precisely opposite reasons.

The trolley, despite the belief of early 20th century planners, did not and could not cause the increasing congestion of central business districts. Transportation can permit travel, but not generate it. Industry in the nineteenth century was scattered throughout the city (Moses and Williamson), but the growing corporate, monopoly capitalism needed central districts in which to organize the administration of its activities. The dynamic growth of central districts as a place for business headquarters led to a dramatic increase in congestion. The reaction of planners, most of whom had close business connections, few of whom were on government payrolls, and none of whom had any professional training as urban planners, was remarkably uniform. The auto and the expressway was necessary to give the central business district some breathing room.

So far I have argued that structural changes in the nature of capitalism implied a particular planning response. I have shown that certain groups of capitalists (the highway lobby and downtown business interests) saw that they could take advantage of these structural trends and enrich themselves. An interesting question still remains: How did the government come to build the expressways? Were they serving as the instrument of these two powerful lobbies, passively doing their bidding? Or was government playing a more active, aggressive role in anticipating the needs of capital accumulation implied in the structural transformations that the economy was undergoing, with the RPA's plan only affecting the timing and specific placement of routes?

The building of urban expressways was a local affair during the 1920s and relatively few were built. By the 1930s the federal government became involved and the nation's cities experienced a boom in expressway construction. Many of the expressways called for in the RPA's plan were built in the 1930s. Many other cities joined the bandwagon, in particular

Los Angeles. The federal government had been subsidizing highways since 1916, but these funds were mandated for rural areas only. Federal urban road building efforts increased dramatically in the 1930s and were financed by the Works Progress Administration and the Public Works Administration as part of the larger depression-fighting program. The WPA spent 38 percent of its budget on roads and highways and almost nothing on other forms of the transportation. The PWA's grants for highways were ten times the size of those for subways (Foster, p. 65). In 1944 the federal government specifically included urban areas in the funding of highways. A great leap forward was taken along this road in 1956 with the introduction of the Interstate Highway system, which financed urban expressways. But the mold had already been set in the 1920s and 1930s.

Since an act of the government is required to validate the private investment in an auto, I have focused so far on the government's role. I have not mentioned pressures from the voting public. There were undoubtedly popular pressures to build roads as more and more autos were bought by voters, but their role is decidedly secondary. One of the reasons for this is that many decisions concerning urban transportation are made by agencies or authorities that are statutorily insulated from electoral pressures. New York is an excellent example of this. The New York Port Authority and the Triborough Bridge and Tunnel Authority have built much of New York City's transportation system. Members of the authorities, however, are not elected. Further, these Authorities can issue bonds in their own names without approval from the electorate or elected officials. The "arrogance" of Robert Moses was thus embedded in statute.

The conventional economists' analysis of the dominance of the auto in urban transportation revolves around consumers' tastes and the convenience and flexibility of the auto. It does offer unparalleled mobility, but as I have argued, this mobility is valuable only in particular social settings. To draw as sharp a contrast as possible, the eighth century European serf with no place to go and with no road on which to go there, would have no use for an auto. The automobile answers human needs (people have a taste for autos) only in a particular social, historical, and economic context. Reformers who wish to limit or eliminate the auto must find a way to change the society which has called it forth.

There have been critics of the automobile who have pointed out the way in which it is congruent with the consumerism alleged to characterize the working classes of affluent capitalist nations (Ashton, p. 85; Walker, 1981, p. 390). Others have pointed to the industry's enormous advertising budgets and annual model changes to explain the dominance of the auto. What is so unsatisfying about these explanations is that they rely upon viewing the consumer as a dupe. Given the choices that workers faced in housing and labor markets, the automobile offered and still offers enormous advantages, allowing a substantial increase in the workers' standard of living. That there are many costs associated with the choice of an automobile is true, but that does not deny the essential rationality of automobile ownership from the individual's point of view.

There is another dimension to this rationality. A higher income encourages automobile ownership for two reasons. Not only can the family more easily afford the purchase price of the auto, but the cost of their time spent in transit increases. With higher income, the automobile becomes more and more of a bargain despite its generally higher budgetary cost because it is considerably faster than public transit in most situations. From this perspective, the widespread ownership of the automobile reflects the enormous victory of the working class in raising its income, and many workers obviously view the matter in these terms.

The search for the ultimate explanation for a phenomenon as integral to modern capitalism as the auto is necessarily frustrating. The system is over-determined, with multiple, overlapping explanations, each reinforcing the other. In many ways the automobilization of society was a process that, once started, acquired a momentum of its own, and one need not look further for The Essential Explanation. Once the first few autos weakened the trolleys even as early as the 1910s, a process was set in motion that needs little further explanation. I have begun this history of the rise of the auto with an account of two factions of capital with an intense interest in getting government to produce the roads and other transport infrastructure which would bring enormous profits and generate an urban form more appropriate for emerging corporate capitalism. This is the appropriate focus. The automobile, like most technologies, is to a substantial degree a neutral technology which can be used in a variety of ways. (There is, for example, no technical attribute of the auto that requires it to be privately owned or prevents its prohibition from intra-urban transportation.) It was the specific form of the urban expressway system advocated by these capitalists that gave the automobile the specific social character that we now take for granted as the nature of the technology itself.

THE DECLINE OF URBAN BUS SYSTEMS

Trolley ridership reached its peak in the year 1920. Heavy rail transit has been stagnant almost since then. Urban buses, however, were growing steadily from the 1910s to the late 1940s (except during the early Depression years), and only began their steady decline after that point. Since the energy crisis of 1973, urban bus ridership has experienced a modest growth, though it has recovered only a small portion of the ridership that had been lost in the preceding 25 years. It is this period of decline in bus ridership to which we now turn our attention.

In many ways the decline of the bus paralleled the decline of the trolley several decades earlier. The primary difference was that since public transit was no longer a growth industry, there were even fewer capitalists than before willing to pick up the franchises of the ailing public transportation companies. In many cases it was a public authority which took over operation of the bus system; in others, the service was simply discontinued. What happened in Washington, D.C. illustrates many of the themes developed so far in this paper (Artabane and Neale; Spake).

O. Roy Chalk bought Washington's bus and trolley system in 1956 from Louis Wolfson, a financier whose franchise was not renewed by Congress because of dissatisfaction over his reaction to a 56-day strike the previous year. Wolfson had ridden the system deeply into debt by paying himself enormous dividends. Even so, Wolfson was able to sell it for $13.5 million, even though it cost him only $2 million.

Three years later, Chalk reorganized D.C. Transit. In retrospect, it is obvious that he was preparing for the inevitable take-over by a public authority. The corporate headquarters was established in Delaware to take advantage of lax corporate regulation and taxation there. More importantly, Chalk set up a series of corporations which were wholly owned subsidiaries of his company and whose only assets were various choice pieces of real estate that had been previously owned by D.C. Transit. For example, D.C. Transit sold to the new subsidiary, M Street Estates, an old car barn located on M street near the heart of fashionable and very expensive Georgetown. The transaction price of $100,000 was the book value of the property, the purchase price minus depreciation. M Street Estates immediately mortgaged the property for nearly $2.5 million. Part of this money was used to refurbish the barn, which then began generating prime rent payable to the M Street Corporation. Nearly $1 million of the money was lent back to D.C. Transit.

This scenario was repeated several times. In the late 1960s when Chalk was finally forced to sell D.C. Transit to a public authority, after years of steady fare increases, he retained ownership of the subsidiary corporations, which owned the lucrative properties once held by the transit company itself. By the end of the 1960s, Chalk was one of the largest land owners in the city. Adding insult to injury, the new public authority paid off the debts that D.C. Transit had incurred with all of Chalk's dummy operations. Without first Wolfson and later Chalk bleeding the company dry, private mass transportation in Washington might have remained a viable undertaking rather than requiring enormous and accelerating deficits which it is now experiencing.

This saga illustrates the way in which public transit operators can, and frequently have exploited transit consumers. More precisely, it illustrates how closely intertwined are investment in land speculation and urban transportation, a theme we observed with the trolleys and elevateds, and will note again in our discussion of the new rapid rail systems of the 1970s. These comments are not meant to suggest that unscrupulous capitalists caused the decline of urban bus transportation, but they surely accelerated the process.

THE NEW RAPID TRANSIT SYSTEMS

In the last twenty-five years, a considerable effort to extend and renovate rapid rail transit has occurred in U.S. cities even as automobile usage increased. San Francisco's new system is nearly a decade old. One third of Washington, D.C.'s system is operating, and Atlanta's carried its first passenger in the summer of 1979. Baltimore and Miami's systems are under construction. Major new additions to or extensive refurbishing of heavy rail lines have been carried out in Cleveland, Chicago, Boston, New York, Philadelphia. A number of other cities are studying proposals to build subways including Honolulu, St. Louis, Pittsburgh, Houston, Minneapolis, and Denver. In addition, new light rail systems (trolleys) are in operation in Newark or under construction in Buffalo. Even in Los Angeles and Detroit, where till now the reign of the auto was uncontested, proposals for elevated transit systems in the downtown areas are being pushed by a federal funding agency and local business interests, and appear likely to be adopted.

This revival of interest in rapid rail transit is merely one extension of the urban expressway boom of the 1920s, 1930s, and 1950s. The continuing transformation of the economy required ever greater efforts to restructure urban areas in a manner compatible with corporate capitalism. The explosive growth in the central business district and the rapid worsening of traffic congestion by the 1920s had required early efforts to decentralize the metropolis by building high-speed highways. The expressway boom had succeeded, to the point that the decentralization process was in danger of going too far, thereby threatening the viability of central business districts and downtown property values. Furthermore, traffic congestion was not improved by the expressways, only changed in form as the automobile replaced the trolley. Urban renewal and regional subway systems were the major new responses to the crisis situation.

The political effort to authorize the construction of new regional subway systems was typically led by coalitions of business executives. Some of them had a very direct economic stake in the survival or growth of central business district property values. Real estate developers, bankers, department store executives, and utility executives were the representatives of this fraction of the capitalist class. There were others in these coalitions who operated nationally or internationally. Their interest was still in profits, but not those that derived from owning a piece of downtown real estate. Rather, they had a broader vision which recognized the need for their corporations and for capital as a whole to have a central district in which to carry out administrative functions.

The beginnings of the revival of rapid transit construction are found in San Francisco in the mid-1940s (Beagle et al., Whitt, Mollenkopf, Hamer, Zwerling). In 1945, a group of major corporations formed the Bay Area Council to formulate business's position with regard to a variety of problems besetting the city. From the beginning, mass transit was considered a key issue. In San Francisco, as elsewhere, the problem was to create a district amenable to the corporate administration function. There was an extra urgency felt by business leaders in San Francisco since the city appeared to be destined to become "Manhattan West," the international headquarters of business operating on the Pacific Coast. It is no accident that San Francisco as well as New York have led the way in planning central business districts.

The Bay Area Council developed plans for a new regional subway system and then lobbied the state legislature to set up the Bay Area Rapid Transit Commission to continue the planning effort. Half of its commissioners were either Bay Area Council trustees or members of its board of governors (Feldman, 1981, p. 33). The Bay Area Council lobbied for the plan's approval by local and state legislative bodies and lavishly financed a public relations campaign that sold the system to the voting public, which had to approve financing arrangements. They were instrumental in getting the legislature to pass a law lowering the proportion of voters required to approve the bond issue from two thirds to three fifths. The referendum succeeded in 1962 with 61.2 percent of the vote, and the system was completed in 1972. (It is interesting to note that urban renewal was planned in San Francisco in much the same manner as the new subway system; many of the same corporate executives were involved in both processes.)

The BART system connects the central business district to suburban housing, hence it is radial rather than circumferential in nature. Indeed, there are only 11 stations in San Francisco and only 8 of the system's 75 miles are within the city's limits. In order to lure commuters out of their automobiles, stops along these radial lines are very widely spaced, averaging 2.5 miles between stations. Fewer stops mean a shorter trip time for through passengers, though at the cost of reduced convenience and flexibility for the short haul passengers. The lack of stations in the central city and the great distance between stations is more pronounced in the BART system than in any other of the new rapid transit systems which copied BART, but the radial nature and widely-spaced stops are found in all of the new systems. The purpose for designing these systems in this way should be obvious. This new breed of rapid rail transit maximizes access to the central business district, thereby stimulating its growth and revitalization.

Not long after the San Francisco business community began organizing itself to push for urban renewal and mass transit, a similar effort occurred in New York City, this time led by the president of the Rockefeller Center, the head of the Chrysler Building, and others. The Regional Plan Association completed a new plan for the city in 1959 and became a leader in the battle for regional transit planning.

In Atlanta, a similar involvement of downtown business leaders is found. There the Chamber of Commerce played a pivotal role in the early 1960s. "MARTA [Metropolitan Atlanta Rapid Transit Authority] was originally the creation of business-oriented civic leaders and their allies in the government" (Coogan et al., p. 59). The mayor at the time of MARTA's creation was a past president of the Chamber. The members and chair of MARTA's board of directors were all business executives. Not surprisingly, MARTA was frequently charged with unresponsive arrogance and in 1968 its first attempt to gain voter approval of the system's financing was rejected (even though the Chamber of Commerce MARTA Lobby had earlier been able to get the voters to approve a change in the state constitution to permit the system to be built). In 1972, after the federal government's agreement to finance most of the system, an intensive public relations campaign, and route changes sought by the black community, voters were persuaded to approve the project.

Plans for another major addition to the nation's rapid rail transit network were laid in Washington, D.C., just as the RPA's planning was begun (Ives et al.; Murin, Chap. 3). By far the largest employer in the Washington area is the federal government, and thus it has a "proprietary" interest in the viability of the central district where federal employment is concentrated. Rapid rail transit has been used everywhere to subsidize a growth in downtown office employment, but in Washington this employment was not primarily in the private sector. Whereas in other cities one sees key business leaders initiating and sustaining the drive for rapid rail transit, in Washington the federal government played the decisive role.

In 1955 Congress mandated that a regional planning agency in the metropolitan Washington area develop a comprehensive transportation plan. Part of its proposal released in 1959 was a 33-mile rapid rail system. The Eisenhower administration subsequently recommended to Congress that it establish the National Capital Transportation Agency to proceed with the plan for the subway system. The 33-mile system was remarkably similar to a plan put forward by a group of downtown-oriented business executives that called itself Downtown Progress, but suburban political pressures appear to have been more influential. The District of Columbia did not have home rule at the time, and District residents had little political leverage. In 1960, just after the Kennedy administration arrived in Washington, Congress acted. The new transportation agency developed detailed plans for a much larger (83-mile) system without any apparent consultation with Downtown Progress, or with any other group for that matter. The program ran into immediate trouble as the national highway lobby and local bus and parking interests lobbied against it, and the arrogant and unresponsive attitude of the agency cost many votes in Congress as well. Not until 1965 was a preliminary program approved. In 1971 the entire leadership of the House opposed the continued funding of METRO even though ground had been broken a year before and millions of dollars in contracts had been let. Lobbying was intense by all parties. With the vigorous support of the Nixon administration, the House repudiated its leadership and METRO was continued. Yet even into the 1980s, with the system only one third finished, there are perennial battles as to whether the entire system should be completed.

San Francisco, New York, and Atlanta were not the only cities to have transportation planning initiated by small groups of downtown business leaders. Indeed, during the 1950s nearly every major city developed a corporate-based planning body. Typically, these included high executives of department stores, banks, utilities, and real estate interests. They were often self-financing. Mollenkopf describes the usual pattern: "these business planning groups first developed their ideas *in camera,* subsequently developed a wider business consensus around them, and then ultimately promoted them by various political means, more especially including connections with growth-oriented mayors" (1975, p. 135).

These downtown business groups were not uniformly successful in implementing their plans for new rapid rail systems. Los Angeles voters in 1968 and 1974 turned down proposals put forward by downtown businesses for a BART-style rapid rail system (Whitt, p. 55), although the principal backers of L.A.'s system were small businessmen and lawyers (Coogan et al., p. 80), not representatives of the large corporations as in San Francisco or Atlanta, or powerful federal administrators as in Washington. Voters in Seattle also failed to approve a regional subway system, but the business community was not active in that campaign either. A civic-minded lawyer began the campaign for Seattle's system (Coogan, p. 82), which was designed to include representatives from as many interest groups as possible. The design team included architects, urban designers, and even sociologists who used social survey methods. But without the leadership of the business community, the proposal failed.

Rapid rail systems were not the exclusive focus of the downtown-oriented business groups. Indeed, some of the groups, especially in smaller cities, were still promoting freeways, not public transit. But nearly all groups were concerned with public transportation in some form. By the early 1960s, New York, Chicago, Boston, Philadelphia, and Cleveland had initiated major rehabilitations or expansion of their rapid rail. Other cities, such as Buffalo, Miami, and New Orleans turned their attention to beefing up their bus systems (Smerk, p. 203). Pittsburgh, led by the Mellon interests, developed the notion of a bus operating on its own grade-separated right-of-way. All of these plans required enormous amounts of money for their fulfillment.

The federal government's response was extraordinarily stingy until the 1970s. Kennedy was put in the White House by a coalition of voters, a prominent segment of whom lived in the central cities, and thus Kennedy had political debts to pay. Within six months after his arrival in Washington, Congress had passed amendments to the Housing Act of 1949 which provided loans for new mass transit equipment and a stipulation that federal monies for highway construction could not be approved unless the planning of the highways was coordinated with the planning of public transportation. By 1964 the Urban Mass Transit Administration (UMTA), an agency within the newly created Department of Transportation, was organized to provide subsidies (though far smaller than federal subsidies of highways) for the construction of public transportation. During the 1960s these subsidies totaled a little over a half billion dollars but rose dramatically after 1970. In 1972 alone a half billion in grants was approved, and by 1980 the grants approved annually neared $3 billion. In 1973, Congress approved diversion of funds from the federal Highway Trust Fund for mass transit. Relatively little of the funds available from this source, however, have been used. The institutional bias of local governments and federal financing formulas that favor highways have discouraged use of highway funds for transit (Yago, 1978).

UMTA during its first decade made grants for capital rather than operating expenditures. It was felt that the subsidy of operating expenses would be a blank check to the unions of operating employees. Funds were available for a wider variety of transportation modes including ferries and inclined planes, but by far the largest share of the grants went to rapid rail transit. The pressures to assist local transit systems by subsidizing operating expenses became so great that UMTA began doing so by 1975. These operating subsidies had risen to over $1 billion a year by 1980.

The federal government's interest in public transit should not be viewed only as a response to the requests of downtown business lobbies or the growing mass transit lobby (composed of corporations that were building the new subway systems). Growing popular resistance to the expressway boom of the 1950s and 1960s undoubtedly played a role in the federal government's newfound interest in mass transit. The taking of land for urban renewal and expressways had displaced thousands of families and destroyed hundreds of communities; this was a major grievance that sparked the urban riots plaguing cities in the mid-1960s. Citizens groups, often with a strong working-class support and leadership, organized to stop expressway construction, most notably in Boston, San Francisco, and Washington. What is remarkable about these protests is how they joined together all manner of people across race, class, ethnic, and even geographic divisions. In Washington, local politicians were caught between Congress, which insisted on miles of central city freeways, and a ferocious popular opposition to any more roads. City council meetings were held under armed guard, but chairs were still thrown at council members on the podium as meetings ended in violent chaos. Demonstrations, mass arrests, and ultimately the dynamiting of construction equipment finally helped end, at least temporarily, the freeway movement in Washington.

In San Francisco, one elevated expressway around the central business district was never finished because of vociferous opposition. More than two decades later, the structure still stands unfinished. The anti-freeway campaign undoubtedly played a role in BART's approval. Kennedy-Johnson liberals struggled against the highway lobby to increase funding for mass transit because of their largely urban constituency. Ironically, it was under a Republican administration (Nixon's) that the rapid growth in mass transit subsidies began. As soon as the energy crisis of late 1973 broke, mass transit finally became politically acceptable (Davies, p. 37).

THE END OF THE RAPID RAIL BINGE

The BART system has now been operating for a decade. Parts of new systems are operating in Washington and Atlanta. It is clear by now that these systems are financial and economic disasters for their central cities. Their purpose was to maximize access to the central business district from suburban residential areas, and they have proved to be a modest success in this regard. Indeed, rapid rail ridership stopped falling for the first time in decades—ridership has stayed roughly the same from 1973 to the present. But the cost has been enormous.

The disadvantages of rapid rail are well known to transportation economists who, for the most part have been resoundingly unenthusiastic about the new rapid rail systems. But outside this small circle of transportation specialists, the disadvantages are not widely understood. Subway construction is still viewed as a progressive reform. Since the rapid rail systems are less than a decade old and only one (BART) is actually completed, little is known with certainty about their impact. The following analysis explains the expected effects of the new systems.

The obvious consequences of designing a transit system with radial routes and widely spaced stops is that access of people living in outlying areas to the central business district is increased, the purpose of these projects. But the new systems make it even easier than before to move to the suburbs while still working downtown, and so suburbanization with all of the consequent problems can be expected to continue or even accelerate. There are, of course, important differences between auto-caused suburbanization and transit-caused suburbanization. Perhaps the most pronounced difference is that in the latter, the central business district is more likely to retain or regain its vitality. But the ring between the central business district (except for the districts immediately surrounding transit stops) and the suburbs is likely to continue to decay from both causes of suburbanization.

The central city outside of the central business district is likely to be hurt by the new transit systems for a second season. The most heavily used bus routes have been on the very same radial arteries as the new rail systems, so the new rail transit is in direct competition with the most heavily used and most profitable parts of the bus system. Both bus and rail systems at best break even in most cities and normally depend upon state, local, or even federal subsidy. In order for the new rail systems to gain an acceptable number of riders, competition with the bus system must be ended since the major share of the new rail systems' riders are former bus riders, rather than former auto commuters. This has been shown by the experience of San Francisco and Washington. (This is facilitated in most cities by a merger of the bus and rail systems under public authority).

Before the advent of the new rail transit systems, the more profitable bus routes (radial, rush-hour routes) subsidized those with lower ridership (non-rush-hour runs and non-radial routes). Now the only way the bus system can maintain a ridership is as a feeder system for the rail transit system, since the number of people who can walk to or park near one of the limited number of rail transit stations is small. Thus the bus system as an independent transportation network is lost, and crosstown transportation becames more difficult and expensive. Because the rail transit system is radial in nature and the bus system has become a feeder system, non-radial trips must be made using a system designed for other purposes. One must take a feeder bus, transfer to rapid rail, and then back to another feeder bus to make a trip which was previously made in one bus. Each transfer from bus to subway or vice versa requires additional time and may require additional fares. Crosstown trip times actually increase and become significantly more expensive.

In Washington, with its 100-mile system one third complete, this process is well underway. Everytime a new station is opened, new feeder bus routes are announced and old routes are cancelled. This process has been so extensive that even some surburban commuters on radial routes have been hurt. Formerly, express buses took the commuters from their homes to the central business district. Now, some of these buses stop at rail stations, making the trip more time consuming and more expensive.

The new rapid rail systems are not designed to serve neighborhoods in which the lower strata of the working class live, but instead connect the central business district with suburban residential areas of the affluent. In Washington, for example, a proposed spur of the METRO system would have extended into one of the neighborhoods at the heart of the central city's slums. This extension was supported by a broad cross-section of community groups, local politicians, and journalists, but was eliminated for "cost reasons" by the METRO authority. This echoes the efforts of urban reformers during the Progressive era to keep subway lines from being built into working class neighborhoods in New York City (Fitch, p. 258). Such transportation would have attracted rather than repelled the working-class residences which depress property values.

The new rail transit systems thus can be expected to benefit primarily the downtown businesses and the suburban commuter. They will actually harm the resident of the central city in a very large number of cases by reducing access of one part of the city to another. The unraveling of the social fabric of the city continues with rapid rail transit, which in turn accelerates the march to the suburbs.

Unless the new rapid rail systems increase the overall efficiency of their metropolitan areas relative to other metropolitan areas, the new systems cannot be expected to create any appreciable local economic development (aside from the small multiplier effect from capital expenditure), but rather to channel it around subway stops. Much economic growth can be expected to be directed by the new transit systems to the central business district (which was why they were built) though Webber argues that this has not happened in San Francisco (pp. 88–89). In Washington, in the 10 years since METRO was begun, the central business district has prospered. Much of the new growth will be channeled to the vicinity of other major rail stations outside the central business district. With widely spaced stops, uneven development becomes even more pronounced. Growth is not spread evenly over the city, but concentrates in certain commercial districts around major transit stations. This has been documented in the case of San Francisco and Toronto (Whitt, p. 123ff). Conversely, decline is distributed unevenly; redevelopment of ghetto neighborhoods is actually retarded (as in Washington).

Since the rail transit routes coincide with major surface arteries, the growing commercial districts around major transit stations sit astride the most congested avenues. Even though new growth is focused around transit stops, the primary mode of transportation in the city remains the auto. This means that most customers or employees in the new shops and offices surrounding the new transit stops arrive by auto rather than by rail. Ironically, automobile congestion may increase as *auto* traffic is concentrated by the *rail* transit system. (See Webber, pp. 85–86, for a discussion of how this process developed in San Francisco.) At any rate, there has been no detectable drop in congestion in the city with the longest experience with a new system (Sherret, p. 184). Even if new rapid rail transit succeeds in reducing the number of automobile drivers, their geographical distribution becomes more uneven than before and congestion is accordingly worsened. This is true even though the ostensible purpose for building these systems was to reduce congestion. This particularly harms central city residents, since their movement about their city either by auto or mass transit becomes more difficult.

The heavy rail systems should be expected to contribute to a worsening of the fiscal crisis of central cities. As we have seen, the new rapid rail systems can be expected to accelerate suburbanization which, in a metropolitan area where central city boundaries are fixed, has in the past been a significant (though certainly not the only) cause of the central city's fiscal crisis. Thus, indirectly rapid rail transit can be expected to worsen the urban fiscal crisis. This effect will be moderated to the extent that the revival of the CBD offsets the decline of the rest of the central city. If the experience of San Francisco—the only city to have completed a new heavy rail system—is any guide, one should not be too optimistic on this score.

Rapid rail transit has another more direct impact on the urban fiscal crisis: it is very expensive. Washington's 100-mile system will cost over $8 billion according to current estimates. San Francisco's 71-mile system (completed in the early 1970s before double-digit inflation) cost $1.6 billion. The first 14 miles of Atlanta's 53-mile system is expected to cost over one billion dollars. This has placed heavy financial burdens on local governments. San Francisco has imposed a one-half percent sales tax and Atlanta, one percent, to finance their systems while the Washington area governments have dipped deeply into general revenues. But the subsidies do not end when construction is completed as some optimists predicted. San Francisco's BART, for example, received 55 percent of its operating budget from federal, state, and local sources in 1977, and the subsidy has grown over the years (Webber, p. 93). In 1976, the subsidy amounted to $3.76 per trip, according to Webber (p. 97) and $12 per trip, according to Lave (p. 301). (The very different estimates arise from different assumptions about capital costs.) Washington's METRO (rail and bus) is receiving nearly half of its operating revenue from subsidies. Total operating subsidy to mass transit (excluding capital subsidies) in the U.S. in 1980 was $3.6 billion (over 2.5 times the 1975 level). From 1970 to 1980 operating subsidies rose nearly 14-fold. Local operating subsidies rose from $700 thousand to $1.7 billion between 1975 and 1980. The new rail systems, despite massive federal subsidies, constitute an important drain on already overburdened local government budgets.[3]

By the late 1970s, as the staggering cost of regional rapid rail transit systems was becoming ever more apparent, mass transit advocates in some cities and their backers in the Urban Mass Transit Administration turned to less comprehensive solutions. In Los Angeles, leading downtown business groups supported by the Community Redevelopment Agency pushed for a downtown "people mover" (Hill). The system would be only three miles long and traverse the central business district on an elevated guideway from the railroad station to the convention center. Vehicles would be automatically operated in order to reduce the labor force operating the system. The $200 million system would be expected to earn in fares only half of its operating expenses. A parking tax would cover part of the deficit, but the rest of the funding is still unclear. Capital grants from UMTA would cover 80 percent of capital costs. Once again we find downtown business interests pushing for central-business-district-oriented public transit, financed by the local and federal tax payer. UMTA was eager to finance similar systems in Miami and Detroit.

It has been two decades since urban public transportation as a whole broke even, and subsidies grew astronomically during the 1970s. Rapid inflation, the building of the new heavy rail systems, and rising bus ridership (since each passenger is subsidized, more passengers require greater total subsidies) fueled the demand for subsidies. It must be emphasized that the growing deficits of public transit systems in part resulted from political decisions by public officials to restrict fare increases. Transit fares adjusted for inflation dropped steeply in the 1970s. In 1982 Birmingham shut down its bus system for more than three months while county officials scrambled to figure out some way to finance it. The buses are now running again but at reduced service levels and higher fares. Boston closed down its subways and buses for one day in late 1981 for the same reason. The Reagan Administration, placed in office without the urban vote, has at this writing announced intentions to end all operating subsidies to urban public transportation (over $1 billion in 1980). This would place a staggering burden on the already impecunious cities. At least forty medium-sized cities have threatened to permanently end service if the present administration carries out its threat to cut off operating subsidies (*Dollars and Sense,* p. 6).

Given the overwhelming drawbacks of the new rapid rail system, it is puzzling to find public officials and civic boosters still enthusiastic about it. Most urban transportation analysts have long favored expansion of bus systems over rapid rail transit since buses are by far the most economical means of expanding public transportation. Even before the construction of BART was initiated, the drawbacks of rail transit were clear (Meyer et al.). Early experience with BART confirmed the worst fears of transportation analysts and the cost-benefit studies supporting other cities' systems have been effectively critiqued before they were begun (Murin). Why did cities in the 1960s and 1970s build rapid rail transit systems without serious consideration of a major expansion of bus transit? Where expressways already serve a particular commuting corridor, metered access of automobiles plus free access of buses to the expressways could reduce congestion and greatly speed the flow of buses. Private automobiles could be banned from certain downtown streets, or perhaps all of them. Separate rights-of-way for express buses would be far cheaper than those for a rail system. Furthermore, the same vehicle could be used for residential feeder and downtown distribution phases of the journey to work and thus significantly reduce trip times when compared with rapid rail. Greatly reduced headways and trip times could be obtained at a considerable expense, but at a small fraction of the enormous sums now being spent on the new rapid rail transit systems.

The perspective offered by this paper suggests two possible explanations. Bus systems are often extolled for their flexibility. Routes, head-ways, and other service characteristics can be adjusted easily as the needs of the passengers change. But this is a drawback for business interests who wish to generate a particular and permanent change in land use (Whitt, 1975, pp. 103ff). A major expansion of bus service can always be re-versed. Metering gates at expressway ramps can be removed and the addi-tional rolling stock can be sold. The new rapid rail system, however, has embedded in concrete and steel a particular urban form for generations to come. This predictability of the consequences of transportation on urban development and property values is a great virtue. An important, and some would argue decisive, element in the coalitions supporting the new rapid transit systems have been business executives with an interest in downtown real estate. It is clear that from the narrow perspective of this group, the bus is the distinctly inferior alternative.

A second reason why there was no major expansion of express buses is because such a choice runs head on into the highway lobby. In order for the greatly expanded bus system to be a success, its ability to compete with the automobile must be enhanced by limiting the mobility of the private car. Access to expressways would be metered; the right to drive on some or all downtown streets at rush hour or all day long might have to be restricted. More buses in other parts of the city would create con-gestion which would slow automobile traffic. This, of course, would be anathema to the highway lobby. The new rapid transit systems, on the other hand, compete to a far smaller extent with the automobile. Many of their riders will come from buses, freeing up more highway space for automobiles.

The preeminence of the automobile is maintained or even strength-ened with the new rapid rail systems. Even trolley systems compete with the automobile in a way that rapid rail systems do not. A major reason for motorization of trolley lines in the 1920s and 1930s was their com-petition with the auto over scarce road space. In the mid-1950s, at the same time that BART was being planned, the last of San Francisco's trolley system was being dismantled. From the point of view of the high-way lobby, rapid rail transit is clearly preferable to either bus or trolley systems.

It is not surprising to find that, at least in some cases, the highway lobby did not oppose the funding of new subway systems or even the diver-sion of Federal Highway Trust Fund monies to mass transit. Whitt docu-ments the unanimity of the capitalist class in California on these transpor-tation issues (see also Zwerling). Coogan et al. have given a detailed analysis of the 1968 defeat of a proposed subway system in Atlanta and a briefer account of similar defeats in Seattle and Los Angeles. Nowhere in their analysis is the highway lobby mentioned, even though the book is about the role of business leaders in transportation planning. Further research is clearly necessary before the definitive statements can be made, but these three studies suggest the tacit approval of highway interests in the production of the new rapid rail systems.

CONCLUDING REMARKS

What lessons can be drawn from this account of the development of urban transportation which might guide progressive political movements? First, the government is not a neutral arbiter. It acts in the interest of capitalists and capital accumulation. Examples of this are found on nearly every page of this paper. Second, beware of blue-ribbon committees, business councils, appointed commissions, and the like. They can be expected to speak only for their own interests, not for the common good, and especially not the good of the working class. Third, any proposal concerning urban transportation necessarily implies a certain effect on urban form whether or not the proposer is aware of it. Usually, he or she is, and that is precisely why it was proposed. The campaign to approve BART in the early 1960s came near the end of a bitter anti-expressway movement. Undoubtedly, BART was approved by the voters because it was billed as an alternative to the automobile rather than a decision about urban form. If the true nature of the program had been clarified to the public, it is less likely that it would have passed the referendum. Fourth, technology is rarely the issue; it is how the technology is used. That, of course, reflects the underlying economic reality and power relationships. Fifth, urban transportation, both public and private, is produced to generate a profit. Occasionally, the transportation services produced contribute to a rational and humane ordering of urban society, but this is almost an incidental byproduct. Sixth, popular movements can and do achieve limited success in influencing decisions concerning urban transportation. The anti-expressway movement, for example, slowed or stopped freeway building in many cities. Progressive movements must expect difficulties since transportation is the key planning sphere in cities, at least in the United States where more aggressive planning is eschewed. Most public transit and all the new subway system are controlled by agencies in which officials are appointed, not elected. Similarly, highway planning and construction is not readily subject to pressures from the ballot box. But to say that difficulties will be encountered only means that the stakes are high, not that failure is inevitable.

NOTES

1. It has been argued that one of the reasons why trolleys developed so rapidly in Europe in the 1890s and 1900s is the very aggressive sales efforts of the giant electrical equipment manufacturers (McKay). They may have played a similarly aggressive role in the U.S.
2. The overwhelming power of the highway lobby is so commonly understood that even establishment-oriented publications frankly admit its existence. After the Senate passed the bill which authorized the Interstate Highway system with a single dissenting vote, and the House passed the measure on a voice vote without debate, the *Saturday Evening Post* commented, "That should answer any questions as to who runs this country" (Davies, p. 22).
3. In the case of Washington's METRO, the fiscal burden, according to a study by Willard Brittain, is disproportionately born by central city residents. It is expected that 34% of METRO's riders will be central city residents who will bear 38% of the costs of the system. However, Brittain estimates that central city riders will receive only 20% of the benefits of the system (which are cost and time savings to riders, time savings to other commuters because of reduced congestion, and parking cost to auto commuters) (p. 441). Note also that San Francisco and Atlanta use the sales tax to finance their heavy rail systems. The sales tax is a regressive tax which places a disproportionate burden on lower-income groups.

REFERENCES

American Public Transit Association, *Transit Fact Book 1981* (Washington: APTA, 1981).

Artabane, Joseph, and F. J. Neale, "A Transit System in Crisis: A Case Study of D.C. Transit," Urban Transportation Center, Consortium of Universities, Washington, D.C., 1972.

Ashton, Patrick, "The Political Economy of Suburban Development," in William Tabb and Larry Sawers, eds., *Marxism and the Metropolis* (New York: Oxford, 1978).

Beagle, Danny, Al Haber, and David Wellman, "Rapid Transit: The Case of BART," in David Gordon, ed., *Problems in Political Economy* (Lexington, Mass.: D. C. Heath, 1971).

Brittain, Willard, "Metro: Rapid Transit for Suburban Washington," in David Gordon, ed., *Problems in Political Economy* (Lexington, Mass.: D. C. Heath, 1971).

Caro, Robert, *The Power Broker* (New York: Alfred Knopf, 1974).

Coogan, Mathew, et al., *Transportation Politics in Atlanta.* A report of the Urban Mass Transportation Study, Harvard Law School, Cambridge, 1970.

Davies, Richard, *The Age of Asphalt* (Philadelphia: Lippincott, 1975).

Dollars and Sense, "Mass Transit: Rocky Road," March 1982.

Due, John, "Urban Mass Transit Policy: A Review Article," *Quarterly Review of Economics and Business* 16, 1, 1976, 93–105.

Feldman, Marshall, "A Contribution to the Critique of Urban Political Economy: The Journey to Work," *Antipode* 1977.

Feldman, Marshall, *The Political Economy of Class and the Journey to Work: The Case of San Francisco,* Ph.D. dissertation, Univ. of California, Los Angeles, 1981.

Fitch, Robert, "Planning New York," in Roger Alcaly and David Mermelstein, eds., *The Fiscal Crisis of American Cities* (New York: Random House, 1977).

Foster, Mark, *From Streetcar to Superhighway: American City Planners and Urban Transportation, 1900–1940* (Philadelphia: Temple University Press, 1981).

Guerin, David, "Urban Transportation: A Practical Analysis Derived from the History of the Conversion of Trolleys to Buses." Unpublished paper, Queens College, New York, 1976.

Hamer, Andrew, *The Selling of Rail Rapid Transit* (Lexington, Mass.: Lexington Books, 1976).

Hill, Gladwin, "Amid Lamenting By Some, Los Angeles Moves to Construct Elevated Railroad," *New York Times,* December 13, 1981.

Ives, Ralph, Gary Lloyd, and Larry Sawers, "Mass Transit and the Power Elite," *Review of Radical Political Economics* 4, 2, 1972.

Lave, Charles, "Transportation and Energy: Some Current Myths," *Policy Analysis* Summer 1978, 297–316.

Meyer, J. R., et al., *The Urban Transportation Problem* (Cambridge, Mass.: Harvard University Press, 1966).

Miller, John, *Fares, Please!* (New York: Dover, 1960).

McKay, John P., *Tramways and Trolleys: The Rise of Urban Mass Transportation in Europe* (Princeton: Princeton University Press, 1976).

Mollenkopf, John, "The Postwar Politics of Urban Development," in William Tabb and Larry Sawers, eds., *Marxism and the Metropolis* (New York: Oxford University Press, 1978).

———, "Theories of the State and Power Struggle Research," *Insurgent Sociologist* 5, 3, 1975, 254–64.

Moses, Leon, and R. Williamson, "Land Use Theory and the Spatial Structure of the Nineteenth-Century City," *Regional Science Association, Papers and Proceedings* 28, 49–80.

Murin, William, *Mass Transit Policy Planning* (Lexington, Mass.: D. C. Heath, 1971).

Pred, Allan, *The Spatial Dynamics of U.S. Industrial Growth: 1800–1914* (Cambridge, MIT Press, 1966).

Sawers, Larry, "American Ground Transportation Reconsidered," *Review of Radical Political Economics* 11, 3, 1979.

Sherret, Allistair, *BART's First Five Years* (Dept. of Transportation [#DOT-BIP-FR-11-3-78] Washington, 1979).

Smerk, George, *Readings in Urban Transportation* (Bloomington: Indiana University Press, 1968).

Snell, Bradford, *America Ground Transportation*, 93rd Congress, 2nd Session. U.S. Senate, Subcommittee on Antitrust and Monopoly, Washington: Government Printing Office, February 26, 1974.

Spake, Amanda, "How Chalk Got His Hand in Your Pocket," *Colonial Times,* March 2, 1972.

Tunnard, Christopher, and Henry Reed, *American Skyline* (Boston: Houghton Mifflin, 1956).

Walker, Richard, "A Theory of Suburbanization," in Michael Dear and Allen Scott, eds., *Urbanization and Planning in Capitalist Society* (London: Methune, 1981).

———, "The Transformation of Urban Structure in the Nineteenth Century and the Beginnings of Suburbanization," in Kevin Cox, ed., *Urbanization and Conflict in Market Societies* (Chicago: Maaroufa, 1978).

Webber, Melvin, "The BART Experience—What Have We Learned?" *Public Interest* Fall 76.

Whitt, J. Allen, "Can Capitalists Organize Themselves," *Insurgent Sociologist* 9, 2–3, 1979–80.

Whitt, J. Allen, "Means of Movement: The Politics of Modern Transportation Systems" (Ph.D. dissertation, University of California, Santa Barbara, 1975).

Yago, Glenn, "The Coming Crisis of U.S. Transportation" (Paper delivered to a conference on New Perspectives on the Urban Political Economy, The American University, Washington, D.C., May 1981).

———, "Current Issues in U.S. Transportation Politics," *International Journal of Urban and Regional Research* 2, 1978.

Zwerling, Stephen, *Mass Transit and the Politics of Transportation* (New York: Praeger, 1974).

II

The Failures of
National Urban Policy

WILLIAM K. TABB

"If we seize our growth as a challenge, we can make the 1970s a historic period when by conscious choice we transform our land into what we want it to become," President Nixon declared in 1970. In that year, Congress, in the Urban Growth and New Community Development Act, decreed that the federal government would adopt a national urban policy. Over the next decade, however, neither presidents nor congresses were able to develop a coherent policy. On the surface the debate was concerned with how much federal aid should be given to localities, and whether the assistance should be targeted to specific groups and goals or simply given to lower levels of government to spend as they chose. By the end of the decade, urban policy appeared in fact to be undergoing a reversal of direction: program development was turning into program dismantlement.

During the 1960s the federal government spent about four times as much money on agriculture as on metropolitan problems (and 50 times as much on military spending). But urban rioting called attention to the need for a War on Poverty, and by the end of the decade the increased dependence of cities on the federal government became evident. In the 1970s direct federal aid to cities more than quadrupled. By the end of that decade, Pittsburgh received 91 cents from the federal government for every dollar it raised locally; Newark, 64 cents; Cleveland, 60 cents. Federal grants to state and local governments as a whole increased from 11.5 percent of the amount of revenue they raised themselves in 1950, to 16.8 percent in 1960, 17.7 percent in 1965, 22.9 percent in 1970, 29.1 percent in 1975 and to 31.7 percent in 1980, according to the Advisory Commission on Intergovernmental Relations. By 1982 the Reagan cuts had reduced federal aid to local government to 24 percent of the amount they raised out of their own sources, or about what it was before President Nixon instituted general revenue sharing.

In the present period of economic crisis the need for transforming our nation's cities by "conscious choice" is no less important than it was when President Nixon spoke of the need to "seize our growth as a challenge." Today the economy is in a period of fundamental restructuring. Old industries are dying or being dramatically restructured, while new growth centers are emerging to challenge the dominance of former leading urban areas.

The role of government in relation to this urban transformation is ambiguous. Because people and built space cannot adjust instantaneously to such shifts, economic and social dislocations can result; affected groups seek political outcomes supportive of their interests. Their bargaining power depends on objective conditions, levels of consciousness, and organization.

In the 1960s, for example, the working poor were in a relatively strong bargaining position. Tight labor markets and civil rights movements helped create, if not a Great Society, at least one concerned with the needs of the urban poor. The decade of the 1970s, however, saw a waning of the optimistic belief that correct policy choices and social engineering could rebuild cities and eliminate poverty, an approach we may call redistributive liberalism. National disenchantment with government programs prevailed by the early 1980s. The Reagan administration's neo-conservative policy-thrust stressed market allocation of resources. Profit-maximizing corporations are encouraged to ignore the social costs of the urban restructuring process. Traditional equity considerations—concern for the poor and an equitable provision of housing, transportation, and other necessities of urban living—have been undermined by the fiscal crisis that afflicts most of urban America. This fiscal crisis is itself caused largely by capital mobility and urban restructuring. Because the social surplus is controlled by private decision-makers whose increasing mobility allows the avoidance of the relatively larger share of taxation that they formerly paid, the cost of reshaping cities rests more heavily on the general taxpayer. This pincer-like pressure—on the one side from declining revenues and on the other from increasing costs of restructuring urban space—has forced a reduction of traditional social programs. This change in the priorities of urban policy in recent years represents a departure from New Deal–Great Society liberalism.

After reviewing the major economic changes and their impact on the development of political and social philosophy in America, the Carter and

Reagan Administration urban policies will be discussed. I shall argue that, despite appearances, the Reagan Administration's carefully articulated philosophy of government generates a coherent urban component. In addition it will be shown that the anti-urban national austerity program of the early 1980s was not the creation of the Reagan Administration; Mr. Reagan accelerated trends that were already underway under Mr. Carter.

Crucial to President Reagan's reversal of New Deal–Great Society programs was the failure of Democrats in the Carter years to develop an updated liberalism consistent with the demands then being placed on the United States' economic and social institutions. Indeed the Reagan approach is prefigured in Mr. Carter's 1978 State of the Union message: "Government cannot solve our problems. It can't set our goals. It cannot define our vision. Government cannot eliminate poverty, or provide a bountiful economy, or reduce inflation, or save our cities."

In April 1977, President Carter designated six Cabinet Department secretaries and the heads of some related agencies as an urban and regional policy group. Their final report, issued in March 1978, enumerated a long list of intentions and general goals. It emphasized the need for welfare reform, fiscal assistance, public works programs, job creation, employment tax credits to employers hiring hardcore unemployed, a national development bank to lend to those investing in cities, an investment tax credit for projects in distressed communities, and funds for low-income housing rehabilitation and neighborhood projects.

The report was premised on two major assumptions: first, that the lack of progress in the past had been due to poor coordination; and second, that market incentives would induce private sector responses adequate to solving urban problems. The Carter urbanists took what were essentially political differences and reduced them to questions of streamlining governmental processes. The politics behind the coordination of programs, the designation of authority, and the levels and effectiveness of inputs were expressed in generalities which were unobjectionable on their face, but which lacked precision, thereby obscuring the economic realities.

In addition, the analysis of the task force ignored the fact that "uncoordinated" policies often had unannounced yet intended effects: Urban renewal removed the poor from valued central city land to the benefit of real estate interests; the interstate highway program subsidized the more affluent, allowing them to leave the cities; and housing programs ostensibly designed to help the poor were raided by profiteers. The list is long and might suggest that more than lack of coordination and other forms of incompetent administration were responsible for the unacceptable federal performance in the urban policy field. The abuses have been structurally determined by the needs of real estate developers, bankers, and other powerful interests.

The Carter urban policy stressed loan guarantees and grants to firms locating in depressed urban and rural areas by allowing businesses to obtain up to three fourths of their capital costs at federally subsidized loan rates (ranging from 2.5% to 7.5%). Between grants and loans, a business could leverage $10,000 of its own money into $100,000 for a new plant in a depressed area. Had the policy been enacted into law, the federal government would have guaranteed bank loans and also stood ready to buy the mortgages issued by the banks. Almost all risk would have been absorbed by the taxpayer. Possibilities for the unscrupulous to profit were, it seemed, almost consciously built in. It was precisely this sort of mechanism that led to the enormous FHA scandal only a few years earlier. At that time banks and real estate speculators were enriched and the government was stuck with hundreds of thousands of overvalued or worthless properties.

President Carter's urban program, which carried a $13.6 billion price tag when first proposed, had been scaled back to about $2.5 billion a little over a year later. The President had not pushed it and Congress was cool to such proposals.

President Carter proposed a Livable Cities Program of funding to establish credit unions and monies for social services, day care, legal assistance, food for the low-income elderly, and for parks, health, and recreation facilities. However, the funding levels proposed were low and did not begin to reverse the decreases in service levels that most cities were experiencing. In the 1960s the War on Poverty had spent billions. In contrast, Carter suggested spending in the low millions. An expansion of well-packaged but gimmicky programs funded at a very low level could not be expected to have a major impact on the nation's urban crisis.

A far more important part of Carter's urban package was the UDAGs. Mr. Carter called these Urban Development Action Grants, which were actually funded by Congress, "the centerpiece" of his urban program. The principle of the program is that federal dollars leverage private funds to revitalize older urban areas. By spending one dollar, HUD officials claimed, they leverage four dollars of private money. Critics on the other hand say that the grant program is welfare for the rich since the program has funded many luxury hotels and shopping malls. Many projects would have been built anyway. A critical 1979 Government Accounting Office review of the program charged that UDAG often simply provided windfall gains to developers. It cited among other cases a $5.8 million grant to Montezuma, Georgia, to build service roads for a new Procter & Gamble pulp mill. The local HUD official had recommended that the grant be turned down since P & G had already announced that it was undertaking the project. The taxpayer's gift came after the commitment and clearly was not necessary. Similarly, high-rent apartment developments in Chicago's Loop were treated to a million dollar subsidy "The project would have gone ahead anyway. . . . The actions grant was a lovely surprise— manna from heaven," said one of the architects (Herbers, 1982b). Typical of the HUD Urban Development Action Grant program are 1979 grants of $8 million for a Trade Center in Miami, $18 million for luxury hotels in Evansville, Indiana; Pontiac, Michigan; and Lynchburg and Roanoke, Virginia; and $32 million for parking garages in Detroit and Pontiac; Jackson, Mississippi; and Chattanooga, Tennessee. By the end of 1979, after two years of UDAG grants, 15 percent had gone to neighborhoods and over half to commercial developments (over a quarter to hotel and hotel-related projects, and the rest to industrial uses).

Clearly Mr. Carter was not anti-private sector. Indeed, more than any other presidential administration in the previous quarter of a century, his had opted for a program of almost total reliance on the private sector. The forces which had created the crisis for working-class urban dwellers not only went unchallenged, but were subsidized in hope of easing the pain of the cities. His aid to the cities was the smallest payoff of political debt to an urban constituency proposed by a Democratic president in decades. It can be argued that Carter's lack of a positive vision set the stage for voter acceptance of Mr. Reagan.

MR. REAGAN AND THE URBAN POOR

Mr. Reagan has a coherent urban program. The component that deals with poverty is based on the belief that poor people need incentives to provide for their own well-being and that federal programs have been counterproductive by reducing incentives to work. A second premise of the Reagan urban program is that the government should rely on the free market as much as possible. The President favors reprivatizing service delivery using a voucher system as his major housing proposal and eliminating other programs such as legal services. Third, Mr. Reagan desires a new federalism, giving back to state and local governments as much responsibility as possible for programs affecting their citizens. The Reagan welfare "reform" which was instituted in October of 1981 is typical in this regard. It cut over 400,000 families from the Aid to Families with Dependent Children program and reduced the benefits of hundreds of thousands more. The goal of the reform was to save a billion dollars.

Most of the savings came from a new formula on how much welfare the working poor could receive. By lowering this limit the Reagan Administration in the short run saved money, but this also decreases the incentive for welfare recipients to find and keep jobs. Under the 1981 Reagan budget, one out of every six families on welfare was forced off the rolls or had its benefits cut. Virtually all of those people had incomes below the federal poverty line ($8410 for a family of four in 1981). This led some to question Mr. Reagan's assertion that his austerity measures would not hurt "the truly needy."

In 1982 Mr. Reagan proposed cutting $2.2 billion more from the federal share of Aid to Families with Dependent Children. Under the proposals the President made for the fiscal 1983 budget, applicants would have to show that they were unsuccessful in seeking jobs before they could be granted welfare aid. Additionally, all states would have to establish "workfare" programs, which were to offer jobs in the public sector when private employment was not available, forcing welfare recipients to work off their benefits at whatever jobs local officials assigned them. Since eighty percent of AFDC recipients are children, they would be the primary victims of harassing recipients off the welfare rolls. All those refusing to work could be denied welfare, no matter how outrageous the working conditions and how inadequate their ability to take care of their families and work at the same time. Reduction of the federal share of welfare financing by over a third, combined with decreases in food stamps, Medicaid, and aid to elementary, secondary and vocational education, appeared to doom children growing up in poverty income households to a dismal future.

THE SIGNIFICANCE OF ENTERPRISE ZONES

In his presidential campaign Mr. Reagan described the enterprise zone as his main remedy for black unemployment. As President, he introduced as his primary domestic initiative an urban enterprise zone proposal at a time when black unemployment was over 17 percent. As the Reagan Administration's only job creation program during its first two years in office, it promised to do little to help joblessness in America's low-income communities. The enterprise zone idea was however an important reversal of past federal job creation and urban programs.

E. S. Savas, Assistant Secretary of Policy Development and Research in Mr. Reagan's Department of Housing and Urban Development, describes the enterprise zone concept as the "mirror image" of the now de-

funct Model Cities program. The Reagan plan proposes federal tax benefits rather than federal spending. It would seek to encourage private
investment and the provisions of local services through private initiative.
Model Cities was a public sector program stressing government provision
of services and infrastructure rebuilding. The cost of the Reagan approach
will not show up as higher expenditures because little federal funding is
involved. There is, however, a longer-term cost to the federal government
in this tax forgiveness proposal. It sets a tone and a direction for future
policy-making by gaining acceptance for the "subsidy of capital" (Reagan).

The ideological underpinning of the approach was clear to the President. "The enterprise zone concept is based on utilizing the market to
solve urban problems, relying primarily on private sector institutions,"
Mr. Reagan said in a message to Congress. "The idea is to create a productive, free-market environment in economically depressed areas by reducing taxes, regulations and other Government burdens on economic
activity" (Raines, p. 1).

A 1982 White House information sheet indicated that 75 percent or
more of the corporate income tax and all capital gains tax would be eliminated for enterprise zone firms under its version of the proposed legislation. The White House expects the 25 enterprise zones to cost the federal
government $12.5 million each with most of this cost coming from lost
tax revenues, for a total cost of $124 to 310 million. In the face of an
84 percent cut in employment and training funds, a 50 percent cut in
vocational and adult education, and other cuts in aid to urban areas and
low wage workers for fiscal 1982, the enterprise zone program is proposed
at funding levels equal to less than one percent of the money Reagan cut
from other urban programs. Not only is this a rather uneven trade, but
the logic of the enterprise zone itself undercuts working conditions and
the local governments' tax base.

The Reagan Administration proposal for the creation of enterprise
zones contained a waiver of Federal minimum wage laws for workers
under 21 years of age. Savas stated that the minimum wage law is destruc-
tive because it "prohibits work for people whose work is not worth that
much money yet" (the statutory $3.25 an hour minimum). He joins many
if not most economists who consider this legal requirement to be a major
obstacle to hiring the unemployed and so wish to see all minimum wage
laws repealed. In proposing no minimum wage guarantee for teenagers,
the Reagan policy-makers seek, in Savas' words "to decriminalize work"
(Hershey, p. 1). Few non-economists have been convinced by such arguments because they know that once one group of workers can be made
to work for less, there will be pressure on other workers. The real nature

of the Reagan Administration's desire to "decriminalize" certain behavior is seen in its accompanying goal to relax health and safety regulations and other protective legislation enforcement in the enterprise zones.

There is also reason to think that the way the Reagan Administration would implement the law would have implications which municipal unions would find objectionable. Savas says that turning over traditional city services to private groups would be one of the factors considered in selecting zones. The American Federation of State, County and Municipal Employees sees the Administration proposal as "an excuse for the creation of company towns" and "a direct assault on public service employees" (Herbers, 1982a, p. A18).

The two New York members of Congress who introduced enterprise zone legislation, Robert Garcia, a Democrat representing the South Bronx and Jack Kemp, a Republican from Buffalo, did not go along with the fast-buck–no-regulation orientation. They were not happy with the Administration's version. Kemp saw the incentives to businesses as inadequate. Garcia believes that there is need for stronger, effective community participation.

Representing the depressed South Bronx, Robert Garcia stresses other directions. His view of the bill is that it be "designed to strengthen neighborhood economies . . . to strengthen the community ties which connect neighbor to neighbor. . . . The enterprise zone approach cannot work by itself—its success requires that it be used in conjunction with the very programs the President wants to eliminate. (Mr. Garcia's statement was made on the house floor June 3, 1981.) From the vantage point of the South Bronx, where 30 percent of the population lives below the poverty line and the unemployment rate is three to four times the national average, enterprise zones are better than nothing. But as Representative Garcia is well aware, there are no substitutes for a full-employment policy supplemented by adequate aid to education and other human capital development programs. Even though the proposal may bring limited benefits to the South Bronx, from the viewpoint of working Americans as a whole, the plan is a potential disaster.

The program is representative of the Reagan approach. It requires very little in direct federal outlays, shifts new burdens to local areas, represents an erosion of the tax base by subsidizing corporations not through direct expenditures but tax forgiveness, and intensifies competition between jurisdictions by lowering wages and tax receipts in other competing locations. The Reagan Administration has made it clear that in determining which of the 2,000 eligible depressed cities, rural areas, and Indian reservations will get aid depends on, among other things, how much tax relief the local jurisdiction grants business. By stimulating such competition, the federal government prompts the erosion of local tax bases, which would be legally sanctioned and extend over the 24-year life of the zones. Elected officials are told to accept whatever changes business interests will want in building codes, licensing laws, and in providing infrastructure and services. These will of course take money from the rather meager resources going to meet the needs of poorer taxpayers.

The enterprise zone idea is a major assault on the American workers' hard-won wage gains and working conditions. There is every reason to believe that it is possible that one day in the not too distant future the entire U.S. will be a tax-free zone. *Business Week* favors the expansion of the enterprise zone to encompass the more far-reaching free trade zone concept, thus encouraging further erosion of customs, laws, tariffs, and other tax concessions. *Business Week* reports: "And although some countries may have gone too far in offering major concessions to attract industry, most economists believe that U.S. companies and government at all levels have fallen far behind the competition" (1980, p. 82). Indeed, it is a fact that in 1979 one percent of our nation's total foreign trade went through U.S. free trade zones while ten percent of international trade passed through free trade zones world-wide. It is also true that U.S. retailers could profitably use such zones to sort, label, and store their clothes and appliance imports. However, such zones can be abused; for example, exporters could ignore U.S. labeling requirements and fire-retardant tests for their garments if they produced them in trade zones. While manufacturers could benefit, workers and consumers would suffer, for free trade zones represent a loss of democratic control over the production process. They weaken consumer protection legislation and worker health-and-safety protection. They also stimulate tax avoidance and promote lower wage structures. If *Business Week* is right that free zones will be handling more than 20 percent of worldwide trade by 1985, competitive devaluation of working conditions and tax policies is certain to occur.

REPRIVATIZATION AND HOUSING VOUCHERS

Another instance of the Reagan reprivatization strategy is to get the federal government out of the business of directly providing services to taxpayers. E. S. Savas, who was quoted so much in our discussion of enterprise zones, came to the Reagan Administration from Columbia University. When he was a professor there he wrote about the desirability of cities contracting out service delivery as a cost reduction method. Contracting out means that work is done by private firms that typically use non-union labor at low wages and pay no retirement, health, or other benefits. Mr. Savas also favored users of a service buying it directly in the market. That way one could seek out exactly the service he or she desired and at the lowest cost. But consider what private contracting of, for example, garbage collection would do. High-income taxpayers would save taxes that formerly went to municipal collection costs and buy private service. Low-income families would find it difficult to buy equivalent services, given their more limited budgets. If tax collection is on a progressive basis, reprivatization can mean cost cuts to the rich, cost increases and poorer services to the poor and working class. Reprivatization of this sort is a key strategy in Reagan's housing policy as well (Tabb, 1982, Ch. 7).

The major, indeed only, housing program favored by the Reagan Administration is the voucher system. It is intended to replace almost all existing housing programs. The Reagan Administration moved to cut federal funding for publicly assisted housing to levels far below those established in federal housing legislation. This policy was not a response to mismanagement on the Housing Authority, which was collecting 97 percent of rents due every month and had a waiting list of 160,000 people (even though with the current rates of turnover it would take 18 years for people at the end of the list to get apartments). New York housing officials said that such a change would have "a traumatic and devastating effect" on the city's public housing program. If the cuts were approved by Congress, the projects would deteriorate quickly, creating a self-fulfilling prophecy by an Administration that rejects public sector housing. Unable at this time to kill public housing without offering an alternative program, the Reagan Administration has proposed a limited housing voucher plan under which qualifying families would get government assistance to meet part of their rent. The advantage of such an approach is that the low-income family could select its own accommodations and federal funds could be spread over more families, since the federal subsidy would ideally fill the gap between market rent and the family's rent-paying ability. This would be less than the cost of building and maintaining public housing. Under such a policy, there would be no need for the federal government either to subsidize new construction or to own actual housing units. However, whether such an approach would improve the housing opportunities of the poor depends on the availability of adequate rental units at a cost the subsidy would allow. Funding levels thus become crucial. Under the Reagan Administration plan, only 107,000 families in the entire U.S. would receive vouchers in fiscal 1983.

Anthony Gliedman, Commissioner of Housing Preservation and Development for New York City, criticized the voucher proposal, saying that "past experience shows that the private sector did not enter certain fragile markets—such as low- and middle-income housing developments—

without being induced by substantial Government support." He said that voucher system of rent subsidies to the poor was unlikely to work in high-rent urban areas where subsidies would be insufficient and coverage too restricted to help many of the poor to obtain adequate housing. The voucher proposal was, however, consistent with the reprivatizing of welfare state functions. Its goal was to minimize the public sector role in providing housing for the poor and to make low-income people even more dependent on market forces.

By spring of 1982 local officials were working out a different relationship with private capital. As William McNichola, Jr., Mayor of Denver, told a gathering co-sponsored by the United States Conference of Mayors and the Atlantic Richfield Company, his "city was in a sense returning to similar practices used at the turn of the century when corporations built parks and other public facilities for the city." Denver had turned over part of the city to a joint private-public committee with power to regulate land use, construction design, pollution control, etc., in a basically private-sector-driven redevelopment. Other cities adopted similar partnership agreements wherein corporations "adopted" schools, fire houses, and other public facilities for which local governments could no longer pay. C. William Verity, Jr., chair of Armco Steel Company and of President Reagan's Task Force on Private Sector, stressed that "these partnerships are not intended to intrude on the mayor's responsibilities" (Herbers, 1982a, p. A25).

It is clear that elected representatives of poverty stricken governments who must beg hat in hand are in a weak position to press priorities to which the charitable corporation objects. The mayor becomes not a public servant but the frontpiece for corporate control. This is the intended effect of Mr. Reagan's urban policy—to return control to capital, to undercut the possibility of local democracy, and to dismantle what was left of an independent public sector and of state policing of corporate behavior.

NEW FEDERALISM

Another pillar of the Reagan urban plan is its new federalism, an effort to return responsibility for urban social services to state and city governments while cutting federal revenue sharing deeply. Mr. Reagan wanted to eliminate a large number of specific grant programs by converting them into a much smaller number of block grants over which state governments would have nearly complete discretion.

In the summer of 1981 President Reagan attempted to reduce Federal authorization for health, transportation, urban aid, education, and other social spending as well. Congress went along with $35 billion in cuts and accepted the conversion of 57 specific grant programs into nine broad block grants, giving the states wider discretion on spending priorities but not the almost complete discretion that the President preferred. In September 1981 President Reagan demanded a second round of cuts, including a 12 percent reduction in the federal revenue sharing program. This was a reversal of Mr. Reagan's previous stance. In October 1980 candidate Reagan had said, "I pledge that when elected, reenactment of revenue sharing will be among my highest domestic priorities." Because one out of every four dollars in federal aid to cities was coming from Washington in the form of revenue sharing, such a cut would have a serious impact, especially since it came after cuts in other social programs which were heavily felt in cities. Richard Conder, president of the National Association of Counties, calculated that while only 14 percent of the total federal budget went to cities, counties, and states, 66 percent of the first set of Reagan budget cuts came from programs directly affecting local and state governments.

Mr. Reagan promised that over the rest of his tenure in office he would further reduce federal social programs and turn fiscal power over to state and local government. Such decentralization has potentially contradictory implications for democracy and accountability. It is possible that people would have more influence over the decisions which affect their lives if more power resides at lower levels of governance. On the other hand, lobbyists and special interests have historically done well in state legislature and city councils where representatives have small staffs and are often themselves flagrantly amenable to financial incentives. Civil rights issues and the needs of the poor are particularly slighted at local levels. These are the reasons why important functions were moved to the federal level in the first place.

On the economic level, decentralization increases the ability of ever more mobile capital to play off one taxing jurisdiction against another. Centralized tax collection by the federal government and revenue sharing to local levels avoids this phenomenon. Returning tax power to local levels also accentuates the impact of differential wealth and revenue-generating capacity on service delivery, another important reason for federal revenue sharing.

Norman Ture, until early 1982 Undersecretary of the Treasury for Tax and Economic Affairs, argued for the Reagan Administration's cutbacks and its policy of shifting responsibilities to local government. Localities could offset these reductions, he said, by increasing their own taxes. People living in jurisdictions that chose not to raise taxes could move to another jurisdiction where programs were maintained (and taxes were raised). The assertion that people can easily uproot and relocate where they will receive benefits they want contains two assumptions: First, people are mobile and not tied by friends and family to a community, and that they would be able to sell a house in a depressed area and afford the moving and relocations costs. Second, one should buy public services the same way one chooses goods in a private market. From such a perspective, if you do not have money for good schooling for your kids and cannot vote with your feet by moving into a posh enclave, you have "chosen" inferior education for your children.

The centralization of economic power and resources in a few hundred large multinational firms and the ability of these corporations to move away from areas of high taxation has meant that there are severe limits to a local community's ability to meet its needs out of local resources. This reality is recognized implicitly in the federal assumption of more and more funding responsibility for functions which had been thought local in nature. By 1970, education, generally recognized as a local responsibility, was 41 percent funded by grants-in-aid. The local level was responsible for 70 percent of direct outlays, but contributed only 40 percent of the financing. In the past most local officials have argued that it is the federal responsibility to pay for income security programs like welfare and food stamps—programs that Mr. Reagan wanted to turn over to them. In return, Reagan offered to take over total responsibility for the Medicaid program, an exchange that would not benefit Medicaid recipients. The cost of the program has been increasing dramatically. It is difficult now for Mr. Reagan to do much about this since it is jointly run with the states. By moving total responsibility to the national level, the stage would be set for dramatic funding cutbacks which cannot now be engineered.

In early April 1982, the Reagan Administration gave up its attempt to transfer welfare and food stamp programs to the states in exchange for federal takeover of all Medicaid costs. Mayors and governors, Democrats and Republicans, saw the swap, the centerpiece of Mr. Reagan's New Federalism, as a ploy to shift responsibility and costs that have been federal responsibilities to local governments. Estimates of future costs and federal grants also showed that the states and municipalities would lose out substantially. (The Congressional Budget Office had estimated a $15 billion loss in its first year; loses would grow over time.) However, even if the states as a whole had come out ahead in narrow "dollars-swapped" terms, they still would have lost out because of what this would have meant—an increase in the unfairness of the distribution of benefits across state and increased inter-state tax competition. If the Reagan proposals were accepted they would undo a decade of progressive legislation. Consider: total federal grants to state and local government more than tripled between 1970 and 1978 (from $24 to $81 billion a year). In 1978 federal grants in aid to state and local governments paid 25 percent of their bills. Many cities are already stepchildren of the federal government, yet the perception is still one of localism, that cities and towns should be able to meet their expenses. They cannot and they should not be expected to do so. The sooner the popular consciousness accepts taxation of the societal surplus at the central level and subsequent distribution to the local one for spending, the better. Local taxes should not be expected to carry a majority of the burden.

CONCLUSION

The pillars of the Reagan urban policy, free market service delivery reprivatization, vouchers, enterprise zones, and the new federalism, have each been resisted in varying degrees by those who see them as anti-urban, anti-poor and anti-working class. The urban policies of the Reagan Administration increase suffering and promote social tension. This is not because the programs do not work—they do work. Most Americans have simply misunderstood their purpose.

In examining the application of the Reagan philosophy it is not difficult to conclude that he is interested in forcing down the individual and social wage of the working class. Denied adequate funds for health, education, and welfare, low-income workers are thrown increasingly into a Dickensian *Hard Times* world, forced to take any job at any wage and under any working conditions, on pain of starvation. The fear of poverty acts as a stick. This is the opposite of liberal programs that offer the carrot of job creation and work incentives made possible through such means as children's day care centers.

The free market premise of the Reagan program also places subsidies to the corporate sector ahead of service provision to those in need and redistributes income and services from the poor and working class to the corporate rich. Placing greater burdens on state and local governments intensifies inter-jurisdictional competition, further reduces corporate tax burden, and lowers the quality of public services. While harsher than Carter in his urban policy, Mr. Reagan, too, is trying to work with market forces in the same fashion as his predecessor did. During the first year and a half after his election, Mr. Reagan had won major contests over policy direction. However as this is written, opposition is steadily growing. While forecasts are always dangerous, the Reagan urban program appears to be a detour on the long road toward increased government responsibility for a different quality of urban life. At the same time it is unlikely that voters will find it desirable to go back to inadequate and yet also wastefully inefficient programs of the past. What are the likely candidates for a different approach to urban social issues? I return to this question as the subject of the final essay in this volume.

REFERENCES

Business Week, "China: How Trades Zones Are Luring Foreign Investors," January 11, 1982.

Business Week, "The U.S. Lags in Trade Zones," November 17, 1980.

Herbers, John, "Cities Seek Aid of Private Concerns to Cope With Budget Cuts," *New York Times,* April 1, 1982. a

Herbers, John, "New Urban Program," *New York Times,* March 26, 1982. b

Hershey, Robert D., "Minimum Wage Waiver Studies for Reagan's Blighted Areas Plan," *New York Times,* January 30, 1982.

Raines, Howell, "Reagan Offers Enterprise Zone Plan for Urban Revitalization," *New York Times,* March 24, 1982.

Reagan, Ronald, "Message to Congress on Urban Enterprise Zones," *New York Times,* March 24, 1982.

Tabb, William K., *The Long Default: New York and the Urban Fiscal Crisis* (New York: Monthly Review Press, 1982).

four

POLITICAL STRUGGLE
AND
FISCAL CRISIS

12

Political Conflict, Urban Structure, and the Fiscal Crisis

ROGER FRIEDLAND, FRANCES FOX PIVEN, and
ROBERT R. ALFORD

During the last few years, many of the older cities in the United States
have experienced in intense form a series of stresses that are sometimes
treated as and called "the urban fiscal crisis."[1] Current dramatics notwithstanding, the so-called fiscal crisis is a familiar feature of urban life. Its
classic symptoms are widening disparities between revenues and expenditures on the one hand, and rising demands for municipal services on the
other. These symptoms are not only a recurrent fact of American urban
history, but also, if often in less intense form, a feature of many other
cities in advanced capitalist nations. In view of the scope of these symptoms, the explanations that have dominated discussion of the so-called
crisis in the United States have been remarkably trivial, emphasizing as
they do such idiosyncratic aspects of contemporary American cities as the
quality of municipal leadership, or the particular functional responsibilities
of particular municipal governments, or the irrationalities in revenue collection and service delivery resulting from fragmented local government
jurisdictions. Even the somewhat more plausible explanations that have
recently come to the fore, emphasizing changing intra-metropolitan and
interregional patterns of capital investment with the resulting erosion of

the municipal tax base, fail to consider these developments in appropriate historical and comparative perspective. (See, for example, Sternlieb and Hughes, 1976; Perry and Watkins, 1977; Starr, 1976; Baer, 1976.) American cities have experienced fiscal strains at earlier historical junctures, at periods when capital was concentrating in the cities, not deserting them. And not all cities, either in the United States or in Western Europe, that are suffering fiscal strains are the victims of territorial shifts in capital investment. In short, while some empirical verification can be found for all of these assertions, they do not propose an explanation of urban fiscal strains commensurate with their perennial and widespread occurrence.

A potentially more illuminating perspective from which to view these urban troubles is suggested by a growing body of work by neo-marxists on the theory of the state. Perhaps the best known exemplar of this new tradition is James O'Connor. Stated simply, O'Connor and others postulate that the capitalist state must provide the infrastructure and subsidies which will ensure the profits of monopoly capital; it must subsidize and protect the accumulation process, while continuing to permit the private appropriation of profits. At the same time, the state must absorb popular discontent generated by the social costs of the accumulation process. The theory of the state argues that the fiscal crisis is the result of the increasing demands on government arising from these dualistic functions.[2] This is a provocative perspective, but it also has certain flaws. The theory asserts a structural and inherent tendency to crisis, although the visible manifestations of the crisis are in fact variable. Also, the theory of the state remains very general and does not deal with variations in symptoms of fiscal stress from one historical period to another, from one city and nation to another, and even from one function or level of the state to another.

In this paper, we begin our argument with the premise that urban areas are critically important sites at which both economic growth and political integration are organized. Government structures in urban areas must therefore perform key functions both to support urban economic processes and to promote the political integration of the urban population. On the one hand, urban governments must be responsive to the infrastructural and service requirements of capital accumulation, and to changes in these requirements generated by economic growth. On the other hand, they must also manage political participation among the masses of the urban population who do not control capital accumulation and may not benefit from it either. Whether or not these dual functions of urban government are, as the theory of the state argues, inherently and consistently contradictory,[3] they are clearly contradictory at certain junctures in the process of capitalist economic development—for example, during extreme downturns in the business cycle when large numbers of people become unemployed and real wages fall, or during periods of rapid economic concentration and modernization that displace workers and uproot or undermine communities.[4]

Considered apart from specific structural arrangements, such periods might be expected to generate extraordinary convulsions in municipal politics. The electoral-representative arrangements which underpin municipal governments make them vulnerable to popular discontent, and also limit their ability to employ extraordinary strategies of collective mobilization or repression to cope with discontent. At the same time, municipal authorities are helpless to intervene in the economic developments which may have triggered discontent and, indeed, find it difficult to resist even new demands arising from the private sector on which they are fiscally dependent. During such periods, the responses required of city government successfully to accomplish political integration and support economic growth might be expected to intensify, and to become antagonistic or contradictory.

However, such convulsions are not frequent. The reason, we will argue, is that specific structural arrangements are developed on the municipal level that mediate these potentially antagonistic functions posited by the theory of the state, and allow urban governments to cope with both the requirements of economic growth and the requirements of political integration, even during periods of potentially intense conflict. Among the structural arrangements that we think are important in mediating economic and popular pressures are

1. the degree of decentralization or centralization of government functions, and

2. the degree of segregation of economic and political functions within urban governments.

All western nations provide for some degree of decentralization in the governance of cities, but the degree of decentralization varies from nation to nation and from city to city, as do the specific forms of government authority which are decentralized or centralized. Similarly, all western nations provide for some degree of structural segregation between those government activities that further economic growth and those that facilitate the political integration of the urban population. And, there is also a widespread but varying tendency for these functions to be fragmented among different agencies and programs. These variations in the scope and substance of decentralization of government authority, and in the segregation and fragmentation of government activities, may help to account for differences among nations and cities in the capacity to cope with periodic eruptions of political conflict.

But while certain structural arrangements help to diffuse and manage conflict, they also lead to the proliferation of government activities and costs, and the contraction of government revenues. The tensions which which might otherwise take the form of direct struggles between business, industry, and finance on the one hand, and workers and consumers on the other hand, take the form instead of escalating demands on municipal agencies—for jobs, services, contracts, tax concessions—with the result that municipal activities and budgets expand, while municipal revenues are reduced. As a consequence, periods of potential social and class conflict become instead periods of fiscal strains.

Finally, the fiscal problems of municipal governments tend to be cumulative as a result of the institutionalization of past concessions. Municipal agencies and activities become a repository of historical demands, and this accumulation of commitments obviously aggravates fiscal strains. Moreover, these existing patterns may inhibit responses to new and emerging requirements of economic growth and political integration. Hence periodic reform efforts to solve the fiscal crisis often concentrate on restructuring local government in order to purge it of obsolete concessions. These efforts may succeed, at least for a time, in managing the recurrent urban fiscal strains.

Before we elaborate on these points, we want frankly to acknowledge that our speculations are based primarily on our knowledge of urban processes and structures in the United States. We have tried to distill from this experience the propositions that might form the basis for more intensive comparative examination of the nature of urban fiscal strains and the institutional arrangements which we think help to explain them. And, although we refer to empirical studies to illustrate our argument, our main object is to suggest a theoretical perspective which at this stage remains largely untested.

ECONOMIC GROWTH VERSUS POLITICAL
PARTICIPATION ON THE URBAN LEVEL

Cities are obviously the location of key production and distribution activities in Western economics, although of course the economic role of cities varies. Cities contain enormous fixed capital investments reflecting their diverse economic functions, in the form of networks of headquarters, offices or manufacturing units, and the agglomeration of what David Harvey has called the "built environment" necessary for these activities (Harvey, 1975). Government at the urban level supports this economic structure in several ways. Government provides public services that help maintain the labor force through subsidized housing, public education, and health care, for example. Government agencies build and operate the public infrastructure necessary for the profitability of urban enterprises, in the form of transportation networks, water and power systems, and pollution control plants. Government agencies provide the authority to make and enforce decisions affecting the spatial efficiency of the urban economy, in the form of zoning plans, the development of industrial parks, urban renewal projects and, increasingly, metropolitan planning activities. Finally, local government agencies implement macroeconomic policies set at the national level, such as public employment programs or counter-cyclical public capital investments.

The concentration of economic activities in urban areas results in the concentration of population in urban areas, and the concentration also of popular political participation. At the same time, therefore, as local governments perform key functions for urban economic enterprises, they also become a primary focus for the political activity and organization of large proportions of the population. While the bare fact of concentrated population might in itself tend to give local governments a large role in maintaining popular political allegiance, certain other features of the urban situation tend to enlarge that role and, from time to time, by heightening the potential for group and class strife, to make it problematic as well.

First, local governments are often important loci for popular political participation because they are structurally accessible, the point of daily contact between citizen and state. The relative visibility of local government policies and the relative accessibility of local government agencies make them a more susceptible target of political opposition than other levels of the state. Oppositional political parties thus frequently develop national political strategies around initial urban political mobilization and electoral victories (e.g., the successes of the Socialists on the local level in the early twentieth century in the United States; the post–World War II local successes of the Communists in Italy; and the recent successes of the French Communists at the municipal level).

Second, local governments are important providers of social services. The quality and quantity of these social services on the one hand, and their tax cost on the other hand, are increasingly significant components of real family income.[5] In cities with a large unionized working class, such public services become an alternative to improvement in real wages through collective bargaining at the workplace, and forms of political participation oriented toward public services become an alternative to trade unionism and political parties oriented toward workplace issues. In cities with large concentrations of non-unionized working class, and of marginal groups unable to find productive employment at all, local public service issues can become the main focus of political organization. Thus the social services provided by urban governments attract the political energies and activism of both organized and unorganized segments of the working class, as well as the politically concerned elements of the middle class.

Rapid economic growth or decline not only tends to increase the demands both of capital and of the working population, but creates a large potential for conflict between these demands. Because urban areas are the location of economic growth, they are also the location where changes in group and class structure, and in political alignments emerging out of group and class structure, find their first political expression.[6] Thus during the late nineteenth century, the expansion of American industry was facilitated by municipal investments in infrastructure as well as municipal contracts, franchises, and even the private appropriation of municipal capital. At the same time, industrial expansion created a new industrial working class, composed of American artisans and tradesmen and of large numbers of immigrants as well. That this working class was rebellious was evident in frequent and bloody strikes. But rarely did working-class mobilizations take the form of challenging business control of municipal government, even when city police were used to break strikes. The structural arrangements which allowed city governments to defuse this potential conflict also produced the recurrent fiscal crises of the late nineteenth century.

Similarly, during the post–World War II period, all Western nations experienced rapid and sustained growth, accompanied by continuous urban concentration. An increasing proportion of production was concentrated in urban areas, and the most productive, technically advanced, and economically powerful enterprises were centralized in a handful of dominant metropolitan centers. Urban economic growth generated large demands for public facilities to complement private investment. Structural economic changes also led to demands for new and expensive urban policies to adapt the city's form and services to expanding coordinative and service functions. Rapid economic growth and concentration generated a continuous flow of population from less developed parts of the country, or from less developed countries, to many major metropolitan centers. Thus millions of southern Italian workers migrated to the northern industrial belt of Italy to find employment, and over a million Italian, Spanish, Portuguese, and Arab workers streamed into the metropolitan centers of France, attracted by the jobs in rapidly developing French industry. Millions of blacks and Latins came to the cities of the United States. These rapid influxes of population created a potential for intense political intra-class and inter-class conflict. But political conflict was muted, we will argue, by structural arrangements on the local level which diverted group and class antagonisms into fiscal claims on local government. Urban governments became the shock absorbers of the upheavals produced by the national political economy. The so-called fiscal crisis is one result.

To summarize, over time urban governments come to be structured in ways which allow them both to support economic growth on the one hand, and to regulate and manage political participation on the other. Urban governments are organized in ways which allow them to absorb political discontent through political participation which is limited to agencies and issues which do not impinge upon economic growth.

URBAN GOVERNMENT STRUCTURES AS MECHANISMS FOR COPING WITH CONTRADICTORY FUNCTIONS

Structural arrangements which we think are important in accounting for the capacity of urban governments to cope with antagonistic pressures are arrangements for the decentralization of state functions, and the structural segregation and fragmentation of accumulation and political integration functions within the state. Some degree of decentralization and structural segregation is common to the urban government structures of advanced capitalist states, but there are variations. We would predict that more advanced forms of decentralization and more advanced forms of structural segregation permit more successful management of the class and group conflicts generated by economic growth and change. However, we would also predict that the structural arrangements which help to mute and channel conflict tend to produce fiscal strains, so that the political convulsions one might otherwise expect come to be realized as intense fiscal stresses. Political conflict may be an alternative to fiscal strain, and may be a strategic alternative under certain historical conditions.

Centralization and Decentralization

Before we can consider the variable arrangements for centralization and decentralization, the fundamental institutional separation of state and economy in capitalist societies must be summarized. In general, the state, including urban governments, has been excluded from profitable activity. Embedded in constitutional arrangements, this exclusion is normally an accepted context rather than a legitimate issue for political participation.[7] Where the state is engaged in productive activity, where the state provides some input into private accumulation, it generally does so where the private market *fails* to supply this input (Offe, 1975, 129–30). Thus state production is usually relegated to unprofitable forms of social service delivery and material production which are nonetheless necessary for accumulation to proceed.

Governments in capitalist societies consequently are dependent on taxes which are ultimately drawn from incomes or profits generated in the private sector. As long as state financing is dependent upon taxation (or public debt to private financial intermediaries), its autonomy is limited by the necessity to avoid policies that might impinge upon capital accumulation.[8] And to the extent that capital accumulation and public fiscal capacity both depend on continued private control of investment, production and location decisions, political issues which question that control are extraordinarily difficult to raise.

The degree of dependence of urban governments on the private sector varies, however, because urban governments occupy different positions in the overall structure of state authority. The level of decentralization of this state structure in terms of financing, policy-making, and implementation responsibilities of urban governments will accentuate the vulnerability of urban governments to capitalist demands for expensive tax and policy subsidies. Conversely, decentralization forces urban governments to resist popular demands for expanded social services or progressive taxes which might impinge upon capitalist interests. Where urban revenues are centrally raised, urban policies nationally formulated, and local implementation constrained by national government, local tax, and expenditure policies will not be as susceptible to the exigencies of local profitability. Under those circumstances, the central government will act as an intermediary, reflecting in its policies the overall fiscal dependency of the state, but buffering municipal governments from the immediate and direct necessity of avoiding any policies which impinge upon capital accumulation (Sbragia, 1976).[9]

By contrast, in political systems where urban government revenues are locally raised, expenditure patterns locally determined, and policies locally implemented, the vulnerability of municipal officials to the vicissitudes of local economic activity is acute. The fracturing of government jurisdictions in metropolitan areas adds to the vulnerability of particular municipal governments, for then investors can bargain among central city and suburban jurisdictions even when they are tied to the metropolitan area by economic considerations. Increasingly, however, the growth of national and international corporations, and improvements in transportation and communications which made this growth possible, have freed capital from dependence on particular locations. Under these conditions, investors can adjust and readjust—or threaten to adjust and readjust—their production and location decisions, bargaining among metropolitan areas and particular governments in metropolitan areas as in a marketplace, so as to secure the most favorable mix of taxes, infrastructure and business-oriented public services.[10] Moreover, just as the exclusion of the national government from profitable activity is taken for granted, and not easily subject to political challenge, so is the restriction of local governments from intervention in the decisions of investors taken for granted, and not easily made a matter of local political contention. Indeed, the ideological supports for this segregation may be stronger on the local level where the conviction that "freedom" consists in the protection of the "free" market from government intervention is joined to the conviction that fiscal decentralization is the foundation of local self-government. Thus voters in local elections, threatened by the loss of jobs that capital flight entails, often support business subsidies or tax favors and spurn proposals to increase business taxes or business costs. Several state referenda increasing the utility charges of large enterprises but reducing the charges paid by individual households were voted down in the 1976 election in the United States.[11]

Such arrangements, ensuring the vulnerability of local government to the requirements of accumulation and preventing political challenge to these requirements, tend, however, to exacerbate fiscal strains. The capacity of private investors to choose among localities leaves local governments not only helpless to regulate the volume and content of private investments within their boundaries, but often helpless even to control public taxation and service decisions. Thus the city government of New York, and state agencies as well, respond to the threatened flight of capital investment from the city by promising to reduce business taxes, relax pollution controls, and enlarge the public infrastructure and subsidies that attract investors.

These structural arrangements make municipal agencies more easily the prey of particular economic interests which secure public expenditure benefits that may increase private profits without necessarily increasing tax revenues. Many of the central city urban redevelopment projects in the United States were promoted on the grounds that they would stimulate private investments that would not otherwise have taken place, thus enlarging the city's tax base. Redevelopment projects certainly increased the tax yield on the development sites. On the other hand, not only did they destroy manufacturing and small retail employment by demolishing older establishments and replacing them with high-rise offices and luxury residential units (Hartman, 1974; Epstein, 1976), but they did not have any net effects on the aggregate level of high-rise residential construction or net industrial investment (Friedland, 1977). Thus it can be argued that in the end they cost municipalities far more in public investment and public services than was regained in increased tax yields.

Similarly, spurred by developer interests, southern U.S. cities have expanded their boundaries and extended public infrastructure to support suburban residential and industrial developments. The lopsided relationship between developers and political officials which yields these public concessions does not necessarily yield tax revenues to finance them.[12] A similar relationship between real estate interests and public officials in declining urban areas results in the use of public funds and authority to acquire properties whose real value is rapidly declining for "urban renewal" which never occurs.

Nor can urban government easily sift through particular economic pressures to reach fiscally wise decisions. Not only are criteria of productivity vague and ambiguous in the public sector, but it is extremely difficult for municipalities to predict the revenue effects of public expenditures when they lack any control over private economic decisions.[13] Moreover, political decision-makers are structurally bound to short-range perspectives by the electoral system itself; profits in politics are earned at the next election, while profits in enterprise are earned over the longer term.

The Structural Segregation of Accumulation and Legitimation Functions

While vulnerable and responsive to economic interests, urban governments resting on electoral support must also provide opportunities and incentives for popular political participation, particularly during periods of mounting discontent, but it must do this in such a way as to insulate the role of municipal government in the accumulation process from political challenge. Another major mechanism to promote participation while deflecting that participation from policies important for economic enterprises is the structural segregation of these potentially contradictory government functions. While such segregation is in no sense strict or complete,[14] it appears to be a common feature of the cities of advanced capitalist nations. The devices by which it is accomplished include locating potentially contradictory functions in different agencies; structuring these agencies so that access to economically important decisions is difficult while access to integrative ones is relatively easy; and locating those different functions at different levels of government. Each of these devices varies *between* cities and nations and changes *within* them historically, partly as a result of the shifting political strategies to deal with the popular discontent which results in moving potential targets "up" or "down" in the political system.

First, authority over policies that impinge upon the profitability of economic processes are often located in one agency, while authority over policies that are designed to absorb political discontents generated by economic processes are located in other agencies. For example, slum clearance for the profitable construction of luxury apartment complexes and office buildings is delegated to an urban renewal agency, while the construction of low-income housing is located in a public housing agency. This arrangement, found in France and the United States, tends to act as a barrier against the effective mobilization of displaced residents to demand adequate replacement housing. When political mobilization against clearance and displacements does occur, it cannot so easily be fused with mobilization for the provision of alternative low-cost housing, whether on the urban renewal site or elsewhere in the city. (Castells, 1976; Friedland, 1977). Another obvious example is the universal separation of agencies responsible for economic development, such as planning or zoning agencies, or industrial redevelopment authorities, from the agencies which are responsible for dealing with those made unemployed by economic development, such as welfare or unemployment or manpower training agencies. By such a separation, agencies which have some authority to determine the structure of employment opportunities are insulated from those agencies that deal with people who cannot find work because of lack of employment opportunities. Not accidentally, when unemployment becomes severe and the unemployed are roused to protest, they direct their discontents against the agencies that manage the unemployed, and not against the agencies that might have some leverage in altering the pattern of economic development and labor market demand.

Second, agencies that control the conditions of economic growth are structured in ways which render them relatively autonomous from popularly elected officials and relatively invisible to the urban population at large.[15] By contrast, agencies that deal with policies related to political legitimation are relatively vulnerable to elected officials, and relatively accessible to the general public.[16] Thus transportation and industrial development policies are often delegated to agencies such as port authorities in the United States whose officials are not elected, whose legislative mandates are not subject to short-term renewal, and whose funding is also protected from legislative review, often because the agency is granted the authority to float its own bonds. Freed in this way from partisan and popular political constraints, these agencies develop external constituencies among those economic interest groups that have a keen interest in public policies that influence the parameters of economic growth. The success of these agencies comes to be dependent upon such clientele relations, a dependency made more intense by the insulation of the agency from electoral or popular pressures. The ideology of technical planning and professionalism with which these agencies cloak themselves not only legitimates their insulation, but it also discourages any attempts at popular intervention, for it argues that what is being done is not political but technical, and so neither relevant nor comprehensible to the wider urban population.

By contrast, agencies which attract the political participation of groups who are excluded from the benefits of economic growth or who may even be its victims, are far less autonomous, their policies are far more visible, and their budgets are allocated from general revenues. The mandate for such agencies is continuously under legislative scrutiny and budgetary review, generating constant concern with the politics of bureaucratic survival. The agencies need constantly to mobilize allies from a diverse urban constituency to ensure renewal of their legislative mandate and funding. To cope with the problem of building political support, these agencies must always deal with conflicting demands for representation on their boards and for patronage through public employment and public services. During periods of economic dislocation, they are likely to be deluged with demands for substantive responses to a host of discontents arising out of larger economic processes. But these agencies do not have the authority or the resources to deal with discontents arising from economic processes. Moreover, such efforts would bring the agencies into conflict with other government agencies, and with the far more powerful economic interests served by those other agencies. Consequently, local agencies charged with maintaining popular political allegiances strive always to convert demands generated by broader economic and social change, which are unmanageable, into demands for symbolic representation and public patronage, which are relatively more manageable.

The observable tendency to respond to popular demands by establishing new programs and new agencies is consistent with this pattern. The new program or agency is a visible, if mainly symbolic, response, and its establishment diverts discontent away from agencies which might make more substantive responses. New programs and agencies also mean the proliferation and fragmentation of symbolic representation and public patronage. Diversified patronage not only fragments broader class alignments, but tends to create the potential for further divisions among the relatively few who are the chief recipients of patronage, and the many who are not. The funding of these agencies through general revenues is also divisive, for the very programs that absorb popular demands are also subject to challenge by the middle- and working-class taxpayers who pay for them.

The third mechanism to structurally segregate accumulation and legitimation functions is to locate them at different levels of government. Policies which affect the rate and direction of urban economic growth are more likely to be decided at a metropolitan-wide, regional or national level, while policies designed to encourage participation and absorb protest are decided locally. Revenues for such programs are, at least in part, likely to be raised locally. In the United States in the 1960s, for example, the anti-poverty program was designed to allow local policy formation, and to encourage participation by the central city poor. Meanwhile, policies providing agricultural subsidies, housing funds and military contracts (all of which had a large effect on urban poverty) were set nationally, without similar provisions for local "participation of residents of the areas to be served." Similarly, the financing of programs which benefit dominant economic interests and the middle class—such as highway construction or home-owner subsidies—tends to be arranged so that these programs are funded by less visible national tax revenues (or invisible tax exemptions). By contrast, programs which are oriented toward lower-class groups, such as medicaid and welfare, are both susceptible to local political decisions and funded in part by acutely visible local taxes.

In Britain, nationally organized commercial and industrial interests have been resistant to any granting of regulatory powers over economic activity to local governments. Scarrow has shown how such capitalist groups have used their institutionalized access at the national level, through national departments for example, to prevent local bills granting such regulatory powers from being passed in Parliament (Scarrow, 1971). Thus local government efforts to regulate economic growth are likely to be consistently thwarted in the national political arena.

The tendency to create supra-municipal jurisdictions to handle the financing and production of public capital investments critical to regional economic growth has occurred in many Western capitalist nations. In the United States, regional special districts with their own taxing and spending powers have rapidly emerged to handle public investments such as water, sewers, mass transit, and airports. Their tax and bond financing have been effectively segregrated from the regional revenue requirements for schools, parks, and social services of all kinds. The emergence of structures to rationalize regionally the allocation of public investment critical to capital accumulation has also been evident in Italy and France, although the scope and success of regional reform is likely to be dependent on patterns of partisan and bureaucratic linkage between existent local governments and the national administration (Tarrow, 1974).

The increasingly regional nature of capitalist economic and political organization is one stimulus for this development. However, the distinction between levels of government as if these levels reflected some enduring reality can be quite misleading, serving to conceal strategies of political domination by making them appear to have legal and technical content rather than political content. "Much so-called imposition by the state is actually policy developed by local groups and interests and implemented through the machinery of state government. Frequently local officials join with other local groups to seek legislation of this kind" (Jones, 1974, p. 4). What this indicates is that decisions to shift either or both policies and agencies from one level to another are themselves a strategy to gain relative political advantage. When dominant economic interests are challenged at lower levels of government, they move to other levels, or create new levels and new agencies beyond the reach of popular opposition.

In short, the formal structure of the state is not socially or politically neutral. To assure that urban governments are responsive to the requirements of accumulation, agencies charged with its management are institutionalized beyond popular or political control. As social needs arising from economic processes are translated into political demands, urban governments attempt to absorb and limit the scope and impact of political participation by channelling it to agencies of limited power and high politicization. This organization of political authority removes some issues from the political arena and makes other fundamental policies relatively invulnerable to popular political challenge. The political relations between social groups and classes are partially mediated through the formal organization of political authority. Thus the structure of urban government is not determined by the technical requirements of public policy optimal to the solution of urban problems. On the contrary, the organization of urban political authority reflects the power relationships among different social groups and their relative ability to institutionalize those programs and agencies upon which their interests are most dependent.

STRUCTURAL DETERMINANTS OF THE PATTERN OF POLITICAL REPRESENTATION

The character of political structures in urban political systems, as in other political systems, shapes political life, determining in large measure the articulation and alignment of groups within those structures, and the issues on which those groups focus.[17] Patterns of class alignment that one might otherwise expect to emerge in cities within capitalist societies are substantially fractured, and conflict diverted, by the political structures of the city.[18] On the one hand, these structures tend to encourage the multiplication and fragmentation of groups focused on relatively minor forms of group recognition, patronage, and service delivery. On the other hand, urban political structures tend to encourage the emergence and coherence of producer groups with larger stakes in the economic benefits yielded by city government activities. Under conditions of relative stability, municipal costs edge slowly upward as a consequence. Under conditions of change and conflict, costs escalate much more rapidly as the demands of producer interests rise, and popular political discontents are channelled into demands for increased recognition, patronage, and services. The structures which normally work to mute conflicts thus become subject to intense fiscal strains.

Even without the mediation of urban political structures, it is probably at the local level that non-class forms of political identification such as territory and ethnicity are most acutely felt. These multiple forms of identification tend of themselves to strain class alignments. But municipal political structures work to heighten non-class bases of identification by organizing formal representation, patronage, and public services on territorial and ethnic bases. The result is that interest groups based on territory and ethnicity predominate in municipal politics, fragmenting broader class interests and encouraging intra-class competition and animosities.

This multiplication of group interests and the promotion of group competition has the consequence of splintering the middle, working, and lower classes, and thus diverting them from demands that would threaten the role of municipal government in the accumulation process, even during periods when economic change stimulates popular discontent. Moreover, the very proliferation of groups and group antagonisms and the complementary proliferation of municipal agencies and programs helps to create an ideological image of the state as a neutral broker between multiple interests, of politics as merely a marketplace in which many buyers and sellers meet to their mutual advantage—in other words, the image of a pluralist democracy.

In general, producer interests operating within insulated agencies are free to remove vast tracts of land from the tax rolls, and at the same time to increase the public debt to private creditors as they continue to produce public works such as roads, bridges, and tunnels in deference to the producer interests to whom they are linked. Despite nominal use of competitive bidding, state contracted production is characterized by cost overruns, byzantine layers of lucrative subcontracting, payoffs and kickbacks, and unproductive expenses of all kinds.

In a similar fashion, producer interests develop around government programs which maximize effective demand,[19] leading to the subsidization of consumption of housing, transportation, and medical services in ways that are responsive to the producer pressure rather than to the overall requirements of either economic growth or popular demand. The use of government by producer groups in this way subverts any popular or consumer control of prices or products. For the urban economy, the results are often the uncontrolled inflation of costs and the anarchic production of services and goods. For urban government, the results are fiscal stress.

STRUCTURAL AND INCREMENTAL EXPANSION

Studies of Western capitalist nations have shown the incremental way in which city, state or provincial, and national expenditures grow (Fried, 1975; Wildavsky, 1964; Meltsner, 1971). Levels of previous expenditure for a given agency, program, or government unit have been found to be the strongest predictor of current expenditures, even controlling for economic and political characteristics. Such incremental budgetary processes are often argued to be due to the non-programmatic decision-making rules used by government officials in a politically and fiscally complicated world. Alternatively, they have been analyzed as deriving from the ability of dominant interests to insulate critical agencies from legislative control (see Alford and Friedland, 1975).

The significance of budgetary incrementalism for the purpose of our analysis of the structural arrangements which produce fiscal crisis is somewhat different. Budget allocations reflect responses to demands arising from the functions of accumulation and legitimation. Once entrenched in agencies and programs, these demands come to be self-perpetuating, protected in part by the development of bureaucratic stakes in the continuation of a particular agency or program.[20] As a consequence, municipal fiscal and legal resources cannot be reallocated to respond to new demands arising from economic processes or from popular political participation. Existing interest groups, often entrenched within the agencies, protect older budgetary commitments. Instead of killing off old programs which may be politically and economically obsolete, new public programs are added to the existing ones, particularly when external demands escalate. These additions contribute to the tendency toward fiscal crisis.

Structural arrangements aggravate this tendency. Because urban governments—as we have argued—are often bureaucratically fragmented into a maze of agencies and jurisdictions, many of which are highly independent of political control, bureaucratic aggrandizement is difficult to control. Once established, public agencies use the web of conflicting political demands and bureaucratic clients to assure their continuation and expansion, and even demonstrate a capacity to activate demands to justify their expansion. As a consequence, city budgets show a continuous tendency for incremental expansion, even in the absence of intense external demands.

The classic studies of budgeting procedures show in great detail how multiple agencies at multiple levels convert the politics of the budgetary process into a series of incremental bargains and negotiations over small increases, with seldom any challenge to the existence of any component budgeting unit, nor to the existence of an ongoing program. (See Wildavsky, 1964, and the various studies of the "Oakland Project.") The consequences are consistent and continuous pressures to increase agency budgets, always protecting historical commitments.

During periods of intense stress and rising demands, these bureaucratic tendencies do not vanish. Instead, the emergence of external pressures becomes the basis on which large new expenditures are added to old ones. Political conflicts do not challenge the fundamental patterns by which public resources are allocated, but rather take the form of demands for additional allocations and additional programs. As a result, public expenditures are rarely restructured, they are only increased, sometimes slowly and sometimes rapidly. As they increase, so do fiscal strains.

To summarize this part of the argument, the segregation of accumulation and legitimation functions in different kinds of agencies or different levels of government insulates the state's role in accumulation from political challenge and absorbs popular participation in accessible locations without substantial power. Yet this structural segregation means that the political authority that orchestrates the causes of social problems is insulated from that which manages their political consequences, and is thus without power to deliver a substantive response. Instead, agencies and programs tend to multiply and budgets expand to cover the flood of demands legitimated by each agency's legislative mandate. The bureaucratization of accumulation functions removes political controls on the growth of these agencies and programs and allows their profitable manipulation by those producer interest groups which have most at stake in their continued operation. Conversely, the channelling of participation of those who do not benefit from accumulation to politicized agencies renders such agencies vulnerable to patronage demands, wasteful stop–go patterns of program expansion, and costly maneuvering for political and bureaucratic allies in a highly unstable environment. Finally, incremental financing and budgeting prevents any fundamental restructuring of tax bases or expenditure priorities. Such patterns of expenditure and revenue growth are encouraged by the structural segregation of accumulation and legitimation functions and the related selective representation of group and class interests. Under conditions of rapid economic and political change, new programs are added rather than old ones replaced, adding to fiscal strains. The general result is that municipal activities at any given historical moment constitute an aggregation of functions, agencies and expenditures which may no longer be functional to the requirements of either accumulation or legitimation.

FISCAL CRISIS AS AN OCCASION AND
STRATEGY FOR COPING WITH FISCAL STRAINS

The post–World War II experience of major metropolitan centers in the West seems to us to reveal the effects of these structural arrangements. The postwar period saw the concentration and expansion of economic activity in many major cities, with accompanying investments in infrastructure and business-oriented services by municipalities. At the same time, the displacement of many people from agriculture, and the need for labor generated by expansion in the cities, led to the concentration in the cities of large new populations, usually distinguished by race or ethnicity from the older populations. The conflicts that erupted during this period of dislocation, however, were mainly conflicts between working and lower-class groups fractured by neighborhood, race, and ethnicity, and focused on competition over the provision of public services and, in some places, the traditional patronage of public employment. To cope with rising conflicts and rising demands, municipal services and patronage expanded.

In response to these different pressures, public expenditure for urban capital projects, social services, and public employment grew by leaps and bounds. By the late 1960s, municipal and regional governments began to suffer budget deficits, rising debt, and increasing dependence on state (or provincial) and national government fiscal aid. "In all of the Western democracies the costs of social programs have grown considerably in the post-war period. In the United States and Western Europe, government spending tended to rise faster than gross domestic product of the economies between 1961 and 1972, with social transfer payments rising even faster than general government spending" (Heidenheimer et al., 1975, p. 275).

Economic decline only exacerbated these fiscal strains, and the political tensions underlying them. In the late 1960s and 1970s, serious recessions in many countries exacerbated the discrepancy between urban revenues and expenditures. Revenues shrank, but popular political demands did not, and in fact were heightened by unemployment, reduced real wages, and inflation. As urban expenditure, taxation, and debt increased together, many cities were thrown into a politically intractable fiscal crisis. Municipal workers were increasingly organized and resisted cutbacks with paralyzing strikes. City residents tried to hold onto existing services, or even to press for improved services, confronting urban bureaucracies with rent strikes, fare reduction campaigns, and housing occupations. Major corporations resisted any threatened service reduction or tax increase that would cut into their profitability with threats of relocation to other cities, and even to other countries.

The dilemma of cities in capitalist societies is how to maintain a structure of expenditure and taxation that can stimulate stable economic growth, while at the same time maintaining the popular legitimacy of government institutions, even when the potential for political conflict becomes intense. The series of structural arrangements described above tend to convert political conflict between groups and classes into demands on the state which force state expansion. But this process also tends to create fiscal strains. Public expenditures increase faster than the state's ability to finance them from its own revenues. Thus fiscal strains are a recurrent feature of capitalist cities.

These fiscal strains result in increased pressures for higher taxes on business and industry, indirectly push up wage costs, and potentially constrain the expansion of public services and infrastructure upon which corporate profitability is dependent. Under these conditions, fiscal strains provide capitalist groups with an occasion and a strategy to increase their control over the city's budget.

The process by which capitalist groups politically manage fiscal strains seems to follow a natural historical sequence, if New York City may be taken as a prototype, although perhaps an extreme one. First, financial and other capitalist interests declare an emergency, publicly redefining fiscal strains as a "fiscal crisis." Second, the fiscal crisis is attributed to natural economic laws beyond the control of political parties, government units, or corporations and banks themselves. Capitalist arguments that urban governments must balance their budgets, that there simply is not enough money, are elaborated by explanations of the inevitable erosion of the economic base of the cities as a mobile capital responds to the "natural laws" of profit maximization.

Third, capitalist interests assert control. Bankers refuse to finance the urban debt. Industrialists and developers make their investments conditional upon expanded subsidies and services, and reduced taxes. Business-backed reform groups push for policy changes to increase public sector productivity and reduce waste and duplication.

Depending on the level of indebtedness, the locational dependency of investors, and the political power of the reform groups, the parameters of urban policy are reorganized. On the one hand, structural changes may be introduced which remove even formal policy and budgetary authority from electoral control, as when an Emergency Finance Control Board was created in 1975 in New York City with the authority to supersede the budgetary decisions of city officials. On the other hand, expenditures and revenues are selectively reorganized to favor business through reduced taxes, enlarged subsidies and a relaxation of public regulation in matters such as environmental pollution. Public employment and neighborhood services which are less necessary to private profitability are cut back. In New York City, for example, half of the Hispanics and two-fifths of the blacks in municipal employment have been fired (Piven and Cloward, 1977, p. 13), most of whom were located in public agencies created to absorb the political protest of the 1960s. Finally, policy proposals for more progressive revenues are suppressed. For example, in the Banker's Agreement of 1932, loans were extended to the city of New York on condition that proposals for taxes on stocks, savings banks, and life insurance companies would be dropped (Darnton, 1977, p. 226).

In conclusion, we believe that municipal expenditures tend to expand, fuelled by the dynamism of group and class conflict. Given the structural arrangements we have described, when popular discontent intensifies, expenditures escalate more rapidly than revenues, producing the various symptoms we have called fiscal strains. At these junctures, capital mobilizes within the framework of these urban structures to declare a fiscal crisis and subdue popular demands. Whether this strategy is viable in the long run seems doubtful, but this conclusion rests on a faith in the possibility of an emergence of political challenges which, at least in the United States, are not yet visible.

NOTES

The authors wish to thank Arnold Heidenheimer, Steven Katz, Ira Katznelson, Mark Kesselman, Theodore Marmor, James O'Connor, Claus Offe, Chris Pickvance, Richard Rose, John Walton, James D. Wright, and a number of students and faculty at the University of California at Santa Cruz, as well as the participants in the Urban Political Economy Conference held in April 1977, on that campus, for their extensive comments. None of our critics are responsible for any of our assertions, of course. We wish to express our thanks also to the Council for European Studies for its support of the Research Planning Group from which this paper developed.

1. For information on growing local government expenditure demands in the face of limited fiscal capacity in the United States, see U.S. Senate, Subcommittee on Housing and Urban Affairs (1973). We use the terms "stress" and "strain" interchangeably, and distinguish these tendencies from the strategies for managing them, which include defining them as a "crisis."

2. O'Connor uses a somewhat different language. He locates the fiscal crisis of the capitalist state in the ways in which public authority must increasingly absorb both the social and the private costs of capital accumulation. On the one hand, monopoly capitalism requires the state increasingly to socialize the costs of constant and variable capital. On the other hand, the tendency toward surplus capacity under monopoly capitalism produces enormous social costs which must also be absorbed by the state. The state's absorption of the social and private costs of accumulation, combined with the continued private appropriation of the social surplus, produces an inherent tendency toward fiscal crisis (O'Connor, 1973). It is of course this last condition, the private appropriation of the social surplus, which distinguishes the capitalist state from the state in other industrial and industrializing societies. These governments may also, as Daniel Bell asserts, face the twin problems of maintaining accumulation and legitimation, but they have greater authority to direct economic development, and are also able to appropriate the surpluses resulting from development, to cope with the problems of legitimacy (Bell, 1974, pp. 37–38).

3. Much of the time, perhaps most of the time, a stable and prosperous economy is also a precondition of the legitimacy of the state, for the breakdown of the accumulation process leads to loss of jobs, declining real income, and the series of dislocations which give rise to political discontent. We are not prepared, therefore, to argue the inherent and continuous contradiction between accumulation and legitimation functions, but argue only that these functions become antagonistic at specific historical junctures.

4. In the past, periods of intense labor—management conflict which have politicized larger urban populations have also made city governments the focus of conflicting demands. This tends not to occur in the contemporary United States, perhaps because of the enlarged role of unions in mediating such conflicts, but it is still important in other Western nations, Italy being one example.

5. Tax revenues, including the payroll taxes that help finance social security, have been rising everywhere as a percentage of Gross National Product. . . . Average annual tax revenue per capita for the period 1965–71 amounted to $1394 in Sweden, $1177 in the United States, $911 in France, $846 in Germany, $795 in the Netherlands and $708 in Britain (Heidenheimer et al., 1975, pp. 227–28).

6. Sammuel Huntington, commenting on O'Connor's thesis, argues that the fiscal crisis is not due to "capitalist economics" but "is in fact a product of democratic politics" which reflected the egalitarian reform movements of the 1960s. It should be clear from our discussion that we think Huntington is partly right; "democratic politics" were an important component of the urban fiscal crisis in the United States. We disagree, however, with Huntington's effort to sever the political demands of the egalitarian movements of the 1960s from the "capitalist economics" which gave rise to them.

7. Claus Offe has defined the capitalist state by this exclusion from profitable activity (1975, pp. 125–26). We think that the extent of control over the capitalist economy and its ability to participate in the production and distribution of a society's surplus should be treated as an historically variable characteristic of capitalist states. States vary, for example, in their ability to produce surplus directly through nationalization of industries or utilities, to capture private surpluses generated by public investment through betterment taxes, or to appropriate them directly through progressive taxation. The determination of this variation and its political and economic correlates remains largely unexplored.

8. There are of course other conditions which ordinarily ensure the subordination of the state to capital, not least its susceptibility to economic interest group pressure, and its overall dependence on relatively stable economic conditions as a precondition of political stability.

9. It is important to note that even in those systems where urban expenditures are financed from central public banking systems, subnational governments nonetheless remain responsible for the discretionary implementation of public capital construction. In the United Kingdom in 1967, local government accounted for 80% of total public capital investment; in France, 66% (Sbragia, 1976, p. 5).

10. In the United States, inter-city competition for private investments allows corporations access to public subsidies for investments that would have been made in any case. A recent study of municipal issuance of industrial aid bonds in the U.S. found that although corporations used alternative location to secure access to publicly subsidized debt financing, the majority of industrial projects, and seven-tenths of the dollar value, would have occurred in the same location without public subsidy (Apilado, 1971).

11. Max Weber pointed out this dilemma of the decentralized municipality: "Within compulsory associations, particularly political communities, all property utilization that is largely dependent on real estate is stationary, in contrast to personal property which is either monetary or easily exchangeable. If propertied families leave a community, those staying behind must pay more taxes; in a community dependent on a market economy, and particularly a labor market, the have-nots may find their economic opportunities so much reduced that they will abandon any reckless attempt at taxing the haves or will even deliberately favor them (Weber, 1963, p. 352).

12. We are indebted to Al Watkins for this point.

13. Offe argues that the capitalist state is not only restricted to unprofitable production, but that it lacks "decision rules" by which to organize the content, method, output and distribution of production. As a result, state activity is inefficient and ineffective, characterized by continuous political conflict, and continuous efforts at organizational reform (Offe, 1975).

14. We readily acknowledge the difficulties of empirically assessing the consequences of specific urban government activities on the urban economy or on the political integration of urban populations. The difficulty is compounded because some activities clearly bear both on the urban economy and on urban politics and, indeed, specific activities may have diverse and contradictory consequences. Some municipal activities, however, clearly relate directly to economic processes, while others directly influence the problems of managing political participation and integration. We present this model of structural segregation as a potentially illuminating way of explaining the allocation of municipal functions, and await the help of our colleagues in dealing with the difficulties of empirically specifying the consequence of diverse municipal government activities.

15. In Oakland, California, city officials "avoid the public in order to bring revenue into the system." By various tactics "indirect taxes and nominal charges are introduced into the tax structure which reduce the tax consciousness of the payer and result in low-yielding taxes and small, attentive tax publics. Public participation is also made difficult, so as to keep these tax publics small, fragmented, and quiet (Meltsner, 1971, p. 8). This is an example of how key public decisions critically affecting accumulation (the tax burden on large property owners) are bureaucratized, rather than politicized, through conscious political decision.

16. Peter Marcuse suggests that our argument that political integration func-

tions are relatively open and visible, while accumulation functions are insulated from popular intervention, has an analogue in the familiar dichotomy between legislative and administrative activities, the one being relatively visible and subject to intervention, while the other is relatively removed from public purview or interference.

17. Our conception of the structural segregation of state agencies and programs, and the consequences of segregation for the political fragmentation of class alignments, has a strong analogue in recent work by leftist economists on the structural arrangements underlying the segmentation and balkanization of the labor force. See, for example, Reich et al. (1973) and Edwards et al. (1975). We are indebted for this point to Ann Markusen.

18. Katznelson refers to the distinctive "serialization" of class in the United States: "What has been 'exceptional' about the American experience of class is that the split between work and community has been reproduced ideologically and institutionally in ways that have fragmented patterns of class in a qualitatively distinct way. Elsewhere in the West, the tendency to parcelization has been partially countered by competing 'global' institutions and meaning systems of class" (Katznelson, forthcoming).

19. Two structural tendencies have necessitated increasing state involvement and particularly urban state intervention in the organization of consumption. On the one hand, the monopolization of capitalist enterprise, combined with enormous increases in industrial and organizational productivity, have rendered the scope of domestic effective demand increasingly problematic for all Western capitalist nations. On the other hand, the increasing spatial and functional complexity involved in the reproduction of labor power through diverse social services and material goods also renders the content and distribution of consumption problematic (Castells, 1976).

20. John Mollenkopf makes the important point that the specific organizational arrangements of particular agencies promotes this effect. For his elaboration of this argument, and his exposition of the functions of specific organizational arrangements for muting conflict, see Mollenkopf (1977).

REFERENCES

Alcaly, E., and D. Mermelstein, eds., *The Fiscal Crisis of American Cities* (New York: Vintage, 1977).

Alford, R., *Health Care Politics* (Chicago: University of Chicago Press, 1975). a

———, "Ideological Filters and Bureaucratic Responses in Interpreting Research: Community Planning and Poverty," in N. J. Demerath III, O. Larsen, and K. F. Schuessler, eds., *Social Policy and Sociology,* New York: Academic Press, 1975). b

Alford, R., and R. Friedland, "Political Participation and Public Policy," *Annual Review of Sociology* 1, 1975, 429–79.

Andersen, G., R. Friedland, and E. O. Wright, "Modes of Class Struggle and the Capitalist State," *Kapitalistate* No. 4–5 (Summer 1976), 186–220.

Apilado, V., "Corporate-Government Interplay: The Era of Industrial Aid Finance," *Urban Affairs Quarterly* 7, 2, 1971, 219–41.

Baer, C., "On the Death of Cities," *The Public Interest* No. 45 (Fall 1976), 3–19.

Bell, D., "The Public Household," *The Public Interest* No. 37 (Fall 1974), 29–68.

Caro, R. A., *The Power Broker* (New York: Vintage, 1974).

Castells, M., "Urban Sociology and Urban Politics: From a Critique to New Trends of Research," in J. Walton and L. H. Masotti, eds., *The City in Comparative Perspective* (Beverly Hills: Sage Publications, 1976).

Castells, M., E. Cherki, F. Godard, and D. Mehl, *Sociologie des mouvements sociaux urbains, enquete sur la region parisienne,* vols. 1 and 2 (Paris: Ecole des Hautes Etudes en Sciences Sociales, Centre d'Etudes des Mouvements Sociaux, 1974).

Cloward, R. A., and F. Fox Piven, *The Politics of Turmoil: Essays on Poverty, Race and the Urban Crisis* (New York: Vintage, 1974).

Congressional Budget Office, United States Congress, *New York City's Fiscal Problem: Its Origin, Potential Repercussions, and Some Alternative Policy Responses* (Washington, D.C.: U.S. Government Printing Office, 1975).

Darnton, J., "Banks Rescued the City in a Similar Plight in '33," in Alcaly and Mermelstein, eds., 1977.

Edelman, M., *The Symbolic Uses of Politics* (Urbana, Ill.: University of Illinois Press, 1964).

Edwards, R., M. Reich, and D. Gordon, *Labor Market Segmentation* (Lexington, Mass.: D. C. Heath, 1975).

Epstein, J., "The Last Days of New York," *New York Review of Books* (February 1976).

Eyestone, R., *The Threads of Public Policy: A Study in Policy Leadership* (Indianapolis: The Bobbs-Merrill Co., 1971).

Fried, R. C., "Comparative Urban Performance," in F. I. Greenstein and N. W. Polsby, eds., *Handbook of Political Science,* vol. 6 (Reading, Mass.: Addison-Wesley, 1975).

Friedland, R., "Class Power and the Central City: The Contradictions of Urban Growth." Unpublished Ph.D. dissertation (Department of Sociology, University of Wisconsin, Madison, 1977).

Friedman, L., *Government and Slum Housing* (Chicago: Rand McNally, 1968).

Hartman, C., *Yerba Buena: Land Grab and Community Resistance in San Francisco* (San Francisco: Glide Publications, 1974).

Harvey, D., "The Political Economy of Urbanization in Advanced Capitalist Societies: The Case of the United States," *Urban Affairs Annual Review* (Beverly Hills: Sage Publications, 1975).

Heidenheimer, A. J., H. Heclo, and C. T. Adams, *Comparative Public Policy, the Politics of Social Change in Europe and America* (New York: St. Martin's Press, 1975).

Huntington, S. P., "The Democratic Distemper," *The Public Interest,* 41 (Fall 1975).

Jones, V., "Bay Area Regionalism." Quoted in F. W. Wirt, *Power in the City: Decision-Making in San Francisco* (Berkeley: University of California Press, 1974).

Katznelson, I., *City Trenches* (New York: Pantheon, forthcoming).

Lupsha, P., "New Federalism: Centralization and Local Control." Paper delivered at the Annual Meeting of the American Political Science Association, San Francisco, 1975.

Marmor, T. R., D. A. Wittman, and T. C. Heagy, "The Politics of Medical Inflation," *The Journal of Health Politics,* Policy and Law I, 1975, 69–84.

McConnell, G., *Private Power and American Democracy* (New York: Alfred A. Knopf, 1966).

Meltsner, A. J., *The Politics of City Revenue* (Berkeley: University of California Press, 1971).

Mollenkopf, J., "Untangling the Logics of Urban Service Bureaucracies: The Strange Case of the San Francisco Municipal Railway." Paper presented at the Conference on Urban Political Economy, American Sociological Association and International Sociological Association, Santa Cruz, California, 1977.

O'Connor, J., *The Fiscal Crisis of the State* (New York: St. Martin's Press, 1973).

Offe, C., "The Theory of the Capitalist State and the Problem of Policy Formation," in *Stress and Contradiction in Modern Capitalism: Public Policy and the Theory of the State.* Associate editor with Colin Crouch and Robert Alford. Principal editor, Leon N. Lindberg (Lexington, Mass.: Lexington Books, 1975).

Perry, D., and A. Watkins, "Contract Federalism and the Socioeconomic Realignment of Yankee and Cowboy Cities, Two Stages of Urban Decay." Paper presented at the Conference on Urban Political Economy, American Sociological Association and International Sociological Association, Santa Cruz, California, 1977.

Piven, F. Fox, and R. Cloward, "The Urban Crisis as an Arena for Class Mobilization," *Radical America* 11 (Jan–Feb 1977), 9–17.

———, *Poor People's Movements: Why They Succeed, How They Fail* (New York: Pantheon Books, 1977).

Pressman, J. L., and A. B. Wildavsky, *Implementation* (Berkeley: University of California Press, 1973).

Reich, M., D. Gordon, and R. Edwards, "The Theory of Labor Market Segmentation," *American Economic Review* LXIII, No. 2 (1973), 359–65.

Sbragia, A., "Public Housing and Private Profit: Some Inferences for Comparative Policy Studies from an Italian Case." Paper delivered at the Annual Meeting of the American Political Science Association, Chicago, 1976.

Scarrow, H. A., "Policy Pressures by British Local Government," *Comparative Politics* 4 (1971), 1–28.

Starr, R., "Making New York Smaller," *New York Times Magazine* (November 14, 1976).

Sternlieb, G., and J. W. Hughes, "New York: Future without a Future?" *Society* 13, 1976, 1–23.

Tarrow, S., "Local Constraints on Regional Reform: A Comparison of Italy and France," *Comparative Politics* 7, 1974, 1–36.

U.S. Senate, Subcommittee on Housing and Urban Affairs, "The Central City Problem and Urban Renewal Policy," 93rd Congress, 1st Session (Washington, D.C.: U.S. Government Printing Office, 1973).

Weber, M., *Economy and Society: An Outline of Interpretive Sociology,* vol. 1, Guenther Roth and Claus Wittich, eds. (New York: Bedminster Press, 1968).

Wildavsky, A., *The Politics of the Budgetary Process* (Boston: Little, Brown, 1964).

13

Fiscal Crisis, Austerity Politics, and Alternative Urban Policies

RICHARD CHILD HILL

So used and therefore so abused, the word "crisis" seems no longer to touch our emotions, move us to action, or even much attract our attention. Rising divorce rates herald a crisis in the family. Dwindling resources denote an energy crisis. Incompetent government leadership is called a crisis in diplomacy. The list goes on *ad nauseum*. Yet when properly used, crisis terminology provides an indispensable tool for social analysis. A crisis occurs when the principles governing the way a society is organized engender contradictions and conflicts, and when these contradictions and conflicts can be ameliorated only through basic changes in the rules themselves.

The fiscal "crisis" of cities poses this sort of issue. New York City, the nation's largest metropolis, virtually went bankrupt in 1975. Cleveland was forced to reorganize its finances in 1978, Detroit in 1981, and dozens of major cities continue to teeter on the brink of fiscal collapse. Falling revenues, municipal wage concessions, cutbacks in services are by now familiar enough to be considered normal. To call this a crisis seems to inflate the significance of routine events. Yet the fiscal contradictions and conflicts facing local governments in the United States do constitute a crisis. And my purpose in this essay is to explore the sources and implications of this urban fiscal crisis.

I have organized this essay into three parts. First, I shall review persistent, structural sources of the urban fiscal crisis. This requires explication of the relationship between capital accumulation, urbanization, and the structure of the state. Next, I turn to the politics of austerity bred by current attempts to manage fiscal contradictions. Here I suggest that austerity measures, meant to renew capital accumulation, may have just the opposite effect. Finally, I review alternative policy responses to the urban fiscal crisis and the imagery of the future city contained within each policy approach.

CAPITAL ACCUMULATION AND URBANIZATION

There is an intimate relationship between capital accumulation and urbanization in the United States. Capital accumulation requires investment in new means of production, production and distribution of commodities to sustain the labor force, a demand for the commodities produced, and additional capital formation through product innovation and market expansion. The capitalist city is a production site, a locale for the reproduction of the labor force, a market for the circulation of commodities and the realization of profit, and a center where these complex relationships are coordinated and controlled (Castells, p. 423). And urbanism is the geographical form taken by the spatial unfolding of the capital accumulation process.

A city manifests its particularity through the relationships it establishes with the broader political economy within which it is located. Capital continuously flows toward new profit-making opportunities. The prestige and vitality of a city is indexed by its capacity to attract investment. So, as David Harvey (1973, p. 250) has argued,

> the geographical pattern in the circulation of surplus can be conceived only as a moment in a process. In terms of that moment, particular cities attain positions with respect to the circulation of surplus which, at the next moment in the process, are changed. Urbanism, as a general phenomenon, should not be viewed as the history of particular cities, but as the history of the system of cities within, between, and around which the surplus circulates.

We can identify periods of urbanization in the United States which correspond to phases in the process of capital accumulation. Each period is characterized by a dominant type of city and a specific pattern of relationships among cities within the evolving urban system (Hill, 1977a; Gordon, essay 2 here). Urban patterns today correspond to the monopoly stage of capital accumulation—the concentration of capital in national and multinational corporate enterprises. Advances in transportation and communication allow corporations to centralize their control over capital, technology, and business organization, and to decentralize their production and commercial activities. Dominant metropolitan centers become the locus of corporate administration, product innovation, and service employment. The rural and urban periphery become more differentiated and stratified providing the agricultural and industrial products necessary for the maintenance and expansion of metropolitan centers (Berry, Hymer). This capitalist production process fosters uneven development within the urban system. The underdevelopment of regional hinterlands, the decline of industrial cities, the rise of new suburbs and metropolitan "growth centers" are all so many manifestations of shifting patterns taken by the process of capital accumulation.

CAPITAL ACCUMULATION, URBANIZATION, AND THE STATE

With the monopoly stage of capitalism, the state assumes an active and expanding role in the economy and society. Following James O'Connor (Chap. 1), we can divide the state budget into three categories corresponding to Marx's departments of production. *Social capital* outlays are state expenditures which facilitate private capital accumulation. There are two kinds of social capital: (1) *social investment* expenditures (social constant capital) are fixed capital outlays on means of production which increase the productivity of labor (e.g., transportation nodes, research and development facilities, utility projects, industrial parks); and (2) *social consumption* expenditures (social variable capital) are consumption fund outlays requisite to the reproduction of labor power (e.g., schools, commuter facilities, health services). *Social expenses* ("luxuries"), the third category of state expenditures, constitute neither fixed nor variable social capital. Rather social expenses are "a lubrication of the social mechanism to avoid an explosion" (Mandel, p. 338). That is, social expenses are projects and services which do not facilitate private capital accumulation but are necessary to maintain political stability. Social expenses are most visible in government expenditures on welfare, prisons, and the police.[1]

There is a direct connection between urbanization and growth in state investment, consumption, and expense outlays. Urban infrastructure, like roads, sewers, and water systems, is capital intensive and indivisible by nature; so are the specialized knowledge and technical skills possessed by the urban labor force. Neither can be funded nor monopolized by one or a few firms. Advanced capitalist countries have therefore socialized a large share of the costs of urban social investment projects (e.g., transportation, job training, R&D facilities, utilities, and urban renewal projects).

As urbanization progresses, subsistence production declines, the market penetrates sphere after sphere of family activity, and the costs of re-producing the urban labor force rise accordingly. So modern capitalist states increase social consumption spending on elementary and secondary schools, hospitals, recreation, and social insurance against economic insecurity. Finally, as monopoly sector productivity outstrips the demand for labor, the state faces increased demands for social expenses by the unemployed and working poor.

We can now see why the state expands in the era of monopoly capitalism. Social investments which increase the productivity of labor, and social consumption expenditures which lower the private reproduction costs of labor power, are indispensable to the growth of private industry. But the growth of concentrated corporate capital fosters unemployment and unutilized capacity requiring increased social expense outlays. In O'Connor's (p. 9) terms, "The greater the growth of social capital, the greater the growth of the monopoly sector. And the greater the growth of the monopoly sector, the greater the state's expenditures on the social expenses of production."

THE URBAN FISCAL CRISIS

As the capitalist state assumes broader responsibilities for maintaining economic growth and social stability, it also incorporates class contradictions intrinsic to capitalist development. The state socializes more capital costs and absorbs more expenses of production, but the social surplus continues to be privately appropriated. The result is a fiscal contradiction: expenditure demands increase more rapidly than revenue to finance them. Fiscal crisis—the gap between expenditure demands and available revenues—becomes the state budgetary expression of class conflict in a monopoly capitalist society.

The form taken by the fiscal crisis, and the intensity with which it is expressed, are influenced by the structure of the capitalist state. Three elements in particular help explain the *urban* fiscal crisis: (1) federalism, (2) the fragmentation of local government in metropolitan areas, and (3) the way city governments accumulate revenue and produce and distribute goods and services.

Federalism

In the United States expenditure levels, trends in outlays, the distribution of expenditures by function, and methods of obtaining revenue vary among federal, state, and local governments and among relatively auton-

omous units within levels of government. The largest share of the federal
budget goes to outlays on social expenses in the form of military expenditures, direct money payments to the indigent, the aged and the infirm,
and the provision of welfare services. The federal government retains a
virtual monopoly over the more "progressive" tax sources: individual and
corporate income taxes and wealth and inheritance taxes (Netzer, p. 80).

State and local governments foot a large share of the welfare bill
and have developed an extensive social control apparatus. But their budget
responsibilities are weighted toward social capital expenditures. Local
governments, for example, assume major responsibility for schools, hospitals, fire protection, sanitation, transportation facilities, and industrial
parks. State and local governments garner their revenues from the most
regressive taxes. Sales taxes are the major source of revenue for states.
Property and flat rate income taxes are the major local sources of revenue
for municipal governments (Netzer, p. 81).

Given the close connection between capital accumulation, urbanization, and the growth of state activity, heavy expenditure demands are
made on state and particularly local governments. But while the federal
government has relatively great tax-raising capabilities and limited responsibility for civilian expenditures, local governments have more cir-
cumscribed tax-raising capabilities to match their heavy expenditure demands. This fiscal "imbalance" between levels of government plays a role
in the urban fiscal crisis.

Fragmentation of Local Government

The U.S. Constitution divides governing responsibility among federal,
state, and local governments. But governing responsibility is also divided
among units within levels of government. Nowhere is this more striking than in the modern metropolis. Metropolitan landscapes are often
dotted with hundreds of municipalities, school districts, and other types
of single- and multipurpose units of local government. This fragmented
system of urban governance also plays a role in the urban fiscal crisis.

First, uneven economic development in a politically fragmented metropolis fosters uneven fiscal development among local governments. The
poor and unemployed tend to concentrate in older central cities and inner-
ring suburban municipalities while capital moves to the expanding suburban fringe and metropolitan centers in growing regions of the country.
The tax base is separated from social needs, and older cities are unable to
marshal sufficient revenue to meet rising expenditure demands (Advisory
Commission on Intergovernmental Relations; Muller).

Second, externalities—where the activity of one local government generates unpriced costs or benefits for other local governments—increase geometrically with the size and complexity of a metropolitan area. For example, central city investments in education redound to the benefit of other jurisdictions when the middle class and those with specialized skills migrate to the suburbs and other metropolitan areas. Central city expenditures on transportation, hospitals, and cultural facilities benefit the region as a whole but the local tax bill is often paid by central city residents alone. Aging central cities also confront added demands for social expenses as displaced people "spill-in" from declining rural areas and as part of their own local labor force is rendered "redundant" by technological change and the international expansion of capital. The burden of these expenditures also falls heavily upon central city property and labor but benefit the suburban fringe and the nation as a whole.

In sum, capital accumulation and urbanization require expanded social investment, social consumption, and social expense outlays by local governments. But the geographical movement of capital according to the criterion of profitability, within a state structure characterized by federalism and a fragmented system of local governments, means the divorce of tax base from social needs and expenditure requirements and a tendency toward fiscal crisis in older urban centers in the United States.

The Organization of Municipal Production

Capital accumulation requires supporting social capital expenditures. Local governments bear primary responsibility for these outlays. It follows that the direction taken by capital movement and the quality of urban life are related to the composition of local government expenditures (Berry, pp. 17–21). Aging central cities confront rising demands for social expense outlays which do not facilitate private accumulation. Yet they find it difficult to make the social capital expenditures required to attract new investment. This contradiction fosters fiscal crises and conflict among groups in the central city political arena. These struggles are shaped by the way central city governments are organized to produce goods and services. Three organizational dimensions are crucial: (1) relations of revenue accumulation, (2) relations of production of goods and services, and (3) relations of distribution of goods and services in the city.

Each element in the structure of central city production underlines a class issue and an axis of conflict in contemporary urban politics. Revenue accumulation refers to the class relations and class distribution of the means of financing city government expenditures (i.e., who pays for what is produced?). Goods and service production denote class relations

setting budget priorities and producing goods and services (i.e., who de-
termines what goods and services are produced and how they are produced?). Distribution points to the social relations between city bureaucracies and residents and the class allocation of city expenditures (i.e.,
who benefits from what is produced?). //

Revenue Accumulation

A city must accumulate revenue to produce goods and services. But the
city, a component of the capitalist state, is subject to three rules governing the relationship between government and the accumulation process in
a capitalist society. (1) Capital accumulation takes place in private enterprises. The state cannot appropriate a surplus to reinvest in its own
enterprises to produce a further surplus. However, (2) the state has the
authority, and the need, to create and sustain conditions of private accumulation. Therefore, (3) the state's ability to produce goods and services
depends upon the continuity of private accumulation. In the absence of
private capital accumulation, state revenues dry up and the power of the
state wanes (Offe).

Moreover, in the U.S. federalist system, rights of local self-government are granted by state governments. The subordinate relationship between city and state government constrains municipal revenue accumulation since state constitutions often limit the range of local tax sources
and the level of local tax rates (Friedman, p. 5). The fragmented, competitive structure of government within metropolitan areas also pressures
local jurisdictions to compete with their neighbors by granting further tax
concessions to attract private investment.

Unlike the federal government, states and cities are prohibited from
funding current expenditures through deficit financing. Municipal and
school district operating expenditures are financed through regressive
property, sales, and flat rate income taxes. The mounting tax burden experienced by a poorer central city population, and the seeming lack of
effectiveness and efficiency of city programs, moves local residents to revolt against further taxation.[2]

Central city capital outlays, in contrast to operating expenditures,
are often financed through borrowing. There is a legal ceiling to local
debt, but since debt limits are usually tied to the total assessed value of
property, they are open to political manipulation. State laws frequently
exempt social capital projects, like pollution control, job development,
and housing, water, and sewage facilities from constitutionally prescribed
limits. Under increasing fiscal pressure, and without a rigid definition of
capital expenditure ceilings, big city governments have transferred oper-

ating expenses into the capital budget. This fiscal sleight of hand merely shifts the fiscal crisis to interest charges paid out of operating expenses. As a city's credit rating drops, the interest rate on new bond issues increases, and the fiscal dilemma is exacerbated (Stern, p. 60; Friedman, pp. 29–30).

In sum, as central cities deteriorate, their bond ratings fall, interest charges as a percentage of current operating expenses rise, and it is increasingly expensive and difficult to borrow to meet social capital expenditure requirements.[3] Concurrently, the taxpayers' revolt presents barriers to increasing, or at times even maintaining, current opeating expenditures through tax increases. So, older cities cannot generate social capital outlays to upgrade their resident labor force, to attract private capital and tax base, or to meet the rising need for social expenses as the impoverished segment of the urban population grows.

Relations of Production

The rules governing the relationship between the state and private capital accumulation in a capitalist society give economic forces "external" to city government marked influence over the urban budget. But within these parameters, the internal structure of city decision-making also plays a role in the urban fiscal crisis. Two facets of central city production merit brief consideration: (1) the process setting budget priorities, and (2) the relations between city management and city workers. Each exerts pressure to expand central city expenditures.

City production of goods and services, in contrast to private capitalist enterprise, is not *directly* dictated by market profit criteria. Rather "budget-making is a political process conducted in the political arena for political advantage" (Friedman, p. 4). City politicians prize the construction of new social capital facilities (capital budget) more than annual expenditures to maintain existing facilities and services (operating budget). Legislators often have pragmatic, short-range interests; capital budgets are politically manipulable; new social capital projects are visible and yield immediate political pay-off. Local capital budgeting, most research reveals, is governed less by long-range planning than by pork-barrel, log-rolling, legislative politics. So there is a tendency to proliferate projects in wasteful and inefficient ways (McConnell).

The municipal operating budget, on the other hand, is shaped by "incrementalism" (Wildavsky). Decision-making is partial, short-range, and pragmatic. The politics of the operating budget reflect the concerns of city agencies and a few elected officials. Public participation is usually "too little, too late" and often is little more than a "democratic ritual."

City bureaus project future funding on the basis of existing appropria-
tions. Past decisions are seldom reexamined, alternatives tend to be neglected, and latent consequences ignored (Friedman, p. 19).

However, since most local government spending goes toward salaries and fringe benefits for the municipal labor force, well-organized city
employee unions have exerted influence over the municipal budgetary
process. During the sixties and early seventies, municipal employee groups
vigorously demanded improved working conditions and wage increases to
advance their level of living and protect against inflation; city collective
bargaining and negotiated wage agreements became the rule, and strikes
to achieve demands increased rapidly (Spero and Capozzola, Chap. 1;
Zack). But class conflict in the state sector has yet to be institutionalized.
Most states outlaw strikes by municipal employees. Binding arbitration
remains anathema to city management and union alike since it shifts responsibility for settlements outside the city political arena. City unions
have not played a regulating role in production relations because, in contrast to capital intensive private enterprises, labor-intensive city services
were not conducive to compensating productivity increases. So in the face
of declining sources of revenue, inflation, and resistance to local tax increases, the wage and benefit demands of municipal employees also fed
the urban fiscal crisis.

Relations of Distribution
The residential location of a social group, relative to the distribution of
city investments, carries with it more or fewer city services, better or
worse schools, more or less access to commercial activities and employment oportunities. With increasing urbanization, social investment, social
consumption, and social expenses mount rapidly. As the city government's share of the total production of goods and services rise, real income becomes more closely tied to the availability and quality of urban
services, and political conflict over the distribution of public goods and
services intensifies.

As city expenditures and contracts increased, who got the action became more important and more divisive as it engaged the class interests
of more people. Expansion in central city government helped absorb part
of the population left unemployed by the dynamics of monopoly capital
accumulation. Municipal and school district government accounted for a
growing share of the dwindling number of *new* employment opportunities
in older central cities. Conflict over access to municipal employment rose
in like measure (Hill, 1977b).

Urban race-relations is a salient example. Post–World War II black
migration to central cities shifted the locus of black liberation struggles

from regional and national civil rights strategies to political mobilization in the arena of central city government. Blacks bore the brunt of unemployment in many inner cities and black urbanization went hand in hand with deterioration in the level and quality of city facilities and services in inner city neighborhoods. Black political struggle in central cities surged forward along three fronts: (1) demands to improve the level and quality of city facilities and services in black neighborhoods; (2) attempts to capture a larger share of city government employment; and (3) a drive to obtain power in City Hall—the necessary prerequisite to changing budget priorities, upgrading the quality of city services in black communities, and providing black access to municipal employment.

Black political demands met stiff resistance from central city service bureaucracies, municipal unions, and professional associations. Urban reform had shifted the political center of gravity—from ward-level patronage to centralized, bureaucratic governance. Municipal bureaucracies were the new urban machines. Monolithic, entrenched in law and tradition, and supported by the local press, middle-class civic groups, and an organized clientele, the new machine opposed black acquisition of power by traditional means.

But whites left central cities in growing numbers while the black percentage grew. Blacks demanded that the allocation of jobs by local government reflect the racial composition of the resident population and asserted that the needs of the black community included dimensions of the black experience that they alone could understand and deal with. This political strategy also denounced "absentee" bureau heads, city professionals, and unionized employees as outsiders, as suburbanites exploiting the central city. In a racially changing central city, territorial claims based upon the right to self-rule proved to be a political stance which improved black access to municipal employment and political power.[4]

Taken together, central city relations of revenue accumulation, production, and distribution divide segments of the urban working class into mutually antagonistic social relationships. Taxpayers rebel against lack of efficiency and effectiveness in municipal expenditures, the service claims of the poor, and the wage and benefit demands of municipal unions. Neighborhood groups attack budget priorities, the lack of accountability of service bureaucracies and municipal unions, and the unequal distribution of city services and employment opportunities. Municipal unions castigate "community witch-hunters" and "tight-fisted" taxpayers alike. Central city politics, an observer once noted, is akin to a bucket of crabs (Baker, p. 27).

In summary, there seems to be a general contradiction between capital accumulation and urbanization in the United States. Capital accumulation requires urbanization, but urbanization requires investment, consumption, and expense outlays which market exchange cannot handle. This increases the role of the state in the economy. But the structure of state production, particularly at the level of local government, is only partially complementary to private accumulation. Federalism, the fragmented system of local governments, and the organization of city government production prevent decaying central cities from accommodating to the requisites of monopoly capital accumulation or to the social needs of central city residents. Fiscal contradictions, conflicts, and crises are the result.

AUSTERITY POLITICS[5]

From the end of World War II to the mid 1970s, growth in state and local government spending far outpaced expansion in the economy as a whole. That trend ended abruptly with the 1974–75 recession—the worst economic slump since the Great Depression. Urban fiscal contradictions could no longer be contained, several of the nation's largest cities hovered on the precipice of fiscal collapse, and a new era of fiscal austerity was born. Set by the example of New York City, urban fiscal retrenchment has meant: city workers giving up millions in wage concessions; city residents paying millions more into increased city taxes and users fees even as services are sharply curtailed; and city governments restructuring their debt and issuing new bonds to pay off accumulated deficits. As economic crisis pinpointed declining U.S. power in the international economy, the politics of fiscal austerity merged with a broader debate over alternative ways to reindustrialize and revitalize the U.S. economy.

With the election of Ronald Reagan to the presidency in 1980, fiscal austerity became national policy. Reagan "supply-siders" argue that shrinking the role of the state in the economy will release capital for private investment and promote a new era of economic expansion. Vast tax and spending cuts, meant to do just that, have been passed. More are on the way. Reagan's "new federalists" also argue that many federal responsibilities should be turned over to state and local governments. To back up that political philosophy, the Reagan administration consolidated 57 federal programs into nine separate block grants to states and localities.

Supply-side economics and the new federalism will surely increase the severity of the urban fiscal crisis. Ironically, these policies may also undermine the very economic expansion they are meant to facilitate. Why? Because social investment projects and social consumption services are a prerequisite to private capital accumulation. And today's national policy is undercutting the ability of local governments to provide urban infrastructure and human services at a time when further public expenditures are desperately needed.

The nation's social investment capital is in a visible state of decay. Recent estimates suggest that 8,000 of the interstate highway system's 42,500 miles must be rebuilt. Two out of five of the nation's bridges must be replaced or repaired, at an estimated cost of $41 billion. $31 billion must be invested in sewer systems and waste-water treatment plants over the next five years to meet pollution control standards. Cities must spend $110 billion over the next two decades to maintain their water systems. And, for lack of revenue, up to one-quarter of the nation's 300 metropolitan transit systems may cease operation by 1985.

The social investment needs of older cities are particularly acute. New York City, for example, must spend $40 billion to repair and rebuild its 6,000 miles of streets, 6,200 miles of sewers, 775 bridges, and 1.5 billion gallons-per-day water system. And Chicago must raise $3.3 billion over the next five years to rehabilitate roads, bridges, sewers, and mass transit. Pollution, congestion, and water shortages also threaten to dry up economic growth in sunbelt boomtowns. Dallas, for example, must raise $700 million for water and sewage treatment facilities and more than $109 million to repair deteriorating streets during the next decade. All told, maintenance of existing infrastructure alone will cost $660 billion over the next 15 years. This is equivalent to total state and local government new investment during the last three decades. _infrastructure_.

. At a time of growing need for public investment, massive reductions in federal aid to state and local governments, a reduced state and local tax base, record-breaking interest rates, and new tax incentives which reduce the attractiveness of state and local bonds further undermine the fiscal capacity of state and local governments. Reagan's first-year budget cuts reduced state and local aid by 25 percent. A substantial part of that reduction will come out of local spending for urban infrastructure. But cities will be forced to compensate most for federal cuts in the area of social services. More than half of the total budget reductions for fiscal 1982 struck income security and health programs (e.g., food stamps, child nutrition, medicaid, Aid to Families with Dependent Children, and trade adjustment assistance) and programs for education, training, and employment (e.g., the Comprehensive Employment and Training Act and public service employment).

Piven and Cloward are right: the Reagan administration is promoting a new class war. Tax cuts are designed to benefit the wealthy at the expense of the less affluent. Expenditure cuts are aimed at income maintenance programs that protect the disadvantaged and social services that benefit the working population. Economic insecurity is meant to breed greater discipline in labor market, factory, and office, and thereby boost the profit rate. Yet Reagan's policy, for all of its transparent class character, misconstrues the role of the state in an advanced capitalist economy. As a more enlightened business publication has noted (*Business Week*, 1981),

> the true test of Reaganomics will come at the state and local level. The President is shifting more of the burden of government away from Washington at a time when the local infrastructure is decaying, when the ability of states and cities to borrow is withering, and when state and local revenues are shrinking. The problems are so severe as to constitute a crisis for state and local governments. (p. 136)

Reagan advisers argue that these cuts will have little consequence for the economy because reduction in state and local government will free resources for the private sector. Reining in government will promote a resurgence in capital investment and business activity which will more than offset the cuts in state spending. But industry cannot long expand without adequate water and sewage systems; without well-maintained roads, bridges, and mass transit systems; without job training, vocational education, and health care.[6] That is, social investment and social consumption expenditures are requisite to sustained economic growth. And social expenses demarcate the boundaries of social stability in a capitalist society.

Reagan's imposed austerity policy sets cities fiscally adrift. And the new federalism assigns them a role they do not have the fiscal resources to fill. It is a politically explosive situation.

TRAJECTORIES OF URBAN CHANGE

The fiscal outlook for many U.S. cities is bleak. Older, industrial cities are in particularly dire straits. These cities may give birth to new economic and political forms for organizing social life. The extent to which transformations in the structure of urban life correspond to the needs of the majority of urban residents will depend upon how the interconnections between the urban fiscal crisis and austerity politics unfold. Current trends and policy debates suggest three possible trajectories of urban change. Cities embody each tendency in varying degrees. Each trajectory, when worked through to its logical conclusion, constitutes a scenario—a relatively distinct image of the future of troubled central cities. Each scenario can also be viewed as an outcome of political strife among antagonistic groups attempting to shape the future of urban life in the United States.)

The Pariah City

In the wake of the 1960s urban rebellions, a number of urban scholars anticipated a pariah-like future for aging industrial cities. The Pariah City is a form of geographical and political apartheid—a "reservation" for the economically disenfranchised labor force in a monopoly capitalist society (Long). The central city was once a location for the concentration of cheap labor. Welfare payments and other social expenses now kept the central city labor force far from cheap. In a global capitalist system, the central city's traditional jobs were being absorbed by labor repressive, low-wage regimes in the Third World. New urban immigrants, if fortunate enough to "make it," soon moved to the suburbs which now had reached a level of population and purchasing power sufficient to provide amenities which only the central city was once capable of sustaining. Left behind were the "poor, the deviant, the unwanted and those who make a business or career of managing them for the rest of society" (Sternlieb, p. 16).

Revenue sharing was a social expense incurred by the outside society to maintain the Pariah City. Part went for the subsistence of the natives, part to the keepers, and the rest to those who managed to make a profit from the reservation. Welfare, housing, food stamps, and medical payments constituted indirect subsidies to local businesses. The unemployed, underemployed, and working poor became "conduits" for the transfer of state revenues to inner city slumlords, merchants, loansharks, and service professionals who transmitted the surplus outside of the city (Hamilton, pp. 40–45).

Professional "keeping" associations made containment a business with little more concern for those confined than is common among security guards in a prison. Social expense outlays sustained a growing municipal bureaucracy feeding on the plight and misery of the poor but yielding few productive resources to the oppressed. Rather, these increasingly expensive programs were placebos, forms of symbolic action, which "provide psychic satisfaction to the patrons of the poor, convince outsiders, especially the media, that something is being done, and indicate to the urban poor that someone up there cares" (Sternlieb, p. 18).

The Pariah City portended dismal prospects for the black liberation struggle. Black control of the Pariah City was a "hollow prize," little more than political possession of an economically sterile environment. Capital outflow and deteriorating tax base made central city leaders de-

pendent on state and federal funds, and white-dominated state and national legislative bodies were indifferent to the problems of the Pariah
City. Co-opted, locked into visible public positions, but without resources
to substantially alter the condition of their constituents' lives, black urban
leaders "dangle on white men's strings while receiving little more than
crumbs" (Friesema, p. 77). The cumulative effect was to convince potential voters and political leaders that the game was not worth the toll in
personal dignity. Despair and apathy defined the political culture of the
Pariah City. An urban "futurist" put the finishing touches on this line of
prognostication when, in an essay entitled "On the Death of Cities," he
concluded that the appropriate metaphor for the industrial city was a
"cemetery" (Baer).

Such, then, seemed to be the trajectory of change in many decaying
cities in the United States. Findings from a recent survey of the fiscal condition of 48 large cities by the Joint Economic Committee of the U.S.
Congress suggest this trend continues apace. Most cities, to balance their
budgets and accommodate cuts in federal and state aid, have reduced expenditures on all services, increased tax rates and user fees, and post-
poned capital projects. But cities with high unemployment and declining
populations are forced to impose the harshest austerity measures. The
cities most in need of assistance are losing the largest share of federal
funds. Federal tax reductions are being partially offset by local tax increases. But since local taxes are more regressive, lower income urban
residents are carrying the burden of this tax shift. The Joint Economic
Committee concluded its investigation with the following observation
(pp. xiii–ix),

> The outlook for cities is bleak. In the declining cities where capital de-
> ferrals are accompanied by reductions in service levels and large tax in-
> creases, it appears that crises cannot long be avoided. . . . This will not
> only leave these cities in a deepening state of distress, but will render these
> cities home for the most dependent segments of society—the underedu-
> cated, the unemployed, the aged, and the minorities. . . . A city which is
> in the process of raising taxes and cutting services and which is resting on
> a decaying infrastructure provides no inducement to business expansion or
> in-migration. . . . As the city service levels and physical plant continue to
> deteriorate in conjunction with increased costs to residents and businesses,
> those that can, will heed the President's advice and "vote with their feet."

But the Pariah City is a house of cards whose imagery stems from a
number of shaky assumptions. A city is not an isolated reservation in
Arizona or New Mexico. It is the core of a complex, interdependent
metropolitan system. Even as they stagnate, central cities remain important control centers for major economic and political institutions, the

mass media, and transportation networks. The urban fiscal crisis threatens the holdings of urban financial institutions and undermines the capacity for renewed economic expansion. And the possibility of violent rebellion by impoverished and desperate inner city residents, convinced they are inheriting the wind, threatens the system at its foundations. Can the metropolitan apple long flourish while its core rots?

The Corporatist City

James O'Connor (pp. 51–55) has outlined a "corporatist" response to the fiscal crisis of the state. In O'Connor's view, a social industrial complex, modeled on the military industrial complex, might alleviate the fiscal crisis by increasing productivity throughout the economy. The social industrial complex increases productivity partly by improving government efficiency, but principally by employing the state budget to raise productivity and profits in the private sector. State contracts with the private sector to produce goods and services now handled by government would transform social expenses into social capital. This would ameliorate the material impoverishment of unemployed and underemployed workers by incorporating them into "a new stratum of indirectly productive workers: technologists, administrators, paraprofessionals, factory and office workers, and others who plan, implement and control . . . new programs in education, health, housing, science and other spheres" (O'Connor, p. 116). In sum, the social industrial complex is a planned "feedback mechanism" which transforms the surplus labor force generated by monopoly capital accumulation into labor productive of further monopoly capital accumulation.

The Corporatist City is an integral unit of the social industrial complex. It combines state, metropolitan, municipal, and special district forms of organization into an urban political system governed according to principles of corporate planning. This requires fundamental alteration in the relations of revenue accumulation, production, and distribution of goods and services in the metropolis. The inadequate handling of spillovers and inequities in service and tax levels of government are alleviated by shifting the fiscal burden and overall coordination and control of service production to higher levels of government. The property tax is replaced by flat-rate income, sales, and value-added taxes levied by metropolitan and state governments. Research projects and conferences develop and refine techniques (e.g., PPBS, operations research, cost accounting) to turn the budget into an instrument to improve efficiency and evaluate the relationship between social capital outlays and private accumulation.

The development of centralized administrative control, budgetary planning, and technocratic procedures provide the organizational means to adjust city budgetary priorities in favor of monopoly capital accumulation. State revenues flow into subsidies for new corporate "solutions" to problems of transportation, labor force development, pollution control, health care, crime prevention, and administration of prisons. Social tensions in the inner city are reduced by creating jobs in the new social capital projects. Minorities are integrated into a hierarchically ordered class structure. The price of social integration is political impotence—a condition minorities share with their majority counterparts in office, factory, and neighborhood.

Variations on the corporatist model range across the political spectrum. The American Enterprise Institute, for example, has been commissioned by the White House to launch a major study of private sector solutions to social problems and how these efforts might be replicated throughout the nation. A new manifesto on "how to shrink government by privatizing the public sector" has just appeared (Savas). And the public-private partnership idea is now being promoted by such diverse groups as the National Alliance of Business, the Committee for Economic Development, the American Council of Life Insurance's Clearinghouse on Corporate Responsibility, and John W. Gardner's Independent Sector (*Business Week,* 1981, p. 181).

But the most ambitious plan to date has been forwarded by Felix Rohatyn, senior partner in the New York investment firm of Lazard Freres and Company. Rohatyn proposes an alternative urban-industrial policy committed to reconstructing urban infrastructure and reorganizing basic industries (e.g., auto, steel, glass, rubber) with the objectives of improving the competitive position of U.S. firms in world markets, evening out the burdens and benefits of economic development across and within U.S. cities and regions, and alleviating the urban fiscal crisis. The catalyst in the Rohatyn strategy is the proposed creation of a national development bank designed to mobilize and coordinate the large sums of equity capital required to reorganize basic industries and reconstruct urban infrastructure. This development bank is also viewed as a key instrument for the creation and enforcement of a "new social contract" between government, business, and labor in the United States. Through a bargained tradeoff, equity capital to firms and job security to workers are to be exchanged for union wage concessions, work rule changes to increase productivity, matching financial commitments by banks and union pension funds, and tax support and reduction in service costs by state and local governments.

The Corporatist City may hold the potential for reversing tendencies toward disaccumulation and urban rebellion generated by the urban fiscal crisis. However, divisions within the capitalist class, the power of organized labor and professional associations, the symbiotic relationship between local businesses and city hall, and the structure of the state, including federalism and a fragmented system of local government, indicate barriers to the realization of the Corporatist City.

The transfer of fiscal responsibility and managerial initiative to state and metropolitan governments assaults the autonomy and privileged status of suburban fiefdoms. But the fragmented system of local government is entrenched in law and tradition, and powerful suburban-rural coalitions dominate the legislatures of most state governments. So far the history of comprehensive metropolitan reform is one of failure (Bollens and Schmandt, Chap. 11). The Corporatist City also implies steeply rising taxes for organized workers and suburban professional groups. Urban scientific management also means the end of pork-barrel, log-rolling local politics, and rationalization of city production and delivery systems at the expense of worker discretion and perogative. So whether the urban fiscal crisis will be ameliorated by Corporatist urban forms depends upon whether new political coalitions can be forged in such a manner as to overcome the resistance of workers, the professions, competitive capital, and the suburbs.

The Socialist City

Perfect model

It seems whimsical to talk of a Socialist City in an era marked by fiscal austerity and right-wing resurgence. Yet, current trends notwithstanding, today's debate over U.S. fiscal and industrial policy foreshadows the necessity for future large-scale government intervention in response to global and regional competition, uneven urban development, renewal of basic industrial and urban infrastructure, and city revitalization. Corporatist state capitalism suggests one alternative trajectory. Democratic socialism foreshadows another.

The Socialist City forms the core of a socialist society. In the short run the development of the Socialist City involves more democratic politics and the creation of a viable local economy. The problem for the emerging Socialist City is to devise democratic alternatives to the market mechanism which would allow for the transfer of productive power and the distribution of surplus to areas where the unfulfilled needs of urban residents are so starkly apparent. In the long run, it means the redefinition of social needs and the concept of surplus itself (Harvey, p. 235).

Revenue accumulation in the Socialist City is governed by the principle of community ownership of the community's wealth. When a city owns and develops itself, the surplus produced goes to the residents. If part of the wealth created by economic activity can be channeled directly to the city treasury, the city is able to expand public services and facilities. Kirshner and Morey, for example, have suggested ways a city can move toward socialist relations of revenue accumulation through "nonreformist reforms" in the parameters governing the capitalist state. Municipal ownership of selected businesses and the generation of a city surplus through user charges on selected social capital investments is one path. Through eminent domain, tax foreclosure, or outright purchase, the city can acquire property in areas surrounding its social capital investments, lease it out to private business, and capture the increment in value. Pension and accrual funds provide potential capital for investment in community-owned ventures. Public assistance recipients can be encouraged to pool their money and, with the aid of low-interest city loans, develop housing, food, and credit cooperatives. Jobs in the community cooperatives are created and the money stays in the community.

In the Socialist City the relations of production and distribution are governed by the principle of social production to meet social needs. The long-term interests of the city and the short-term interests of its residents coincide. Community ownership of the community's wealth, and social production to meet social needs, imply massive investment in public sector activities and employment to revitalize the city and improve the quality of urban life. The emerging Socialist City implies a major redistribution of wealth. But the mature Socialist City implies more. It implies stability in the material standard of living coupled with improvements in the way in which people relate to one another and their environment through more earth-preserving and life-sustaining forms of work and play.

In the Socialist City the market is subordinated to a decentralized planning process. City-wide hearings provide continuous community representation. Neighborhoods have independent sources of information, staff, and other resources so they can play a more autonomous part in the decision-making process. With maturation, technology is demystified, economies of scale are debated, and science and technology are put in the service of human needs, aspirations, and imagination. In part this means development of "soft" technologies whereby people in neighborhoods can help feed, heat, and transport themselves in a way that "reduces stress on the environment, is low in capital demands, frugal in its use of resources and decentralizing in its social impact" (Morris and Hess). In part it means the development of broader and more ambitious plans for democratic socialist reindustrialization.

The outlines of just such a redevelopment strategy have emerged in work done by the National Center for Economic Alternatives and like-minded groups grappling with the issues of capital flight, uneven regional development, and workers and community dislocation in the U.S. (Alperovitz and Faux). Like Rohatyn's corporatist plan, this strategy argues the merits of focusing upon basic industries, increasing government authority in the economy, developing new structures to pool investment capital, and linking industrial policy to efforts at urban revitalization. But the two strategies part company over the methods for achieving these objectives.

A democratic socialist strategy focuses less upon the reorganization of basic industries than upon the planned public conversion of idle and underutilized infrastructure, plant, and equipment to the production of alternative goods for which there is a clear social need and a potential economic demand. The calculus governing what is to be produced encompasses social benefits beyond private profits—indirect benefits derived from employment retention, including lower unemployment insurance, welfare, health, and crime control costs which are born today by the public sector rather than by the private investor. Here the role of government in the economy encompasses the current range of public incentive tools and the proposed national development bank but also extends to the creation of joint public and private or fully public enterprises capable of producing a reinvestible surplus. And the meaning of bargained development planning is extended to include workplace governance, employee ownership plans, and combined business, worker, neighborhood, and city representation at the enterprise and redevelopment planning levels.[7]

The creation of the Socialist City faces obvious barriers. Capitalist parameters govern the state and tend to limit redistribution and city production of goods and services to the point where they seriously threaten the production and circulation of private profit. Mutually antagonistic relations among city workers, community groups, and private sector workers (in their role as taxpayers) confound the mobilization of the urban labor force into a political coalition capable of transforming the character of city and society. Clearly a scenario of the Socialist City which remains unconnected to concrete political struggles pressuring urban administrations in a socialist direction, and which fails to confront the central problem of how public control over production and distribution of surplus in the private sector is to be politically achieved, represents little more than a pipedream.

Yet there is a socialist undercurrent in local and state politics in the United States. Over the past two decades a plethora of grass-roots direct action, electoral, and alternative institution groups emerged from the civil rights, anti-war, women's, welfare rights, consumer, and ecology movements (Perlman; Herbers). These movements catapulted representatives into political office who in turn have placed public ownership and control over some forms of capital on legislative agendas in many cities and states across the country.

Annual national conferences on Alternative State and Local Public Policies, sponsored by the Institute for Policy Studies, bring together mayors, judges, state legislators, city council members, state and city department heads, and school board members from state and local governments throughout the United States. Workshops range from land-use planning and comprehensive tax reform to job creation and housing co-operatives, and revolve around an overarching theme: public control over capital. Conferences have produced sourcebooks of policy proposals, legal initiatives, and legislative enactments related to public ownership of banks, insurance companies, lotteries, liquor stores, and electric companies, and new mechanisms to enhance citizen participation and government accountability. The Institute for Policy Studies runs a national legislative clearing house and coordinates a network for the communication of shared experiences among state and local political activists around the country.

It means little to talk about constructing socialism on an urban island amidst a capitalist sea. Yet any theory of socialist transition in late capitalist societies must afford a central role to the dynamics of urban political movements. Political efforts to construct and implement socialist urban institutions are primitive, yet dynamic and evolving local foundations for the construction of a socialist society. Nonreformist reforms can bend capitalist parameters, but success requires a popular socialist movement. Local politics must be linked to vertically integrated organizations influential in state capitols and in Washington. This is crucial due to the commanding role played by state and federal governments in the allocation of resources and programs. Without vertical political integration, political and economic development of the central city will be constrained.

Alternative state and local policies are unlikely to be effective unless they unite rather than divide key segments of the working population in urban areas. The absence of a united labor constituency leaves left-oriented, elected and appointed officials vulnerable to conservative attack by a corporatist urban reform movement riding the crest of shifting electoral mood. Nonetheless, there are reasons to believe current divisions among private sector workers, the municipal labor force, and activist community groups may eventually be overcome. Unions and associations of municipal employees occupy a strategic importance in central city politics. As fiscal resources decline, and as city workers are threatened with loss of jobs and are forced to make wage concessions, pressures mount for a coalition between municipal unions and neighborhood activists around a program to upgrade the quality of urban services through expanding and decentralizing municipal employment. In almost every declining central city, blacks and other minorities are a large share of the municipal labor force and the deprived population. Blacks have assumed political leadership positions in many central cities. Issues of economic impoverishment and race and sex oppression may also help cement a coalition between city workers and community groups (O'Connor, pp. 241–44).

Municipal workers are dependent on the city budget to meet their material needs. But their demands encounter hostility from a highly taxed central city working class. Union demands for improved wages and working conditions will at some point have to be tied to changes in methods of revenue accumulation and overall city budget priorities. To the extent that city workers demand that their material needs and conditions of work be met more by reallocating available resources than by increasing taxes, and to the extent that they challenge the priorities of corporatist reforms, present divisions between private and state workers and neighborhood organizations will narrow. Demands for public service jobs to meet community needs, supported by changes in budget priorities and the regressive tax structure, may yet prove a means for uniting the fragmented urban working class.[8]

CONCLUSION

All three paths of change—Pariah, Corporatist, and Democratic Socialist—are currents in contemporary urban politics. Deeply distressed Northern cities suggest the Pariah scenario, but the dominant tendency is toward corporatist urban institutional arrangements (Hill, 1977b). There is a democratic socialist alternative to corporate capitalist urban reform. But to be effective, democratic socialist policy alternatives must meet the concrete needs and interests of various segments of a divided working population. To do so, alternative policies must clarify the class character of current government arrangements and evoke a vision of a better social order. For until "a vision of a better social order can be made concrete and related to present possibilities, people will struggle for what they can get within the existing system" (Kirshner and Morey, p. 19).

NOTES

1. As O'Connor, Chap. 1) is careful to point out, a policy expenditure can rarely be allocated to one budget category. Rather, "nearly every state expenditure is part social investment, part social consumption, and part social expense." Transportation facilities, for example, are means of production

when used by industry, but social variable capital when used by individual households. State-financed health care represents social consumption when consumed by the productive work force but is a "luxury" when consumed by retired workers. Measuring the class composition of the state budget is thus a difficult and complex task. Nonetheless, O'Connor's categories are conceptually clear, and a rough approximation of the distribution of expenditures among the three categories of the state budget seems possible (Gough).

2. Proposition 13 in California and Proposition 2½ in Massachusetts are the most visible, but similar movements to limit taxation and government spending have taken place in 17 other states (*Business Week*, 1981, p. 136).

3. According to *Business Week* (1981, p. 154), "All in all, the combination punch of high interest rates and blocked borrowing will mean more financial pressure on states and cities at a time when they can least afford it because of sharp federal cutbacks in aid. Debt service as a percentage of total expenditures will rise for those who can borrow, local governments' credit ratings will erode, and they will be forced to resort more and more to short-term financing, which will make long-term planning for upwards of $700 billion in capital needs in the 1980s all but impossible."

4. The number of black, elected officials rose from 103 in 1964 to 3,500 in 1975; nearly half were municipal officials.

5. Unless otherwise noted, data presented in this section are drawn from *Business Week*, 1981.

6. For example, "U.S. Steel Corporation is losing $1.2 million per year in employee time and wasted fuel rerouting trucks around the Thompson Run Bridge in Dusquesne, Pa., which is posted for weight restrictions because it is in such disrepair. Companies wanting to locate in certain parts of downtown Boston must bear the additional cost of a sewage holding tank to avoid overloading the system in peak hours. And companies in Manhattan lose $166 million a year for each additional five-minute delay on the subways and buses" (*Business Week,* 1981, p. 151).

7. For an innovative plan embodying these themes see Luria and Russell, 1981.

8. For example, a potentially powerful coalition among mayors, the American Federation of State, County & Municipal Employees (AFSCME) and the American Federation of Teachers (AFT) has formed to fight the new federalism. This coalition's alternative to Reaganomics calls for spending $24 billion in fiscal 1983 on programs to improve urban infrastructure, training and employment, housing, railroads, maternity and child care plans, and promote economic development (*Business Week,* 1982, p. 36).

REFERENCES

Advisory Commission on Intergovernmental Relations, *City Financial Emergencies: The Intergovernmental Dimension* (Washington, D.C.: U.S. Government Printing Office, 1973).

Alperovitz, Gar, and Jeff Faux, "Beyond Bailouts: Notes for Next Time," *Working Papers for a New Society* (Nov/Dec 1980).

Baer, William C., "On the Death of Cities," *The Public Interest* (Fall 1976).

Baker, Ross, "The Ghetto Writ Large: The Future of the American City," *Social Policy* (January/February 1974).

Berry, Brian J. L., *Growth Centers in the American Urban System,* vol. 1 (Cambridge, Mass.: Ballinger Publishing Company, 1973).

Bollens, John C., and Henry J. Schmandt, *The Metropolis* (New York: Harper & Row, 1970).

Business Week, "State and Local Government in Trouble," October 26, 1981.

———, "Reagan's Plan Forges a Coalition of Rivals," February 22, 1982.

Castells, Manuel, "Vers une Theorie Sociologique de la Planification Urbaine," *Sociologie du Travail* (1969).

Friedman, Lewis, "City Budgets," *Municipal Performance Report* (August 1974).

Friesema, H. Paul, "Black Control of Central Cities: The Hollow Prize," *Journal of the American Institute of Planners* 35 (March 1969).

Gough, Ian, "State Expenditure in Advanced Capitalism," *New Left Review* (July–August 1975).

Hamilton, Charles, "Urban Economics, Conduit-Colonialism and Public Policy," *Black World* (October 1972).

Harvey, David, *Social Justice and the City* (Baltimore: Johns Hopkins University Press, 1973).

Herbers, John, "Citizen Activism Gaining in Nation," *New York Times* (May 15, 1982).

Hill, Richard Child, "Capital Accumulation and Urbanization in the United States," *Comparative Urban Research* (1977).a

———, "State Capitalism and the Urban Fiscal Crisis in the United States," *International Journal of Urban and Regional Research* (1977).b

Hymer, Stephen, "The Multinational Corporation and the Law of Uneven Development," in J. W. Bhagvati, *Economics and the World Order* (New York: World Law Fund, 1971).

Institute for Policy Studies, *"What Do I Do Now?: A Reader on Public Policy* (Washington, D.C.: Institute for Policy Studies, 1975).

Joint Economic Committee, Congress of the United States, *Emergency Interim Survey: Fiscal Condition of 48 Large Cities* (Washington, D.C.: U.S. Government Printing Office, January 14, 1982).

Kirshner, Edward M., and James Morey, "Controlling a City's Wealth," *Working Papers for a New Society* (Spring 1973).

Long, Norton, "The City as Reservation," *The Public Interest* (Fall 1971).

Luria, Dan, and Jack Russell, *Rational Reindustrialization: An Economic Development Agenda for Detroit* (Detroit, Mich.: Widgetripper Press, 1981).

Mandel, Ernest, *Marxist Economic Theory* (New York: Monthly Review Press, 1970).

McConnell, Grant, *Private Power and American Democracy* (New York: Knopf, 1967).

Morris, David, and Karl Hess, *Neighborhood Power: The New Localism* (Boston: Beacon Press, 1975).

Muller, Thomas, *Growing and Declining Urban Areas: A Fiscal Comparison* (Washington, D.C.: The Urban Institute, 1975).

Netzer, Dick, *Economics and Urban Problems* (New York: Basic Books, 1970).

O'Connor, James, *The Fiscal Crisis of the State* (New York: St. Martin's Press, 1973).

Offe, Claus, "The Theory of the Capitalist State and the Problem of Policy Formation" (Paper presented at the Eighth World Congress of Sociology, Toronto Canada, 1974).

Piven, Frances Fox, and Richard Cloward, *The New Class War* (New York: Pantheon, 1982).

Perlman, Janice, "Grassrooting the System," *Social Policy* (Sept.–Oct. 1976).

Reischauer, Robert, and Robert Hartman, *Reforming School Finance* (Washington, D.C.: Brookings Institution, 1973).

Rohatyn, Felix, "The Coming Emergency and What Can Be Done About It," *New York Review of Books* (December 4, 1980).

————, "The Older America: Can it Survive?" *New York Review of Books* (January 22, 1981).

Savas, E. S., *Privatizing the Public Sector* (Chatham, N.J.: Chatham House Publishers, Inc., 1982).

Shearer, Derek, "Dreams and Schemes: A Catalogue of Proposals," *Working Papers for a New Society* (Fall 1975).

Spero, Sterling, and John M. Capozzola, *The Urban Community and its Unionized Bureaucracies* (New York: Dunellen Publishing Co., 1973).

Stern, Michael, "Fiscal Experts See the City in Severe Financial Crisis," *New York Times* (October 27, 1974).

Sternlieb, George, "The City as Sandbox," *The Public Interest* (Fall 1971).

Wildavsky, Aaron, *The Politics of the Budgetary Process* (Boston: Little, Brown, 1973).

Zack, Arnold M., "Meeting the Rising Cost of Public Sector Settlements," *Monthly Labor Review* (May 1973).

14

The
New York City
Fiscal Crisis

WILLIAM K. TABB

The New York City fiscal crisis which began in the mid-1970s is conventionally attributed to greedy bankers, corrupt politicians, selfish municipal unions, and malingering welfare recipients. Such explanations of social causation are essentially misleading. They personalize and, in so doing, seriously obscure the larger social processes at work. At the same time apportioning blame correctly helps focus policy options when the larger economic and national urban context is taken as given.

A careful look at the data shows New York City's municipal unions and its welfare population are not the "cause" of the city's problems. Compared with those in other large cities in the United States, their costs are not out of line. These costs appear sizable only against the background of severe overall economic downturn and a long-term loss of employment that is found not only in New York City but also in much of the Northeast, Mid-Atlantic, and industrial Midwest. The movement of capital, and thus of jobs, lies at the heart of the crisis of most older industrial cities. The attempt to transform New York City into the world corporate capital has imposed a higher cost structure on the city. Overextension of borrowing by shortsighted and opportunistic politicians was the immediate trigger to the crisis, but the extent of city borrowing itself cannot be explained away without full consideration of this restructuring process.

This continuing crisis was caused by decisions based on private profit calculations and the failure of society through the political process to place social needs ahead of the imperatives of the market. The present trend is not inevitable but results from forces that can be subjected to conscious democratic control.

Incorrect explanations are the rationale for centralization of decision-making and the seizure of power by the city's financial community, which has been instrumental in causing the crisis and has been administering its own solution. The "solution," however, is iatrogenic, the very cure creates the disease. When this is understood, far different cures are called for, and indeed the dismissal of the discredited "doctors" is demanded.

Beyond the individual actors lies a second level of cause-blame categories: social forces—for example, migration of capital, jobs, people, the way technological change in production and transportation impact on where and how economic activity take place, and of course the political and institutional contexts that mediate such shifts in the mode of production.

In contextualizing the New York City fiscal crisis in these terms, we are able to distinguish the key actors—individuals, interest groups, strata within the working class and the capitalist classes; and at the second level of analysis—social forces within our economic and political system.

The traditional "explanations" are dealt with first. Considering them in some detail is important because they are the rationales for present urban policies. Almost all analysts are now willing to admit that New York City's fiscal problem is rooted in the loss of jobs and the failure to generate sufficient new ones to employ the city's work force and support its municipal services.[1] The tasks are to explain the erosion of the city's economic base and to discuss the issue of whether New York is unique, and if not, as I shall argue, then why has the city's crisis been so dramatic?

FISCAL IRRESPONSIBILITY

To date the New York City fiscal crisis from the default of the Urban Development Corporation (UDC) in early 1975, as most analysts would do, is to define the crisis in terms of the specter of default. The temporary failure of the UDC, an agency of the state of New York, focused attention on the fiscal situation of other agencies and jurisdictions in the state. A review of New York City's debt structure led to a decision by the banks to stop purchasing New York City obligations and to sell many of the bonds they held.

With the problem defined as the insecurity of New York City's financial capacity, the solution to the crisis was to create new agencies which would creditably raise funds by offering satisfactory security to lenders. In the same manner, the state of New York attempted to prevent default

by the city, which would mean the city would be unable to pay wage, welfare, and other obligations. Such an event could destroy for years to come
the City's ability to borrow, with obvious implications for the state. Most
elected officials in New York believed default had to be prevented at almost any cost. The Municipal Assistance Corporation (MAC) was consequently created in mid-1975, empowered by the state legislature to offer
investors guarantees on repayment with secured tax revenues earmarked
exclusively for the bonds MAC issued.

MAC soon proved inadequate. The next step was to create another
governmental agency with more clout. In the Financial Emergency Act
and the Emergency Moratorium Act, the former creating the Emergency
Financial Control Board (EFCB), the latter mandating a stretch-out for
repayment of existing debt, the state of New York acted to provide fiscal
security for the city and financial guarantees to investors. The adoption
of a financial plan subject to EFCB approval, review, audit, and EFCB
control over the disbursement of city funds was seen as guaranteeing
sound budgeting practices for the city that had chosen to be fiscally irresponsible. The EMCB, a tough watchdog agency with full powers to demand model behavior, would see to it that strict accounting principles
were followed.

The powers of the EFCB amounted to control of the governance of
New York City.[2] This was thought to be a good thing since the board
could force city officials to impose the painful austerity which elected
representatives would find unpopular and so difficult to carry out. Democracy was thus protected from itself by a healthy dose of authoritarian control. Stated in these terms, the city fiscal crisis was created, in terms used
in wider context by Samuel Hunnington, from "an excess of democracy."
This lesson (that politicians wishing to be popular will appropriate funds
beyond responsible program levels unless discipline can be imposed) is
the one Ronald Reagan drew from the history of twenty years of federal
deficits. By the early eighties the national government was dismantling key
elements of welfare state policy that had been in place for half a century.
The New York City fiscal crisis and how its causes and solution were
popularly understood initially played a part in gaining acceptance for the
Reagan initiatives. In the mid-seventies, however, those favoring austerity
in domestic social policy areas asserted that New York, unique among
American cities, had spent more on wages for its municipal workers and
welfare programs for its poor than other local government. It had prac-
ticed socialism in one city and had painfully learned the cost of good intentions, that the streets were not paved with gold. To judge this unique-
ness requires a closer examination of the history of New York's fall.[3]

RETELLING THE STORY

In the late 1960s Dick Netzer, who later was to join the Municipal Assistance Corporation board, wrote of the city's fiscal problem: "The City on its own has a very limited ability to solve the problem. The City government must devise a program which will maximize the probability that the fiscal problem will in fact be solved from without, by higher levels of government" (p. 653). New York, like almost all older industrial cities, was suffering from no growth. Its aging physical plant housed a growing lower-income population. Job loss was a serious problem, and tax revenues lagged behind rising expenditure levels. Urban financial experts had come to the decision that "there are few, if any, untapped revenue sources of any quantitative consequence." Since taxes on New Yorkers were already "higher than elsewhere in the nation by wide margins," and since there were "few business activities indeed that would not substantially reduce their total tax liabilities by leaving New York City" (Netzer, pp. 673–74), increasing taxes seemed to make little sense. New York's higher personal tax levels also created incentives to individuals to migrate to suburbia. Unable to raise taxes further while refused more aid by the federal and state governments, city officials turned to chicanery.

In the spring of 1974, Mayor Abraham Beame presented the usual kind of city budget—one that mislabeled nearly three-quarters of a billion dollars in expenditures so that they could be construed as part of the capital budget. (The cost of constructing schools and bridges may be included in the capital budget and amortized bond issues; pencils, wages and other day-to-day expenses should go in the operating budget, paid out of current tax revenue.) Beame created a Stability Reserve Corporation to facilitate borrowing a half billion dollars to be repaid over the years. In an intricate juggling of books, he arranged the estimates of anticipated revenues, dates of tax collections, and expenditures so as to "balance the city's budget." In the previous year, the last Lindsay budget had done much the same. In it, $564 million of current expenditures had been placed into the capital budget (double the amount for the previous year). By postponing payment on previous debts, still new obligations could be and were contracted. The city budget was widely considered by those with even a casual acquaintance with such matters as nigh unto fraud.

Answering the charge before a Senate Committee that New York's fiscal crisis was "caused" by the irresponsible borrowing of irresponsible politicians, Mayor Beame excused his own actions by saying:

> I have long acknowledged that the City was resorting to undesirable budgeting practices to meet its responsibilities to the public—practices which have already been known to the underwriters. But, those sophisti-

cated in city finances recognized that the borrowing and the gimmickry were the product of common consent of all concerned—by all political leaders—and by all levels of government, and with the full knowledge of the financial community, in recognition of the very special and enormous burdens which the City of New York must bear.

When I assumed office in January 1974, I publicly recommended programs to eliminate it. Yet, financial institutions which had provided the City with credit when they knew of this large gap have become reluctant to loan money in the very face of reforms and economies already underway. (U.S. Senate, p. 5)

The Mayor's statement is, I submit, essentially correct. The question then becomes: Why was such a course taken? And *did* everyone "cooperate"? The City's legal overborrowing required the state's approval. The person who extended this permission through his hold on the legislature was the New York State Governor Nelson Rockefeller. Under his aegis, the state itself went heavily into debt. To exceed constitutional borrowing limits, Mr. Rockefeller asked the help of a friend, a Wall Street lawyer and bond expert, later to become the law-and-order Attorney General indicted in the Watergate burglaries, John Mitchell. He invented the "moral-obligation bond," which allowed New York State to borrow beyond constitutional limits (and to avoid the possibility of rejection in a public referendum). The legality of these bonds—certainly their financial soundness—has been questioned by many, including the then Secretary of the Treasury William Simon, who, in refusing help to New York, said its own irresponsible borrowing was to blame. But when Simon was the ace bond salesperson for Salomon Brothers, he enthusiastically sold many of these very questionable debt instruments. These "innocents" very clearly knew what they were doing.

In the six-month period between October 1974 and March 1975, the city's large banks bailed out of the New York bond market, selling $2.3 billion in city securities. Then, realizing that their loans in the past had overextended New York's obligations, they rushed to pull out fast, before others saw how serious the situation was becoming. In so doing, they pulled the rug out from under the city, which was attempting to roll over $3 billion of its short-term debt. As one report recounts (Newfield and DuBrul, p. 11), "This sudden avalanche of New York City bonds and notes set off a panic among municipal investors. As a result, the City was barred from capital markets—perhaps for decades. New York City didn't jump; it was pushed."

The New York bankers sold heavily, dumping city obligations, and then claimed, after they themselves had saturated the market by unloading their portfolios, that the city could no longer borrow and that first

MAC and then EFCB needed to be created to run the city. Once the market for New York City's securities collapsed and interest rates rose to record levels, the banks returned to the market. This led many observers to blame the banks for the city's painful suffering, saying they caused the panic and then took control of the city to ensure they would profit from the solution of the crisis.

The bankers had chosen which loans they preferred to call in. They did not choose the least viable. To the bankers, it made sense to keep rolling over the billions upon billions in real estate loans. New York City's six largest banks held $3.6 billion in face-value loans backed by bankrupt condominiums, hotel developments, and unsold second-home and retirement villages. This $3.6 billion was far less secure in a real sense than the $1.7 billion these banks held in city securities. The city was an amateur in shoddy budgeting and gimmickry compared with the Real Estate Investment Trust entrepreneurs who pyramided loans and leveraged their accounts by four dollars for every dollar they may have had. Cases abound such as the one in which, in a declining market, an $8.5 million hotel is magically (and for a mere $50,000 fee) revalued at $26 million.

As President Ford was giving his "Drop Dead" speech (from the *Daily News* headline of October 30, 1975: "FORD TO CITY: DROP DEAD"), Chase Manhattan Mortgage and Realty Trust was negotiating with its forty-one creditor banks to reduce the interest on its more than three-quarter billion dollar debt—from 9.75 percent to 2 percent. But the banks did not scale down their loans to the city; indeed, they raised interest rates. By 1977, 20 percent of New York's budget went to interest payments—the largest and fastest-growing item. Bank self-interest imposed a suden chilling austerity on the city instead of the longer, gradual readjustment banks extended to other borrowers.

The key point is that the interests of the banks and those of most of the city's residents and workers were in sharp conflict. Indeed, the banks turned crisis to profitable advantage. Since the bankers have some influence on making the rules and the ways they are enforced, "suffering" has not been spread evenly. The key bankers' meetings to decide whether to extend the city credit were held in bank offices at 23 Wall Street, a building on which real estate taxes were reduced that year by a quarter of a million dollars. The Stock Exchange building's taxes were reduced by a similar amount (on top of other reductions the two previous years). When Dun and Bradstreet pondered the rating to be given the "irresponsible" city, they themselves pled poverty and obtained a $200,000 reduction in the property-tax assessment for their building at 99 Church Street.

Nearby stood the tax-exempt World Trade Center, which the Port Authority could build by dubbing it a "port facility." If the Trade Center were regarded as private, the city would have received about $50 million in property taxes in the mid-1970s. Instead, taxpayers were (1) paying interest to the banks for the money lent to build the structure, (2) paying its operating deficit, (3) paying higher taxes to the state, which are turned over to the World Trade Center for the high-cost office facilities, and (4) forcing the tax reductions granted to other office buildings with vacant space due to offices moving to the World Trade Center. The details of how David Rockefeller as head of the Lower Manhattan Association prevailed upon his brother, the then Governor Nelson Rockefeller, to appropriate the taxpayer's money in the four ways mentioned above would only be one small chapter in the story of how banks both cause fiscal problems and profit from their "resolution." The Trade Center example is not untypical of how the large banks and real estate interests use city government.

In periods of financial stress (there have been twenty such business cycles in the United States since the Civil War), restructuring is carried out by the largest banking houses and corporations at the expense of smaller firms and of workers, who have less bargaining power at the trough of the cycle. In the cities, this takes the form of an unwillingness of business to reinvest and the intensification of their search for new low-wage areas at home and abroad upon which to base the next period of growth. In the twentieth century, these cycles create a surplus work force in the older centers, and deprive the cities of the tax revenues needed to meet the cost of maintaining this swollen reserve army of now-redundant workers—workers who will be absorbed only at the peak of the cycle.

In the history of New York City, there have been many similar cycles. In an expanding economy, expenditures rise to meet the needs of citizens for services as well as the needs of politicians for patronage jobs, contractor's contributions, and votes at election time. Special-interest groups swarm, each trying to get as much of the sweet pork barrel as possible. In an economy prone to business cycles, optimistic projections of growth give way (after overexpansion in the upturn) to talk of the need for austerity and responsible government (Boss Tweed was elected to throw the rascals out). If the crisis is a severe one, a coalition of "good-government" activists backed by the banks, large real estate interests, and major downtown retailers may take a very direct role in guiding local politics. In the two most recent disaster periods—the Great Depression and the current period (the worst economic debacle since the 1930s)—bankers have directly assumed management of the city over the opposition of elected officials.

The extent of the economic upswing of the 1960s is a rare occurrence in U.S. history. The most recent parallel to it is the 1920s. In both of these decades of sustained expansion, New York City experienced a major boom in office construction. Each ended with a glutted market. In both instances, the city optimistically projected growth rates in a period of affluence, then became overextended and went into receivership. The 1935 Bankers Agreement abdicating power to the financiers was a less disguised transfer of power than the creation of the Emergency Financial Control Board.[4]

Unless the current New York City fiscal situation is seen in the historical context of cyclical crisis and structural transformation, the role of the bankers can be given too volunteerist a cast. While the names and faces change, the process is part of the normal working of our political economy. It is a systemic fault and that makes it difficult to really resolve crises brought about either by the normal business cycles or by the long waves of urban restructuring described by David Gordon earlier in this book. We need to combine an understanding of these larger economic forces with a keener awareness that solutions proposed are almost always class based.

The city's fiscal crisis has been about defaulting on the service needs of citizens to bail out the banks. The strategy has been accepted because it was accompanied by a shifting of blame to those who suffered most from the fiscal crisis, the municipal workers and the service recipients, especially the poor. The "solution" served those who profited most, the bankers, developers, and gentrifiers. Our first step in correcting widely held misconceptions of causation is to begin with the erroneous nature of this conventional scapegoating.

BLAMING THE VICTIM

The conventional explanations for the New York City fiscal crisis assert that excessive municipal wages and exorbitant welfare payments caused the increased tax squeeze; that the proper solution was to "bite the bullet" by reducing these expenditures. But does the hard data really proclaim the guilt of city workers and welfare recipients? The answer depends, of course, on how comparisons are made.

Arguing against assisting New York City, then Treasury Secretary William Simon said: "New York spends in excess of three times more per capita than any [other] city with a population over 1,000,000." He proffered a comparison that turns out to be exceedingly misleading: "Looking at the payroll, Census Bureau data shows that New York employs some 49 employees per 1,000 residents. The payrolls of most other major cities range from 30 to 35 employees per 1,000 inhabitants." The fault lies in Simon's comparing apples and oranges.

The U.S. Congressional Budget Office, a high-caliber non-partisan agency, made a serious effort to calculate comparative costs. It found that New York City has not spent far more. Many of the services that in New York are provided by the city government are in other cities provided by state, county, school-board, special-district, and other non-municipal jurisdictions. A truly comparable estimate must be based only on standard city functions: elementary and secondary education, roads, police, fire, sanitation, parks, and general and financial administration. In 1974, New York's actual per capita expenditure for all city functions was $1,224 a year, as compared with the highs of $858 for Boston and $806 for Baltimore, and with the lows of $248 for Los Angeles and $267 for Chicago. But when we compare standard city functions only, the figure for New York City is less than that for many large older cities (New York, $435; Boston, $441; Baltimore, $470; San Francisco, $448), and only slightly higher than that for Los Angeles ($408). From this view it is clear that New York's per capita expenditures were not out of line (p. 146).

When the same standard-functions adjustment is made for comparability with other older cities, we find that Philadelphia, Newark, and Baltimore each has more employees per capita. The Scott Commission study found that expenditures by the New York City government for "common municipal functions" during the pre-crisis period (1965–72), measured by both per capita level and growth rate, appear relatively "normal" (pp. III–ii).

Labor costs, a focus of growing concern in all cities, also do not appear "abnormal" in New York City as compared with these other cities. Both the rates of city government employees per city resident and the average level of wages appear well within the range experienced by most large cities (p. 37).

In another careful study of the data, Professor Charles Brecher concluded:

> Once allowance is made for the variations in functions, New York's rate of increase in expenditure is typical of large cities. Among the 10 largest cities, New York ranked seventh in rate of increase in per capita expenditures for functions common to all cities, and for those cities with responsibilities similar to New York's, there was little variation in rate of expenditure growth. (p. 3)

Between 1965 and 1972, 31 percent of the city's increased labor cost was due to increased work force, 46 percent to increased prices, and 23 percent represented higher real wages for city employees. Interestingly, with respect to increases in retirement costs, 33 percent was due to more workers covered, 50 percent to price increases, 4 percent to increases in contribution rates, and only 12 percent to real-wage increase. While city expenditures in this period had increased by over 150 percent, labor costs rose by about 90 percent and retirement costs even less. These were the years of the alleged "giveaways" (see Scott Commission).

The data on common municipal functions shows that between 1966 and 1973 average salaries fell in New York relative to other large cities. Percentage increase for New York over this period was ninth lowest out of the ten largest cities. After adjusting for cost of living, New York's workers ranked sixth out of the ten in 1973. New York was also not the most generous in pension benefits; fringe benefits are more difficult to compare, but it is doubtful that they made up for relative lower standing in basic pay. After 1975 New York City's workers' wages have increased at half the rate of inflation.

Similarly, while New York City's welfare levels are said to be "generous," in real terms they are lower than those of Chicago, Detroit, Philadelphia, and even Milwaukee. In February 1975, average monthly public-assistance payments per person in the city were $94 (hardly a munificent sum). The 973,000 persons receiving such payments constituted 12.6 percent of the population. New York City was far from having the highest incidence of welfare recipients. In Baltimore the proportion of the population on welfare was 16.8 percent, in St. Louis 16.4 percent, Boston 17.0 percent, Washington, D.C., 14.9 percent.

Of New York City's city and state welfare expenditures, two thirds are Medicaid payments to doctors, pharmacists, nursing homes, and hospitals—not cash payments to the poor. A proper investigation of where the welfare dollar goes, of who benefits from "welfare abuse," of who the "chiselers" are, would not focus on the poor. Almost 10 percent of the city's population receive Medicaid benefits, at an average cost per recipient of $2,000 per year. The city, with its disproportionate share of the metropolitan area's aged poor, pays one fourth of these staggering costs. Indeed, the fastest-growing cost in city government is not wages or welfare; it is the costs of Medicaid. Medicaid costs had risen by 25 percent each year between 1971 and 1976.

Furthermore most errors are not caused by client malfeasance. More recipients are harassed off welfare or have their cases closed by fiat than cheat the government. This is evidenced by the findings that half the appeals brought by recipients against city agency actions are accepted by the state, and that in another 30 percent of the cases appealed, the city concedes prior to decision. Clearly, thousands of recipients do not contest unfair decisions. Many do not know they can appeal, and others believe that they cannot "fight City Hall." In the early 1980s the New York solution to alleged fraud, waste, and abuse in the welfare system had been adopted by the Reagan Administration which cut billions of dollars from income transfer programs.

If, as we have demonstrated, New York City's wages and welfare were not seriously out of line with other large cities as critics charged, what accounted for the city's brush with insolvency? The most important real causes fall into two categories. The first is the erosion of the city's economic base. The loss of jobs and tax revenues was central. Second, the consequence of overextension of public debt and the dramatic 1974–75 business-cycle downturn left the city more vulnerable than other cities, also suffering a loss of jobs and tax revenues, that had not borrowed so heavily.

THE MATERIAL BASE OF THE CRISIS

New York City's loss of 542,000 jobs between 1969 and 1976 lies at the root of the city's fiscal crisis. In 1975 the rate of job loss was twice the average for the preceding seven-year period. The city lost 61,000 public-sector jobs in 1975, bringing the number of government employees to the lowest level since 1966. In addition, another 25,000 manufacturing jobs were lost. That was nothing new: close to half the jobs lost since 1969 had been in factory employment, making the factory work force nearly a third lower at the end of the period than at the beginning. These figures can also be compared with 1950–69, when the city lost an average of 11,000 factory jobs a year, and with 1969–75, when losses averaged 43,000 a year (U.S. Bureau of Labor Statistics).

Job loss is inevitably followed by tax-revenue loss. Economists at the Maxwell School, Syracuse University, estimated that the city lost from $651 to $1,035 in tax revenues, depending on wage level and job category, for each job lost. The city's Finance Administration estimates were lower but still sizable: the loss of a $6500 blue-collar job resulted in a loss in sales- and income-tax collection of $320 a year; a $10,500 clerical job, of $532; and a $15,500 professional job, of $950. If the half million jobs that disappeared between 1969 and 1975 were today providing income for New Yorkers, the city would be receiving $1.5 billion more in tax revenues.

The dramatic job loss is itself an effect, not a basic cause. The origin of the problem lies in the cyclical nature of our economy and in secular trends brought about by private and public decision structures, which minimize private costs and ignore externalities, specifically the social costs of development patterns. The results are, of course, felt not only in New York City. Geographic mobility of capital and privatized decision-making result in the growth and then the decay of cities and, increasingly, in their troubled older suburbs. It can be predicted that the same pattern will take place in the now-growing parts of the country, the so-called "Sunbelt" in the South and Southwest, in the decades to come.

NEW YORK IS NOT ALONE

New York City's problems are part of a larger trend. In almost all of the older manufacturing cities, the same problems are encountered. To avoid the burdens imposed by the decline in central cities that are occasioned by corporate investment policies, upper-income residents move to exclusive and excluding suburbs. Free choice in the private sector leads mobile capital to move to low-wage areas, leaving behind urban social problems requiring increased taxation from a dwindling tax base.

If, as headline writers suggested in the mid-1970s, the New York economy was crumbling, then the city was not going downhill alone. Between 1965 and 1972, while New York City lost nearly 16 percent of its jobs, Philadelphia lost 17 percent and New Orleans nearly 20 percent. The recessions of the mid-1970s and early 1980s had dire effects on most of the nation's older cities, particularly in New England and the Middle Atlantic regions. The economic epidemic has been characterized by a decline in the old manufacturing areas, and by growth in some parts of the Sunbelt and the Northwest. The decline in the quality of life in the older central cities is spreading to their suburbs; the rot of a deteriorating infrastructure and housing stock and the curtailment of public services are metastasizing.

The Advisory Commission on Intergovernmental Relations issued a report entitled "City Financial Emergencies" two years before the highly publicized fiscal crisis in New York. The commission had focused on the "incredible and seemingly insoluble array of financial difficulties" facing urban governments due to a wide spectrum of deep structural problems: outmoded capital facilities, inability to increase the tax base, and irreversible soaring demands of public services. Debt ceilings, taxpayer rebellion, and competition with other jurisdictions placed limits on the cities' ability to raise funds—despite the fact that the basic needs of the citizenry were not even then being adequately met. The "general inability to make the revenue sources stretch to fit the expenditures mandated by the state and demanded by the people" had reached, in the commission's view, emergency proportions (pp. 2–4).

In the cities of almost all of the older industrial states of the northern Midwest and Northeast, stringent cutbacks in municipal services were made. A national survey in 1975 by the Joint Economic Committee found state and local governments eliminating some 140,000 jobs, raising taxes by $3.6 billion, cutting services by $3.3 billion, and canceling or deferring some $1 billion in construction projects. A similar study in 1980 showed service cuts in an overwhelming majority of U.S. cities. In the mid-1970s, even while New York filled the headlines other cities were in serious trouble.

In Chicago, Cook County Hospital had to borrow $1.5 million every two weeks in order to meet its $4 million payroll; in 1975, the County Board decreased the hospital allocation by $8.8 million and, as a result, matching funds were lost. In Detroit, museums were open only on alternate weekends. Police were forced to take off two weeks without pay. When Detroit firemen refused a similar package, hundreds were laid off. Bumper stickers and billboards sprouted with pictures of Detroit burning, captioned "What if you had a fire and nobody came?" Small businessmen in the northwest, a middle-class part of the city, talked of seceding from Detroit on the grounds that the city has failed to meet its obligations to the community. Cleveland has actually defaulted on its outstanding bonds. It would be difficult to find a city in the Northeast or the industrial Midwest that is not experiencing serious financial problems and cutting service levels.

INDUSTRIAL DECLINE

New York was typical in another important way as well. When we look at the people who were working in New York City during the sixties, we find the number of commuters rising by 29 percent (150,000 jobs), and the proportion of city-resident workers falling by 5 percent (or 170,000 jobs). The commuters held the better jobs and earned more: in 1969, despite the higher cost of living, the average Manhattan worker living in New York City earned only $6,719—half of what commuters earned ($13,862 for Westchester residents working in Manhattan; $13,642 for Rockland County; $13,614 for Nassau). City residents were twice as likely to be service workers, operatives, and laborers; half as likely to be clerical, professional, technical, and managerial employees. Among blue-collar jobs, commuters were twice as likely to be craftsmen and foremen as operatives.

The job mix in the mid- to late-1960s translates increasingly into one labor market for the poor and another separate one for the better paid professionals. In 1968, over a fifth of all jobs in the city paid less than $80 a week; at that time a wage of $75 per week, 50 weeks a year, was at the poverty threshold for a family of four. The office-headquarters labor market for professional workers in finance, insurance, communications, law, advertising, and the nonprofit foundations was large and growing. Manhattan, which had only a quarter of the metropolitan area's employment, had close to half the jobs paying $25,000 or more.

With the decline in low-wage manufacturing and the need for more office workers with more substantial education, a large proportion of the students in New York City public schools were potentially unemployable in the local labor market. A study of the high school class of 1980 showed a dropout rate in New York City public schools approaching 50 percent. These youth could look forward to unemployment rates of nearly twice those of their peers who did graduate and almost three times the average unemployment rate. In 1981, the Bureau of Labor Statistics estimated that in New York City, of the 105,000 jobs opening each year through 1985, only 9000 would be open to high school dropouts.

Between the city's millions of unemployed welfare recipients and young people who were growing up to be unemployable in existing labor market conditions, social service costs on the one side and rising crime rates on the other led many to view the poor (of whom only a small proportion were criminals or welfare dependent) as the problem. The mismatch of jobs and jobless in New York gave rise to a new purpose in government policy: attempting to get rid of the poor and take away the better situated housing stock to reallocate to the workers who were needed by corporate New York. The emerging strategy of "planned shrinkage" calls for the dismantling of services to lower-income communities with the goal of pushing their residents out of the city. This is an integral part of the Emergency Financial Control Board's transformation strategy—get rid of the poor, break the power of the municipal unions, and reduce services, except to the business and upper-income areas.

PLANNED SHRINKAGE

Jay Forrester, a Massachusetts Institute of Technology professor, had used a computer-simulation "urban dynamics" model to work out the likely effect of various city policy options. The one that maximized a city's well-being called for tearing down poor people's homes. It is very simple. The computer coldly and logically spewed out its conclusion: if we destroy people's homes and they have nowhere to live in the city, they will have to leave. As a result, the average income of the city rises and the city's well-being increases. By concerning itself with the city instead of with its people, computers can come to such conclusions.

Not only computers but also flesh-and-blood people can and do think this way. A most important recent development in the New York City fiscal crisis has been the public surfacing of just such a policy formulation. Roger Starr, the City's Housing and Development Administrator in early February 1976, sent up a trial balloon. He suggested, as an alternative to continued across-the-board cuts in city services, that the city "thin out services" in certain slum areas: that the city close fire and police stations and curtail public education as a way of accelerating population decline. Such action would make whole areas of the city uninhabitable, and then the land could be bulldozed. By offering "inducements" for people to move elsewhere (hopefully out of the city?), the "city" could be saved. The acceleration of housing abandonment emerges as a major strategy proposed by some conservative thinkers for solving the city's crisis. "We should not encourage people to stay where their job possibilities are daily becoming more remote," Starr asserts (p. 104). The city governments appears to have followed this approach. Indeed even as basic services to low-income residents were cut, funds were directed toward subsidizing corporate interests on a lavish scale.

SUBSIDIZING THE AFFLUENT

In 1968, New York State began a program to help small manufacturers create jobs in low-income urban areas. In response to its fiscal crisis of the mid-to-late 1970s the state increased its aid under this program, the State Commerce Department's Job Incentive Board, by granting hundreds of millions of dollars in tax credits, usually without discussion, to businesses, most of which would have made their investments without the aid. Investigative journalists found among other instances:

> Alien & Company, investment bankers. The company got an estimated $1.3 million, 10-year tax benefit by moving from Wall Street to new, larger offices in midtown Manhattan. The state gave it credit for creating six jobs and "retaining" 114 others.
> WKBW-TV, an ABC affiliate in Buffalo. It built a $2.5 million studio, added five new employees and retained 98 others. It got an estimated $1.7 million, 10-year credit. "I found out about the program after we started the project," said Philip R. Beuth, the general manager. "It had nothing to do with our going ahead." (Fleetwood and McFadden, p. B4)

Other beneficiaries included the Long Island newspaper *Newsday* ($16.2 million), Lehman Brothers ($3.4 million), Morgan Stanley ($5.6 million), Procter & Gamble ($14 million), and Hooker Chemical Company ($40 million). State officials acknowledged that many of the recipients did not appear to need the ten-year tax credits. (Pressure has mounted to cut such giveaway programs, but they are at this writing still in place.)

The Industrial and Commercial Incentive Board is a mayoral body whose task it is to encourage economic development in New York City. In theory it offers tax abatement to projects that would not be realized without such assistance. In point of fact the Board also hands out millions of dollars to some of the largest corporations and well-connected campaign contributors. Subsidies to developers typically go to projects in the Wall Street and midtown areas that would be completed without such gifts. The head of the Board is the Deputy Mayor for Economic Development, who comes to the city job from a vice presidency for urban affairs at one of the city's largest banks.

Other subsidy programs were earmarked to underwrite gentrification. Tax abatements were given to those who would buy up decaying housing stock (low-cost apartments for low-income people) and refurbish it for a more affluent clientele. In a study of Columbia University political scientist Gerald Finch, compiled for City Council President Carol Bellamy in 1981, it was estimated that if this housing program (the J-51 program) were to be continued in its existing form and development proceeded at its present pace, by the end of 1984 the city will have given away $2 billion in tax revenues by the end of the century. (Under the program, taxes on a rehabilitated building are frozen for up to 20 years.) There is a huge incentive involved, one that has prompted many unscrupulous landlords to illegally harass the lower income and elderly tenants who occupy convertible apartments. Such use of public funds has prompted New York's Terrence Cardinal Cooke, in a rare public intervention in New York's politics, to criticize the J-51 program.

In cities where developers are anxious to put up major projects, it hardly seems necessary to pay them to do what they already see profit in doing. Indeed progressive city governments have learned to require certain benefits from the developers to defray costs to the taxpayer that a development may impose. For example, in Santa Monica, California, where a leftist coaliation is in power, a 1981 agreement with the Greenwood developers for 312,000 square feet of commercial office space included provisions calling for:

> 30 units of "very low, low, and moderate-income housing" to be ready within 18 months of completion of the office space, housing to be provided by the developer for 40 years or the life of the project (whichever is longer). The developer was also required to provide 1500 square feet of community room space, a free day-care center for apartment tenants' and office workers' young children, an affirmative action hiring program for construction workers, and a public park. (Lindorff, p. 20)

In New York City where a continuing mid-Manhattan building boom threatens to add 25 percent more workers (according to some projections) to the already overcrowded midtown area, burdening rush-hour commuting still further, Dave Lindorff asks:

> If the Santa Monica approach were taken, this picture would change. Clearly mid-Manhattan is a goldmine for office tower developers. What if the city were to demand housing in return for each profitable office they wanted to erect? A 1.3 million-square-foot tower like the Citicorp Building would require provision of 130 low-income housing units within walking distance if the same ratio were used as was applied to Greenwood Development.
>
> Of course, these are not magic numbers. If the relative attractiveness of mid-Manhattan were greater for developers than that of Santa Monica, even more housing, or funds for transit renewal and expansion, could be demanded. (p. 20)

In practice the rising tax dollars needed to pay for redevelopment impoverished the public sector further. The physical displacement of lower-income individuals makes them easier to ignore. As a group associated with the Indiana Christian Leadership Conference said in a careful study of Indianapolis:

> Initially, we must emphasize the misleading way in which the word revitalization is used by downtown development advocates. What they see under the heading turns out eventually to be the direct replacement of poor residents by new well-to-do residents. For us, a genuine revitalization can only by an improvement in the condition of existing residents. If there is to be any diversification, it should be limited to what can be done without uprooting current central-city residents. The integrity of the neighborhood should be preserved and enhanced, not undermined. (p. 43)

Tax policy, as Santa Monica has shown, can pursue such goals if local government is controlled by groups committed to progressive localism.

CONCLUSIONS

The difficulties engendered by changes in the economic base, as David Gordon has shown (essay two), place strains on older cities which cannot easily adjust to their new functional role. The New York City fiscal crisis is a reflection of true costs of transformations. This argument is to be made in a number of steps: *first,* it is shown that job loss has been the cause of the fiscal crisis; *second,* that the situation is as serious in many other older cities (except that because they have not borrowed as much, their crisis does not outwardly appear as dramatic), and that a larger process of regional stagnation in the old industrial heartland of the nation is advancing at an alarming rate; *third,* that the solutions being offered by most politicians and urban experts are inflicting still greater pain and demanding more sacrifice from the cities' poor and working class; *fourth,* the problems of older cities and regional strife are reflective of an underlying contradiction between the interests of our giant corporations and the nation's citizens, both in their role as taxpayers and as workers; and *fifth,* local governments can, as Santa Monica has, pursue a pro-people urban policy. (In the final essay in this book such an alternative is developed.)

The overextension of New York City borrowing has been described in great detail because the very people and interest groups which encouraged the borrowing controlled and profited from the austerity-restructuring policies that "solved" the city's fiscal crisis. As we look to the future more austerity will be demanded not only of New Yorkers but most urban residents. The mismatch of needs and resources insures this.

Continuing to "solve" New York City's fiscal crisis is relatively easy. Someone must continue to pay. If the poor, the unionized workers, and the poorer neighborhoods accept mammoth reductions of all kinds, the problem goes on being solved.

Under this solution, what is in store for the city? Not one set of sacrifices, but continuing severe cutbacks in service and a cycling downward into further decay are to be expected—to be ended only when "planned shrinkage" gets rid of enough of the poor, and unionization among municipal workers has been adequately beaten back.

American social scientists are fond of denying that there is such a thing as class struggle. In the case of the New York fiscal crisis, they speak in value-neutral terms of increasing efficiency. Politicians urge us all to pull together, share the burden, bite the bullet. The perspective offered in the present analysis suggests that class conflict in fact lies at the heart of the problem—it explains why the crisis exists, why those in power choose the scapegoats they do, why they seek to impose the "solutions" they do. The fiscal crisis is in fact a form of class struggle. Alternative answers that do not require the poor and the workers to bear the burden of the crisis must begin with an analysis that does not blame them for the existence of the crisis. The conventional analyses, when subjected to scrutiny, have been found to be incorrect, misleading. The simplest of class analyses is strongly suggestive of which forces are, in fact, to blame and of how to conceptualize alternative answers to the crisis.

We can trace the problem then—not to welfare and wages, corruption and overborrowing, but to the loss of jobs and taxable resources, to the workings of the profit motive and the political system that has solved our economic problems by creating even more severe ones.[5] The increased mobility of capital, along with its ability to plan on a global basis, undercuts the power of workers as individuals. To the extent that workers have access to institutional representation in unions and local governments, the possibility of defensive action there is also undercut. The effect of workers in one area having to compete for jobs with those in another, and of jurisdictions being able to encourage plant location through tax giveaways and free services, mean lower wages and higher tax levels for working people in all areas.

As things now stand, disastrously high levels of unemployment blight the U.S., especially its older industrial cities. The failure of the private sector to create jobs leads not to rational planning of full employment policies but to demands by the corporate sector to still more tax giveaways. Neither at the local level, as the New York experience has shown, or at the national level, as the Reagan Administration appears bent on proving, can such policies deal adequately with our problems. The real answer, then, is in the social control of investment.

The New York crisis will spread, not just to other older cities (it is there already), but also to newer ones and their more affluent suburbs. As the Gross National Product rises, we become poorer in our quality of life. Instead of helping to offset social costs through progressive social programs—in health, housing, mass transit, income maintenance, and job creation—a planned-shrinkage policy is being advocated. We Americans are asked to be realistic about what government can do, and told that we should not throw money at problems. It is time to discuss the alternative to perpetual deterioration. That alternative is the social control of investment, which of necessity would include planned full employment and price controls. The distribution of jobs and resources is already a political issue. The central question is whether it will be decided under democratic control by consumers and workers, or by corporations and their politician friends who claim there is little they can do to meet social needs.

NOTES

1. The conventional wisdom seems ever to lag behind changing reality. The best expert opinion of the early 1970s was that New York was alive and well, and that it really had no serious problems. Consider the following:
   "The City's funded debt has not been increasing at all rapidly in recent years, as debt repayment more or less matches new borrowing. If this policy persists, debt service costs will grow only slowly in the years immediately ahead. There is no reason to expect the policy to change, unless the capacity of city agencies to actually consume larger Capital Budget allocations improves rapidly; even so, until the market for municipal bonds

eases substantially, it is improbable that any administration would feel comfortable about an aggressively expanded new borrowing program" (Netzer, in Fitch, 1970, pp. 664–65).

Of the commonly accepted proposition that "New York City's economy is shrinking, the facts do not support this view of the local labor market." Another "currently accepted proposition is that the unique role of New York City as a stronghold of corporate headquarters is being eroded and that it is only a matter of time before this trend will lead to the decline of the City's economy. Again, a look at the facts will help set the record straight" (Ginsburg, 1973, pp. 70–71).

"Predictions of rapid decay for New York's economy are likely to be proved wrong. The City's employment base grew substantially over the last decade and at a rate equivalent to that of most similarities. Although the manufacturing sector has declined somewhat, this is true of manufacturing relative to total employment in every large city" (1973) (Friedlander and Brecher, p. 28).

2. The seven voting members of the EFCB were: the governor of New York, who was to chair the group, the state and city comptrollers, the mayor, and three public members appointed by the governor with the advice and consent of the state senate. City officials could be outvoted should the need arise.

The areas of EFCB responsibility were determining and estimating revenues for the city, consulting with the city in preparing a fiscal plan, prescribing the form and information required from the city and exercising the authority to approve, disapprove, or modify the plan. Control extended to detailed review of operations and of all contracts prior to their implementation. The city not only had to submit a copy of any contract to the EFCB with an analysis but also a certification that the contract would be in accordance with the financial plan. Any city official failing to comply with an order from the EFCB was subject to administrative discipline including suspension from duty without pay or removal from office. The FEA also subjected any person who "knowingly or willfully violate[d]" an order from the EFCB to criminal charges.

3. Professor Terry W. Clark and associates of the University of Chicago have sought to put the New York fiscal crisis in perspective through a comparison with a representative sample of places of residence of the U.S. urban population. Leading newspapers popularized their contention that "population size is associated with many variables affecting fiscal matters but has minimal direct effect on fiscal strain" (p. 5). This may be a misleading generalization, since it is drawn from an analysis of a sample of fifty-one cities that range in population from 50,000 to only 750,000, with which New York City, Chicago, and Los Angeles are compared.

Thomas Muller, comparing U.S. cities with populations of half a million or more, comes to somewhat different conclusions. The choice of samples reflects an underlying difference in approach. The Clark study sees the crucial comparison to be the amount New York spends per capita compared with the average of American cities. In a competitive economy, in this view, the relevant comparison is the urban average, for given freedom of movement, the affluent will relocate to avoid taxation.

Muller, on the other hand, is interested in comparing the fiscal status of growing and declining larger cities. Interestingly, public spending per capita in U.S. cities, arranged by population size, does not increase markedly up to cities of a half million (see table reproduced below). This is of significance in comparing the findings of the two studies.

**Expenditure for Common Services Per Capita
for U.S. Cities by Population Size**

City Size	Dollars per Capita
50,000 to 99,999	129
100,000 to 199,999	157
200,000 to 299,999	180
300,000 to 499,999	177
500,000 to 999,999	232
1,000,000+	283

Source: *City Government Finances in 1972–73* (Washington, D.C.: Bureau of the Census, 1974).

Muller's conclusion (that declining large cities in the North and industrial Midwest are in trouble compared wtih "Sunbelt" cities) is in Clark's view oversimplified. "The stereotypes," Clark writes, "are false, or at least misleading" (p. 5). Clark's more limited sample, weighted as it is to smaller cities, does not find the trend Muller observes. However, the expanded sample, and the more representative one, does in fact show the "stereotype" view to be supported. The excellent statistical work of both studies forms the basis of very different policy emphases.

Most decision-makers and the general public are exposed to such scholarly studies only in the simplified form in which they appear in newspaper accounts. The public may reach opinions, and decision-makers may act on the views, formed in this manner. It is important to explain why these different results come about—in this case because of different sample cities used for comparison.

4. The press for the most part treated the transfer of power with awe and respect for the banks, generally praising their willingness to get involved. The takeover was greeted with editorial assurance by the *New York Times*:

"The intricate series of maneuvers, commitments, and legislative action through which New York City has been rescued from the disaster of default provides much needed reassurance of democratic society's capacity to overcome partisanship and selfish interest in the face of crisis."

The *Times* sees not disfranchisement, but a boom to democracy. It also characterized the teachers' strike to preserve past gains in working conditions as a "shameful desertion" by teachers of their classrooms—while the governor and Big MAC are praised for their stand in opposition.

The only New York newspaper with any significant circulation to print a different position was the *Village Voice*. In its pages, Pete Hamill wrote of the banks:

"They managed their coup d'état with an extraordinary gift for the Big Con. They gave the impression that only New York was profligate, that only New York had trouble paying for its paper, that only New York was wasting money.

"The junta's bankers did not mention their own responsibilities in reducing New York to panhandler status: how they manipulated the huge office building boom of the '60s that has left us with 32 million empty feet of office space; redlined marginal neighborhoods that could have been saved with an infusion of private capital; recklessly shot craps in the stock market;

and exported New York capital to distant parts of the United States and the world.

   "The central tactic of the Big Con is to place the blame elsewhere. The bankers have placed the blame for their own bottomless greed on New York. It is like the mugger blaming the victim for not having money" (1975, p. 7).

5. The inability of the U.S. capitalist economy to create full employment and the phenomenon of manufacturing leaving the industrial Northeast, on the one hand, and the militance of the working-class poor in the 1960s demanding humane levels of social-service benefits, on the other, set the terms of the urban fiscal crisis of the 1970s. The reformist achievements of the 1960s did not address the causes of the problem but rather sought to ameliorate conditions through expanded welfare measures. These benefits, while far from adequate, look relatively overgenerous in a period of economic crisis and retrenchment. The "right" to such services in a market economy can never be absolute, since it violates the very logic of the allocation process. Welfare in a market society is demeaning because it must be extended in a manner that does not interfere excessively with work incentives. It must perpetuate stratification and hierarchy by characterizing recipients not as victims of the economic system but as parasites on the social order. The demand for minimal income for the nonworking drives a wedge between them and overtaxed workers.

   Similarly, the demands of municipal workers are portrayed as coming at the expense of these same taxpayers. Price increases in the private sector, a far more important source of declining living standards, while disliked, are taken as inevitable. Further, the argument that unless profits are protected, "they" will not be able to create jobs for us, reflects an acceptance that the key decisions that affect our lives are beyond our control. The function of government may be to promote full employment, but the only acceptable way to do so is to bribe the corporations through higher profits. Textbook notions that ours is a pluralistic society in which contending interest groups vie for influence seem naive in the face of the power of capital.

REFERENCES

Advisory Commission on Intergovernmental Relations, *City Financial Emergencies: The Intergovernmental Dimension* (Washington, D.C.: U.S. Government Printing Office, 1973).

Auletta, Ken, "An Agenda to Save Our City," *New York,* March 22, 1976.

Brecher, Charles, *Where Have All the Dollars Gone? Public Expenditures for Human Resource Development in New York City, 1961–1971* (New York: Praeger, 1974).

Business Week, "The Second War Between the States," May 17, 1976.

Clark, Terry Nichols, Irene Sharp Rubin, Lynne C. Pettler, and Erwin Zimmerman, "How Many New Yorks?: The New York Fiscal Crisis in Comparative Perspective" (draft of a study in progress; September 15, 1976, version, University of Chicago, Department of Sociology). Also see Terry Nichols Clark, "Fiscal Strain in New York and Elsewhere—Is New York Still First?" *New York Affairs,* in press.

Fainstein, Susan S., and Norman I. Fainstein, "The Federally Inspired Fiscal Crisis," *Society,* May–June, 1976.

Fitch, Robert, "Planning New York," in Roger E. Alcaly and David Mermelstein, eds., *The Fiscal Crisis of American Cities* (New York: Vintage Books, 1977).

Fleetwood, Blake, and Robert D. McFadden, "State Programs for Corporate Tax Relief in Dispute," *New York Times,* March 10, 1981.

Forrester, Jay W., *Urban Dynamics* (Cambridge, Mass.: MIT Press, 1969).

Friedlander, Stanley, and Charles Brecher, "A Comparative View," in Eli Ginzburg, ed., *New York Is Very Much Alive* (New York: McGraw-Hill Book Co., 1973).

Ginzburg, Eli, "The Manpower Record," in Eli Ginzburg, ed., *New York Is Very Much Alive* (New York: McGraw-Hill Book Co., 1973).

Hamli, Peter, "Welfare Must Be Abolished," *Village Voice,* Sept. 29, 1975.

Kaiser, Charles, "Black and Puerto Ricans—a Bronx Majority," *New York Times,* Apr. 19, 1976.

Lindorff, Dave, "Tomorrow the World?" *Village Voice,* December 2-8, 1981.

Muller, Thomas, "Growing and Declining Urban Areas: A Fiscal Comparison," (Washington, D.C.: Urban Institute, Nov. 1975, with minor revisions Mar. 1976).

Netzer, Dick, "The Budget: Trends and Prospects," in Lyle C. Fitch and Annmarie Hauck Walsh, eds., *Agenda for a City: Issues Confronting New York* (Beverly Hills: Sage Publications, 1970).

New York Times, "State of the City: Industry and Labor," May 13, 1975.

Newfield, Jack, and Paul DuBrul, "Banks to City: Drop Dead," *Village Voice,* Nov. 22, 1976.

(Scott Commission) Maxwell Research Project in the Public Finances of New York City, *New York City: Economic Base and Fiscal Capacity* (New York: State Study Commission for New York City, 1973).

Starr, Roger, "Making New York Smaller," *New York Times Sunday Magazine,* Nov. 14, 1976.

Tabb, William K., *The Long Default: New York and The Urban Fiscal Crisis* (New York: Monthly Review Press, 1982).

U.S. Bureau of the Census, "Population Estimates and Projections," *Current Population Reports,* Series P-25, number 615 (Washington, D.C.: U.S. Government Printing Office, 1976).

U.S. Bureau of Labor Statistics, Middle Atlantic Region "1975 Year End Report on Employment, Prices and Earnings in New York City." *Regional Labor Statistics Bulletin,* Number 39, Jan. 1976.

U.S. Congressional Budget Office, *New York City's Fiscal Problems: Its Origins, Potential Repercussions and Some Alternative Policy Responses* (Washington, D.C.: U.S. Government Printing Office, 1975).

U.S. Senate, Committee on Government Operations, *Federal Response to Financial Emergencies of Cities* (Washington, D.C.: U.S. Government Printing Office, 1975).

15

Management Strategies in Public Sector Labor Law: A Case Study of New York City

MARK MAIER

There is a popular tale making the rounds these days about municipal labor relations in New York City. Raymond Horton calls it "The Decline of Public Management," Charles Morris titles it "The Cost of Good Intentions," and Ken Auletta labels it "The Failure of Democracy."[1] All are part of a new trend in political thinking which seeks to blame our current economic problems on mistakes made during the 1960s. The purpose of this paper is to show that the neoconservative account inadequately describes events during this period. As a result it is a poor guide for policy decisions, even though it is couched in currently popular rhetoric.

Briefly the neoconservative story about New York City goes as follows: John Lindsay, elected Mayor of New York City in 1965, approached city governance with an idealistic zeal unknown in prior administrations. The result, however, was disastrous, nowhere more so than in the City's relationship with its employees. Under Lindsay, unions were encouraged to sign up members and petition the City for recognition as official bargaining agents for City workers. An independent commission was set up to certify these unions and so-called impartial mediation panels were empowered to resolve disputes between the unions and City officials. In previous administrations, City labor policies had been the exclusive responsibility of City Hall, where skillful ward-heeling mayors used sometimes less-than-honest, but usually effective means to hold down the costs of City services. However, the new liberal policies tipped the balance of power to union leaders who could always resort to a strike if they did not win what they wanted through negotiation. Wages and benefits skyrocketed, while City services suffered under union-imposed restrictions on the workload of City employees. Liberal politicians, needing union support for re-election, refused to resist the increasingly unaffordable contract demands by the unions.

In the neoconservative view, mismanagement by public officials during the 1960s led directly to near-bankruptcy for New York. Unable to obtain further credit from banks in the summer of 1975, the City handed over control of its finances to the Emergency Financial Control Board, which had the power to veto contracts including those negotiated with labor unions. Thus, although unions continued to represent workers, the clout of the unions was unquestionably diminished at the bargaining table. By 1980, over 60,000 City jobs had been eliminated and newly bargained contracts called for wage deferrals as well as work-rule changes long sought after by management. As a final blow City unions were forced to pledge a large portion of their pension fund money to New York City bonds, which no one else was willing to buy.

Soon it became clear that New York City unions were not the only ones in trouble. As Detroit, Cleveland, Boston, and a number of smaller cities also sank into red ink, they were rescued from the bankruptcy court only by last-minute financial arrangements.[2] In these cities as well, bankers required cutbacks in spending as the price for access to the credit market. As a result, lay-offs and wage freezes threatened whatever gains were made by workers since the 1960s. However, even though austerity policies are no longer limited to New York City, according to the neoconservatives New York City remains the prime evidence for *why* retrenchment in municipal services is necessary. Allegedly New York City is a case study of misguided liberalism in public sector labor relations.

There is superficial plausibility to the neoconservative account. More than any other urban politician of the time, John Lindsay represented the Camelot approach to politics with his snappy dress, eagerness to espouse moral crusades, and his coterie of Ivy League aides. Linday's confident campaign style in the election of 1965 contrasted sharply with the stormy period that characterized New York City politics during his term in office. Foremost among his travails were labor negotiations with City unions, beginning on his first day in office with the City's first complete transit shutdown. By the time Lindsay left office in 1973, most groups of City workers had gone on strike, including for the first time police and firefighters. During his eight years in office Lindsay came to terms with the "power broker" labor leaders he so disdained in the 1965 campaign, so that by the time he sought reelection in 1969 he had support from most of the City's municipal labor leaders. Labor officials also have lived up

to their stereotyped reputations. Michael Quill, leader of the transit workers and John DeLury, president of the sanitations workers union, in particular, seemed to relish their role as gruff, public-be-damned labor bosses
who could stand up to the Yale graduates at City Hall and win large
contract concessions for their members.

WHAT'S WRONG WITH THE
NEOCONSERVATIVE ACCOUNT?

Despite the current popularity of the neoconservative story, there are
some serious inaccuracies and omissions in their account. Three errors
stand out as particularly significant.

First, it is not true that New York City collective bargaining procedures are the responsibility of John Lindsay alone. The groundwork was
laid by previous mayors, especially by Robert Wagner, Jr., who commissioned a report in 1965 that almost word-for-word became the City's collective bargaining law in 1968.[3] Thus, ironically, it is Wagner, one of the
darling boss-style mayors, exalted in the neoconservative reading of history, who is most responsible for public sector collective bargaining in
New York City.

Second, the neoconservative history is in error in placing worker
militancy exclusively in the Lindsay years. Since there were many strikes
before Lindsay was elected mayor, it is difficult to ascribe public sector
strikes to the permissive attitude of the mayor's office after 1966. In fact
it appears that causation worked in precisely the opposite direction: labor
militancy during the 1960s spawned efforts by the City to contain it within
collective bargaining procedures.

Third, unlike the neoconservative account, there is not a simple correlation between strong labor leaders such as Quill or DeLury and successful negotiation of contracts by unions. Just the reverse is true: those
unions *without* strong centralized leadership won the best contracts, and
transit and sanitation workers were successful only at times when the
strong leadership of Quill and DeLury was threatened by militant rank-
and-file movements within the unions.

A DIFFERENT INTERPRETATION

Similar criticisms have been made of the conventional historical account
of another period in U.S. labor history: the rise of industrial unionism
during the 1930s. Traditionally, the National Labor Relations Act (NLRA)

of 1935 had been viewed as a good-hearted act on the part of President Roosevelt to promote fair treatment of workers. However, recent scholarship has pointed to the strike wave of 1934 as an important factor in Roosevelt's support of collective bargaining.[4] Fear of left-wing insurgency (the strikes included three socialist-led general strikes) rather than a concern over the rights of workers removed Roosevelt's reservations about the NLRA. Similarly, large corporations such as General Motors and U.S. Steel, not surprisingly, initially opposed recognition of industrial unions, then decided that certification of unions under the NLRA was preferable to the continuation of sit-down strikes and left-wing political activity, which swept through these industries during 1936 and 1937. Both Roosevelt and these large corporations were attracted to the NLRA because it set up a structure for collective bargaining, which they hoped would contain worker militancy. So although under the NLRA, workers gained government enforcement of their right to join unions, the new structures were set up in ways favorable to management.

The revised interpretation of events during the 1930s suggests a new way of looking at public employee labor relations in New York City several decades later. Between 1954 and 1975 a series of mayoral proclamations, State laws, and City Council bills dramatically changed the rules for public sector labor relations in New York City. Parallels with the rise of industrial collective bargaining during the 1930s are numerous. One advocate of collective bargaining for public sector workers was Mayor Robert Wagner, Jr., son of Senator Robert Wagner, Sr., chief architect of the National Labor Relations Act. More substantially, New York City labor legislation occurred in response to an upsurge of worker militancy, as did Depression-era legislation on the national level. And, the rules adopted for collective bargaining in New York's public sector contained the same management strategies used in the 1930s. The following pages describe in detail this history using a typology of management strategies to keep track of how the changes in collective bargaining affected different groups of workers.[5] By examining labor relations as a series of management strategies in response to worker militancy, it is possible to understand events in New York City far more satisfactorily than with the neoconservative model. The alternative view is more comprehensive in that it explains more of the changes in labor relations without recourse to ad hoc interpretations involving individual whim by political leaders. In a final section the implications of the alternative view for the current period are examined.

RECOGNITION STRATEGIES

The company union stands at the extreme of possible management strategies for union recognition. It is not a present policy in New York, but one with a legacy earlier in the century. The streetsweepers, for example, antecedents of today's sanitation workers, were granted a company union in 1896, known as the Committee of 41. Because it was the policy of a reform government, the experiment lasted only two years until Tammany Hall was voted back into office. Significantly, however, the company union created a nucleus of organization and leadership that led to an employee-controlled union local that carried out a nine-day strike in 1911. After the strike was defeated, organizing attempts in the sanitation department languished until the 1930s, when during that decade's upsurge of industrial organizing, a CIO affiliate, the State, County and Municipal Workers of America (SCMWA), signed up large numbers in the department. In order to nip this organizing drive in the bud, Mayor LaGuardia arranged to deal with the SCMWA's rival, an amalgam of several AFL locals, brought under the affiliation of the American Federation of State, County and Municipal Employees (AFSMCE). As a result, the CIO group could not represent workers at City Hall, causing the union to stagnate until it was wiped out by the anti-red purges of the 1950s.

The favored locals, under the leadership of John DeLury, broke away from AFSCME in 1952, joined the Teamsters, and in 1958 became the first union outside of transit to sign a contract with the City. In return for their 1958 contract, the union would not only abandon claims in a pension dispute but would sacrifice wage claims for previous years and for the two years of the contract. DeLury tried to sell the contract to his members by arranging for supporters to carry him victoriously from the signing ceremony. But back at the union hall the reception was different; members voted down the contract overwhelmingly and demanded a strike the following morning, forcing DeLury back to negotiations where he won changes in the contract. During the 1960 contract negotiations the union leadership called a one-day strike in advance of reaching an agreement. Mayor Robert Wagner, Jr., pretended the strike did not take place, thus avoiding imposition of otherwise mandatory and quite severe penalties under the State's Condon-Wadlin Act, under the assumption that the union would call off the strike and sign a contract that evening. However, once again the nays at the union meeting clearly outnumbered the yeahs on acceptance of the contract. Nonetheless, DeLury declared the strike over and left the hall with a squad to protect him from the fistfights that broke out. With the new contract in effect, any sanitation worker not on the job the following morning faced stiff penalties without protection from the union.[6]

On the basis of this example alone, the neoconservative story is called into question. Here is a union striking and winning formal recognition long before Lindsay came into office. More significantly, it appears that collective bargaining was a response rather than the initiating factor: incipient organizing by the CIO during the 1930s and later an angry rank and file were what prompted the city to meet with the union and to sign contracts with it. By outright favoritism in the case of LaGuardia's relationship with the SCMWA and AFSCME and by selective enforcement of State law in the case of Mayor Wagner, city management was able to influence which union would be recognized and, within that union, which leader would stay in power.

Labor relations for transit workers in New York City tells a similar history. Prior to the Great Depression, a combination of yellow dog contracts, individual working agreements, and large funds to pay for scabs kept union organizing in check. Then during the 1930s a CIO group, the Transport Workers Union of America (TWU), succeeded in signing contracts with the private companies that ran the subways—just in time to see them go bankrupt and be bought up by the City. The union thought it had a deal worked out with Mayor LaGuardia that representation would be guaranteed under "unification," as the City buy-out of the subway lines was called. But the City ducked out of the agreement on the grounds that it would be against civil service regulations for them to give a union exclusive bargaining rights, thus imposing union representation on a group of workers who may not have voted for the union.

In 1946, when the country was hit by a wave of strikes (particularly in the public sector), the City was forced once again to confront the union. At this time, one leader in the TWU, Michael Quill, was able to make a deal with the City at the expense of another TWU leader, Austin Hogan, whom the City feared for his ties with the Communist Party and as the leader of more militant rank-and-filers within the union. During the following years the City had a sudden change of heart about exclusive representation, concluding that, not only was it necessary, but that a *single* exclusive unit was the most democratic union structure for the transit system. Not incidentally, of course, the rule change gave Michael Quill control over all sections of transit labor and enabled him to negotiate the first written contact with the Transit Authority in 1954. Like the sanitation workers' contract of 1958, the transit contract came at a high price, including a workers' pay sacrifice for the first day of sick leave, an aspect of the contract not known by transit workers at voting time.

The sick-leave change and subsequent contracts negotiated by TWU leadership led to a number of rank-and-file revolts between 1954 and 1958. Most successful were the motormen, organized in the Motormens Benevolent Association (MBA), who shut down the subway system in 1956 and 1957. The motormen's solution to what they saw as unsatisfactory contracts negotiated by the TWU was to redraw the representation system: specifically they wanted to bargain separately from the Quill-dominated unit. TWU leadership, of course, was opposed to such a split and helped the City put down the MBA strikes. Management and the union were able to work together in several ways, including transferring dissident workers to distant and undesirable job assignments (a practice also found in the City's sanitation department).

The most publicized occasion of City involvement in union affairs occurred in 1957 when MBA leaders discovered City agents with electronic eavesdropping devices in the MBA office. During those pre-Watergate days such revelations were big news and reversed the then-sagging fortunes of the MBA, forcing all parties—the City, the MBA, and the TWU—to reach a compromise in which the MBA agreed to drop their suit concerning the surveillance in return for partial rescinding of the sick-leave rules and a small pay increase. Perhaps more significant for future negotiations, however, the MBA had to agree to a merger with TWU, thus stifling effective rank-and-file protest within the union for several years.[7]

THE SINGLE UNIT

In the case of transit in New York, favoritism is evident not only toward a certain union and particular leaders, but also for a specific union structure—the large, exclusive bargaining unit. Such bias came under the guise of anti-communism and in favor of union democracy, but it appears obvious that the decision to create one large unit was prompted instead by a need to control rank-and-filers within an authoritarian union. The same trend toward single-unit representation also occurred for clerical workers, laborers, and other non-uniformed members of the City's civil service. Initially, however, City strategy was precisely the opposite, favoring fragmentation of bargaining units. During the 1950s Mayor Wagner tried to keep one union balanced off against another: one bargaining unit would be granted to the Teamsters, then one to AFSCME, and then another to the Communication Workers so that all unions were kept small, fighting one another, and without resources to mount more significant organizing campaigns. Wagner had a number of tools available for favoring unions, especially gerrymandering of bargaining units, which allowed Wagner to all but guarantee a union's victory or loss in a bargaining election. (A similar tactic is used today by management against fast food and clerical workers in order to defeat unions in representation elections.) Wagner could also control when an election occurred, thus helping or hindering unions in their efforts to interest workers.

During the 1960s New York City management shifted away from this crazy-guilt of fragmented bargaining units toward recognizing one union for all non-uniformed civil service workers. One reason for this change in strategy was the success of some unions in using the fragmented system to their own advantage. The Social Service Employees Union (SSEU), for example, broke away from the AFSCME district council in 1964, a move supported by Wagner in order to erode the strength of the larger AFSMCE unit. But on their own, the SSEU was able to win several outstanding contracts, thus encouraging the City to impose single-unit representation as had been done in the case of transit to keep the motor-men in check. Wagner wanted a Teamster local to be the single-unit union, but his finagling with the timing of representation elections back-fired among hospital aides and clericals. AFSCME's District Council 37 stressed their connections with the civil rights movement and the upgrad-ing of low-level jobs to win a key representation election in 1965. Two years later DC 37 signed a "citywide" contract, establishing its role as dominant union among non-uniformed civil servants.[8]

NEGOTIATING STRATEGIES

Successful collective bargaining from management's standpoint also re-quires strategies for negotiations. In this regard two features have been emphasized in recent years: management control over what can be nego-tiated (the scope-of-bargaining question); and control over enforcement of contracts, especially the requirement that unions guarantee worker com-pliance with contract terms. New York City restrictions on the scope of bargaining have become more carefully defined in the last twenty years. Originally, the City was vague about the definition of working conditions, a situation allowing the social workers' union (mentioned above) to win major concessions in their 1965 and 1967 contracts, including: reduction in caseload, changes in City hiring procedures so that reduction in case-load was sure to occur, an education fund, control of transfers, and an increase in clothing grants for clients. Some observers have discounted SSEU members as crazy leftist kids, more interested in social policy than "trade union" goals. SSEU publications make it clear, however, that mem-bers saw a connection between service delivery and working conditions.

As long as caseload was high, paperwork burdensome, and "home visits" mandatory, then the workplace was oppressive for worker and welfare recipient alike. What made the SSEU unusual was their recognition of mutual interests with their clients, a coalition they were able to maintain even during their several work stoppages.[9] The New York City Collective Bargaining Law of 1967 was intended to offset SSEU success in negotiating wide-ranging contracts. In that law the City affirmed its absolute right to "determine the method and means by which government operation would be conducted and complete control over the organization and technology used in performing work." No longer were any of these topics permitted at the bargaining table.[10]

The second negotiating strategy used by management in addition to controlling the scope of bargaining has been gaining union enforcement of contracts. The strategy obviously is closely related to management favoritism toward certain unions or particular union leaders: it is precisely a trustworthy union that will guarantee enforcement of a contract. In the case of the 1954 contract in New York City transit, TWU not only guaranteed to negotiate changes in the sick leave rule and helped deflect rank-and-file pressure for a strike when the changes were put into effect, but also promised the Transit Authority a minimum saving as a result of loss of pay for the first day of sick leave. If not forthcoming, this minimum amount would be conceded in other areas of the contract. Consequently, management had good reason to believe Michael Quill when he assured the City of "greater stability" in labor relations once splinter groups competing with the TWU were eliminated from the system.[11]

The most recent use of union enforcement of contracts occurred under the banner of "productivity." Interestingly, management began to *expand* the scope of bargaining during the mid-1970s, once again making work rules a mandatory topic for negotiations. At this time management was confident that it could control the direction of work-rule changes since wage increases, even cost-of-living allowances, were permitted only when accompanied by so-called productivity improvements. Almost without exception, the productivity program of 1976–77 involved speed-up of the work pace or cutbacks in service.[12] Secretaries, for example, were expected to perform the same work in an office pool with fewer employees. Asphalt crews needed to fill more potholes in the same time period. And, in a more recent example, the transit workers' 1980 contract included such productivity improvements as reduced break time between train runs.

All management strategies discussed here are interrelated. Productivity deals, for example, are more likely when management has been able to influence which union represents workers and when the scope of bargaining is also management-defined. Together these union recognition and negotiating strategies begin to explain the inability of unions to effectively resist cutbacks in employment and wages experienced in recent years, most especially in New York City, but also in other cities afflicted by budgetary crises. The paucity of union response has been attributed by some to "sell out" leadership or an apathetic rank and file. Based on the evidence provided here, however, the *structure* of labor relations itself appears to be a strong inhibiting factor on union activity in the public sector. The inability of unions to make coalitions with consumers, for example, is restricted by state laws concerning the scope of bargaining. Moreover, even the anti-democratic tendencies within many public sector unions are attributable, not just to the internal relationships within those unions, but also to management strategies which fostered the growth of authoritarian control in unions and large units with leadership quite distant from rank-and-file members.

SUCCESSFUL UNION STRATEGIES

We need not be entirely pessimistic about the state of public sector unions. Management-imposed regulations on collective bargaining do not necessarily preclude effective union activity. Consider two examples from New York City indicative of the possibility for democratic union structures and successful collective bargaining.

Police and firefighters in New York City have negotiated the most successful contracts among City workers during the last fifteen years and have been more successful than other groups of City workers in resisting strong attempts by management to change the organization of work. Such victories are in large part due to the highly democratic structures of the police and fire unions. There is no tradition of dominance by a single union leader—both groups throw out their leaders with great regularity. Also the structure of the delegate assembly, in which representatives are directly accountable to quite cohesive work groups, allows each rank-and-file member to monitor union decisions. It is perhaps surprising to find a model of union democracy in the most militaristic of city professions; the structure appears to have developed because of the firehouse/police station organization of work combined with the ability of individual workers to communicate easily with one another by radios.[13] In recent years the City has reduced staffing on firefighting equipment, and introduced the one-person police patrol car. These changes had been resisted successfully for several decades and imposed only with guarantees demanded by the union. It is doubtful that, without the democratically run union, either group would have been able to resist these changes in the face of City law designating management control over "means and methods of work."[14]

A democratic union structure also developed in the social workers union, SSEU, in which there also was representation and accountability from the work group to the decision-making body of the union. The union went to great lengths to foster member participation through welfare center newsletters, new member orientations, and rules not permitting leaders to succeed themselves in office. Although the union was forced to merge with DC 37 because of City bargaining rules that limited the ability of independent unions such as SSEU to negotiate on its own, the merger itself is a model of democratic decision-making. The process is also marvelous for labor historians because the debate was carried out in public. All three sides (those wanting to join DC 37, those opposed to affiliation, and those wanting a merger with another union) had access to the union paper in which lengthy position papers spelled out the important factors in a self-conscious discussion of the union's policies.[15]

SUMMARY OF EVENTS IN NEW YORK CITY

The history of labor relations in New York City's municipal sector is best understood if divided into three stages, each characterized by a particular management strategy: first, outright refusal to deal with unions; second, recognition of unions under restrictive labor laws; and third, a period of retrenchment in employment and wage levels. This periodization is not intended to indicate an inherent evolutionary process; it is quite possible for labor relations to stagnate at one stage indefinitely as they in fact did for many decades when non-uniformed City workers were refused union representation.

The stages of management strategy did not necessarily occur for the same groups of workers at the same time. Thus transit workers negotiated contracts under highly specific rules for union recognition during the early 1950s when the City claimed that other employees had no legal right to join labor organizations. The simultaneous application of different management strategies highlights their pragmatic nature: rules for dealing with workers changed depending on the level of organization and militancy reached by a particular group of workers. In short, labor relations policies in New York City developed not because of varying political philosophies of elected officials as the neoconservatives describe it, but because of an ongoing struggle between management and labor.

APPLICATION TO OTHER U.S. CITIES

The typology of management strategies outlined above helps us understand events in New York City. Can the approach be applied to other U.S. cities? The following examples, admittedly limited in number, suggest that remarkable similar management strategies were adopted outside of New York. Generalization of the analysis serves not only as verification of the approach used here, but also as a corrective to an error in the neoconservative view: the emphasis on New York City as the leader in public sector labor relations. Although in most respects New York City is not a typical U.S. city, it is quite representative of other large cities in its dealing with municipal unions. Popular accounts notwithstanding, New York City is not unusual in its compensation of public sector workers. For every category of workers there are other large cities with higher wages, pensions, and total compensation.[16] And, as shown below, other large cities recognized unions for almost their entire work force before New York City even began certifying bargaining units for workers, other than those in the transit system.

Examples of management strategies outlined above, both recognition and negotiating strategies, can be found in other cities. Management favoritism toward single-unit representation is evident in Philadelphia beginning in the 1930s when the city first permitted consultation with labor representatives. In 1957 one union was formally recognized as the exclusive bargaining agent for large numbers of Philadelphia workers. At this time Mayor Dilworth explained: "Municipal management has been plagued with wasteful union competition over grievances and a lack of centralized union responsibility required for stable and efficient collective bargaining."[17] Similarly in Cincinnati a single unit was recognized in 1960 in order to stop an organizing drive by the United Mine Workers of America. A city official stated at the time, "We did not want the city to serve as a battleground between two rival groups."[18]

Management strategy for restricting the scope of bargaining is also found outside New York. Thirty-two states define the scope of bargaining as "wages, hours and working conditions." And, as in New York City, this vague definition has been given more careful interpretation by legislative mandate and by boards set up to administer procedures for public sector bargaining. Many states distinguish between mandatory, permissible, and prohibited topics for bargaining, language drawn from procedures set down by the National Labor Relations Board (NLRB) for private sector labor relations. Under NLRB rules, mandatory topics are those which must be negotiated and are defined as "rates of pay, wages, hours of employment and other conditions." Prohibited topics are those such as discriminatory practices (violations of civil rights statutes, criminal arrangements such as kick-backs, and "hot cargo" agreements[19]), all of which are not allowed in collective bargaining contracts. In between mandatory and prohibited topics lie permissible topics, those which *may* be discussed if both sides agree. Here the NLRB has ruled that employers must bargain over topics traditionally included in collective bargaining, but may exclude what are called "normal management prerogatives."[20] Such language is obviously vague and has led to considerable controversy when applied to issues of current concern such as plant closings and the movement of capital.[21]

The three-part division of the scope of bargaining between mandatory, permissible, and prohibited topics has been adopted by several states in their statutes regulating public sector collective bargaining rules. However, in general, state legislation specifies many more topics to be prohibited and many fewer as mandatory than under federal law for the private sector. The Montana state law is typical in giving management the unabridged right to hire, fire, direct workers, and determine the methods and processes of work. These topics are prohibited from collective bargaining. Other states exclude similar issues from collective bargaining, which in the private sector would commonly be a matter of union-management negotiations. Nevada state law gives local governments the right to lay off workers without going to collective bargaining. New Mexico law precludes bargaining over safety regulations. Pennsylvania statutes prohibit bargaining over the use of new technology. Class size for public schoolteachers, one of the most litigated issues in public sector bargaining, is a prohibited topic in six states. (It is, however, a mandatory topic in four states.[22])

Finally, management strategy in many states aims to enlist unions in carrying out the enforcement of collectively bargaining contracts. For the private sector, the courts have interpreted the no-strike clauses found in almost all union contracts to be a binding commitment on the part of union officials to prevent unauthorized walk-outs by their members. In the public sector, however, an additional restriction has been placed on union officials: state no-strike laws which apply even after the expiration of a contract. (Several states permit public sector strikes, but in each case only for certain groups of workers and then only in limited circumstances.) Normally unions and union officials face severe penalties when a strike occurs.[23]

But no-strike laws have not meant the absence of strikes in the public sector. There have been strikes by public workers in most U.S. cities.[24] And, similar to the pattern noted for New York City, many of these strikes took place despite the active opposition of union leaders. Typical of such strikes were wildcat walkouts in 1978 by District of Columbia bus drivers, which prompted a *Washington Post* headline: "Union Loses Control of Workers."[25] The reluctance of union officials to support strikes no doubt has many sources, but one frequently overlooked factor is management strategy in writing labor law. In New York City, Cincinnati, Philadelphia, and Washington, D.C., the lack of union leadership support for strikes can be traced to management initiatives: large bargaining units and the recognition of highly centralized unions were adopted as strategies with the express purpose of setting union leadership against its own rank and file.

IMPLICATIONS OF THE ANALYSIS

Undoubtedly, the 1980s will see a new set of management strategies. Collective bargaining is now standard practice for public workers in the U.S. (outside of the South) and the structures for recognizing unions and conducting collective bargaining are already in place. Management now must relate to workers *within* the framework of collective bargaining established in the 1960s and 1970s. Among corporate-sponsored research groups and labor relations professional organizations there is a consensus about the best management strategies for the 1980s.[26] They recommend: productivity deals, contracting out of services,[27] education of the public about the cost of public services, and increased business influence over government affairs. None of these policies is completely new; productivity deals were introduced into the New York City transit system as early as 1954. Neither public education nor business influence are untested policies; there is a long tradition in many cities of "good government" groups based on downtown business interests, attempting to monitor public spending.

What is new is the effort by public managers to coordinate all of these activities. The result has been an unprecedented reversal of gains made by public sector workers. William Tabb describes elsewhere in this volume how in 1975 the New York City Emergency Financial Control Board sidestepped established democratic procedures and took control of the City budget, an effort that was later copied in Cleveland. The trend of pay deferrals, lay-offs, and work-rule changes now affects workers in the private sector as well, including such core industries as steel, automobiles, and trucking.

Why were New York City municipal unions so ineffective in resisting the cutbacks of the late 1970s? If we accept the neoconservative version of events, we are hard-pressed to explain the ease with which wage deferrals, lay-offs, and work-rule changes were enforced. After all, if union leaders were really so politically astute and so powerful during the 1960s (as the neoconservatives claim), why were they cutbacks so easily accomplished? The apparent paradox results from an incomplete picture reported by the neoconservatives. The history recounted here suggests that, contrary to popular opinion, municipal unions did not build an unassailable bastion of power during the 1960s. In fact, although unions and collective bargaining rights were granted to workers for the first time during this period, city managers were careful to do so in a manner that had an inhibiting effect on the power of those unions. Favoritism, large units, restricted scope of bargaining, and union enforcement of contracts all created an environment in which unions were relatively ineffective when the cutbacks were proposed during the 1970s.

If our interest is in reversing the policies of retrenchment, then we need to address the structural problems that have made resistance difficult. The success of social workers, police, and firefighters in New York City points to one potentially successful labor strategy: worker control over their own unions.[28] Union democracy, based on the experiences of these three unions, is most successful when it includes not only formal accountability of union officials through elections, but also union structures that promote participation by union membership. Independent caucuses within large bargaining units and communication between workers on the job through newsletters, two-way radios, or roving personnel are used to maintain involvement by large numbers of workers.

Several observers of public sector unions have suggested a second strategy for workers: alliances with community groups, in particular users of public services.[29] Social service workers in New York City provide an example of such an attempt. At present, union-community alliances could counter the educational campaigns described above in which management attempts to link high taxes and allegedly high public sector wages. Since both unions and community residents suffer from cutbacks in service, unions could emphasize the commonality of interest between the two groups. Moreover, unions could argue that funds for services need not come out of the pockets of low- and middle-income city residents.

The neoconservative account, with its emphasis on actions by individual union and government leaders, obscures the source of restrictions on union activity. We have seen how events in New York City tell a complicated story about the 1960s, when unionization was achieved for the first time by many public sector workers. However, in the process of setting up procedures for collective bargaining, city leaders were careful to influence the legal apparatus of union recognition and the rules for negotiations so the power of these unions was restrained. Even though management strategies were at times contradictory (for example, in moving from the advocacy of small bargaining units to large single units), the intention remained the same: dissipate the growing power of unions.

When the full story is told about the development of labor relations in the public sector, we see that the absence of a successful response by unions to the current fiscal crisis in U.S. cities is, in part, a result of successful management strategies of past years. By undercutting the militant potential of unions during the 1960s, public managers are able today to enforce far more stringent cutbacks than would otherwise be possible. Nonetheless, there is evidence that public sector unions may once again actively resist this management offensive. Despite the current legal and institutional restraints on unions, documents of the 1930s and 1950s show that while management appeared to have the upper hand, there was an upsurge of rank-and-file activity which revitalized public sector unions. This is a history conveniently forgotten in the neoconservative story and, today, when unions are at a distinct disadvantage, it is a history desperately in need of remembering.

NOTES

Valuable assistance was received from Roger Waldinger, Matthew Edel, Kristie Jayne and participants in the Conference on New Perspectives in Urban Political Economy.

1. Raymond Horton, *Municipal Labor Relations in New York City* (New York: Praeger, 1973); Ken Auletta, *The Streets Were Paved With Gold* (New York: Vintage Books, 1980); Charles Morris, *The Cost of Good Intentions* (New York: W. W. Norton, 1980). Morris does write that "there appears to be little warrant for the belief that the Lindsay administration was the unusual pushover for the municipal unions" (p. 184). Nonetheless, he concludes that pay increases granted during the Lindsay administration were unjustified (p. 193) and that Lindsay's labor relations policies were inept (p. 184).

2. See A. J. Winnick, J. Gregory, and J. Mandina, "The Financial Crisis in Cleveland," in *Crisis in the Public Sector* (New York: Monthly Review Press, 1981), and "State and Local Government in Trouble," *Business Week* (October 26, 1981).

3. American Arbitration Association, Labor-Management Institute. "Agreement Between City, Labor and Public Members" (March 1966); City of New York Consolidated Rules of the Office of Collective Bargaining *City Record* (January 11, 1968).

4. Richard Hurd, "New Deal Labor Policy and the Containment of Radical Union Activity" *Review of Radical Political Economics* 8, 3, 1976; F. F. Piven and R. Cloward, *Poor People's Movements* (New York: Pantheon, 1977); David Brody, "Radical Labor History and Rank and File Militancy," *Labor History* 16, 1, 1975; James Green, "Working Class Militancy in the Depression," *Radical America* 6, 6, 1972; Michael D. Yates, "Public Sector Unions and the Labor Movement," in Economics Education Project, loc. cit.

5. The examples used here are described in greater detail in Mark H. Maier, "The City and the Unions: Collective Bargaining in New York City 1954–1973" (Ph.D. dissertation, New School for Social Research, 1980).

6. Ralph T. Jones, "City Employee Unions in New York and Chicago" (Ph.D. dissertation, Harvard University, 1972); *New York Times*, 1958–1960.

7. J. J. McGinley, *Labor Relations in the New York Rapid Transit System"* (New York: King's Crown Press, 1949). Peter Freund, "Labor Relations in New York City's Rapid Transit Industry" (Ph.D. dissertation, New York University, 1964); L. H. Whittemore, *The Man Who Ran the Subways* (New York: Holt, Rinehart & Winston, 1973); *The New York Times, 1954–1959.*

8. A. H. Raskin, "Politics Up-ends the Bargaining Table" in Sam Zagoria, *Public Workers and Public Unions* (Englewood Cliffs, N.J.: Prentice-Hall, 1972); *The New York Times 1954–1968.*

9. Joyce L. Miller, "Constraints on Collective Bargaining in the Public Sector: A Case Study," *Urban Analysis* vol. 1; Richard Mendes, *"The Professional Union: A Study of the Social Service Employees Union"* (Ph.D. dissertation, Columbia University, 1975); *The New York Times, 1961–1969.*

10. City of New York "Consolidated Rules," loc. cit.

11. *The New York Times,* September 23, 1955.

12. City of New York, "The Joint Labor Management Productivity Committee Program to Fund the Cost of Living Adjustments for the Period October 1, 1976 to March 31, 1977," December 6, 1976.

13. For further discussion of this point see: David M. Gordon, "The Best Defense is a Good Defense," in M. Carter and L. Leahy, *New Directions in Labor Economics* (South Bend, Ind.: University of Notre Dame Press, 1980).

14. *The New York Times, 1958–1974.*

15. Maier, 1980, loc. cit., Chap. five.

16. See, for example, *New York Times,* February 3, 1978, p. 38; Municipal Labor Committee, "New York Revisited," undated; U.S. Department of Labor, Bureau of Labor Statistics," 1973–1974 Pay Gains of New York City Municipal Government Workers Lag Behind Private Sector," May 18, 1975; and Tabb (essay 14 here).

17. Irving Beller, "Collective Bargaining by the City of Philadelphia," in Jack Barbash, *Unions and Union Leadership* (New York: Harper & Row, 1959).

18. W. D. Heisel, "Anatomy of a Strike," *Public Personnel Review* 30, 4; *The New York Times,* 1957, 1968–1970.

19. Commerce Clearing House, *1976 Guidebook to Labor Relations* (Chicago: Commerce Clearing House, 1976), pp. 212–16, 260–62.

20. Under "hot cargo" agreements, a union contract prevents an employer from hiring non-union labor for work not covered by the contract. Such practices are illegal under NLRB rulings, with the exception of the garment and construction industries.

21. For discussion of this issue see, "Plant Closings," *Labor Update,* vol. 1, No. 4 (February 1981).

22. Commerce Clearing House, *Public Employee Bargaining* (Chicago: Commerce Clearing House, 1981).

23. Sector Collective Bargaining and the Right to Strike in D. Lewin, *Public Sector Labor Relations* (Glen Ridge, N.J.: Thomas Horton and Daughters, 1977).

24. Mark H. Maier, "Public Sector Labor Law," in Economics Education Project, op. cit.

25. *Washington Post,* July 21, 1978, p. 1; Maier, 1980, loc. cit., p. 270.

26. H. H. Wellington and R. K. Winter, *The Unions and the Cities* (Washington, D.C.: The Brookings Institution, 1971); David Stanley, *Managing Local Government under Union Pressure* (Washington, D.C.: The Brookings Institution, 1971); A. L. Chickerling, *Public Employee Unions* (San Francisco: Institute for Contemporary Studies, 1976); The Tax Foundation, *Unions and Government Employment* (New York: The Tax Foundation, Nov. 27, 1972); Committee for Economic Development, *Improving Productivity in State and Local Government* (New York: C.E.D., 1976).

27. For discussion of this issue see Suzanne Sankar, "Contracting Out: Attrition of State Employees," in Economics Education Project loc. cit.

28. For a thorough introduction to democratic rights of union members in the private sector see H. W. Benson, *Democratic Rights for Union Members* (New York: Association for Union Democracy, 1979).

29. For further discussion of the need for union-community alliances in the public sector see Michael Yates, op. cit. and Paul Johnston, "Public Sector Unionism" in Economics Education Project, loc. cit.

five

EPILOGUE

16

A Pro-People Urban Policy

WILLIAM K. TABB

Articles in this book have discussed the historical development of cities, suburbs, and regions. They have described the complex interaction between economic forces and public policy. Authors have examined governmental housing and transportation policies, and traced the impact of urban economic trends on racial minorities, women, the urban poor, and industrial workers. They have suggested that our urban policies have been either inadequate or ill-conceived, having failed dismally to address social and economic problems. This failure is rooted in the larger inability to adequately analyze the deleterious mechanics of the capitalist marketplace. Government policy has come in after market forces (and government subsidies) have done their damage in order to undo some of the harm and to assist victims. Our argument is that the urban crisis was not inevitable, but was caused by unwillingness in the political process to control capital mobility. The disastrous social costs of urban decay were the result of allowing socially crucial decisions to be controlled by private profit calculations and of intensifying these harmful trends with perverse government tax incentives.

In this essay the failures of urban policies based on redistributive liberalism are explained in the context of the way that the U.S. political economy operates. The views of free market conservatives are also examined against the background of the increased mobility of capital and its impact on employment and the tax base. The remainder of this article builds an alternative framework—a pro-people urban policy.

Important community goals are predicated on equity or fairness considerations which characteristically conflict with market-based allocation.

367

The political process can address this conflict between equity and efficiency by legislating new definitions of property rights, by requiring that the social cost imposed by private decisions be taken into account, and by financing collective rather than individual forms of ownership and control. This article explores how democratic decision making can be applied to urban economics.

LIBERALISM, THE FREE MARKET, AND THE ROLE OF GOVERNMENT

Those who favor income redistribution and equity in public service provision and taxation must understand the causes of liberalism's failure to adjust to changed circumstances from the 1960s to the 1970s and early 1980s. Put simply, in a period of rapid economic growth like the 1960s, people regarded redistribution favorably. There was reason to upgrade the labor force and invest in human resources. As our economic crisis developed in the 1970s, a period of stagflation and falling living standards, there appeared to be less generosity and no need to train the unemployed. The availability of skilled, unemployed workers makes Great Society retraining programs cost-inefficient. As long as Keynesian policies could produce growth, the needs of the poor could be met out of the economic surplus. In turn, more growth was stimulated through expansionary fiscal policies. In a period of expansion it seems less important that subsidies are conditioned by the needs of special interests. In any case it seemed difficult, if not in most cases impossible, to regulate corporations in ways that challenge profitability or corporate prerogatives. In periods of contraction stimulation policies continue to favor this trickle-down approach. However, results are disappointing because in contractionary periods there is little or no trickle-down, only redistribution from the poor and working class to the corporate rich.

Ironically, liberalism could not provide adequate services even in periods of growth because redistribution programs are conceived as being only for the poor; resistance from tax-paying workers excluded from program benefits was inevitable. Most fundamentally, since liberalism stays at the level of redistribution, changes that challenge the class nature of society (for instance, production for exchange rather than directly for use values) or deal with the root causes of alienation are precluded from consideration. Under the rules of the market, society continues to need low-wage workers. This means that benefit levels have to be kept low to avoid work disincentives. Full employment at adequate levels seems beyond the system's capacity. Without full employment liberalism cannot make good its promises to the urban poor. It can redistribute income to a limited extent but it cannot productively integrate the urban poor into the labor markets.

At the macro level the failure of the Keynesian model—the inadequacy of fiscal and monetary policy—is tied both to the inability to influence investment and production decisions directly, and especially to the ability of the multinational corporations to escape restrictive policies through their mobility. Further, since economic policy must be pursued within the context of a basically "free" market system, it is difficult to escape the conclusion that workers in one city, state, or nation must accept lower wages and a deterioration in public services so that jobs are not relocated to a more favorable business climate. It is important here to challenge the misguided use of localism, which suggests that any region should have to solve its problems on its own resources, for given the mobility of capital, it does not have control of these resources.

Social welfare expenditures in the United States rose from 16 percent of government spending (at all levels) in 1950 to 35 percent by 1970. As in all other countries of the world, in the U.S. there has been a positive income elasticity of demand for civilian government expenditures over time. As nations get richer, government takes over more functions everywhere. At first governments pay to build harbors, dams, canals, and railroads in order to subsidize economic development. As the economy matures, the state steps in to clean up after the private market by providing the losers with public relief and unemployment insurance. It tidies up urban decay, pollution, and congestion. Thus government spending must rise as a byproduct of capitalist "development." If the basic productive system did not create unemployment, poverty, other forms of economic insecurity, and disease (physical, emotional, and social), there would be less need for the Welfare State to pick up the broken pieces of destroyed and deformed lives. If firms produced in socially responsive ways because consumer desires were paramount in product design and worker needs uppermost in workplace design and organizations, government's formal role could be small indeed.

Free market advocates, on the other hand, see competition as providing the lowest possible prices, innovation, and quality goods. If a problem subsequently arises, they say, it can only be due to the unwarranted intervention of some external force, like government. In classical economic theory a firm seeks out the low-cost location for its plant, using criteria based on transportation, energy, labor, and materials costs, local taxes, and services and markets. The classical theory also assumes atomistic competition in which no single firm can influence markets by itself. Full employment is a given of the model.

The real world of today features high unemployment and inter-jurisdictional competition. Rather than passively taking the best of given opportunities under these conditions, companies negotiate and exert pressure to create the terms they want. Because capital is increasingly mobile among cities, states, and countries, corporations can play one against the other, and corporate behavior includes maximizing profits by relocating and constantly threatening to relocate.

The multinational firm attracted to low wages in the periphery sets in motion changes that encourage international labor mobility. Products move not so much by courtesy of the invisible hand of the market but rather by the subcontracting and inter-subsidiary shipments of the global corporation. The upshot of these trends, as Richard Hill writes, "is a new global spatial division of labor which increasingly corresponds to the internal organization of the transnational corporation." Far from being some new and mysterious process, "the logic which produced the detailed division of labor and the separation of conception from execution within the enterprise in the past is the same logic which underlies the spatial differentiation, extension, and global reorganization of the labor process today" (Hill, p. 8).

CAPITAL MOBILITY AND TAXATION

In 1959, corporations paid just under a third of all federal income taxes (32 percent). By 1978, they paid only 25 percent. This means, of course, that individuals paid slightly over two thirds of federal income taxes in 1959 but three fourths two decades later. The gambit of those who wanted to reduce business' share still further was to urge reduction in public services. In the last two years of the Carter Administration and in the first of Reagan's, steps were taken to all but abolish the corporate income tax.

The same trend was evident at the state and local level, where the personal income tax share rose from 61 to 73 percent and the corporate burden decreased from 39 to 27 percent. At the local level, tax revolts also lowered other taxes in ways which favored the corporations and the wealthy. The extent of tax loss is enormous, although difficult to measure comprehensively. These erosions in the tax system combined with increasing regressivity were the result in large measure of corporate threats to leave high-tax jurisdictions, which pressured citizens, frightened by worsening economic conditions, into granting whatever concessions were asked.

Confirming the findings of most previous studies, in November 1981 the National Governors Association reported that tax incentives to attract industrial development have had little effect on where corporations choose to build their plants. Tax incentives are such a small factor in the plant location decision that half the companies responding to the survey did not even know if they were available in areas where they had decided to build or expand existing facilities.

As the economic crisis continues (we are writing in 1982), citizens at the state and local level have begun to move against both runaway plants and tax giveaways. In Michigan, Representative Perry Bullard, introducing legislation in 1980 that would limit the mobility of capital, explained, "The bill is intended to prevent the kidnapping of capital earned by employees in this state by employers who take the money to build someplace else." He added, "much of General Motors' or Ford's profits come from the work of a large number of workers in Michigan, and management's claim is that they have the right to take the profit of all that work and invest it in Alabama or Spain or Mexico and not take into consideration the impact on all those workers and communities that made those profits possible." An awareness is growing in many areas that are losing jobs that property rights can be redefined to protect workers by restricting the loss of capital, capital they have created.

Resistance to unwarranted tax abatement is also growing. In November 1981, *The Wall Street Journal* featured an article describing the rebellion of home owners in some cities against tax breaks to business in the face of increasing evidence that abatements haven't paid off. It increasingly appeared to such groups of irate citizens that they were giving up more to downtown hotels and convention centers than they would recoup from their tax dollar. Tax incentives can be unfair, unnecessary, and dangerous. Over time, erosion of the tax base can take a serious toll on the fiscal capacity of a city. In the sixties, Congress acted on the understanding that because higher taxes in local jurisdictions most in need of services would lead to capital flight, enlarged federal revenue sharing was necessary. The centralization of economic power and resources in a few hundred large, multinational firms and the ability of these corporations to move from areas of high taxation has meant, Congress implicitly acknowledged, that taxing nationally and spending locally made sense. But federal controls accompanied the money and, it was complained, there was too much bureaucratic interference in local affairs. Undoubtedly some of the forms were overly burdensome and guidelines were written in incomprehensible language. Often, however, the guidelines were all too clear. The federal bureaucrats could ask for reports on how policies affected poor communities. They might want neighborhood involvement in the planning process. Bureaucrats sometimes questioned funding which suspiciously favored well connected developers. Controls often grew because of local abuse, waste, and fraud as well as discrimination based on race and class.

If bureaucrats had always respected local wishes, minimized red tape, and carried out congressional intent, balancing competing goals with the skill of heavenly angels, there would still have been problems in the basic premise of redistributive liberalism that markets should be encouraged to work freely. To accept this premise is to accept deindustrialization of our older cities and their transformation into white-collar office-service complexes. Strong market forces are prompting the conversion of space from industrial underutilization to office use and higher-income residential use. Subsidies to the corporate sector facilitate this shift in urban function. However, the cost to present residents is almost totally ignored by public policymakers.

The role of government has been a major force in the restructuring of our cities, not through bold Marshall Plans but through deep tax subsidies to developers. Because the market process carries out much of the displacement, a "minimalist government" image, from a developer's viewpoint, optimizes the state's role in the transformation process.

COMMUNITIES VS. THE MARKET

Community organizers would do well to reject the minimalist government viewpoint and to approach gentrification as a situation open to negotiation, attempting to use the government and the legal system where they can. Tenants may not wish to be displaced, but owners are nearly always happy to sell if the price is right. The task is twofold. It would be better (for tenants) if the concept of ownership rights in tenancy were strengthened. To some extent, laws which prevent eviction without just cause (the right to statutory tenancy) and which provide for rent control serve this purpose. They increase the rights and bargaining power of tenants. Where landlords have to buy out tenants before they can gentrify a building, the process becomes very costly and, consequently, displacement more difficult. Second, negotiation with large-scale developers, especially where tax subsidies are involved (which is most of the time), and with city officials can be initiated. The key demand is likely to be that comparable housing be provided for tenants well before a development project starts destroying old dwellings, a demand which should be backed by the right of tenants to challenge their removal if a satisfactory alternative dwelling is not made available. Neighborhood groups might also seek concessions for local merchants in new long-term leases so that they are not priced out of new structures. They could also bargain for a fixed percentage of new units to be subsidized for existing neighborhood residents seeking to remain in the community. Such concessions from developers and city officials make gentrification more costly, but do so by reassigning costs more fairly than under present arrangements in which low-income residents and small shopkeepers pay a large part of the cost and are not compensated financially while being forced out of their neighborhood.

Costing out our present patterns of urban development is conceptually and technically a difficult process. In terms of tax incentives, much of the calculation of what the city will get for its investment is conjectural. After the fact no one has much of an interest in retrospectively seeing what has been bought for the tax benefits previously granted. We have few solid case studies, but evidence accumulates that many incentives are not justified. It would seem useful for local officials to follow a two-stage process. The first step would involve a closer inspection of the likelihood that subsidies are required for the desired investment to take place. In order to be considered necessary, the tax abatement would have to create a certain number of jobs of a specified pay grade and skill level for city residents in accordance with a local community's ability to meet its needs out of local revenues. Second would be a performance contract that specifies what beneficiaries of subsidies would pledge to do for the local jurisdiction. Auditing the contract would ensure that promises were kept; recapturing subsidies plus other penalties would be imposed on those who did not meet obligations. Local officials could issue housing permits only if a portion of housing units were available for low- and moderate-income families. They could require parking on site for commercial structures and issue a set of building standards and specify working conditions. They could require periodic review of compliance with recapture clauses to take back privileges not earned.

Even with careful consideration and follow-up, local officials cannot prevent intensified inter-jurisdictional competition. This requires federal assumption of more funding responsibility for functions which are thought to be local in nature. For example, by 1970 education, generally recognized as a local responsibility, was 41 percent funded by grants-in-aid. Overall in 1970 local governments were responsible for 70 percent of direct outlays but contributed only 40 percent of financing. (The Reagan Administration in the early 1980s moved to reduce the federal role drastically and force the funding of welfare state programs back on to the local governments.)

A pro-people urban policy would go beyond the minimal defense strategy described above to attempt revitalization in low-income, working-class areas based upon community-oriented, non-profit criteria, rather than upon the individualistic market approach that has victimized the urban poor.

COMMUNITY DEVELOPMENT

Before turning to an examination of what such alternatives might entail,
it is useful to take a quick view of the last period in which alternatives to
market hegemony were put forward in a mass way, the 1960s. This was
a decade in which the most oppressed and excluded groups in American
society were able to build movements which changed the consciousness of
far broader sectors of the American people, and a new consensus on
social policy began to emerge. Consider that one of the major accomplish-
ments of the civil rights movement—especially in its later phase, which
moved from the 1964 March for "Freedom Now" to a demand for "Jobs
and Income"—was its relative success in bringing economic issues to the
fore. The War on Poverty was a recognition that these issues could no
longer be avoided. The National Welfare Rights Organization's demand
for an adequate standard of living for all, regardless of their attachment
to the job market, was a major challenge to the system. It resulted in some
reform of the welfare system and serious consideration by Congress of a
Family Assistance Plan that would establish an income floor for all Americans. The black liberation movement's demand for community control
led to the creation of economic development corporations (though these
brought few new jobs). The demands for jobs-or-income were made with
increasing frequency in the sixties. At the ideological level, there was a
growing consensus that individuals had a legitimate claim on society's
resources and a right to protection from oppressive conditions. Direct
action—from rent strikes to sit-ins in government offices—was seen as a
legitimate response to government failures in countering abuses of greedy
landlords, merchants, employers, and public-sector bureaucrats. In auto
plants and the U.S. Post Office, for instance, through wildcat strikes and
slowdowns, black workers often spearheaded direct action. These activities
had a wide impact.

Day-to-day struggle on the job over control of the workplace—always
a factor in antagonistic production relations—was accentuated. These struggles escalated most impressively in the older industrial cities. The difference in the cost of labor between these areas and the Sunbelt widened
both quantitatively and, more importantly, qualitatively. Class-conscious
actions of the more sophisticated and militant workers in the old industrial
Northeast, involving resistance and sabotage in response to speedups and
work stretch-outs, meant rising costs of production. Productivity is a matter of work attitude, and companies found worker discontent on the rise
and labor discipline eroding; they sought more docile workers in the South
and Southwest.

Public-service recipients became increasingly militant, demanding more responsive and high-quality services from hospitals, schools, and welfare agencies—all of which were overcrowded and offered services far inferior to the official, though still inadequate, standards. The failure of city officials to respond adequately gave rise to further demands for community control of schools, civilian review boards, co-ops, and other institutions. The need for a coordinated effort to deal with socioeconomic problems led community activists away from market solutions in the economic realm toward new forms of cooperation. Early academic development theorists advocated the concept of the "big push," a unified effort on a number of fronts which would create input-output linkage tie-ups. It seemed just the right strategy for neighborhood development. In housing the problem was described as "the neighborhood effect"; it was difficult to upgrade one property when it was surrounded by others continuing to deteriorate. But if a whole block could be upgraded as a joint effort all residents would benefit. Similarly if vocational training programs in the schools led their qualified graduates into locally owned businesses which in turn provided work for accountants, printers, and so on, a process of cumulative growth could be initiated. This of course would require massive infusions of federal monies, but the price was certainly worth the expense, or so it was believed in the optimism of the sixties.

The idea of the Community Development Corporation was based on a simple yet profound recognition that the cities need direct public investment to meet the basic needs of the low-income people, who have no prospects of work at decent pay, whose housing is unfit for human habitation, whose children go to inadequate schools, whose understaffed and overcrowded hospitals don't give adequate service. Each locality must be given, out of the centrally collected social surplus, the resources to meet the food, shelter, education, and health needs of its residents unable to do so on their own, and to do so in a way which promotes independence and meaningful participation. Planning for decentralized priorities

> would entail a cumulative series of steps to subsidize those forms of local social and political organization that could be expected to further the replacement of hierarchical by egalitarian social relationships. Political life is shaped by work life and by home life in particular neighborhood contexts. The interactions that take place at this level either encourage or frustrate use of people's active and creative faculties. Where work life is a hierarchically structured system of domination and subordination, where neighborhoods are powerless to affect their own development, passivity and fatalism, rather than social activism and political participation are encouraged. National public policies to encourage experiments in worker-controlled work settings and the devolution of real political power to neighborhoods can do much to alter this pattern. The goal of such sub-

sidies would be to redistribute political experience. This goal would be achieved by (1) gradually introducing major changes in the structure of social interaction (hierarchy) that heretofore has characterized work life; and (2) devaluing policy-making controls down to a level that local social networks can have a real chance to influence." (Smith, p. 283)

Smith's vision is one which requires not so much a restructuring at the community level as a reorientation of national priorities, modes of decision making, and resource allocation. Unfortunately, in the 1960s a widespread disenchantment with local control movements followed the shift in demand from asking for more funding for community organizations to a re-examination and modification of the fundamental structures of the political economy. In retrospect, there are questions of whether poverty programs and neighborhood revitalization could have restructured relationships of exploitation, discrimination, and dependency without still greater changes in the macro economy. There were also practical operational questions. Could community development corporations succeed within the confines of funding and responsibility that they had been given?

Listening to some community development corporation (CDC) officials recounting their mistakes—the all-night pharmacy in the wrong location, the equipment bought rather than leased that was almost immediately outdated, the investments made at the urging of patrons who died soon after the money was committed, and the contracts negotiated by people with pull which tied the CDC politically into being nice to the right people, one gets a feel for the difficulty of building viable vehicles of local power even under favorable political conditions. In the eighties, austerity and an anti-government mood create an even more difficult environment for new neighborhood democracy movements. On the other hand, President Reagan's stress on localism might offer some opening to community-based organizations. While not the total solution, local organizations can play an important role.

Progressive government could take the bull by the horns and do what it thinks needs to be done—that is, create public enterprises on a large scale. Unlike "public service," which aids private enterprises in building and maintaining airports, industrial parks, and other infrastructural and supportive projects, public enterprises provide goods and services directly to consumers. Public enterprises bring investment location decisions into the realm of public decision-making and accountability and replace the profit motive with other goals, such as job creation, low cost service, consumer and worker decision-making, and strengthening certain parts of a jurisdiction's economic base.

When confronted with such ambitious functions for government, critics ask: "And just who is going to do all this? Look around you. Public enterprises as they exist today are run, and bungled, by bureaucrats, sheltered by subsidies (paid for by taxpayers), and plagued by patronage appointment. They deliver inferior service at high cost." Defenders point to the well-run TVA, which provides low-cost electricity while offering recreational and flood control services that have allowed a vast, formerly underdeveloped region to prosper where "private enterprise" saw no profit. Public enterprise also has a good record in Western Europe where steel mills, auto plants, and high-speed railroads are operated efficiently by governments. Advocates say that once public enterprises in the United States are free to pay competitive salaries and are controlled by worker, consumer, and technically competent, politically sensitive government representatives, they will be open to public scrutiny and responsive to public needs. Some advocates see the process dynamically coming about through struggle which builds public concern and involvement and which establishes widespread genuine citizen participation from below. For those who believe in effective democracy, there may be no alternative to such an approach.

We suggest that those who are being abandoned by the corporate sector and their own government in the older industrial areas, and indeed in depressed rural areas as well, would benefit by coalescing around a threefold strategy: first, by building institutions responsive to local need and under neighborhood control, and by trying to channel, where possible, federal revenue sharing funds to these grassroots organizations. Second, a renewed liberal-labor coalition revitalized by neighborhood minority, women, and consumer groups must enter the political arena and fight to defend people's rights in a period of withering attack. Finally, as the perception deepens that we are in a structural crisis for capitalism as a world system, we will have to develop concepts of collective decision-making and a participatory version of American economic democracy. The national counterpart to the social efficiency planning discussed earlier is *not* centralized, bureaucratically controlled nationalized industries. In short, a progressive local strategy cannot succeed unless it is part of a national movement which rejects laissez-faire thinking and poses an alternative macroeconomics.

THE NATIONAL CONTEXT

Prevailing market-oriented policies allow capital to play region against region and city against city to the detriment of the tax base and service delivery everywhere. To ameliorate this situation, our national government would have to control capital mobility; this would help enable cities to meet social needs and carry out effective urban programs. Beyond the control of economic activity is the even more substantial goal of the social allocation of investment. Such a program would stress the primacy of sector goods and service provision over unrestricted incentives to the corporate rich. It would require a fair, progressive tax structure, and encourage forms of collective ownership of capital (for example, the use of pension funds and Social Security to take ownership of the means of production) and economic democracy—worker and consumer control. A national economic development program would replace our existing inadequate stabilization and growth policies.

Such an orientation is not a return to redistributive liberalism but a step into the new world of democratic control of production. With social control, government regulation does not have to compensate for harmful, profit-oriented production decisions. Socially costly decisions would not be taken in the first place. Where and how production takes place and the allocation of society's resources would be made consistent with democratically established priorities. The challenge for those advocating economic democracy as the answer to the current crisis of our cities and the larger society is to clearly enunciate the ways in which our political institutions can adjust to these challenges.

Just as the devastation of Europe in World War II provided the opportunity for reindustrialization using up-to-date technologies, so the urban infrastructure collapse provides the possibility of replacing decaying systems with new energy efficient, ecologically sound and democratically run alternatives. The need for new sewage capacity, for example, could provide the opportunity for instituting decentralized methane gas–producing sewage treatment processes, and the product could be used to run cogenerators for neighborhood hot water and electricity, saving transportation and conventional fuel costs. Urban energy needs could be reduced by a program to retrofit housing and public buildings. Solar collectors could be installed as well. By putting human needs before profit considerations and investing in neighborhoods, a people-oriented economic policy could be developed.

Successful democracy at the neighborhood and municipal level would require analogous changes in the larger political economy. To avoid economic disruption of a community, labor unions and progressive public officials endorse "early warning" legislation requiring advance notification before plants are closed to give communities and workers time to offer alternative plans to keep the plant open. These can include new tax incentives and wage and working condition concessions. But they can also involve worker-community buy-outs and public investment. Worker control is seen by some to offer the opportunity to qualitatively change capitalism. Workers could, and sometimes do in employee-owned plants, make decisions democratically and run their workplaces. Yet they often are owners of a rundown plant that a private owner has allowed to optimally deteriorate. The workers may be more productive if they are working for themselves, but they still must buy and sell in cruelly competitive markets. This may require self-exploitation, especially if a factory is short on investment capital and saddled with an outmoded physical plant.

Under capitalist economics, nationalization is seen as a fairly extreme step, undertaken only when private management, even with heavy public subsidies, is unable to avoid bankruptcy. Only then is government ownership considered. Effective government ownership can, however, be based on different premises. For example, banks, military contractors, and oil companies in America are quite successful. Together they make far more money than the rest of our corporations put together; yet they typically pursue policies that many Americans see as counter to the public's interest. Why not nationalize the banks? The French government has done so. Most European governments have national energy corporations and follow coherent energy programs, consuming half the energy per capita that the U.S. does (and, in the case of nine countries in Europe, enjoying a higher standard of living). The arms race would be both cheaper and politically easier to slow down and reverse if it were not so profitable to powerful interests.

Publicly owned firms could have efficient managers trained at MIT and Stanford just as private corporations do. Under public control they would have other goals to guide their decision making. Renault, the largest auto maker in Europe, is owned by the French government. It is efficiently managed, as is Volkswagen with controlling German government ownership. A nationalized Chrysler corporation could make buses, subway cars, and specialized vehicles to transport the physically handicapped as part of a national energy program stressing conservation and spatial access. Public planning would not maximize private profit but societal well-being. It could also go well beyond simply giving new goals to traditionally trained managers. Economic democracy would mean restructuring work and the workplace as part of a larger societal transformation which would include education and training so that citizens could run their society.

COLLECTIVE CONSUMPTION

The struggle over how much of people's needs will be met by collective decision-making and a sharing of resources is perhaps *the* question of the twentieth century. It is central in urban areas where interdependencies abound and where the social costs of not providing for people's basic needs are so clearly visible.

As collective consumption issues have moved to center stage in the urban drama, the politics of service delivery and funding has become more important. "The realm of the public" is determined by the extent of perceived interdependencies on the one hand and the struggle of group and classes to use the state to meet their own purposes on the other. In some societies entitlements on the basis of citizenship are more extensive than others. Similarly, restrictions on individual freedom differ. Few would abolish all such government intervention. Building code requirements arose from the perception that given close proximity, an easily combustible building endangered neighboring properties. Such interdependence is the rationale for other restrictions on freedom from traffic lights to zoning regulations. We fight more over the content of such government coercion than its propriety.

Public domain entitlements and restrictions imply uniformity of treatment. While in richer neighborhoods streets may be better cleaned and garbage collected more frequently, such service differences are far smaller than in the private sector with its extremes of housing, food, and material wealth. In the case of publicly provided goods, equality is acknowledged as the norm we strive toward; in private markets wide disparities of resources ordain that the consumption of goods and services will be grossly unequal. Both are "natural" in their sphere as long as a socioeconomic system maintains this separation. But just how far should the sphere of each sector extend?

The welfare state can be seen as a defensive halfway house. At one extreme is the unbridled rule of the market, which would have each individual and family fully rsponsible for its own actions, either reaping the benefits of hard work and diligence or suffering deprivations caused by laziness or lack of skill or luck—all as measured by the impersonal rule of supply and demand. At the other is a societal definition of rights which accords each a share of the collective wealth, and which assigns to the realms of human decisions and policy control not only the production of goods and services but also the conditions for self-realization for each individual.

Attempting to devise a direct-needs strategy in a market-oriented economy is difficult. Government must give the financial incentive for behavior that is irrational in market terms. Because production takes place only when profit is anticipated, building housing beyond the potential tenant income level is foolish unless government subsidies are forthcoming. Similarly, leaving open space in crowded areas can be achieved by public sector purchase of land or tax subsidies to land owners. Such incentives are difficult to devise when the desired outcome involves a major change from the dictates of market profitability.

Consider the goal of building stable communities which encourage the participation of local residents in neighborhood governance. To achieve such a goal we would need taxation at a higher level of government, preferably federal, to avoid capital flight. Second, stability of tenure would be desirable. Rather than people changing communities when their income rose, upward mobility would be achieved through a mixture of income levels within each jurisdiction. Each neighborhood unit would be small enough to be responsible for its major services. Citizens could then have effective control, and participation would be encouraged. Each of these conditions is necessary. Expanded revenue sharing would decrease interjurisdictional differences in fiscal capacity; diversity within communities would reduce tensions which now come from the striking contrasts between upper-class enclaves and concentrations of low-income people in slum areas. Localism would work if scale and responsibility were properly matched.

These structural prerequisites would allow decision-making and implementation to be united. Public workers would be members of their community, service providers, and recipients encouraged to work together, and citizenship would be more than voting, since it would be expressed through ongoing continuous involvement with checks and balances provided by the active participation of the community. The answers to the questions of what services are being provided and for whose gain become directly observable.

Technological developments may be creating the possibility of such a decentralized spatial patterning, but only if the questions of political-economic control can be adequately addressed. The multinational corporations, which by moving capital, jobs, and tax revenues at will have undermined fiscal integrity of large cities and nations, and a governance structure unwilling to address the social control of capital, are profound constraints on the possibility of stable community. Social priorities and the dictates of private profitability clash jarringly as the internationalization of labor and capital undermine democratic preferences throughout the international economy. The urban fiscal crisis is a derived problem. Its cause is intimately intertwined with the freedom of capital from democratic control. Democracy and the collective needs of society, the specific requirements of those most oppressed by poverty or discrimination, and the goals of meaningful citizenship are subverted by the inability to use the resources and the wealth produced by the collective efforts of the society. Change involves taking control of forces which now seem uncontrollable—retrieving power from the banks and the multinationals rather than granting them more power. Solving urban crisis at the local level goes hand in hand with building democratic control of the larger political economy.

REFERENCES

Hill, Richard Child, "Transnational Capitalism and the Crisis of Industrial Cities" (paper presented at the International Studies Association, Cincinnati, March 27, 1982).

Peterson, Iver, "States Seeking to Curb Impact of Closing Industrial Plants," *New York Times,* March 16, 1980.

Smith, Michael P., *The City and Social Theory* (New York: St. Martin's Press, 1979).

Contributors

Robert Alford teaches sociology at the University of California, Santa Cruz. Alford is the author of *Health Care Politics,* and is finishing a book with Roger Friedland on theories of the state in capitalist democracies, titled *The Power of Theory.* Alford is currently working on the unobserved economy and its place in political and economic analysis.

Patrick J. Ashton was born and grew up in the city of Detroit. That city has also provided the context for his research on the political economy of suburbanization, the urban fiscal crisis, black politics, and police relations with the black community. Ashton currently teaches in the Sociology Department at Indiana University–Purdue University at Fort Wayne. His current research focuses on economic redevelopment in declining industrial cities and strategies for community organization and empowerment. With a colleague, Peter Iadicola, he has recently completed a book on the history of an inner-city neighborhood association in Fort Wayne.

Barry Checkoway is associate professor in the School of Social Work at the University of Michigan in Ann Arbor. He received his Ph.D. from the University of California at Berkeley. His research interests include urban social policy and planning, citizen participation, and community organization.

Peter Dreier is Assistant Professor of Sociology at Tufts University. He received his B.A. in journalism from Syracuse University and his

Ph.D. in sociology at the University of Chicago. He has published widely in academic and popular publications and is now writing a book with John Atlas entitled *The Renters' Revolt,* to be published by Temple University Press. He is on the National Executive Committee of Democratic Socialists of America, founder of the Massachusetts Tenants Organization, and an associate of Massachusetts Fair Share.

Roger Friedland teaches sociology at the University of California, Santa Barbara. Friedland is the author of *Power and Crisis in the City,* published by MacMillan (London) and Schocken (New York). Friedland is currently working on a study of corporate headquarter relocation and the social structuring of corporate mergers with Donald Palmer of the Stanford Business School.

David M. Gordon teaches economics at the Graduate Faculty of the New School for Social Research and is director of the Center for Democratic Alternatives in New York. He is the author of, among recent books and articles, *Segmented Work, Divided Workers* (co-authored with R. Edwards and M. Reich).

Charles Hoch is a native of Minnesota, but spent most of his youth in the suburbs of Dallas and San Diego. The experience of growing up suburban stimluated his curiosity about the political origins of suburban municipalities and, as he suspected, things were not as they had appeared. At present he is teaching courses in planning theory, housing, land use planning, and urbanization in the Urban Planning and Policy Program at the University of Illinois at Chicago Circle.

Richard Child Hill teaches urban studies and political economy in the Department of Sociology at Michigan State University. He has published articles on urban theory, race-relations, employment policy, and the postwar history of Detroit. He is currently doing comparative research on the crisis and global reorganization of the automobile industry.

Nancy Kleniewski teaches urban sociology at the State University of New York at Geneseo, near Rochester. She previously lived, studied, and taught in Philadelphia, where she became interested in the problems of urban decline and revitalization. She is active politically, currently serving on the Executive Committee of the Democratic Socialists of America.

Richard LeGates is a Professor of Urban Studies at San Francisco State University where he teaches housing and community development policy, land use law, and social science urban theory. He received M.C.P. and J.D. degrees from the University of California, Berkeley, and is a member of the California bar. He has taught at Berkeley, Stanford, and The University of Chile (Allende era), worked as a planner for many community based organizations and governments, and represented many groups in housing and land use conflicts. His recent books include *City Lights: An Introduction to Urban Studies* (New York, Oxford: 1981) with E. Barbara Phillips, and *Displacement: How to Fight It* (Berkeley, National Housing Law Project, 1982).

Mark Maier teaches economics at the College of New Rochelle (New Rochelle, New York). He has written for *Dollars and Sense, The Progressive, Radical Teacher* and for several publications of the *Union for Radical Political Economics*. His doctoral dissertation (New School for Social Research, 1980) studied the rise of municipal unionism in New York City.

Ann Markusen is an Assistant Professor of City and Regional Planning at the University of California, Berkeley. She teaches regional economics and planning, and has written extensively on regional change, regional politics, national urban policy, and women's issues. Her book, *Regional Political Economy,* will be published this year.

Karen A. Murphy, M.C.P. Berkeley, is currently employed by the Garth Group directing research for political campaigns. Her most recent publication, co-authored with Manuel Castells, is "Cultural Identity and Urban Structure: The Spatial Organization of San Francisco's Gay Community," in *Urban Policy Under Capitalism,* Urban Affairs Annual Reviews (volume 22).

Frances Fox Piven teaches political science at the City University of New York. Piven is a co-author of *Regulating the Poor, Poor People's Movements* and *The New Class War,* with Richard Cloward. Piven is currently working on women and the welfare state in comparative perspective.

Larry Sawers is a Professor of Economics at The American University in Washington, D.C., where he has taught since he received his doctorate from the University of Michigan in 1969. He teaches urban economics, labor history, and political economy. He is co-editor of *Sunbelt/Snowbelt* (Oxford 1983) with William Tabb and has published numerous articles in scholarly journals.

William Tabb teaches economics at Queens College, City University of New York, and is on the Graduate Faculty in Sociology. He is author of *The Long Default: New York and the Urban Fiscal Crisis* (New York: Monthly Review Press, 1982) and is involved in economic education with church, community, and labor groups. For a number of years, he has had a monthly call-in program "Behind the Economic News" on listener-sponsored WBAI in New York.

Index